Beginning Rails 6

From Novice to Professional

Fourth Edition

Brady Somerville
Adam Gamble
Cloves Carneiro Jr.
Rida Al Barazi

Apress®

Beginning Rails 6: From Novice to Professional

Brady Somerville
Bowling Green, KY, USA

Adam Gamble
Gardendale, AL, USA

Cloves Carneiro Jr.
Hollywood, FL, USA

Rida Al Barazi
FONTHILL, ON, Canada

ISBN-13 (pbk): 978-1-4842-5715-9
https://doi.org/10.1007/978-1-4842-5716-6

ISBN-13 (electronic): 978-1-4842-5716-6

Managing Director, Apress Media LLC: Welmoed Spahr
Acquisitions Editor: Steve Anglin
Development Editor: Matthew Moodie
Coordinating Editor: Mark Powers

Cover designed by eStudioCalamar

Cover image by Boris Stromar on Unsplash (www.unsplash.com)

Distributed to the book trade worldwide by Apress Media, LLC, 1 New York Plaza, New York, NY 10004, U.S.A. Phone 1-800-SPRINGER, fax (201) 348-4505, e-mail orders-ny@springer-sbm.com, or visit www.springeronline.com. Apress Media, LLC is a California LLC and the sole member (owner) is Springer Science + Business Media Finance Inc (SSBM Finance Inc). SSBM Finance Inc is a **Delaware** corporation.

For information on translations, please e-mail editorial@apress.com; for reprint, paperback, or audio rights, please email bookpermissions@springernature.com.

Apress titles may be purchased in bulk for academic, corporate, or promotional use. eBook versions and licenses are also available for most titles. For more information, reference our Print and eBook Bulk Sales web page at http://www.apress.com/bulk-sales.

Any source code or other supplementary material referenced by the author in this book is available to readers on GitHub via the book's product page, located at www.apress.com/9781484257159. For more detailed information, please visit http://www.apress.com/source-code.

Printed on acid-free paper

*To my parents, who sparked my love of technology
with a Macintosh Classic many years ago and have encouraged,
supported, and loved me unconditionally.*

Brady Somerville

Table of Contents

About the Authors

Brady Somerville is a professional web developer and senior engineer at Eezy in Bowling Green, Kentucky. He has over 15 years of professional web development experience, using languages and frameworks such as Ruby on Rails, Hypertext Preprocessor (PHP), and Perl. He earned a bachelor's degree in computer science and mathematics from his hometown university, Western Kentucky University.

Adam Gamble is a professional web developer and currently works as CTO for Eezy in Birmingham, Alabama. He has over 10 years' experience building web applications for everything from start-ups to multiple Fortune 500 companies. His passion for technology has enabled him to turn a hobby into a career that he loves.

Cloves Carneiro Jr is a software engineer who's been building software since 1997, especially web-based applications. He's also the original author of *Beginning Rails* and *Beginning Ruby on Rails* for Apress. His experience includes both Ruby and Java. He is currently working for LivingSocial in Florida.

Rida Al Barazi is a passionate web developer experienced in building smart web applications for start-ups. He has been designing and building for the Web since 2002. He started working with Rails in 2005 and has spoken at different web and Rails conferences around the world.

About the Technical Reviewer

Eldon Alameda is a web developer who currently resides in the harsh climates of Kansas. He works as a regional webmaster for the US National Weather Service; prior to this, he did development for a variety of companies including local start-ups, advertising firms, Sprint PCS, and IBM. During the 1990s, he also acquired a nice stack of worthless stock options from working for dot-com companies.

Acknowledgments

First of all, I want to thank my beautiful bride, Heather, for giving me the freedom to pursue writing this book. Without your support, this simply could not have happened; thank you, my love! And thank you, Owen, James, and Reuben, for letting Dad work at his computer just a "little" bit more than usual; I hope I'm fair in saying I do this for you.

And thank you, Mom and Dad, for modeling so many great characteristics for my siblings and me: how to have a strong work ethic, but still have fun; how to disagree, but still love; and how to have high expectations, but still show grace. It's simply not fair that I was fortunate enough to grow up under your loving care.

I also want to thank my colleagues and bosses along my professional journey, both for challenging me to be better and for giving me freedom and opportunities to make choices and fail. Philip at ICA—you showed me what a strong senior developer looks like and encouraged me to step up my game. Chris and Clinton at Hitcents—for many years, you trusted me to make good decisions and try new things; thank you! And to my leaders and colleagues at Eezy, thank you for making me part of your team; we are a close-knit bunch who grow and learn together every day, and I love working with you all.

And most literally, this book could not have happened without the excellent guidance and support from the folks at Apress publishing. Steve, thank you for setting the wheels in motion and doing everything you did to make this happen. Mark, thank you for (mostly) keeping me on track and for your encouragement along the way. And thank you to Matthew and the countless others at Apress whose involvement I wasn't aware of, but whose involvement was no less important and critical. Thank you all!

Finally, this book would have been of a markedly lesser quality had it not been for the excellent, careful feedback of our technical reviewer, Eldon Alameda. By having a careful eye for detail, Eldon saved you, dear reader, from exasperation due to typos, omissions, and other sundry errors which may have left you wondering where *you* went wrong in following code samples, when it had really been *my* mistake. But Eldon also kept a bigger picture and gave great feedback at a higher level for improving the flow of chapters. Thank you, Eldon! We were all fortunate for your involvement in this book.

—Brady Somerville

What Is This Book About?

In the past several years, the popularity of the Web has exploded to the point that it touches nearly every facet of our lives. It touches everything we do; ordering food, getting rides, and match-making are easy examples to think of. Even some *refrigerators* now integrate with the Internet. Ruby on Rails has played a part in fueling that explosion. This book will equip you with the knowledge you need to build real production web applications. It leads you through installing the required prerequisites on Windows, OS X, or Linux and then jumps straight into building applications. It is meant for the novice programmer who has some command-line experience but little or no programming experience. At the end of the book, you should have a firm grasp on the Ruby language and the Rails framework.

Chapter 1 introduces you to the current web landscape and then goes over some of the ideals and principles that the Rails framework is built on. It teaches you about the MVC paradigm and shows how Rails implements each piece of that paradigm (model, view, and controller).

Chapter 2 walks you through installing Ruby, Rails, and the SQLite database. It is broken down by operating system and, when finished, will give a level platform among all three. You should be able to follow along with the book no matter which platform you choose. It also will show you how to build a quick "Hello World" application to make sure everything is working correctly.

Chapter 3 dives right in and starts the blog application that we'll use throughout the rest of the book. We'll continually build on this application, enhancing and refactoring as we go along. You'll create your first model in this chapter, the Article model. We'll cover how migrations work and even get Rails to construct our first scaffold. At the end of this chapter, you'll have a working blog application, although it will be lacking features. We'll add those in the following chapters.

Chapter 4 slows down a little bit from the previous chapter and takes you on a tour of the Ruby language. If you've used Ruby for a while and feel comfortable with it, feel free to skim over this. If you're new to Ruby, this chapter will teach you everything you need to know to get started with Rails. Ruby is an easy language to pick up, as the syntax is very inviting and easy to read. Although we won't add any code to our blog application here, you will get to use the Ruby language inside the Ruby console.

Chapter 5 shows you how Rails uses Active Record to let you interact with a variety of databases. Rails abstracts away the difficult bits (unless you need them) and lets you interact with databases in an object-oriented (OO) way. You'll learn how to create new records, find records, and even update and delete them. We'll also apply some basic validations so we can be sure our data are just the way they should be.

Chapter 6 expounds on the previous chapter. You'll dive deeper into Active Record and your models. You will build more complex validations and custom instance methods. A major component of this chapter is the relation between your models and how Rails lets you define those relations. Your models for the blog application will have complex relations and validations.

In Chapter 7, we'll cover the view and controller parts of MVC. We will flesh out the blog application and walk through the code that Rails generated for the scaffold of our controllers and views.

Chapter 8 modifies the controllers and views in more advanced ways, and at this point, the features of our blog application have come together. You'll learn about controller callbacks and strong parameters that were added in Rails 4. We'll also give our application a fresh coat of paint with some Cascading Style Sheets (CSS).

Chapter 9 goes over the Asset Pipeline that was added in Rails 3.2, as well as Webpacker which was added in Rails 6, and shows how to add JavaScript and CSS to your application. We'll enhance our application with JavaScript dabbling in Ajax and DOM manipulation. At the end of this chapter, your application will have a nice layer of spit and polish.

Chapter 10 provides a tour of Active Storage, a component introduced in Rails 5, which provides an out-of-the-box experience for storing, processing, and retrieving uploaded files in your Rails application. We will use Active Storage to add the ability to add cover images to our blog's articles.

Chapter 11 introduces Action Text, a new component introduced in Rails 6, which provides a batteries-included approach to adding rich text capabilities to your Rails application. We'll use Action Text to allow article authors to include HTML in their articles using a WYSIWYG editor.

Chapter 12 adds email capabilities to our application. We'll show how to send emails from your Rails application. We'll add the ability to suggest articles to friends and even be notified when your article has new comments. We'll also cover a new addition to Rails 6, Action Mailbox, which allows your Rails application to *receive* emails and process them. We'll add the ability for authors to send an email to our blog application, which will create a draft article on their behalf. Amazing!

Chapter 13 covers Active Job, a component of Rails which allows us to defer certain tasks to be processed *later*. First, we'll explore the capabilities of Active Job, and then we'll improve our blog's performance by changing our emails to be sent outside of the request cycle, using Active Job.

Chapter 14 covers a very useful Rails module—Active Model. We'll explore how it can be used to enhance plain Ruby classes with impressive behaviors and then apply our knowledge to our blog by adding validations to our Email a Friend submission form.

Chapter 15 introduces Action Cable—a sophisticated, yet simple framework for using WebSocket technology to allow real-time, bidirectional communication between the server and the client. After getting familiar with some new concepts it introduces, we'll add an impressive new feature—instant, in-page notifications to all readers whenever a new article is published.

Chapter 16 covers one of the most important topics in Rails applications: testing. We'll discuss the benefits of automated testing, discuss some of the various types of tests, and then begin adding tests to our blog application. You can be sure that after this chapter you'll be able to add new features without breaking old ones. You'll test whether your application behaves exactly the way you think it should.

Chapter 17 covers internationalization. After all, it is the World Wide Web, and not everyone speaks the same language. We'll translate our web application into another language, and along the way you'll learn how to translate the application into as many languages as you like.

Chapter 18 will show you how to deploy your web application to Heroku, one of the leading Platform as a Service (PAAS) providers. This will allow you to present your application to the world quickly and easily so you can start building a user base.

Finally, the three appendices cover using SQLite and some basic SQL, where to find help in the Rails community, and some basics for working with the Git version control system.

CHAPTER 1

Introducing the Rails Framework

Rails is a web application framework for the Ruby programming language. Rails is well thought out and practical: it will help you build powerful websites quickly, with code that's clean and easy to maintain.

The goal of this book is to give you a thorough and complete understanding of how to build dynamic web applications with Rails. This means more than just showing you how to use the specific features and facilities of the framework, and more than just giving you a working knowledge of the Ruby language. Rails is quite a bit more than just another tool: it represents a way of thinking. To completely understand Rails, it's essential that you know about its underpinnings, its culture and aesthetics, and its philosophy of web development.

If you haven't heard it already, you're sure to notice the phrase "the Rails way" cropping up every now and again. It echoes a familiar phrase that has been floating around the Ruby community for a number of years: "the Ruby way." The Rails way is usually the easiest way—the path of least resistance, if you will. This isn't to say that you can't do things your way, nor is it meant to suggest that the framework is constraining. It simply means that if you choose to go off the beaten path, you shouldn't expect Rails to make it easy for you. If you've been around the UNIX circle for any length of time, you may think this idea bears some resemblance to the UNIX mantra: "Do the simplest thing that could possibly work." You're right. This chapter's aim is to introduce you to the Rails way.

© Brady Somerville, Adam Gamble, Cloves Carneiro Jr and Rida Al Barazi 2020
B. Somerville et al., *Beginning Rails 6*, https://doi.org/10.1007/978-1-4842-5716-6_1

The Rise and Rise of the Web Application

Web applications are extremely important in today's world. Almost everything we do today involves web applications. We increasingly rely on the Web for communication, news, shopping, finance, and entertainment; we use our phones to access the Web more than we actually make phone calls! As connections get faster and as broadband adoption grows, web-based software and similarly networked client or server applications are poised to displace software distributed by more traditional (read, outdated) means.

For consumers, web-based software affords greater convenience, allowing us to do more from more places. Web-based software works on every platform that supports a web browser (which is to say all of them), and there's nothing to install or download. And if Google's stock value is any indication, web applications are really taking off. All over the world, people are waking up to the new Web and the beauty of being web based. From email and calendars, photos, and videos to bookmarking, banking, and bidding, we're living increasingly inside the browser.

Due to the ease of distribution, the pace of change in the web-based software market is fast. Unlike traditional software, which must be installed on each individual computer, changes in web applications can be delivered quickly, and features can be added incrementally. There's no need to spend months or years perfecting the final version or getting in all the features before the launch date. Instead of spending months on research and development, you can go into production early and refine in the wild, even without all the features in place.

Can you imagine having a million CDs pressed and shipped, only to find a bug in your software as the FedEx truck is disappearing into the sunset? That would be an expensive mistake! Software distributed this way takes notoriously long to get out the door because before a company ships a product, it needs to be sure the software is bug free. Of course, there's no such thing as bug-free software, and web applications aren't immune to these unintended features. But with a web application, bug fixes are easy to deploy.

When a fix is pushed to the server hosting the web application, all users get the benefit of the update at the same time, usually without any interruption in service. That's a level of quality assurance you can't offer with store-bought software. There are no service packs to tirelessly distribute and no critical updates to install. A fix is often only a browser refresh away. And as a side benefit, instead of spending large amounts of money and resources on packaging and distribution, software developers are free to spend more time on quality and innovation.

Web-based software has the following advantages:

- Easier to distribute

- Easier to deploy

- Easier to maintain

- Platform independent

- Accessible from anywhere

The Web Isn't Perfect

As great a platform as the Web is, it's also fraught with constraints. One of the biggest problems is the browser itself. When it comes to browsers, there are several contenders, each of which has a slightly different take on how to display the contents of a web page. Although there has been movement toward unification and the state of standards compliance among browsers is steadily improving, there is still much to be desired. Even today, it's nearly impossible to achieve 100% cross-browser compatibility. Something that works in Internet Explorer doesn't necessarily work in Firefox, and vice versa. This lack of uniformity makes it difficult for developers to create truly cross-platform applications, as well as harder for users to work in their browser of choice.

Browser issues aside, perhaps the biggest constraint facing web development is its inherent complexity. A typical web application has dozens of moving parts: protocols and ports, the HTML and Cascading Style Sheets (CSS), the database and the server, the designer and the developer, and a multitude of other players, all conspiring toward complexity.

Despite these problems, the new focus on the Web as a platform means the field of web development is evolving rapidly and quickly overcoming obstacles. As it continues to mature, the tools and processes that have long been commonplace in traditional, client-side software development are beginning to make their way into the world of web development.

Why Use a Framework?

Among the tools making their way into the world of web development is the framework. A *framework* is a collection of libraries and tools intended to facilitate development. Designed with productivity in mind, a good framework provides a basic but complete infrastructure on top of which to build an application.

3

Having a good framework is a lot like having a chunk of your application already written for you. Instead of having to start from scratch, you begin with the foundation in place. If a community of developers uses the same framework, you have a community of support when you need it. You also have greater assurance that the foundation you're building on is less prone to pesky bugs and vulnerabilities, which can slow the development process.

A good web framework can be described as follows:

- *Full stack:* Everything you need for building complete applications should be included in the box. Having to install various libraries or configure multiple components is a drag. The different layers should fit together seamlessly.

- *Open source:* A framework should be open source, preferably licensed under a liberal, free-as-in-free license like the Berkeley Software Distribution (BSD) or that of the Massachusetts Institute of Technology (MIT).

- *Cross-platform:* A good framework is platform independent. The platform on which you decide to work is a personal choice. Your framework should remain as neutral as possible.

A good web framework provides you with the following:

- *A place for everything:* Structure and convention drive a good framework. In other words, unless a framework offers a good structure and a practical set of conventions, it's not a very good framework. Everything should have a proper place within the system; this eliminates guesswork and increases productivity.

- *A database abstraction layer:* You shouldn't have to deal with the low-level details of database access, nor should you be constrained to a particular database engine. A good framework takes care of most of the database grunt work for you, and it works with almost any database.

- *A culture and aesthetic to help inform programming decisions:* Rather than seeing the structure imposed by a framework as constraining, see it as liberating. A good framework encodes its opinions, gently guiding you. Often, difficult decisions are made for you by virtue of convention. The culture of the framework helps you make fewer menial decisions and helps you focus on what matters most.

Why Choose Rails?

Rails is a best-of-breed framework for building web applications. It's complete, open source, and cross-platform. It provides a powerful database abstraction layer called *Active Record*, which works with all popular database systems. It ships with a sensible set of defaults and provides a well-proven, multilayer system for organizing program files and concerns.

Above all, Rails is opinionated software. It has a philosophy of the art of web development that it takes very seriously. Fortunately, this philosophy is centered on beauty and productivity. You'll find that as you learn Rails, it actually makes writing web applications pleasurable.

Originally created by David Heinemeier Hansson, Rails was extracted from Basecamp, a successful web-based project management tool. The first version, released in July 2004, of what is now the Rails framework, was extracted from a real-world, working application: Basecamp, by 37signals. The Rails creators took away all the Basecamp-specific parts, and what remained was Rails.

Because it was extracted from a real application and not built as an ivory tower exercise, Rails is practical and free of needless features. Its goal as a framework is to solve 80% of the problems that occur in web development, assuming that the remaining 20% are problems that are unique to the application's domain. It may be surprising that as much as 80% of the code in an application is infrastructure, but it's not as far-fetched as it sounds. Consider all the work involved in application construction, from directory structure and naming conventions to the database abstraction layer and the maintenance of state.

Rails has specific ideas about directory structure, file naming, data structures, method arguments, and, well, nearly everything. When you write a Rails application, you're expected to follow the conventions that have been laid out for you. Instead of focusing on the details of knitting the application together, you get to focus on the 20% that really matters.

Since 2004, Rails has come a long way. The Rails team continues to update the framework to support the latest technologies and methodologies available. You'll find that as you use Rails, it's obvious that the core team has kept the project at the forefront of web technology. The Rails 6 release proves its maturity; gone are the days of radical, sweeping changes. Instead, the newest version of Rails makes a few incremental improvements to maintain relevancy and facilitate common needs.

Rails Is Ruby

There are a lot of programming languages out there. You've probably heard of many of them. C, C#, Lisp, Java, Smalltalk, PHP, and Python are popular choices. And then there are others you've probably never heard of: Haskell, IO, and maybe even Ruby. Like the others, Ruby is a programming language. You use it to write computer programs, including, but certainly not limited to, web applications.

Before Rails came along, not many people were writing web applications with Ruby. Other languages like PHP and Active Server Pages (ASP) were the dominant players in the field, and a large part of the Web is powered by them. The fact that Rails uses Ruby is significant because Ruby is considerably more expressive and flexible than either PHP or ASP. This makes developing web applications not only easy but also a lot of fun. Ruby has all the power of other languages, but it was built with the main goal of developer happiness.

Ruby is a key part of the success of Rails. Rails uses Ruby to create what's called a *domain-specific language* (DSL). Here, the domain is that of web development; when you're working in Rails, it's almost as if you're writing in a language that was specifically designed to construct web applications—a language with its own set of rules and grammar. Rails does this so well that it's sometimes easy to forget that you're writing Ruby code. This is a testimony to Ruby's power, and Rails takes full advantage of Ruby's expressiveness to create a truly beautiful environment.

For many developers, Rails is their introduction to Ruby—a language with a following before Rails that was admittedly small at best, at least in the West. Although Ruby had been steadily coming to the attention of programmers outside Japan, the Rails framework brought Ruby to the mainstream.

Invented by Yukihiro Matsumoto in 1994, it's a wonder Ruby remained shrouded in obscurity as long as it did. As far as programming languages go, Ruby is among the most beautiful. Interpreted and object oriented, elegant, and expressive, Ruby is truly a joy to work with. A large part of Rails' grace is due to Ruby and to the culture and aesthetics that permeate the Ruby community. As you begin to work with the framework, you'll quickly learn that Ruby, like Rails, is rich with idioms and conventions, all of which make for an enjoyable, productive programming environment.

In summary, Ruby can be described as follows:

- An interpreted, object-oriented scripting language

- Elegant, concise syntax

- Powerful metaprogramming features

- Well suited as a host language for creating DSLs

This book includes a complete Ruby primer. If you want to get a feel for what Ruby looks like now, skip to Chapter 3 and take a look. Don't worry if Ruby seems a little unconventional at first. You'll find it quite readable, even if you're not a programmer. It's safe to follow along in this book learning it as you go and referencing Chapter 3 when you need clarification. If you're looking for a more in-depth guide, Peter Cooper has written a fabulous book titled *Beginning Ruby: From Novice to Professional*, Third Edition (Apress, 2016). You'll also find the Ruby community more than helpful in your pursuit of the language. Be sure to visit `http://ruby-lang.org` for a wealth of Ruby-related resources.

Rails Encourages Agility

Web applications aren't traditionally known for agility. They have a reputation of being difficult to work with and a nightmare to maintain. It's perhaps in response to this diagnosis that Rails came onto the scene, helping to usher in a movement toward agile programming methodologies in web development. Rails advocates and assists in the achievement of the following basic principles of software development:

- Individuals and interactions over processes and tools

- Working software over comprehensive documentation

- Customer collaboration over contract negotiation

- Responding to change over following a plan

So reads the Agile Manifesto,[1] which was the result of a discussion among 17 prominent figures (including Dave Thomas, Andy Hunt, and Martin Fowler) in the field of what was then called "lightweight methodologies" for software development. Today, the Agile Manifesto is widely regarded as the canonical definition of agile development.

Rails was designed with agility in mind, and it takes each of the agile principles to heart almost obsessively. With Rails, you can respond to the needs of customers quickly and easily, and Rails works well during collaborative development. Rails accomplishes this by adhering to its own set of principles, all of which help make agile development possible.

---

[1]`http://agilemanifesto.org`

Dave Thomas and Andy Hunt's seminal work on the craft of programming, *The Pragmatic Programmer* (Addison Wesley, 1999), reads almost like a road map for Rails. Rails follows the *don't repeat yourself* (DRY) principle, the concepts of rapid prototyping, and the *you ain't gonna need it* (YAGNI) philosophy. Keeping important data in plain text, using convention over configuration, bridging the gap between customer and programmer, and, above all, postponing decisions in anticipation of change are institutionalized in Rails. These are some of the reasons that Rails is such an apt tool for agile development, and it's no wonder that one of the earliest supporters of Rails was Dave Thomas himself.

The sections that follow take you on a tour through some of Rails mantras and, in doing so, demonstrate how well suited Rails is for agile development. Although we want to avoid getting too philosophical, some of these points are essential to grasp what makes Rails so important.

Less Software

One of the central tenets of Rails' philosophy is the notion of *less software*. What does less software mean? It means using convention over configuration, writing less code, and doing away with things that needlessly add to the complexity of a system. In short, less software means less code, less complexity, and fewer bugs.

Convention over Configuration

Convention over configuration means that you need to define only configuration that is unconventional.

Programming is all about making decisions. If you were to write a system from scratch, without the aid of Rails, you'd have to make a lot of decisions: how to organize your files, what naming conventions to adopt, and how to handle database access are only a few. If you decided to use a database abstraction layer, you would need to sit down and write it or find an open source implementation that suited your needs. You'd need to do all this before you even got down to the business of modeling your domain.

Rails lets you start right away by encompassing a set of intelligent decisions about how your program should work and alleviating the amount of low-level decision making you need to do up front. As a result, you can focus on the problems you're trying to solve and get the job done more quickly.

Rails ships with almost no configuration files. If you're used to other frameworks, this fact may surprise you. If you've never used a framework before, you should be surprised. In some cases, configuring a framework is nearly half the work.

Instead of configuration, Rails relies on common structures and naming conventions, all of which employ the often-cited *principle of least surprise* (POLS). Things behave in a predictable, easy-to-decipher way. There are intelligent defaults for nearly every aspect of the framework, relieving you from having to explicitly tell the framework how to behave. This isn't to say that you can't tell Rails how to behave: most behaviors can be customized to your liking and to suit your particular needs. But you'll get the most mileage and productivity out of the defaults, and Rails is all too willing to encourage you to accept the defaults and move on to solving more interesting problems.

Although you can manipulate most things in the Rails setup and environment, the more you accept the defaults, the faster you can develop applications and predict how they will work. The speed with which you can develop without having to do any explicit configuration is one of the key reasons why Rails works so well. If you put your files in the right place and name them according to the right conventions, things *just work*. If you're willing to agree to the defaults, you generally have less code to write.

The reason Rails does this comes back to the idea of less software. Less software means making fewer low-level decisions, which makes your life as a web developer a lot easier. And easier is a good thing.

Don't Repeat Yourself

Rails is big on the DRY principle, which states that information in a system should be expressed in only one place.

For example, consider database configuration parameters. When you connect to a database, you generally need credentials, such as a username, a password, and the name of the database you want to work with. It may seem acceptable to include this connection information with each database query, and that approach holds up fine if you're making only one or two connections. But as soon as you need to make more than a few connections, you end up with a lot of instances of that username and password littered throughout your code. Then, if your username and password for the database change, you have to do a lot of finding and replacing. It's a much better idea to keep the connection information in a single file, referencing it as necessary. That way, if the credentials change, you need to modify only a single file. That's what the DRY principle is all about.

The more duplication exists in a system, the more room bugs have to hide. The more places the same information resides, the more there is to be modified when a change is required, and the harder it becomes to track these changes.

Rails is organized so it remains as DRY as possible. You generally specify information in a single place and move on to better things.

Rails Is an Opinionated Software

Frameworks encode opinions. It should come as no surprise then that Rails has strong opinions about how your application should be constructed. When you're working on a Rails application, those opinions are imposed on you, whether you're aware of it or not. One of the ways that Rails makes its voice heard is by gently (sometimes forcefully) nudging you in the right direction. We mentioned this form of encouragement when we talked about convention over configuration. You're invited to do the right thing by virtue of the fact that doing the wrong thing is often more difficult.

Ruby is known for making certain programmatic constructs look more natural by way of what's called *syntactic sugar*. Syntactic sugar means the syntax for something is altered to make it appear more natural, even though it behaves the same way. Things that are syntactically correct but otherwise look awkward when typed are often treated to syntactic sugar.

Rails has popularized the term *syntactic vinegar*. Syntactic vinegar is the exact opposite of syntactic sugar: awkward programmatic constructs are discouraged by making their syntax look sour. When you write a snippet of code that looks bad, chances are it *is* bad. Rails is good at making the right thing obvious by virtue of its beauty and the wrong thing equally obvious by virtue of ugliness.

You can see Rails' opinion in the things it does automatically, the ways it encourages you to do the right thing, and the conventions it asks you to accept. You'll find that Rails has an opinion about nearly everything related to web application construction: how you should name your database tables, how you should name your fields, which database and server software to use, how to scale your application, what you need, and what is a vestige of web development's past. If you subscribe to its worldview, you'll get along with Rails quite well.

Like a programming language, a framework needs to be something you're comfortable with—something that reflects your personal style and mode of working. It's often said in the Rails community that if you're getting pushback from Rails, it's probably because you haven't experienced enough pain from doing web development the old-school way. This isn't meant to deter developers; rather, it means that in order to truly appreciate Rails, you may need a history lesson in the technologies from whose ashes Rails has risen. Sometimes, until you've experienced the hurt, you can't appreciate the cure.

Rails Is Open Source

The Rails culture is steeped in open source tradition. The Rails source code is, of course, open. And it's significant that Rails is licensed under the MIT license, arguably one of the most "free" software licenses in existence.

Rails also advocates the use of open source tools and encourages the collaborative spirit of open source. The code that makes up Rails is 100% free and can be downloaded, modified, and redistributed by anyone at any time. Moreover, anyone is free to submit patches for bugs or features, and hundreds of people from all over the world have contributed to the project over the past nine years.

You'll probably notice that a lot of Rails developers use Macs. The Mac is clearly the preferred platform of many core Rails team developers, and most Rails developers are using UNIX variants (of which macOS is one). Although there is a marked bias toward UNIX variants when it comes to Rails developers, make no mistake; Rails is truly cross-platform. With a growing number of developers using Rails in a Windows environment, Rails has become easy to work with in all environments. It doesn't matter which operating system you choose: you'll be able to use Rails on it. Rails doesn't require any special editor or Integrated Development Environment (IDE) to write code. Any text editor is fine, as long as it can save files in plain text. The Rails package even includes a built-in, stand-alone web server called Puma, so you don't need to worry about installing and configuring a web server for your platform. When you want to run your Rails application in development mode, simply start up the built-in server and open your web browser. Why should it be more difficult than that?

The next chapter takes you step by step through the relatively painless procedure of installing Rails and getting it running on your system. But before you go there, and before you start writing your first application, let's talk about how the Rails framework is architected. This is important because, as you will see in a minute, it has a lot to do with how you organize your files and where you put them. Rails is a subset of a category of frameworks named for the way in which they divide the concerns of program design: the model-view-controller (MVC) pattern. Not surprisingly, the MVC pattern is the topic of our next section.

Rails Is Mature

You may have heard murmurs that "Rails is dead." You may have seen graphs that show the popularity of Rails declining. Don't let that worry you! Though other frameworks may be *trendier*, don't assume that means they are *better*. Rails is still highly effective for building modern web applications and has the benefit of having proved its effectiveness for years. Rails has entered adulthood.

A High-Level Overview of Rails

Rails employs a time-honored and well-established architectural pattern that advocates dividing application logic and labor into three distinct categories: the model, view, and controller. In the MVC pattern, the model represents the data, the view represents the user interface, and the controller directs all the action. The real power lies in the combination of the MVC layers, which Rails handles for you. Place your code in the right place and follow the naming conventions, and everything should fall into place.

Each part of the MVC—the model, view, and controller—is a separate entity, capable of being engineered and tested in isolation. A change to a model need not affect the views; likewise, a change to a view should have no effect on the model. This means changes in an MVC application tend to be localized and low impact, easing the pain of maintenance considerably while increasing the level of reusability among components.

Contrast this to the situation that occurs in a highly coupled application that mixes data access, business logic, and presentation code (PHP, we're looking at you). Some folks call this *spaghetti code* because of its striking resemblance to a tangled mess. In such systems, duplication is common, and even small changes can produce large ripple effects. MVC was designed to help solve this problem.

MVC isn't the only design pattern for web applications, but it's the one Rails has chosen to implement. And it turns out that it works great for web development. By separating concerns into different layers, changes to one don't have an impact on the others, resulting in faster development cycles and easier maintenance.

The MVC Cycle

Although MVC comes in different flavors, control flow generally works as follows (Figure 1-1):

- The user interacts with the interface and triggers a request to the server (e.g., submits a registration form).

- The server routes the request to a controller, passing any data that was sent by the user's request.

- The controller may access one or more models, perhaps manipulating and saving the data in some way (e.g., by creating a new user with the form data).

- The controller invokes a view template that creates a response to the user's request, which is then sent to back to the user (e.g., a welcome screen).

- The interface waits for further interaction from the user, and the cycle repeats.

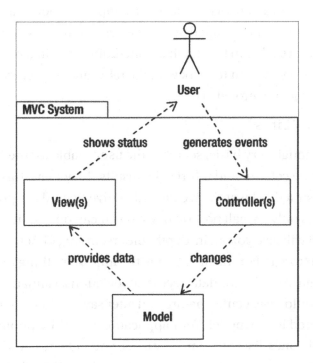

Figure 1-1. *The MVC cycle*

If the MVC concept sounds a little involved, don't worry. Although entire books have been written on this pattern and people will argue over its purest implementation for all time, it's easy to grasp, especially the way Rails does MVC.

Next, we'll take a quick tour through each letter in the MVC and then learn how Rails handles it.

The Layers of MVC

The three layers of the MVC pattern work together as follows:

- *Model:* The information the application works with

- *View:* The visual representation of the user interface

- *Controller:* The director of interaction between the model and the view

Models

In Rails, the model layer represents the database. Although we call the entire layer the model, Rails applications are usually made up of several individual models, each of which (usually) maps to a database table. For example, a model called User, by convention, would map to a table called users. The User model assumes responsibility for all access to the users table in the database, including creating, reading, updating, and deleting rows. So, if you want to work with the table and, say, search for someone by name, you do so through the model, like this:

```
User.find_by name: 'Linus'
```

This snippet, although very basic, searches the users table for the first row with the value Linus in the name column and returns the results. To achieve this, Rails uses its built-in database abstraction layer, Active Record. Active Record is a powerful library; needless to say, this is only a small portion of what you can do with it.

Chapters 5 and 6 will give you an in-depth understanding of Active Record and what you can expect from it. For the time being, the important thing to remember is that models represent data. All rules for data access, associations, validations, calculations, and routines that should be executed before and after save, update, or destroy operations are neatly encapsulated in the model. Your application's world is populated with Active Record objects: single ones, lists of them, new ones, and old ones. And Active Record lets you use Ruby language constructs to manipulate all of them, meaning you get to stick to one language for your entire application.

Controllers

For the discussion here, let's rearrange the MVC acronym and put the *C* before the *V*. As you'll see in a minute, in Rails, controllers are responsible for rendering views, so it makes sense to introduce them first.

Controllers are the conductors of an MVC application. In Rails, controllers accept requests from the outside world, perform the necessary processing, and then pass control to the view layer to display the results. It's the controller's job to field web requests, like processing server variables and forming data, asking the model for information, and sending information back to the model to be saved in the database. It may be a gross oversimplification, but controllers generally perform a request from the user to create, read, update, or delete a model object. You see these words a lot in the context of Rails, most often abbreviated as CRUD. In response to a request, the controller typically performs a CRUD operation on the model, sets up variables to be used in the view, and then proceeds to render or redirect to another action after processing is complete.

Controllers typically manage a single area of an application. For example, in a recipe application, you probably have a controller just for managing recipes. Inside the recipes controller, you can define what are called *actions*. Actions describe what a controller can do. If you want to be able to create, read, update, and delete recipes, you create appropriately named actions in the recipes controller. A simple recipes controller would look something like this:

```
class RecipesController < ApplicationController
  def index
    # logic to list all recipes
  end

  def show
    # logic to show a particular recipe
  end

  def create
    # logic to create a new recipe
  end

  def update
    # logic to update a particular recipe
  end
```

15

```
def destroy
  # logic to delete a particular recipe
end
end
```

Of course, if you want this controller to do anything, you need to put some instructions inside each action. When a request comes into your controller, it uses a URL parameter to identify the action to execute; and when it's done, it sends a response to the browser. The response is what you look at next.

Views

The view layer in the MVC forms the visible part of the application. In Rails, views are the templates that (most of the time) contain HTML markup to be rendered in a browser. It's important to note that views are meant to be free of all but the simplest programming logic. Any direct interaction with the model layer should be delegated to the controller layer, to keep the view clean and decoupled from the application's business logic.

Generally, views have the responsibility of formatting and presenting model objects for output on the screen, as well as providing the forms and input boxes that accept model data, such as a login box with a username and password or a registration form. Rails also provides the convenience of a comprehensive set of helpers that make connecting models and views easier, such as being able to prepopulate a form with information from the database or the ability to display error messages if a record fails any validation rules, such as required fields.

You're sure to hear this eventually if you hang out in Rails circles: a lot of folks consider the interface to *be* the software. We agree with them. Because the interface is all the user sees, it's the most important part. Whatever the software is doing behind the scenes, the only parts that an end user can relate to are the parts they see and interact with. The MVC pattern helps by keeping programming logic out of the view. With this strategy in place, programmers get to deal with code, and designers get to deal with templates called ERb (Embedded Ruby). These templates take plain HTML and use Ruby to inject the data and view specific logic as needed. Designers will feel right at home if they are familiar with HTML. Having a clean environment in which to design the HTML means better interfaces and better software.

The Libraries That Make Up Rails

Rails is a collection of libraries, each with a specialized task. Assembled together, these individual libraries make up the Rails framework. Of the several libraries that compose Rails, three map directly to the MVC pattern:

- *Active Record:* A library that handles database abstraction and interaction.

- *Action View:* A templating system that generates the HTML documents the visitor gets back as a result of a request to a Rails application.

- *Action Controller:* A library for manipulating both application flow and the data coming from the database on its way to being displayed in a view.

These libraries can be used independently of Rails and of one another. Together, they form the Rails MVC development stack. Because Rails is a full-stack framework, all the components are integrated, so you don't need to set up bridges among them manually.

Rails Is Modular

One of the great features of Rails is that it was built with modularity in mind from the ground up. Although many developers appreciate the fact that they get a full stack, you may have your own preferences in libraries, either for database access, template manipulation, or JavaScript libraries. As we describe Rails features, we mention alternatives to the default libraries that you may want to pursue as you become more familiar with Rails' inner workings.

Rails Is No Silver Bullet

There is no question that Rails offers web developers a lot of benefits. After using Rails, it's hard to imagine going back to web development without it. Fortunately, it looks like Rails will be around for a long time, so there's no need to worry. But it brings us to an important point.

As much as we've touted the benefits of Rails, it's important for you to realize that there are no silver bullets in software design. No matter how good Rails gets, it will never be all things to all people, and it will never solve all problems. Most important, Rails will never replace the role of the developer. Its purpose is to assist developers in getting their job done. Impressive as it is, Rails is merely a tool, which when used well can yield amazing results. It's our hope that as you continue to read this book and learn how to use Rails, you'll be able to leverage its strength to deliver creative and high-quality web-based software.

Summary

This chapter provided an introductory overview of the Rails landscape, from the growing importance of web applications to the history, philosophy, evolution, and architecture of the framework. You learned about the features of Rails that make it ideally suited for agile development, including the concepts of less software, convention over configuration, and DRY. Finally, you learned the basics of the MVC pattern and received a primer on how Rails does MVC.

With all this information under your belt, it's safe to say you're ready to get up and running with Rails. The next chapter walks you through the Rails installation so you can try it for yourself and see what all the fuss is about. You'll be up and running with Rails in no time.

CHAPTER 2

Getting Started

For various reasons, Rails has gained an undeserved reputation of being difficult to install. This chapter dispels this myth. The truth is that installing Rails is relatively easy and straightforward, provided you have all the right ingredients. The chapter begins with an overview of what you need to get Rails up and running and then provides step-by-step instructions for the installation. Finally, you'll start your first Rails application.

An Overview of Rails Installation

The main ingredient you need for Rails is, of course, Ruby. Some systems, such as macOS, come with Ruby preinstalled, but it's often outdated. To make sure you have the best experience with this book, it's best if you start from a clean slate, so you'll install it. After you have Ruby installed, you can install a *package manager* (a program designed to help you install and maintain software on your system) called RubyGems. You use that to install Rails.

If you're a Ruby hacker and already have Ruby and RubyGems installed on your computer, Rails is ridiculously easy to get up and running. Because it's packaged as a gem, you can install it with a single command:

```
> gem install rails
```

That's all it comes down to—installing Rails is a mere one-liner. The key is in having a working installation of Ruby and RubyGems. Before you get there, though, you need one other ingredient to use Rails: a database server.

As you're well aware by now, Rails is specifically meant for building web applications. Well, it's a rare web application that isn't backed by a database. Rails is so sure you're using a database for your application that it's downright stubborn about working nicely without one. Although Rails works with nearly every database out there, in this chapter you use one called SQLite. SQLite is open source, easy to install, and incredibly easy to develop with. Perhaps that's why it's the default database for Rails.

19

© Brady Somerville, Adam Gamble, Cloves Carneiro Jr and Rida Al Barazi 2020
B. Somerville et al., *Beginning Rails 6*, https://doi.org/10.1007/978-1-4842-5716-6_2

Rails 6 introduces the use of *webpack* for processing CSS and JS files. This also means we'll need to install Node.js to run JavaScript on the server and Yarn to manage our JavaScript dependencies.

You start by installing Ruby and RubyGems, and you use the magical one-liner to install Rails. Then, you install SQLite, Node.js, and Yarn and make sure they are working properly. Here are the steps in order:

1. Install Ruby.

2. Install Rails.

3. Install SQLite.

4. Install Node.js.

5. Install Yarn.

Before you begin, note that the "many ways to skin a cat" adage applies to Rails installation. Just as the Rails stack runs on many platforms, there are as many ways to install it. This chapter describes what we feel is the easiest and most reliable way to install Rails for your platform. You go about the process differently for macOS, Linux, and Windows, but they all amount to the same thing.

No matter which platform you're using, you need to get familiar with the command line. This likely isn't a problem for the Linux crowd, but it's possible that some macOS users and certainly many Windows users don't have much experience with it. If you're using macOS, you can find a terminal emulator in `/Applications/Utilities/Terminal.app`. If you're on Windows, you can open a command prompt by clicking Start, typing `cmd`, and clicking "Command Prompt." Note that you'll use the command line extensively in your travels with Rails. A growing number of IDEs make developing applications with Rails even simpler, and they completely abstract the use of a command-line tool; but stick to the command line to make sure you grasp all the concepts behind many commands. If you later decide to use an IDE such as JetBrains' RubyMine, you'll have a great understanding of Rails and will understand even better where the IDE is speeding up your work.

Also, a quick note for macOS users: If you're using a Mac and would prefer to use a package manager such as Fink or MacPorts, the Linux instructions will prove useful.

Go ahead and flip to the section that describes your platform (macOS, Windows, or Linux), and let's begin.

Installing on macOS Catalina

You'd think that given the prevalence of macOS among Rails developers, installing Rails on macOS would be easy. And you'd be correct. First, we need to install Apple's Developer Tools so that we can compile packages. Note that SQLite is preinstalled on macOS, so that's one thing we don't need to worry about.

Installing the Command Line Tools for Xcode

Some RubyGems you may need in the future require compilation, so you'll need to install a compiler. Apple's Command Line Tools for Xcode includes a compiler and provides the easiest way to set up a development environment on your Mac. Run the following command:

```
> xcode-select --install
```

Follow the prompts to continue installation.

Installing Homebrew

For this next piece, you'll need to dig into the terminal a bit, but don't worry, we'll guide you through it. Homebrew is a great package manager for macOS that is written in Ruby no less. It will help you to install the other pieces you'll need as you go. To install Homebrew, enter the following command into the terminal (Applications ➤ Utilities ➤ Terminal):

```
> ruby -e "$(curl -fsSL https://raw.githubusercontent.com/Homebrew/install/master/install)"
```

Installing RVM

Now you'll need to install a common Ruby tool called the Ruby Version Manager (RVM). It helps you manage versions of Ruby and various gems that you may use for projects. Its install is just as simple as Homebrew. It's just one command:

```
> \curl -sSL https://get.rvm.io | bash -s stable --ruby
```

You can test to see if Ruby is installed correctly by asking Ruby for its version number:

```
> ruby --version
```

```
ruby 2.6.5p114 (2019-10-01 revision 67812) [x86_64-darwin19]
```

If your output isn't exactly like this, don't panic. Ruby is often updated with new security patches and features, but it should at least say Ruby 2.5.0 in order to support Rails 6.

Installing Rails

To install Rails, use the command line:

```
> gem install rails -v '~> 6.0.2'
The "-v '~> 6.0.2'" part of the command ensures you'll get the most recent
version of Rails 6.0.
```

That's it! Rails is installed. Let's check the version to make sure everything went well:

```
> rails -v
```

```
Rails 6.0.2.1
```

Again, if your output isn't exactly like this, don't panic. Quite likely a newer version of Rails 6.0 has been released. But to ensure compatibility with this book, please make sure your version number begins with 6.0.

Installing Node.js

To install Node.js, use the command line:

```
> brew install node
```

To verify Node.js installation succeeded, issue the following command:

```
> node --version
```

If everything went well, you should see output that includes something like

```
v13.2.0
```

Installing Yarn

To install Yarn, we'll use *npm*, the Node.js package manager, which was installed for you when you installed Node.js:

```
> npm install -g yarn
```

To verify Yarn installation succeeded, issue the following command:

```
> yarn --version
```

If everything went well, you should see output that includes something like

```
1.21.0
```

Great! Ruby, Rails, SQLite, Node.js, and Yarn are installed and working correctly.

Installing on Windows

Installation on Windows is easy thanks to installer packages. You start by installing Ruby.

Installing Ruby

Installing Ruby on Windows is marvelously easy thanks largely to the one-click installer for Ruby. You can read more and download the installer from its website: `http://rubyinstaller.org/`.

The latest version of the installer at the time of this writing is Ruby 2.6.5-1. While a newer version of Ruby would *probably* still be compatible with Rails 6.0 and the code in this book, a safer bet would be to install the most recent stable Ruby 2.6 version.

After you've downloaded the installer, start the installation by double-clicking its icon. What follows is standard installer fare, and the defaults are sufficient for your purposes. When you select the location where you want to put Ruby (usually C:\Ruby26-x64), as shown in Figure 2-1, select the "Add Ruby executables to your PATH" checkbox; the installer takes care of the rest. You have a fully functioning Ruby installation in minutes.

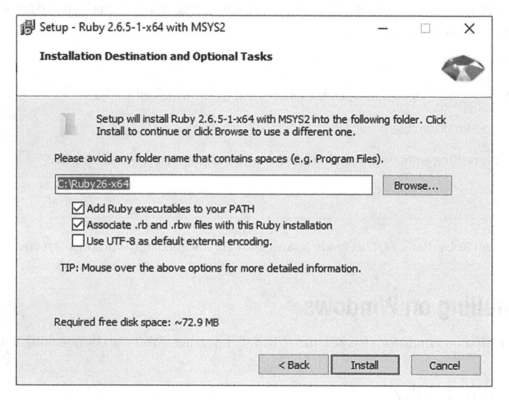

Figure 2-1. *Ruby installer for Windows*

When the installer is finished, you can test to see if Ruby is working and that your environment is correctly configured by opening your command prompt and asking Ruby its version number:

```
> ruby --version
```

```
ruby 2.6.5p114 (2019-10-01 revision 67812) [x64-mingw32]
```

Installing Rails

You'll be pleased to know that Ruby 2.6 comes bundled with RubyGems, a package management system for Ruby (`http://rubygems.org`), which makes installing Ruby libraries, utilities, and programs a breeze. This includes Rails installation.

First, let's update RubyGems and its sources list. Open your command prompt and issue the following `gem` command:

```
> gem update –system
```

Now, to install Rails, issue the following `gem` command in your command prompt:

```
> gem install rails -v '~> 6.0.2'
```

The "-v '~> 6.0.2'" part of the command ensures that the most recent version of Rails 6.0 is installed—important for making sure you can follow along with this book. Be forewarned that the `gem` command can take some time. Don't be discouraged if it seems to be sitting there doing nothing for a few minutes; it's probably updating its index file. RubyGems searches for gems in its remote repository (`https://rubygems.org`), so you need to be connected to the Internet for this command to work.

After spitting out some text to the screen and generally chugging away for a few minutes, the gem program should exit with something like the following before dumping you back at the command prompt:

```
Successfully installed rails-6.0.2.1
```

That's all there is to it! The one-click installer takes care of most of the work by installing and configuring Ruby; and because Rails is distributed as a RubyGem, installing it is a simple one-liner.

You can double-check that Rails was installed successfully by issuing the `rails -v` command at the command prompt:

```
> rails -v
```

```
Rails 6.0.2.1
```

Installing SQLite

To install SQLite on Windows, visit the SQLite website (`www.sqlite.org/download.html`), find the "Precompiled Binaries for Windows" section, and download the two files you'll need: the "sqlite-tools-*.zip" file and the "sqlite-dll-*.zip" file which matches your system—either the 32-bit (x86) version or the 64-bit (x64) version. (Most relatively modern computers should be x64 instead of x86. If unsure, open the "About your PC" program, and look at "Device specifications ➤ System type." For Windows versions other than Windows 10, you might need to use your favorite search engine to learn how to determine this). For example, the following is for our x64 system:

> `www.sqlite.org/2019/sqlite-dll-win64-x64-3300100.zip`

> `www.sqlite.org/2019/sqlite-tools-win32-x86-3300100.zip`

Note that the version number may be different by the time you read this. Unzip the zip files, and move their contents to the Ruby bin directory created by the preceding ruby installation step—in our case, `C:\Ruby26-x64\bin`. When you're done, you can test that you've correctly installed SQLite by issuing the following command from the command prompt:

```
> sqlite3 --version
```

```
3.30.1 2019-10-10 20:19:45
18db032d058f1436ce3dea84081f4ee5a0f2259ad97301d43c426bc7f3df1b0b
```

Now that you've installed SQLite, let's install its Ruby binding—a Ruby library that allows you to talk with SQLite. To install the SQLite3 Ruby binding, issue the following gem command from the command prompt:

```
> gem install sqlite3
```

If everything went well, you should see output that includes something like

```
Successfully installed sqlite3-1.4.1
```

Installing Node.js

To install Node.js on Windows, simply visit `https://nodejs.org/`, and download the installer which is "recommended for most users." (At the time of this writing, that's version 12.13.1 LTS.) Run the installer, accepting most of the defaults, but be sure to check "Automatically install the necessary tools" to avoid more manual steps. Follow the remaining steps to complete installation of Node.js.

To verify Node.js installation succeeded, open a new command prompt and issue the following command:

```
> node --version
```

If everything went well, you should see output that includes something like

```
v12.13.1
```

Installing Yarn

To install Yarn on Windows, simply visit `https://yarnpkg.com/`, click "Install Yarn," and download the installer for the current stable version for Windows. (At the time of this writing, that's version 1.19.2.) Run the installer, accepting the defaults, and complete the installation.

To verify Yarn installation succeeded, open a new command prompt and issue the following command:

```
> yarn --version
```

If everything went well, you should see output that includes something like

```
1.19.2
```

With Ruby, Rails, SQLite, Node.js, and Yarn happily installed, it's time to take them for a test drive. Unless you feel like reading the installation instructions for Linux, you're free to skip ahead to the "Creating Your First Rails Application" section.

Installing on Linux

Linux (and UNIX-based systems in general) comes in a variety of different flavors, but they share a lot in common. These instructions use a Debian-based variant called Ubuntu Linux, but they should apply to most UNIX systems with varying mileages.

Note   Ubuntu Linux is a top-notch distribution that has rapidly gained mindshare in the Linux community. At the time of this writing, it's one of the most popular Linux distributions for general use and is largely responsible for the increased viability of Linux as a desktop platform. It's freely available from `http://ubuntu.org` and highly recommended.

Just about all Linux distributions (including Ubuntu) ship with a package manager. Whether you're installing programs or code libraries, they usually have dependencies; a single program may depend on dozens of other programs in order to run properly, which can be a struggle to deal with yourself. A package manager takes care of these tasks for you, so you can focus on better things.

Ubuntu Linux includes the Debian package manager `apt`, which is what the examples in this book use. If you're using a different distribution, you likely have a different package manager, but the steps should be reasonably similar.

Before you begin installing Ruby, Rails, SQLite, Node.js, and Yarn, update the package library using the `apt-get  update` command:

```
$ sudo apt-get update
```

The `apt-get` program keeps a cached index of all the programs and their versions in the repository for faster searching. Running the `update` command ensures that this list is up to date, so you get the most recent versions of the software you need.

Installing Ruby

Before you install Ruby, you need to install a few libraries required by the components you're installing. Enter the following command:

```
$ sudo apt-get install build-essential curl git
```

You're going to use the Ruby Version Manager to let Ruby install it for you. This makes everything a snap! First, install the GPG keys for RVM (as found on `https://rvm.io/rvm/install`):

```
$ gpg --keyserver hkp://pool.sks-keyservers.net --recv-keys \
  409B6B1796C275462A1703113804BB82D39DC0E3 \
  7D2BAF1CF37B13E2069D6956105BD0E739499BDB
Next, run the command to install RVM.
$ \curl -sSL https://get.rvm.io | bash -s stable --ruby
```

Note   If using Gnome Terminal, you'll need to enable its "Run command as a login shell" option for RVM to work. Go to its Preferences ➤ Profile ➤ Command, and enable that option. Then close and reopen the terminal.

You can test that this is working by asking Ruby for its version number:

```
$ ruby --version
```

```
ruby 2.6.3p62 (2019-04-16 revision 67580) [x86_64-linux]
```

Installing Rails

Now you can use RubyGems to install Rails. Enter this command:

```
$ gem install rails -v '~> 6.0.2'
```

The "-v '~> 6.0.2'" part of the command ensures that the most recent version of Rails 6.0 is installed—important for making sure you can follow along with this book. After spitting out some text to the screen and generally chugging away for a little while, the gem program should exit, with a message like the following somewhere in the output:

```
Successfully installed rails-6.0.2.1
```

You can verify this claim by asking Rails for its version number:

```
$ rails --version
```

```
Rails 6.0.2.1
```

With Ruby and Rails happily installed, you're ready to move on to the next step: installing SQLite.

Installing SQLite

To install SQLite with apt-get, issue the following command:

```
$ sudo apt-get install sqlite3 libsqlite3-dev
```

If all goes according to plan, you can test your SQLite3 installation by invoking the sqlite3 program and asking for its version number:

```
$ sqlite3 --version
```

```
3.29.0 2019-07-10 17:32:03
```

Now that you've installed SQLite, let's install its Ruby binding—a Ruby library that allows you to talk with SQLite. To install the SQLite3 Ruby binding, issue the following gem command from the command prompt:

```
$ gem install sqlite3
```

Installing Node.js

To install Node.js, use the command line:

```
> curl -sL https://deb.nodesource.com/setup_12.x | sudo -E bash -
> sudo apt-get install -y nodejs
```

To verify Node.js installation succeeded, issue the following command:

```
> node --version
```

If everything went well, you should see output that includes something like

```
v12.13.0
```

Installing Yarn

To install Yarn, we'll use *npm*, the Node.js package manager, which was installed for you when you installed Node.js:

```
> sudo npm install -g yarn
```

To verify Yarn installation succeeded, issue the following command:

```
> yarn --version
```

If everything went well, you should see output that includes something like

```
1.21.1
```

With Ruby, Rails, SQLite, Node.js, and Yarn happily installed, it's time to take them for a test drive.

Creating Your First Rails Application

You'll start by using the `rails` command to create a new Rails project. Go to the directory where you want your Rails application to be placed; the `rails` command takes the name of the project you want to create as an argument and creates a Rails skeleton in a new directory by the same name. The newly created directory contains a set of files that Rails generates for you to bootstrap your application. To demonstrate, create a new project called (what else?) `hello`:

```
$ rails new hello
```

```
      create
      create  README.md
      create  Rakefile
      create  .ruby-version
      create  config.ru
      create  .gitignore
      create  Gemfile
 ...
```

```
    create   app
    create   app/controllers/application_controller.rb
    create   app/helpers/application_helper.rb
...
    create app/models/application_record.rb
...
    create   app/views/layouts/application.html.erb
...
```

If you look closely at the output, you see that the subdirectories of app/ are named after the MVC pattern introduced in Chapter 1. You also see a name that was mentioned briefly in Chapter 1: *helpers*. Helpers help bridge the gap between controllers and views; Chapter 7 will explain more about them.

Rails generated a new directory called hello. If you look at the folder structure, you'll see the following:

app/	db/	node_modules/	README.md	yarn.lock
babel.config.js	Gemfile	package.json	storage/	
bin/	Gemfile.lock	postcss.config.js	test/	
config/	lib/	public/	tmp/	
config.ru	log/	Rakefile	vendor/	

Starting the Built-In Web Server

Next, let's start up a local web server so you can test your new project in the browser. True, you haven't written any code yet, but Rails has a nice welcome screen that you can use to test whether the project is set up correctly. It even gives you some information about your Ruby environment.

Ruby ships with a built-in, zero-configuration, pure Ruby web server that makes running your application in development mode incredibly easy. You start up the built-in web server using the rails server command. To start the server now, make sure you're inside the directory of your Rails application, and then enter the following command:

```
$ cd hello
$ rails server
```

```
=> Booting Puma
=> Rails 6.0.2 application starting in development
=> Run `rails server --help` for more startup options
Puma starting in single mode...
* Version 4.3.1 (ruby 2.6.3-p62), codename: Mysterious Traveller
* Min threads: 5, max threads: 5
* Environment: development
* Listening on tcp://127.0.0.1:3000
* Listening on tcp://[::1]:3000
Use Ctrl-C to stop
```

The message from the `rails server` command tells you that a web server is running at the IP address 127.0.0.1 on port 3000. That means that the server is running locally on your machine. The hostname `localhost` also resolves to your local machine and is thus interchangeable with the IP address. We prefer to use the hostname variant.

With the server running, if you open `http://localhost:3000/` in your browser, you'll see the Rails welcome page, as shown in Figure 2-2. Congratulations! You've put Ruby on Rails.

Figure 2-2. Rails welcome page

The welcome page is nice, but it doesn't teach you much. The first step in learning how Rails works is to generate something dynamic. You're about to learn why you called this project "hello"!

We're sure it would be in violation of the law of programming books if we didn't start with the ubiquitous "Hello World" example. And who are we to disobey? In the next few steps, you make your Rails application say hello; and in doing so, you learn a few new concepts. Your goal is to have a request with the URL `http://localhost:3000/salutation/hello` respond with a friendly "Hello World!" message.

First things first: Stop the web server by pressing Ctrl+C in the command prompt window. That should bring you back to your prompt.

Note   Notice how easy it is to start and stop a local server? That's the whole point of the built-in server in a nutshell. You shouldn't need to be a system administrator to develop a Rails application.

Generating a Controller

You use the `rails` command's `generate` option to create certain files within your project. Because you're dealing with the request and response cycle (you request a URL, and the browser receives a response), you generate a controller that is responsible for handling salutations:

```
$ rails generate controller salutation
```

```
create    app/controllers/salutation_controller.rb
invoke    erb
create      app/views/salutation
invoke    test_unit
create      test/controllers/salutation_controller_test.rb
invoke    helper
create      app/helpers/salutation_helper.rb
invoke      test_unit
invoke    assets
invoke      scss
create        app/assets/stylesheets/salutation.scss
```

Not unlike the `rails` command you used to generate your application, the `rails generate controller` command creates a bunch of new files. These are mostly empty, containing only skeletal code (often called *stubs*). You could easily create these files on your own. The generator merely saves you time and the effort of needing to remember which files to create and where to put them.

The salutation controller was created in the `app/controllers` directory and is sensibly named `salutation_controller.rb`. If you open it with a text editor, you see that there's not much to it, as shown in Listing 2-1.

Listing 2-1. The app/controllers/salutation_controller.rb File

```
class SalutationController < ApplicationController
end
```

Creating an Action

If you want `SalutationController` to respond to a request for `hello`, you need to make an action for it. Open `salutation_controller.rb` in your text editor and add the `hello` action, as shown in Listing 2-2.

Listing 2-2. The Updated app/controllers/salutation_controller.rb File: `http://gist.github.com/319866`

```
class SalutationController < ApplicationController
  def hello
    @message = 'Hello World!'
  end
end
```

Actions are implemented as Ruby methods. You can always tell a method definition because of the `def` keyword. Inside the action, you set a Ruby instance variable called @ `message`, the value of which you output to the browser.

Creating a Template

With your action successfully defined, your next move is to add some HTML into the mix. Rails makes it easy by separating the files that contain HTML into their own directory as per the MVC pattern. In case you haven't guessed, HTML is the responsibility of the view.

If you look in the app/views directory, you see another product of the controller generator: a directory called salutation. It's linked to the salutation controller, and it's where you put template files that correspond to your salutation actions.

Note   Because Rails allows you to embed Ruby code in your HTML by using the ERb templating library, you use the .html.erb (HTML + ERb) extension for your templates.

The default way to render a template in response to a request for an action is remarkably simple: name it the same as the action. This is another case of using a predefined Rails convention. Because you want to show a response to the hello action, name your file hello.html.erb, and Rails renders it automatically. This is easy to grasp in practice. Figure 2-3 gives a visual cue as to how controllers and templates correspond.

Figure 2-3. *Controllers correspond to a directory in app/views*

Start by creating a new, blank file in app/views/salutation/. Name it hello.html.
erb, and add the code shown in Listing 2-3. Notice the <%= %> syntax that surrounds
the @message variable: these are known as Embedded Ruby (ERb) output tags. Chapter 7
explains more about ERb. For now, it's only important to know that whenever you see
<%= %> in a template, whatever is between the tags is evaluated as Ruby, and the result is
printed out.

Listing 2-3. The app/views/salutation/hello.html.erb File: https://gist.
github.com/nicedawg/0a45eae95abb3ff0e7993b9fd2120d59

```
<h1><%= @message %></h1>
```

If familiar with HTML, you may be wondering why we don't need to include tags like
<html> or <body> in our view! By default, our views will be wrapped inside of the code
found in app/views/layouts/application.html.erb, which contains the <html> and
<body> tags, as well as other HTML which we want to include in most of our pages.

You now have to tell your Rails application how to respond to a URL. You do that by
updating the config/routes.rb file. You don't need to worry about the details of how
the routes file works for now, Chapter 7 will cover that. Replace the contents of your
config/routes.rb file and make sure it looks like Listing 2-4.

Listing 2-4. The config/routes.rb File: https://gist.github.com/nicedawg/
29b16f5d5fefeea7c3f5293b7dddb0da

```
Rails.application.routes.draw do
  get 'salutation/hello'
end
```

It looks like you're all set. The salutation controller fields the request for hello
and automatically renders the hello.html.erb template. Start up the web server again
using the rails server command, and request the URL http://localhost:3000/
salutation/hello in your browser. You should see the result shown in Figure 2-4.

Hello World!

Figure 2-4. The "Hello World" application

Sure enough, there's your greeting! The hello template reads the @message variable that you set in the controller and, with a little help from ERb, printed it out to the screen.

In case you didn't notice, the URL http://localhost:3000/salutation/hello maps directly to the controller and action you created because of the change you made to your config/routes.rb file. Rails saw your "salutation/hello" route and figured out it should execute the "hello" action in your SalutationController. By following Rails naming conventions like this, you can avoid a lot of extra configuration code!

Summary

This chapter covered a lot, so you should be proud of yourself. You went from not having Rails installed to getting a basic Rails application up and running. You learned how to install Ruby and how to manage packages with RubyGems (which you used to install Rails). You also learned how to create a new Rails project using the rails command and how to use the generator to create a new controller. And you learned how controller actions correspond to templates. The stage is now set for the next chapter, where you begin building a more full-featured project.

CHAPTER 3

Getting Something Running

The best way to learn a programming language or a web framework is to dig in and write some code. After reading the first two chapters, you should have a good understanding of the Rails landscape. Chapter 4 will lead you through the Ruby language, but first let's write a little code to whet your appetite. This chapter builds a foundation and will get you excited by walking you through the construction of a basic application. You will learn how to create a database and how to connect it to Rails, as well as how to use a web interface to get data in and out of the application.

You will receive a lot of information in this chapter, but it shouldn't be more than you can absorb. The goal is to demonstrate, not to overwhelm. Rails makes it incredibly easy to get started, and that's a feature this chapter highlights. There are a few places where Rails really shines, and getting something running is one of them. By the end of this chapter, you'll have a working web application to play with, explore, and learn from. You'll build on this application throughout the rest of the book, adding features and refining functionality.

An Overview of the Project

This chapter will walk you through building a simple blog application that lets you create and publish articles, like WordPress or Blogger. The first iteration focuses on the basics: creating and editing articles.

Before you start coding, let's sketch a brief summary of the goals and flow of the application at a very high level. The idea isn't to focus on the nitty-gritty, but instead to concentrate on the general case.

Your application will have two kinds of users: those who post and publish articles and those who wish to comment on existing articles. In some cases, people will play both roles. Not all users will need to create an account by registering on the site. It will also be

© Brady Somerville, Adam Gamble, Cloves Carneiro Jr and Rida Al Barazi 2020
B. Somerville et al., *Beginning Rails 6*, https://doi.org/10.1007/978-1-4842-5716-6_3

nice if people can notify their friends about interesting articles using a feature that sends a friendly email notification to interested parties.

You will add some of these features in later chapters. Other application requirements will likely come up as you continue, but these are enough to get started. In the real world, specifications evolve as we learn how real users interact with our web applications. Don't let this frustrate you or surprise you—that's what the Agile methodology of software development recognizes and celebrates. Rails doesn't penalize you for making changes to an application that's under construction, so you can engage in an iterative style of development, adding and incrementing functionality as you go.

You start with what matters most: articles. You may wonder why you don't begin with users. After all, without users, who will post the articles? If you think about it, without articles, what could users do? Articles are the epicenter of the application, so it makes the most sense to start there and work out the details as you go. Ready? Let's get started!

Creating the Blog Application

As you saw in Chapter 2, the first step is to create a new Rails application. You could come up with a fancy name, but let's keep it simple and call the application blog. It's not going to win any awards for creativity, but it works.

To begin, from the command line, go to the directory where you want to place your new application; then, issue the rails command to generate the application skeleton and base files:

```
$ rails new blog
  create
  create   README.md
  create   Rakefile
  create   .ruby-version
  create   config.ru
  create   .gitignore
  create   Gemfile
...
```

As you recall from the example in Chapter 2, the rails command takes as an argument the name of the project you want to create and generates a directory of the same name that contains all the support files. In this case, it creates a subdirectory called `blog` in the current working directory. Change into the `blog` directory and get oriented. Figure 3-1 shows the directory structure.

Figure 3-1. *The Rails directory structure*

You'll quickly get used to the Rails directory structure, because all Rails applications follow this standard. This is another benefit of conventions: you always know where to locate files if you have to work on a Rails project that was developed by someone else. Table 3-1 briefly explains the directory structure.

Table 3-1. *Rails Directory Structure*

Folder/File	Description
app	All the components of your application.
bin	Executables to support Rails.
config	Configuration files for all of the components of your application.
db	Files related to the database you're using and a folder for migrations.

(continued)

Table 3-1. (*continued*)

Folder/File	Description
`lib`	Libraries that may be used in your application.
`log`	Log files that your application may require.
`node_modules`	External javascript dependencies.
`public`	Static assets served by your application, such as images, JavaScript, and CSS files.
`storage`	Contains uploaded files when using Active Storage's disk service.
`test`	Directory containing unit tests for your application.
`tmp`	Contains temporary files supporting your application.
`vendor`	External libraries, such as gems and plug-ins, that your application bundles.
`.browserslistrc`	Configuration file which declares what types of browsers your frontend (JS/CSS) tools should try to support.
`.gitignore`	Contains patterns of files/directories to ignore when saving changes to version control.
`.ruby-version`	Declares which version of Ruby to use with this Rails project.
`babel.config.js`	Configures babel so you can write javascript code with new features and syntax that can still work on older browsers.
`config.ru`	A file used by rack servers to start the application.
`Gemfile`	Used by the bundler gem to keep a list of gems used in your application.
`Gemfile.lock`	Canonical resource of what gems should be installed.
`package.json`	Declares javascript dependencies and configuration.
`postcss.config.js`	Config for PostCSS (a tool that lets you process CSS with javascript).
`Rakefile`	Lists available for tasks used by Rake.
`README.md`	Human-readable file generated to describe an application.
`yarn.lock`	Canonical resource of which javascript dependencies should be installed (like Gemfile.lock, but for javascript!).

Your first stop is the config directory. Of the little configuration there is to do in a Rails application, most of it takes place in this aptly named location. To get an idea of what Rails expects as far as databases go, open the config/database.yml file in your editor and take a peek. You should see something like the file shown in Listing 3-1 (comments are omitted here).

Listing 3-1. The config/database.yml File

```
default: &default
  adapter: sqlite3
  pool: <%= ENV.fetch("RAILS_MAX_THREADS") { 5 } %>
  timeout: 5000

development:
  <<: *default
  database: db/development.sqlite3

test:
  <<: *default
  database: db/test.sqlite3

production:
  <<: *default
  database: db/production.sqlite3
```

The first thing you should notice is the different sections: development, test, and production. Rails understands the concept of *environments* and assumes you're using a different database for each environment. Therefore, each has its own database connection settings, and different connection parameters are used automatically. Rails applications run in *development* mode by default, so you really only need to worry about the development section at this point. Still, other than the database names (db/*.sqlite3), there should be little difference between the connection parameters for each environment.

This example uses the default SQLite database because it's easy to use and set up. However, you can use the database management system of your choice by passing the -d or --database= option to the "rails new" command with one of the following options as per your preference: mysql, oracle, postgresql, sqlite3, sqlserver, or other supported database servers. (See "rails new --help" for a complete list.)

If you select a database other than SQLite, the `rails` command may prefill the `database` parameter based on the database server and project name: `blog` in this case. If you give your application a different name (say, a snazzy Web 2.0 name like `blog.ilicio.us *beta`) with a database server such as MySQL, you'll see something different here. It doesn't matter what you name your databases, as long as `database.yml` references the correct one for each environment. Let's stick with the convention and create the databases using the default names.

WHAT IS YAML?

The `.yml` extension refers to a YAML file. YAML (a recursive acronym that stands for "YAML Ain't Markup Language") is a special language for expressing objects in plain text. Rails can work with YAML natively and can turn what looks like plain text into Ruby objects that it can understand.

YAML is whitespace sensitive: it uses spaces (not tabs) to convey structure and meaning. Make sure your editor knows the difference between tabs and spaces, and be sure that when you're editing YAML files, you use only spaces.

Creating the Project Databases

You may think that to create a new database, you'll use your favorite database administration tool. However, because you already told Rails the database connection details, you can now run a Rails command that talks to the database and issues all the necessary commands to set up the databases. Jump to the command prompt and type:

```
$ cd blog
$ rails db:create
```

When using SQLite, you aren't forced to create the database, because a new database file is automatically created if one doesn't exist; but it will come in handy when you try a different database engine. You also may see some messages like *db/development.sqlite3 already exists*. Don't be afraid—this is an indication that an SQLite file was found. If you see that message, rest assured that your existing database was left untouched and no database file has been harmed.

Regardless of the database management system you select, you should notice that the databases you want to use are created. This is another case in which Rails removes some complexity from your mind and helps you focus on your application.

Note   Depending on how your environment is set up, you may not need to specify the username, password, and other options in your `config/databases.yml` file to create the database.

Although you're only concerned with the development environment at this time, it doesn't hurt to create the other databases while you're at it. Go ahead and create two more databases, one each for the test and production environments:

```
$ rails db:create:all
```

Rails provides an easy way to interact directly with the database via its command-line interface. You can confirm the creation of the database by using the `rails dbconsole` program to interact with your development database:

```
$ rails dbconsole
```

```
SQLite version 3.29.0 2019-07-10 17:32:03
Enter ".help" for usage hints.
sqlite> .databases
main: /path/to/your/blog/db/development.sqlite3
sqlite> .exit
```

At this point, you can issue any number of SQL (Structured Query Language) statements and look at the tables and records that eventually will be in your application. (If you aren't familiar with SQL, you can learn more about it in Appendix B.) When you're finished with the SQLite console, type the `.exit` command to go back to your regular prompt. You can test to see if your connection is working by running the following command:

```
$ rails db:migrate
```

If nothing exceptional is returned, congratulations! Rails can connect to your database. However, if you're using a database engine other than SQLite and you may see something like this

```
rake aborted!
Access denied for user 'root'@'localhost' (using password: NO)
```

then you need to adjust your connection settings. If you're having problems, make sure the database exists and that you've entered the correct username and password in the config/database.yml configuration file.

Creating the Article Model

Now that you can connect to the database, this section will explain how you create a model. Remember that models in Rails usually correspond to database table names. Because you want to model articles, let's create a model named Article. By convention, model names are camel-cased singular and correspond to lowercased plural table names. So an Article model expects a table named articles; a Person model expects a table named people.

Note   Camel case means that each word begins with a capital letter and is written without spaces. For instance, a class that described blog images would be written as BlogImage. Refer to http://en.wikipedia.org/wiki/CamelCase for more information.

Rails is smart enough to use the correct plural name for most common words; it doesn't try to create a persons table.

Like most things in Rails, models have their own generator script that makes it easier to get started. The generator automatically creates a new model file in the app/models directory and also creates a bunch of other files. Among these are a unit test (for testing your model's functionality, as discussed in Chapter 16) and a database migration. A *database migration* contains instructions for modifying the database table and columns. Whenever you generate a new model, a migration is created along with it.

Note   If you want to skip generation of the migration when generating a new model, you can pass the `--no-migration` argument to the generator. This may be useful if you're creating a model for an existing database or table.

To see the generator's usage information, run it without arguments:

```
$ rails generate model
```

```
Usage:
  rails generate model NAME [field[:type][:index] field[:type][:index]]
  [options]
...
```

As you can see from the usage banner, the generator takes a model name as its argument and an optional list of fields. The model name may be given in camel-cased or snake-cased format, and options can be provided if you want to automatically populate the resulting migration with column information.

Note   Snake-cased words are written in all lowercase with underscores replacing spaces, for instance, blog_image. For more information, visit `http://en.wikipedia.org/wiki/Snake_case`.

Let's run the generator now to create the first model, `Article`:

```
$ rails generate model Article
```

```
  invoke   active_record
  create   db/migrate/20191219235126_create_articles.rb
  create   app/models/article.rb
  invoke   test_unit
  create   test/models/article_test.rb
  create   test/fixtures/articles.yml
```

If you look at the lines that start with `create`, you see that the generator has created an Article model, an Article test, an articles fixture (which is a textual representation of table data you can use for testing), and a migration named **20191219235126_create_ articles.rb**. From that, your model is generated.

Note   The first part of the migration file name is the timestamp when the file was generated. So the file on your computer will have a slightly different name.

Creating a Database Table

You need to create a table in the database. You could do this with a database administration tool or even manually using SQL, but Rails provides a much more efficient facility for table creation and maintenance called a *migration*. It's called a migration because it allows you to evolve, or migrate, your schema over time. (If you're not familiar with databases, tables, and SQL, consult Appendix B for the basics.)

Note   *Schema* is the term given to the properties that make up a table: the table's name, its columns, and its column types, as well as any default values a column will have.

What's the best part about migrations? You get to define your schema in pure Ruby. This is all part of the Rails philosophy that you should stick to one language when developing. It helps eliminate context switching and results in higher productivity.

As you can see from the output of the model generator, it created a new file in db/ migrate called 20191219235126_create_articles.rb. As mentioned before, migrations are named with a numeric prefix, which is a number that represents the exact moment when the migration file was created. Because multiple developers can create migrations in a development team, this number helps uniquely identify this specific migration in a project.

Let's open this file and take a peek. It's shown in Listing 3-2.

Listing 3-2. The db/migrate/20191219235126_create_articles.rb File

```
class CreateArticles < ActiveRecord::Migration[6.0]
  def change
    create_table :articles do |t|
```

```
      t.timestamps
    end
  end
end
```

In its initially generated form, the migration is a blank canvas. But before you go any further, let's note a few important items. First, notice the instance method: change. In previous versions of Rails, there would be an up and down class method, but now Rails is smart enough to figure it out based on the modifications you make in this method. You can roll back without ever writing a method that explicitly drops the table. Pretty slick, isn't it?

Listing 3-3 has the details filled in for you. Even without ever having seen a migration before, you should be able to tell exactly what's going on.

Listing 3-3. Completed db/migrate/20191219235126_create_articles.rb File

```
class CreateArticles < ActiveRecord::Migration[6.0]
  def change
    create_table :articles do |t|
      t.string    :title
      t.text      :body
      t.datetime :published_at

      t.timestamps
    end
  end
end
```

Let's step through the code. First, you use the create_table method, giving it the name of the table you want to create. Inside the code block, the string, text, and datetime methods each create a column of the said type named after the parameter; for example, t.string :title creates a field named title with the type string. The timestamps method, in the t.timestamps call, is used to create a couple of fields called created_at and updated_at, which Rails sets to the date when the record is created and updated, respectively. (For a full description of the available method types you can create in your migrations, see https://api.rubyonrails.org/classes/ActiveRecord/Migration.html.)

On its own, this migration does nothing. Really, it's just a plain old Ruby class. If you want it to do some work and create a table in the database for you, you need to run it. To run a migration, you use the built-in db:migrate Rails command that Rails provides.

From the command line, type the following to run the migration and create the articles table. This is the same command you used to test the database connection. You sort of hijack it for this test, knowing that it will attempt to connect to the database and thus prove whether the connection works. Because there were no existing migrations when you first ran it, it didn't do anything. Now that you have your first migration, running it results in a table being created:

```
$ rails db:migrate
```

```
== 20191219235126 CreateArticles: migrating =================================
-- create_table(:articles)
   -> 0.0028s
== 20191219235126 CreateArticles: migrated (0.0029s) ======================
```

Just as the output says, the migration created the articles table. If you try to run the migration again (go ahead, try it), nothing happens. That's because Rails keeps track of all the migrations it runs in a database table, and in this case there's nothing left to do. If for some reason you decide you need to roll back the migration, you can use the db:rollback task to roll back. Try it and you will notice that it dropped the articles table. Remember that we never wrote any code to drop the table, Rails just handled it for us. Imagine if you would have edited the database schema directly with a database management tool; if you wanted to roll back, you'd have to remember what it looked like before and exactly what you changed. This makes your life much easier. Okay, before we move on, don't forget to run migrations again since we rolled back.

Generating a Controller

You've created a model and its supporting database table, so the next step is to work on the controller and view side of the application. Let's create a controller named articles (remember controllers are plural and models are singular) to control the operation of the application's articles functionality. Just as with models, Rails provides a generator that you can use to create controllers:

```
$ rails generate controller articles
```

```
create  app/controllers/articles_controller.rb
invoke  erb
create     app/views/articles
invoke  test_unit
create     test/controllers/articles_controller_test.rb
invoke  helper
create     app/helpers/articles_helper.rb
invoke     test_unit
invoke  assets
invoke     scss
create        app/assets/stylesheets/articles.scss
```

The controller generator creates four files:

- *app/controllers/articles_controller.rb:* The controller that is responsible for handling requests and responses for anything to do with articles.

- *test/controllers/articles_controller_test.rb:* The class that contains all functional tests for the `articles` controller (Chapter 16 covers testing applications).

- *app/helpers/articles_helper.rb:* The helper class in which you can add utility methods that can be used in your views (Chapters 7 and 8 cover helpers).

- *app/assets/stylesheets/articles.scss:* This is a SASS (Syntactically Awesome Style Sheets) file where you can put style sheets for the associated views.

Note   SASS is a language that compiles into CSS. SASS extends CSS with enhanced syntax that helps developers organize their CSS and simplify their code. (See `https://sass-lang.com/` for more info.) Rails supports SASS out of the box by precompiling it into CSS automatically via the Asset Pipeline.

The controller generator also creates an empty directory in `app/views` called `articles`. This is where you place the templates for the `articles` controller.

Up and Running with Scaffolding

One of the most talked-about features that has given a lot of exposure to Rails is its scaffolding capabilities. *Scaffolding* allows you to create a boilerplate-style set of actions and templates that makes it easy to manipulate data for a specific model. You generate scaffolding using the scaffold generator. You're probably getting used to generators by now. Rails makes heavy use of them because they help automate repetitive tasks and generally remove the chances for errors when creating new files. Unlike you probably would, the generator won't ever forget how to name a file; nor will it make a typo when creating a class. Let's use the scaffold generator now and solve the mystery of how this works.

First, we need to remove the files we generated in the previous steps. Rather than having to find all the files we generated and delete them by hand, we can use the "rails db:rollback" and "rails destroy" commands to undo previous operations. Run the following commands:

```
$ rails destroy controller articles
$ rails db:rollback
$ rails destroy model Article
```

Now, we'll run the following commands to generate scaffolding for our Article model, complete with controllers, views, and other files, and then to create the database table:

```
$ rails generate scaffold Article title:string body:text published_
at:datetime
$ rails db:migrate
```

The scaffold provides methods and pages that allow you to insert, update, and delete records in your database. That's all you need to generate a working scaffold of the Article model. Let's fire up the web server and test it. Start your local web server from the command line (rails server), and browse to the articles controller in your browser:

```
http://localhost:3000/articles
```

You should see the results displayed in your browser, as shown in Figure 3-2.

Figure 3-2. *Articles scaffolding*

Click the New Article link, and you're taken to a screen where you can enter articles. Notice that the URL is http://localhost:3000/articles/new, which means you're invoking the new action on the articles controller. Go ahead and add a few articles and generally play with the application. Figure 3-3 shows an example of an article entered on this screen.

Figure 3-3. *Adding an article*

Notice that every time you add an article, you're redirected back to the show action, where you see the details of the article you just created. You can click "Back" to go the index action, where you see all of your articles listed. You can edit them, delete them, or create new ones. You've got to admit, Rails gives you a lot of functionality for free.

Speed is the key benefit here. The scaffold generator allows you to quickly get something running, which is a great way to test your assumptions.

Caution   Scaffolding comes with an important disclaimer. You shouldn't use it in production. It exists to help you do exactly what you just did: get something running. By its definition, it's a temporary or unfinished product.

Adding More Fields

Now that you can see the model represented in the browser, let's add some more fields to make it a little more interesting. Whenever you need to add or modify database fields, you should do so using a migration. In this case, let's add the excerpt and location fields to the articles table.

You didn't need to generate the last migration (the one you used to create the articles table), because the model generator took care of that for you. This time around, you can use the migration generator. It works just like the model and controller generators, which you've seen in action. All you need to do is give the migration generator a descriptive name for the transformation:

```
$ rails generate migration add_excerpt_and_location_to_articles
excerpt:string location:string
```

```
      invoke  active_record
      create    db/migrate/20191220013103_add_excerpt_and_location_to_articles.rb
```

As you've already seen, the generator creates a migration class in db/migrate prefixed by a number identifying when the migration was created. If you open the 20191220013103_add_excerpt_and_location_to_articles.rb file, you see the migration class with the code shown in Listing 3-4. As with the model generator, which prefilled the migration to some extent, passing field names and types as options to the migration generator prefills the generated class for you as long as you refer to the correct table name at the end of the migration name—in this case, to_articles.

Listing 3-4. The db/migrate/20191220013103_add_excerpt_and_location_to_articles.rb File

```ruby
class AddExcerptAndLocationToArticles < ActiveRecord::Migration[6.0]
  def change
    add_column :articles, :excerpt, :string
    add_column :articles, :location, :string
  end
end
```

Looking at the add_column method, the first argument is the table name (articles), the second is the field name, and the third is the field type. Remember that the change method knows how to migrate up or down, so if in the unlikely event you want to remove these columns, Rails will know how.

With this new migration in place, use the following Rails command to apply it and make the changes to the database:

```
$ rails db:migrate
```

```
== 20191220013103 AddExcerptAndLocationToArticles: migrating ============
-- add_column(:articles, :excerpt, :string)
   -> 0.0030s
-- add_column(:articles, :location, :string)
   -> 0.0017s
== 20191220013103 AddExcerptAndLocationToArticles: migrated (0.0052s) =====
```

If all goes according to plan, the articles table now has two new fields. You could edit the view templates in the app/views/articles folder to add form elements for the new fields, but instead let's call the generator again (you'll learn about views in Chapter 7):

First, we need to remove a few files again, so that the generator won't refuse to run:

- app/models/article.rb

- app/controllers/articles_controller.rb

- app/helpers/articles_helper.rb

And now, we can rerun the scaffold generator with our new options:

```
$ rails generate scaffold Article title:string location:string excerpt:string
body:text published_at:datetime --no-migration
```

Press Y when asked if you want to overwrite some files, and you're finished, as you can see in Figure 3-4.

← → C ⌂   🛡 ⓘ localhost:3000/articles/2/edit

Editing Article

Title

Beginning Rails 6

Location

Bowling Green, KY

Excerpt

Body

```
Beginning Rails 6 is the practical
starting point for anyone wanting
to learn how to build dynamic web
applications using the latest
release of the Rails framework for
Ruby. You'll learn how all of the
components of Rails fit together
and how you can leverage them to
create sophisticated web
applications with less code and
more joy.
```

Published at

2019 ∨   December ∨   20 ∨ — 01 ∨ : 16 ∨

Update Article

Show | Back

Figure 3-4. *Additional fields added to the new article form*

This exposes one of the issues of this type of scaffolding: when you generate new versions of the scaffold files, you run the risk of overwriting custom changes you may have made. We're doing it this way as an illustration, but you wouldn't normally do this.

Adding Validations

You may wonder what happens if you try to save a new article without giving it any information. Try doing that: Rails doesn't care. Actually, it's the `Article` model that doesn't care. This is because in Rails, the rules for data integrity (such as required fields) are the responsibility of the model.

To add basic validation for required fields, open the `Article` model in `app/models/article.rb` and add the validation method shown in Listing 3-5 inside the class body.

Listing 3-5. Validation Added to the `app/models/article.rb` File

```ruby
class Article < ApplicationRecord
  validates :title, :body, presence: true
end
```

Save the file, and try creating an empty article again. Instead of saving the record, Rails displays a formatted error message, as shown in Figure 3-5.

Figure 3-5. *Error messages for an article*

If you've done any web development before, you know that validating fields is a major nuisance. Thankfully, Rails makes it easy.

Note   Notice that you don't need to restart the web server when you make changes to your project files in the app/ directory. This is a convenience provided by Rails when running in development mode.

Chapter 6 goes through all the specifics of model validations. For now, you're using only the most primitive methods of protecting your data. It shouldn't surprise you that Active Record is capable of much more involved validations, such as making sure a numeric value is entered, validating that data are in the correct format using regular expressions, and ensuring unique values, among other checks.

Note   *Regular expressions* (regex for short) are expressions that describe patterns in strings. Like most programming languages, Ruby has built-in support for regular expressions.

Generated Files

Now that you've seen the pages in action, let's look at the articles controller again. As you can see in Listing 3-6, the controller is now chock-full of actions. There's one for each of index, show, new, create, edit, update, and destroy—the basic CRUD actions.

Listing 3-6. The app/controllers/articles_controller.rb

```ruby
class ArticlesController < ApplicationController
  before_action :set_article, only: [:show, :edit, :update, :destroy]

  # GET /articles
  # GET /articles.json
  def index
    @articles = Article.all
  end

  # GET /articles/1
  # GET /articles/1.json
  def show
  end

  # GET /articles/new
  def new
    @article = Article.new
  end
```

```ruby
# GET /articles/1/edit
def edit
end

# POST /articles
# POST /articles.json
def create
  @article = Article.new(article_params)

  respond_to do |format|
    if @article.save
      format.html { redirect_to @article, notice: 'Article was
      successfully created.' }
      format.json { render :show, status: :created, location: @article }
    else
      format.html { render :new }
      format.json { render json: @article.errors, status: :unprocessable_
      entity }
    end
  end
end

# PATCH/PUT /articles/1
# PATCH/PUT /articles/1.json
def update
  respond_to do |format|
    if @article.update(article_params)
      format.html { redirect_to @article, notice: 'Article was
      successfully updated.' }
      format.json { render :show, status: :ok, location: @article }
    else
      format.html { render :edit }
      format.json { render json: @article.errors, status: :unprocessable_
      entity }
    end
  end
end
```

```
# DELETE /articles/1
# DELETE /articles/1.json
def destroy
  @article.destroy
  respond_to do |format|
    format.html { redirect_to articles_url, notice: 'Article was
    successfully destroyed.' }
    format.json { head :no_content }
  end
end

private
  # Use callbacks to share common setup or constraints between actions.
  def set_article
    @article = Article.find(params[:id])
  end

  # Only allow a list of trusted parameters through.
  def article_params
    params.require(:article).permit(:title, :location, :excerpt, :body,
    :published_at)
  end
end
```

As you did in this chapter, after you've generated scaffolding, if you change your model, you have to regenerate it if you want your application to follow suit. Most of the time, however, you make the changes by hand and have a variation of the default scaffold.

It's important to realize why scaffolding exists and to be aware of its limitations. As you've just seen, scaffolding helps when you need to get something running quickly to test your assumptions. It doesn't take you very far in the real world, and eventually you end up replacing most (if not all) of it.

Explore the generated code and see if you can figure out how it hangs together. Don't worry if you can't understand all of it—the chapters that follow will discuss it in depth. With everything you know about Rails already, you should be able to piece together most of it.

Try changing a few things to see what happens. If you inadvertently break something, you can always run the scaffolding generator again to revert to the original. Can you see how the views in `app/views/articles` are related to the actions? What about the response messages, like `Article was successfully created`? What happens when you change them? See if you can find where the error messages for failed validations are rendered. If you remove the message, does the record still get saved? You can learn a lot by exploring, so take as much time as you need.

Summary

This chapter started by outlining the basics of the sample application. Then, you rolled up your sleeves and created a database and configuration files. Based on the goals of the application, you began by creating the tables necessary to run the core of your `Article` model and got a first look at the simplicity and flexibility that migrations give the development process. The scaffolding allowed you to test your assumptions about the model and table you created by getting a firsthand look at it in action. You also took a first crack at adding in validations that ensure you maintain the integrity of your data. The chapters that follow investigate these concepts in depth, starting with the first part of the MVC principle: models.

## CHAPTER 4

Introduction to the Ruby Language

Rails is a great framework for the development of web-based applications. One of its greatest advantages over other web frameworks is that it's written in Ruby, a very consistent and elegant object-oriented programming language. In order to increase your productivity as a Rails developer, it's important that you master Ruby. If you're new to programming, don't worry: we explain the concepts in a way you can understand.

Ruby was made to make developers happy. This should be exciting to you because you're a developer, and you want to be happy! Some languages feel like the creator was in a bad mood and hated you. Ruby tries its best to make you feel at ease and in control. As you grow as a developer, you'll understand the importance of this fact more and more, especially if you do this for a living.

This chapter gives you an overview of the features of the Ruby language. It explains how the language is organized and presents its fundamentals. After reading this chapter, you should better understand how the Ruby language that Rails is built on works, and you should be able to create classes and methods and use control-flow statements in your code. The best way to learn is to explore the language using this chapter as a guide. It's important that you run the examples given yourself and also to try things on your own.

Ruby has far more features than we can mention in this short introduction. We encourage you to investigate more of the complex features of Ruby as you continue using Rails.

Instant Interaction

A lot of languages require that you write some code, compile, and then run the program to see the results. However, Ruby is *dynamic*, which means you can work with the language live. You will get instant feedback from your commands.

Ruby comes with a great little tool: an interactive interpreter called irb (for Interactive Ruby). You can start up an irb session whenever you want by typing **irb** at the command prompt. Using irb, you can play around with code and make sure it works as you expect before you write it into your programs.

You can execute any arbitrary Ruby code in irb and do anything you would otherwise do inside your Ruby programs: set variables, evaluate conditions, and inspect objects. The only essential difference between an interactive session and a regular old Ruby program is that irb echoes the return value of everything it executes. This saves you from having to explicitly print the results of an evaluation. Just run the code, and irb prints the result.

You can tell when you're in an irb session by looking for the irb prompt, which looks like `irb(main):001:0>`, and the arrow symbol (`=>`), which indicates the response.

To start an irb session, go to the command prompt and type **irb**. You should see the irb prompt waiting for your input:

```
$ irb
irb(main):001:0>
```

Look at that. You're inside Ruby! If you press Enter, Ruby ignores the line and gives you another prompt, but it ends with an asterisk instead of the greater-than sign to indicate that Ruby is expecting something from you to execute. It can only get more exciting from here.

Note   Your **irb** prompt might look slightly different depending on your version of Ruby and your computer environment. This is perfectly okay.

When learning a new programming language, traditionally, the first thing you do is make the language print the string "Hello, World!" Let's go ahead and do that. Type the following after the irb prompt:

```
irb(main):001:0>  "Hello, World!"
=> "Hello, World!"
```

Excellent. You just wrote your first bit of Ruby! Some languages require many more lines of code to write the Hello, World! application, but in Ruby it only took one. One of the ways Ruby makes developers happy is by being concise. One line is certainly concise, wouldn't you say?

So what exactly happened here? Well, first, you created a string with the content "Hello, World!" The irb command always outputs the value of the last command to the screen; thus, you have "Hello, World!" written to the screen. You will notice as you type valid Ruby commands and press Enter that irb will continue to output the value of those commands. Try adding two numbers together:

```
irb(main):001:0>  1 + 1
=> 2
```

Now let's try something a little more difficult. Let's ask Ruby for the current time:

```
irb(main):001:0>  Time.now
=> 2020-01-20 19:38:17 -0600
```

So Ruby dutifully reported the current time to us, including the date no less. What if you just wanted the current year?

```
irb(main):001:0>  Time.now.year
=> 2020
```

You can see how easy and concise Ruby is. The code is simple and almost reads like an English sentence. If you're wanting a description of exactly what you did in the last two examples, here it is: You called a method (now) on a class (Time). In the second example, you chained another method call onto the previous one. We'll cover this in depth later, but first let's talk about data types.

Ruby Data Types

A *data type* is a constraint placed on the interpretation of data. Numbers and strings are just two of the data types the Ruby interpreter distinguishes among, and the way Ruby adds numbers is different from the way in which it adds strings. For example, 2 + 3 evaluates to 5, but "2" + "3" evaluates to "23". The second example may seem surprising at first, but it's simple: anything, including numbers, surrounded by quotes is interpreted as a string. Read on to find out more.

Strings

A *string* is a sequence of characters that usually represents a word or some other form of text. In Ruby, you can create `String` objects by putting the characters inside single or double quotation marks:

```
irb(main):001:0>  'Ruby is a great language'
=> "Ruby is a great language"

irb(main):002:0>  "Rails is a great framework"
=> "Rails is a great framework"
```

The main difference between strings delimited by single and double quotes is that the latter are subject to substitutions. Those substitutions are identified by Ruby code inside the #{} construct, which is evaluated and replaced by its result in the final `String` object. The technical term for this technique is *string interpolation*:

```
irb(main):003:0>  "Now is #{Time.now}"
=> Now is 2020-01-20 19:39:45 -0600"

irb(main):004:0>  'Now is #{Time.now}'
=> "Now is \#{Time.now}"
```

Note   In general, most developers only use double quotes when using string interpolation or if the actual string includes single quotes. This is technically faster, if only slightly.

When you use the hash symbol (#) with the curly braces, Ruby notices and tries to evaluate whatever is between the braces. To *evaluate* means to process it like any other code. So, inside the braces, you say `Time.now`, which returns the current time. However, when you use single quotes, Ruby doesn't check the string for substitutions before sending it through.

The `String` class has a large number of methods you need when doing string manipulation, like concatenation and case-changing operations. The following examples list a few of those methods:

```
irb(main):005:0>  "Toronto - Canada".downcase
=> "toronto - canada"
```

```
irb(main):006:0>  "New York, USA".upcase
=> "NEW YORK, USA"

irb(main):007:0>  "a " + "few " + "strings " + "together"
=> "a few strings together"

irb(main):008:0>  "HELLO".capitalize
=> "Hello"
```

Tip   To get a list of methods available for any object, call the "methods" method using an instance of the object you want to inspect. Type **"a string".methods** in irb to see all the methods you can call on the String object. If you want to find a certain method, try using grep on that method too. For example, typing **"a string".methods.grep /case/** shows all string methods containing the word *case*. Other examples would be

4.methods

["some", "array", "elements"].methods

Numbers

Ruby has a couple of classes to represent numbers: Integer and Float. Integer represents whole numbers, while Float objects represent real numbers, meaning numbers with a fractional part. As in most programming languages, you can perform basic arithmetic operations in Ruby as you would using a calculator:

```
irb(main):001:0>  1 + 2
=> 3

irb(main):002:0>  2323 + 34545
=> 36868

irb(main):003:0>  9093 - 23236
=> -14143

irb(main):004:0>  343 / 4564
=> 0
```

```
irb(main):005:0>  3434 / 53
=> 64

irb(main):006:0>  99 * 345
=> 34155

irb(main):007:0>  34545.6 / 3434.1
=> 10.059578928977025
```

Note   Notice that when whole numbers are divided, the result is always a whole number even if there is a remainder. If one of the numbers is a decimal, then a decimal will always be returned:

```
irb(main):001:0> 6/4
=> 1
irb(main):002:0> 6/4.0
=> 1.5
```

Symbols

Symbols aren't a common feature in most languages. However, as you'll learn when reading this book, they're extremely useful. Symbol is a data type that starts with a colon, like :controller. Symbols are objects that work just like any other object in Ruby. They're used to point to some data that isn't a traditional String object, in a human-readable format. In fact, they're almost like strings, except you can't modify them:

```
irb(main):001:0>  :my_symbol
=> :my_symbol

irb(main):002:0>  :my_symbol + :second
Traceback (most recent call last):
     ...
     1: from (irb):22
NoMethodError (undefined method `+' for :my_symbol:Symbol)

irb(main):003:0>  "my_string" + "second"
=> "my_stringsecond"
```

Fancy computer science types refer to this condition as being *immutable*, which really just means you can't modify something. Use symbols when you want to name something nicely and you don't want it changed at all—for example, by having something appended to the end of it. There are also memory advantages to using symbols, but that is out of the scope of this book. The importance of symbols will become clear as you use Ruby more.

Arrays and Hashes

Sometimes you have a lot of data that you need to keep track of—maybe a list of students, users, or anything that you may keep in a collection. Ruby has two different types of *container* objects for storing collections: arrays and hashes.

Arrays are part of almost every modern language. They keep information in order. You can ask for the first item or the last item or put items in a certain order. You can think of an Array object as a long series of boxes in which you can put things. You define arrays by using the [ ] notation. Note that in most programming languages, including Ruby, arrays are 0 indexed. This means you always refer to the first element in an array as 0. Read carefully what happens here:

```
irb(main):001:0>  city_array = ['Toronto', 'Miami', 'Paris']
=> ["Toronto", "Miami", "Paris"]

irb(main):002:0>  city_array[0]
=> "Toronto"

irb(main):003:0>  city_array[1] = 'New York'
=> "New York"

irb(main):004:0>  city_array << 'London'
=> ["Toronto", "New York", "Paris", "London"]

irb(main):004:0>  city_array + ["Los Angeles"]
=> ["Toronto", "New York", "Paris", "London", "Los Angeles"]
```

In the first example, we created the array of cities and assigned it to the variable named city_array. In the second example, we referenced the city array and asked for the object at the index position 0 (remember, with arrays, 0 is the first index). "Toronto" is returned. In the third example, we are replacing the object at index 1 with the string "New York." Notice in the next example when the array is printed to the screen, Miami is no longer in the list but has been replaced. The fourth example uses what is commonly called the *shovel* operator. Simply put, this just adds the object to the end of the array. So we added the string "London" to the end of our array. Finally, in the last array, we added the array that contains "Los Angeles" to our previous array. This returns a new single dimensional array with the contents of both arrays. Arrays are extremely common and useful in Ruby.

The Hash object offers another way to keep a collection. Hashes are different from arrays, because they store items using a *key*. *Hash objects* preserve order, just like arrays, which enables you to call certain methods on them—for example, hash.first to get the first key-value pair. In Ruby, you often use symbols for hash keys, but in reality, *any* object can function as a key.

You define hashes with curly braces, {}. You can create a Hash object by defining it with {key: "value", other_key: "other value" }. Then, you can pull out data by using square brackets on the end of the list. For instance, you retrieve a value by typing my_hash[:key] from the my_hash variable. Here are some examples:

```
irb(main):005:0> my_hash = {canada: 'Toronto', france: 'Paris', uk: 'London'}
=> {:canada=>"Toronto", :france=>"Paris", :uk=>"London"}
```

Notice how the return value doesn't quite look like what you typed in—the format of the hash changed. What you typed in is referred to as JavaScript Object Notation (JSON) style, whereas the format shown in the return value is referred to as the Hashrocket style. (See the rockets in the hash?) In a sense, the two styles are equivalent. Many prefer the more compact JSON-style hash, though it has some limitations; with JSON-style hashes, the keys *must* be symbols, whereas Hashrocket supports any object as a key. You will see both styles regularly used.

We've created a hash and assigned it to the "my_hash" variable. In this example, the keys of our array are countries, and the values are cities. To reference a specific value of a hash, you pass the hash a key, and it will return the value to you:

```
irb(main):006:0>  my_hash[:uk]
=> "London"
```

We've passed the hash a key of :uk, and it returned the value of "London."

```
irb(main):007:0>  my_hash[:canada] = 'Calgary'
=> "Calgary"
```

This is the same idea, but here we're changing the value out for the key Canada. So the value of "Toronto" goes away and is replaced by "Calgary."

```
irb(main):008:0> my_hash.first
=> [:canada, "Calgary"]
```

In this example, we use the `first` method, which returns the first key-value pair. Notice in this case the return value is an array. The first element in the array is the key, and the second is the value. The keys method will return an array of all the keys contained in the hash. Here is an example:

```
irb(main):010:0> my_hash.keys
=> [:canada, :france, :uk]
```

It is important to note that in all of our examples, we have assigned strings to different positions to both our hashes and arrays, but any object could be stored in an array or hash. For instance, you might want to store numbers or even another array or hash. The possibilities are unlimited:

```
irb(main):001:0> numbers_array = [1, 2, 3, 4, 5]
=> [1,2,3,4,5]

irb(main):002:0> numbers_hash = {one: 1, two: 2, three: 3}
=> {:one => 1, :two => 2, :three => 3}
```

Language Basics

Like other programming languages, Ruby includes variables, operators, control-flow statements, and methods. This section shows you how to use them.

Variables

Variables are used to hold values you want to keep for later processing. When you perform a calculation, you probably want to use the result of that calculation somewhere else in your application code, and that's when you need a variable. In Ruby, variables are easily created. You just need to give a variable a name and assign a value to it; there's no need to specify a data type for the variable or define it in your code before you use it.

Let's create a few variables to hold some values you may need later. Notice that you can reuse a variable name by reassigning a value:

```
irb(main):001:0>  test_variable = 'This is a string'
=> "This is a string"

irb(main):002:0>  test_variable = 2010
=> 2010

irb(main):003:0>  test_variable = 232.3
=> 232.3
```

You've created a variable named `test_variable` and assigned a few different values to it. Because everything in Ruby is an object, the `test_variable` variable holds a reference to the object you assigned.

Variable names can be any sequence of numbers and letters, as long as they start with a letter or an underscore; however, the first character of a variable indicates the type of the variable. Variables also have a *scope*, which is the context in which the variable is defined. Some variables are used in a small snippet of code and need to exist for only a short period of time; those are called *local variables*. Table 4-1 lists the different types of variables supported by Ruby and shows how to recognize them when you're coding. Type some variable names in `irb`, and you'll get results similar to those shown here.

Table 4-1. *Ruby Variables*

Example	Description
$user	*Global variables* start with $. Global variables are not constrained by any scope—they're available anywhere. While this sounds convenient, global variables can also lead to bugs which are difficult to diagnose. Global variables should generally be avoided except in unique circumstances.
@@count	*Class variables* start with @@. Class variables exist in the scope of a class, so all instances of a specific class have a single value for the class variable.
@name	*Instance variables* start with @. Instance variables are unique to a given instance of a class.

(continued)

Table 4-1. (*continued*)

Example	Description
SERVER_IP	You can create a *constant* in Ruby by capitalizing the first letter of a variable, but it's a convention that constants are written in all uppercase characters. Constants are variables that don't change throughout the execution of a program. In Ruby, constants can be reassigned; however, you get a warning from the interpreter if you do so.
my_string	*Local variables* start with a lowercase letter or an underscore, and they live for only a short period of time. They usually exist only inside the method or block of code where they're first assigned.

In Ruby, it's considered best practice to use long and descriptive variable names. For example, in Java, you may have a variable named phi; but in Ruby, you write out place_holder_variable for clarity. The basic idea is that code is much more readable if the person looking at it (probably you) doesn't have to guess what phi stands for. This is extremely important when you come back to a piece of code after a year or so.

Operators

You can combine Ruby code using operators. Many classes implement operators as methods. Table 4-2 lists the most common operators and their functions.

Table 4-2. *Ruby Operators*

Operator	Description
[] []=	Assignment
* / % + **	Arithmetic
<= >= < >	Comparison
.. ...	Range
& ^ |	AND, exclusive OR, regular OR (bitwise)
|| && not or and	Logical operators

Ruby contains a ternary operator that you can use as a short notation for if-else-end. The ternary operator uses the form expression ? value_if_true : value_if_false:

```
a = 10
b = 20
a > b ? a : b
# => 20
```

In plain English, we're saying if a is greater than b, then return a; otherwise, return b. The ternary operator is very concise but still easy to read.

Blocks and Iterators

Any method in Ruby can accept a *code block*—a fragment of code between curly braces or do..end constructs. It determines whether the method in question calls the given block. The block always appears immediately after the method call, with the start of the block coming on the same line as the method invocation.

Here's an example using the times method; times executes the given code block once for each iteration. In this case, "Hello" is printed five times:

```
5.times { puts "Hello" }
```

```
Hello
Hello
Hello
Hello
Hello
```

If a method yields arguments to a block, the arguments are named between two pipe characters (|) on the same line as the method call. In the next example, the block receives one argument, *item:*

```
[1,2,3,4,5].each { |item| puts item }
```

```
1
2
3
4
5
```

Here, each number is yielded to the block in succession. You store the number in the block variable `item` and use `puts` to print it on its own line.

The convention is to use braces for single-line blocks and `do..end` for multiline blocks. Here's an example similar to the previous one; it uses `each_with_index`, which yields the item and its index in the array:

```ruby
["a", "b", "c"].each_with_index do |item, index|
  puts "Item:  #{item}"
  puts "Index: #{index}"
  puts "---"
end
```

```
Item:  a
Index: 0
---
Item:  b
Index: 1
---
Item:  c
Index: 2
---
```

Comments

Sometimes developers feel the need to annotate their code with information to help future developers understand some code. Such annotations are called *comments*. In Ruby, comments are most often identified by an unquoted #, and anything between the # and the end of the line of code is ignored by the Ruby interpreter. You can also use a # to "comment out" a line of code—essentially temporarily disabling it while developing or debugging. Here's an example with both an "informative" comment and a commented-out line:

```ruby
# This method creates a widget
def create_widget
  widget = Widget.new
```

```
  # widget.forge!
  widget
end
```

To make the best use of comments, avoid using them to state the obvious (like the preceding example). Instead, reserve comments for explaining difficult sections of code. (Or better yet, rewrite the code so it's intuitively understood without comments.) Comments can be a liability when they add too much clutter to the code or when they're not updated to accurately reflect changes to the code since they were first written.

Control Structures

In all of the previous examples, the Ruby interpreter executed the code from top to bottom. However, in the majority of cases, you want to control which methods are to be executed and when they should be executed. The statements you want to be executed may depend on many variables, such as the state of some computation or the user input. For that purpose, programming languages have *control-flow statements*, which allow you to execute code based on conditions. Here are a few examples of how to use if, else, elsif, unless, while, and end. Notice that control structures in Ruby are terminated using the end keyword:

```
now = Time.now
# => 2020-01-20 20:00:37 -0600

if now == Time.now
  puts "now is in the past"
elsif now > Time.now
  puts "nonsense"
else
  puts "time has passed"
end
# => time has passed
```

The first if statement will never trigger because there is a slight bit of time that passes between when you set the now variable and when you test it against Time.now. The second conditional won't trigger because the now variable will obviously be in the past, if only slightly. The third conditional "else" will always trigger, because neither of the first two conditionals triggered.

A trick that makes simple conditionals easy to read is to place `if` and `unless` conditional statements at the end of a code line so they act as *modifiers*. Here's how it looks:

```
a = 5
b = 10
puts "b is greater than a" if a < b
```

```
b is greater than a
puts "a is greater than b" unless a < b
nil
```

The `unless` structure was confusing for us at first. Once we started reading it as "if not," it made sense. In the previous example, reading the statement as "puts 'a is greater than b' if not a < b" makes the most sense.

You can also use `while` statements, as in all major programming languages:

```
a = 5
b = 10

while a < b
  puts "a is #{a}"
  a += 1
end
```

```
a is 5
a is 6
a is 7
a is 8
a is 9
```

Methods

Methods are little programmable actions that you can define to help your development. Let's leave `irb` for the moment and talk about pure Ruby code. (All of this also works if you type it into `irb`.)

Suppose that, several times in the application you're writing, you need to get the current time as a string. To save yourself from having to retype `Time.now.to_s` over and over, you can build a method. Every method starts with `def`:

```
def time_as_string
  Time.now.to_s
end
```

Anywhere in the application that you want to get the time, you type `time_as_string`:

```
puts time_as_string
```

```
"2020-01-20 20:03:15 -0600"
```

See how easy that is? Obviously with this code, you didn't do much, but methods can be much more complex. Methods can also take in variables:

```
def say_hello_to(name)
  "Hello, #{name}!"
end

puts say_hello_to("John")
```

```
"Hello, John!"
```

Here you defined a method named `say_hello_to` that accepts one argument *name*. That method uses string interpolation to return a string of "Hello, *name that was passed to the method*!" The `puts` then sends the response of that method to the screen.

Next, let's look at how to put methods together into classes to make them really powerful.

Note   You already know that local variables must start with a lowercase letter and can't contain any characters other than letters, numbers, and underscores. Method names are restricted to the same rules, which means they often look like variables. Keywords (like `if`, `or`, `when`, and, etc.) share the same set of properties. How does the Ruby interpreter know the difference? When Ruby encounters a word, it sees it as a local variable name, a method invocation, or a keyword. If it's a keyword, then Ruby knows it and responds accordingly. If there's an equals sign (=) to the right of the word, Ruby assumes it's a local variable being assigned. If it's neither a keyword nor an assignment, Ruby assumes it's a method being invoked and sends the method to the implied receiver, `self`.

Classes and Objects

You've reviewed all the basic types of items in a Ruby application, so let's start using them.

Objects

Ruby is an *object-oriented* (OO) programming language. If you've never worked in an OO language before, the metaphors used can be confusing the first time you hear them. Basically, *objects* are simple ways to organize your code and the data it contains. Objects are just like objects in the real world. You can move them around, make them do things, destroy them, create them, and so forth. In OO programming, you act on objects by either passing messages to them or passing them in messages to other objects. This will become clearer as we go along.

To better understand OO programming, let's start out with some *procedural* code (which is decidedly *not* object oriented) first. Let's say you're writing a program to help track the athletic program at a school. You have a list of all the students who are currently participating in a team, along with their student IDs. This example looks at the rowing team. You could keep an array of arrays representing the students on the team:

```
rowing_team = [[1975, "Smith", "John"], [1964, "Brown", "Dan"], ...]
```

Note   This is called a *multidimensional array*. It's simply an array that contains more arrays as elements. You could reference the first array in the array like so:

```
rowing_team.first=>
[1975, "Smith", "John"]
```

This is an array of [`id`, `first_name`, `last_name`]. You'd probably need to add a comment to explain that. If you wanted multiple teams, you could wrap this in a hash:

```
teams = { :rowing => [[1975, "Smith", "John"], [1964, "Brown", "Dan"], ...],
          :track  => [[1975, "Smith", "John"], [1900, "Mark", "Twain"], ...]
        }
```

That works for now. But it's kind of ugly, and you could easily get confused, especially if you kept adding teams. This style of coding is referred to as *procedural*, and it's not object oriented. You're keeping track of huge data collections that are made up of simple types. Wouldn't it be nice to keep all these data more organized? You'll need to define what your objects will look like, so you'll need a pattern, called a *class*. Then you will instantiate your class to make an *instance*.

Classes

A *class* is like a blueprint for creating an object. You've been using classes all over the place—Array, String, User, and so on. Now, let's construct a Student class and a Team class.

Here is the basic blueprint for a Student class:

```
class Student
  # Setter method for @first_name
  def first_name=(value)
    @first_name = value
  end

  # Getter method for @first_name
  def first_name
    @first_name
  end

  # Setter method for @last_name
  def last_name=(value)
    @last_name = value
  end

  # Getter method for @last_name
  def last_name
    @last_name
  end
```

```
  # Returns full name
  def full_name
    last_name + ", " + first_name
  end
end
```

Note   "Getter" and "setter" methods are methods that get an instance variable or set an instance variable, respectively. It's that simple. They are used to expose this functionality both inside and outside your instance. In this case, you have a getter and setter method for `last_name` and `first_name`. They use instance variables (as opposed to local variables) so that the getter and setter methods can share the same data. Otherwise, if they used *local* variables, the getter and setter methods for `last_name`, for example, would have their *own* data for the last name— meaning you couldn't "get" what you "set."

Right now, you're keeping track of the student's `first_name` and `last_name` strings. As you can see, you define a method named `first_name=(value)`, and you take value and put it into an instance variable named `@first_name`. Let's try using this class:

```
# Take the Class, and turn it into a real Object instance
@student = Student.new
@student.first_name = "Bob"
@student.last_name = "Jones"
puts @student.full_name
```

```
"Jones, Bob"
```

Instead of building a dumb array, you've built a smart class. When you call new on the class, it builds a version of itself called an *object*, which is then stored in the `@student` variable. In the next two lines, you use the = methods to store the student's first and last names. Then, you use the method `full_name` to give a nicely formatted response.

It turns out that creating getter and setter methods like this is a common practice in OO programming. Fortunately, Ruby saves you the effort of creating them by providing a shortcut called `attr_accessor`:

```ruby
class Student
  attr_accessor :first_name, :last_name, :id_number

  def full_name
    last_name + ", " + first_name
  end
end
```

This behaves in exactly the same way as the first version. The `attr_accessor` bit helps by automatically building the methods you need, such as `first_name=`. Also, this time you add an `@id_number`.

Let's build a Team class now:

```ruby
class Team
  attr_accessor :name, :students

  def initialize(name)
    @name = name
    @students = []
  end

  def add_student(id_number, first_name, last_name)
    student = Student.new
    student.id_number  = id_number
    student.first_name = first_name
    student.last_name  = last_name
    @students << student
  end

  def print_students
    @students.each do |student|
      puts student.full_name
    end
  end
end
```

You've added something new to this class: the `initialize` method. Now, when you call new, you can pass in the name. For example, you can type `Team.new('baseball')`, and the `initialize` method is called. Not only does initialize set up the name but it also sets up an instance variable named `@students` and turns it into an empty array. The method `add_students` fills the array with new `Student` objects.

Let's see how you use this class:

```
team = Team.new("Rowing")
team.add_student(1982, "John", "Smith")
team.add_student(1984, "Bob", "Jones")
team.print_students
```

```
Smith, John
Jones, Bob
```

Containing things in objects cleans up your code. By using classes, you ensure that each object only needs to worry about its own concerns. If you were writing this application without objects, everyone's business would be shared. The variables would all exist around one another, and there would be one *huge* object. Objects let you break things up into small working parts.

By now you should have a general idea of what's going on with some of the Ruby code you've seen floating around Rails. There is a *lot* more to Ruby that we haven't touched on here. Ruby has some amazing metaprogramming features you can read about in a book that specifically focuses on Ruby, such as *Beginning Ruby: From Novice to Professional,* Third Edition, by Peter Cooper (Apress, 2016).

RUBY STYLE

Style is important when you're programming. Ruby programmers tend to be picky about style, and they generally adhere to a few specific guidelines, summarized here:

- Indentation size is two spaces.
- Spaces are preferred to tabs.
- Variables should be lowercase and underscored: `some_variable`, not `someVariable` or `somevariable`.

- Method definitions should include parentheses and no unnecessary spaces: `MyClass.my_method(my_arg)`, not `my_method( my_arg )` or `my_method my_arg`.

Whatever your personal style, the most important thing is to remain consistent. Nothing is worse than looking at code that switches between tabs and spaces or mixed and lowercase variables.

Ruby Documentation

You can refer to the following documentation for more information about Ruby:

- *Core library:* The Ruby distribution comes with a set of classes known as the Ruby Core library, which includes base classes such as `Object`, `String`, `Array`, and others. In the Ruby Core application programming interface (API) documentation, you can find all the classes and methods included in the Core library. In this short chapter, you've already seen a few classes in action. One of the secrets to effectively using Ruby is to know which classes and methods are available to you. We recommend that you go to the Ruby Core API documentation page at `www.ruby-doc.org/core/` and start to learn more about Ruby classes and methods.

- *Standard library:* In addition to the Core library, the Ruby distribution comes bundled with the Ruby Standard library. It includes a set of classes that extends the functionality of the Ruby language by helping developers perform common programming tasks, such as network programming and threading. Make sure you spend some time reading the Standard library documentation at `www.ruby-doc.org/stdlib/`.

- *Online resources:* The Ruby documentation project home page is located at `www.ruby-doc.org`. There you can find additional reading resources to help you learn Ruby, such as articles and tutorials, as well as the Core and Standard Ruby API documentation.

Summary

This chapter gave a strong introduction to the Ruby language. You now have the tools to start learning the Rails framework and start building web applications. As you progress, you'll more than likely come to love Ruby, especially if you have a background in other languages. Its power is only matched by its simplicity, and it's genuinely fun to program with. The next chapter will dive into Active Record and learn how Rails lets you easily interact with your database.

CHAPTER 5

Working with a Database: Active Record

Earlier, you took a whirlwind tour through creating a basic Rails application using the built-in scaffolding feature. You sketched out a basic model for a blog application and created the project databases. You used the built-in web server to run the application locally and practiced adding and managing articles from the web browser. This chapter will take a more in-depth look at how things work, starting with what is arguably the most important part of Rails: Active Record.

You may recall from Chapter 1 that Active Record is the Ruby object-relational mapping (ORM) library that handles database abstraction and interaction for Rails. Whether you realized it or not, in Chapter 3 all access to the database—adding, editing, and deleting articles—happened through the magic of Active Record.

If you're not sure what exactly object-relational mapping is, don't worry. By the end of this chapter, you'll know. For now, it's best if you think of Active Record as being an intermediary that sits between your code and your database, allowing you to work with data effectively and naturally. When you use Active Record, you communicate with your database using pure Ruby code. Active Record translates the Ruby you write into a language that databases can understand.

This chapter teaches you how to use Active Record to talk to your database and perform basic operations. It introduces the concepts you need to know about communicating with databases and object-relational mapping. Then, you will look at Active Record and walk through the techniques you need to know to effectively work with a database from Rails. If you don't have a lot of database experience under your belt, don't worry. Working with databases through Active Record is a painless and even enjoyable experience. If you're an experienced database guru, you'll find that Active Record is an intelligent and efficient way to perform database operations without the need for low-level database-specific commands.

© Brady Somerville, Adam Gamble, Cloves Carneiro Jr and Rida Al Barazi 2020
B. Somerville et al., *Beginning Rails 6*, https://doi.org/10.1007/978-1-4842-5716-6_5

Note   If you need to get the code at the exact point where you finished
Chapter 3, download the zip file from GitHub (`https://github.com/
nicedawg/beginning-rails-6-blog/archive/chapter-03.zip`).

Introducing Active Record: Object-Relational Mapping on Rails

The key feature of Active Record is that it maps tables to classes, table rows to objects,
and table columns to object attributes. This practice is commonly known as *object-
relational mapping* (ORM). To be sure, Active Record isn't the only ORM in existence,
but it may well be the easiest to use of the bunch.

One of the reasons Active Record is so easy to use is that almost no configuration
is required to have it map a table to a class. You just need to create a Ruby class that's
named after the table you want to map and extend the Active Record `Base` class:

```
class Book < ApplicationRecord
end
```

Notice the part that reads < `ApplicationRecord`. The less-than sign indicates that
the `Book` class on the left is a subclass of the one on the right, `ApplicationRecord`. In
Ruby, when you inherit from a class like this, you automatically gain access to all the
functionality in the parent class. ApplicationRecord is defined in your app/models/
application_record.rb. Initially, it simply inherits from ActiveRecord::Base. There's a
lot of code in the `ActiveRecord::Base` class, but you don't need to look at it. Your class
merely inherits it, and your work is finished.

Assuming Active Record knows how to find your database and that you have a table
called books (note that the table name is plural, whereas the class name is singular), the
table is automatically mapped. If you know your books table contains the fields `title`,
`publisher`, and `published_at`, you can do this in any Ruby context:

```
book = Book.new

book.title = "Beginning Rails 6"
book.publisher = "Apress"
book.published_at = "2020-04-15"

book.save
```

These five lines write a new record to the books table. You gain a lot of ability by the simple act of subclassing! And that's why Active Record is easy to use. Notice how the table's fields (title, publisher, and published_at) can be read and written to using methods on the object you created (book). And you didn't need to tell Active Record what your fields were named or even that you had any fields. It figured this out on its own. Of course, Active Record doesn't just let you create new records. It can also read, update, and delete records, plus a lot more.

Active Record is database agnostic, so it doesn't care which database software you use, and it supports nearly every database out there. Because it's a high-level abstraction, the code you write remains the same no matter which database you're using. For the record (no pun intended), in this book you use SQLite. As explained in Chapter 2, SQLite is open source, easy to use, and fast, and it's the default database used for Rails development. (Along with the SQLite site, https://sqlite.org, the Wikipedia entry on SQLite is a good resource: https://en.wikipedia.org/wiki/SQLite.)

At some point, you may need to switch to another database backend. (SQLite is great for development, but not appropriate for many production apps.) Rails 6 has added a command—*rails db:system:change*—which makes it easy to switch databases. We won't run this command for this book, but just know this command exists.

Note   Rails is also ORM agnostic: it allows you to hook up your ORM of choice. There are several alternatives to Active Record which you can use if you think Active Record has some deficiencies. (See www.ruby-toolbox.com/categories/orm for a list of popular ones.) However, we feel that sticking to the default ORM is the best way to learn. We don't cover alternative ORMs in this book.

What About SQL?

To be sure, you don't need Active Record (or any ORM) to talk to and manipulate your database. Databases have their own language: SQL, which is supported by nearly every relational database in existence. Using SQL, you can view column information, fetch a particular row or a set of rows, and search for rows containing certain criteria. You can also use SQL to create, drop, and modify tables and insert, update, and destroy the information stored in those tables. The problem with SQL is that it's not object oriented. If you want to learn the basic SQL syntax, look at Appendix B.

Object-oriented programming and relational databases are fundamentally different paradigms. The relational paradigm deals with relations and is mathematical by nature. The object-oriented paradigm, however, deals with objects, their attributes, and their associations to one another. As soon as you want to make objects persistent using a relational database, you notice something: there is a rift between these two paradigms—the so-called *object-relational gap*. An ORM library like Active Record helps you bridge that gap.

Note   Active Record is based on a design pattern. *Design patterns* are standard solutions to common problems in software design. Well, it turns out that when you're working in an object-oriented environment, the problem of how to effectively communicate with a database (which isn't object oriented) is quite common. Therefore, many smart people have wrapped their minds around the problem of how best to bring the object-oriented paradigm together with the relational database. One of those smart people is Martin Fowler, who, in his book *Patterns of Enterprise Application Architecture* (Addison Wesley, 2002), first described a pattern that he called an Active Record. In the pattern Fowler described, a one-to-one mapping exists between a database record and the object that represents it. When Rails creator David Heinemeier Hansson sought to implement an ORM for his framework, he based it on Fowler's pattern.

Active Record lets you model real-world things in your code. Rails calls these real-world things *models*—the *M* in MVC. A model might be named `Person`, `Product`, or `Article`, and it has a corresponding table in the database: `people`, `products`, or `articles`. Each model is implemented as a Ruby class and is stored in the `app/models` directory. Active Record provides the link between these classes and your tables, allowing you to work with what look like regular objects, which, in turn, can be persisted to the database. This frees you from having to write low-level SQL to talk to the database. Instead, you work with your data as if they were an object, and Active Record does all the translation into SQL behind the scenes. This means that in Rails, you get to stick with one language: Ruby.

> **Note**   Just because you're using Active Record to abstract your SQL generation doesn't mean SQL is evil. Active Record makes it possible to execute SQL directly whenever that's necessary. The truth is that raw SQL is the native language of databases, and there are some (albeit rare) cases when an ORM won't cut it.

Active Record Conventions

Active Record achieves its zero-configuration reputation by way of convention. Most of the conventions it uses are easy to grasp. After all, they're conventions, so they're already in wide use. Although you can override most of the conventions to suit the particular design of your database, you'll save a lot of time and energy if you stick to them.

Let's take a quick look at the two main conventions you need to know:

- Class names are singular; table names are plural.

- Tables contain an identity column named id.

Active Record assumes that the name of your table is the plural form of the class name. If your table name contains underscores, then your class name is assumed to be in *CamelCase*. Table 5-1 shows some examples.

Table 5-1. *Table and Class Name Conventions*

Table	Class
events	Event
people	Person
categories	Category
order_items	OrderItem

All tables are assumed to have a unique identity column named id. This column should be the table's *primary key* (a value used to uniquely identify a table's row). This is a fairly common convention in database design. (For more information on primary keys in database design, the Wikipedia entry has a wealth of useful information and links: https://en.wikipedia.org/wiki/Unique_key.)

The belief in convention over configuration is firmly entrenched in the Rails philosophy, so it should come as no surprise that there are more conventions at work than those listed here. You'll likely find that they all make good sense, and you can use them without paying much attention.

Introducing the Console

Ruby comes with a great little tool: an interactive interpreter called irb (for Interactive Ruby). irb is Ruby's standard REPL—a Read-Eval-Print Loop. Many programming languages have REPL tools, and Ruby has REPL tools other than irb. (pry is a popular alternative REPL for ruby with some great features.)

Most of the time, you invoke irb using the *rails console* command that ships with Rails, but you can start up an irb session whenever you want by typing `irb` at the command prompt. The advantage of the console is that it enjoys the special privilege of being integrated with your project's environment. This means it has access to and knowledge of your models (and, subsequently, your database).

You use the console as a means to get inside the world of your `Article` model and to work with it in the exact same way your Rails application would. As you'll see in a minute, this is a great way to showcase the capabilities of Active Record interactively.

You can execute any arbitrary Ruby code in irb and do anything you might otherwise do inside your Ruby programs: set variables, evaluate conditions, and inspect objects. The only essential difference between an interactive session and a regular old Ruby program is that irb echoes the return value of everything it executes. This saves you from having to explicitly print the results of an evaluation. Just run the code, and irb prints the result.

You can tell whenever you're inside an irb session by looking for the double greater-than sign (>>)—or a slightly different sign depending on your environment—which indicates the irb prompt, and the arrow symbol (=>), which indicates the response.

As you continue to progress with both Ruby and Rails, you'll find that irb is an essential tool. Using irb, you can play around with code and make sure it works as you expect before you write it into your programs.

If you've been following along with the previous chapters, then you should have a model called `Article` (in `app/models/article.rb`), and you've probably already entered some sample data when playing with scaffolding in Chapter 3. If not, make sure you get up to speed by reading Chapters 2 and 3 before moving on.

Let's load irb and start to experiment with the `Article` model. Make sure you're inside the blog application directory, and then type `rails console` on your command line. This causes the irb console to load with your application's *development* environment and leaves you at a simple prompt, waiting for you to enter some code:

```
$ rails console
Loading development environment.
>>
```

From the console, you can interrogate your `Article` model for information. For instance, you can ask it for its column names:

```
>> Article.column_names
=> ["id", "title", "body", "published_at", "created_at", "updated_at",
"excerpt", "location"]
```

Look at that! All your columns are presented as a Ruby array (you can tell by the fact that they're surrounded by square brackets). Another quick trick you may use often is to type just the name of your model class in the console to find out not only the column names but also the data type of each column:

```
>> Article
=> Article(id: integer, title: string, body: text, published_at: datetime,
created_at: datetime, updated_at: datetime, excerpt: string, location: string)
```

You get the `column_names` class method courtesy of the `ActiveRecord::Base` class from which your `Article` class ultimately inherits. Actually, you get a lot of methods courtesy of `ActiveRecord::Base`. To see just how many, you can ask

```
>> Article.methods.size
=> 690
```

Note   Depending on the version of Rails you are using and what gems you have installed, the number of methods might be different from 690. This is normal.

That's a lot of methods! You may get a different number of methods depending on your environment. Many of the methods are inherited from ActiveRecord, but many of them come from classes that Active Record ultimately inherits from—like Ruby's base Object class and *its* parent classes. Don't worry—you don't need to memorize all of these methods. Most of them are used internally so you'll never have to use them directly. Still, it's important, if for no other reason than to get a sense of what you get for free just by subclassing Active Record. Although in this case ApplicationRecord is considered the *superclass*, it sure makes your lowly Article class super, doesn't it? (Sorry, enough bad humor.)

A CRASH COURSE IN RUBY CLASS DESIGN

Object-oriented programming is all about objects. You create a class that encapsulates all the logic required to create an object, along with its properties and attributes, and use the class to produce new objects, each of which is a unique instance, distinct from other objects of the same class. That may sound a little abstract (and with good reason—abstraction, after all, is the name of the game), but if it helps, you can think of a class as being an object factory.

The obvious example is that of a car factory. Contained within a car factory are all the resources, tools, workers, and processes required to produce a shiny new car. Each car that comes off the assembly line is unique. The cars may vary in size, color, and shape, or they may not vary from one another much at all. The point is that even if two cars share the exact same attributes, they aren't the same car. You certainly wouldn't expect a change to the color of one car to affect all the others, would you? Well, in object-oriented programming, it's not much different. The class is the factory that produces objects, which are called *instances* of a class. From a single factory, an infinite number of objects can be produced:

```
class Car
end

car1 = Car.new
car2 = Car.new
```

car1 is a Car object, which is to say it's an instance of the class Car. Each car is a different object, created by the same factory. Each object knows which class it belongs to (which factory created it), so if you're ever in doubt, you can ask it:

```
car2.class #=> Car
```

Your Car class doesn't really do anything that useful—it has no attributes. So let's give it some. You start by giving it a make—something like Toyota or Nissan. Of course, you need to define a way to read and write these attributes. You do this by creating aptly named *reader* and *writer* methods. Some object-oriented languages refer to these as *getters* and *setters*. The two sets of terms are pretty much interchangeable, but Ruby favors the former. Let's add a reader and writer for the make attribute:

```
class Car
  # A writer method. Sets the value of the @make attribute
  def make=(text)
    @make = text
  end

  # A reader method. Returns the value of the @make attribute
  def make
    @make
  end
end
```

The methods you just defined (make() and make=()) are instance methods. This is because they can be used only on instances of the class, which is to say the individual objects that have been created from the class. To create a new instance of the Car class, you use the new constructor:

```
my_car = Car.new
```

That's all that's required to create a new instance of the class Car in a local variable called my_car. The variable my_car can now be considered a Car object. Although you have a new Car object, you haven't yet given it a make. If you use the reader method you created to ask your car what its make is, you see that it's nil:

```
my_car.make #=> nil
```

Apparently, if you want your car to have a make, you have to set it. This is where the writer method comes in handy:

```
my_car.make = 'Toyota'
```

This sets the value of the make attribute for your car to Toyota. If you had other Car objects, their makes would remain unchanged. You're setting the attribute only on the my_car object. Now, when you use the reader method, it confirms that the make attribute has been updated:

```
my_car.make #=> 'Toyota'
```

Of course, you can change the value any time you want:

```
my_car.make = 'Mazda'
```

And again, if you ask your Car object its make, it will tell you:

```
my_car.make #=> 'Mazda'
```

That's a simple example, but it illustrates a couple of very important points: classes are used to create objects, and objects have attributes. Every object has a unique set of attributes, different from other objects of the same class.

The reason for this crash course in Ruby class design is to illustrate the point that modeling with Active Record is a lot like modeling with standard Ruby classes. If you decided to think of Active Record as being an extension to standard Ruby classes, you wouldn't be very far off. In practice, this fact makes using Active Record in Ruby quite natural. And because Active Record can reflect on your tables to determine which fields to map automatically, you need to define your attributes in only one place: the database. That's DRY (don't repeat yourself)! See Chapter 4 to learn more about Ruby's syntax, classes, and objects.

Active Record Basics: CRUD

Active Record is a big topic, so let's start with the basics. You've seen the so-called big four earlier, but here they are again: create, read, update, and delete, affectionately known as CRUD. In one way or another, most of what you do with Active Record in particular, and with databases in general, relates to CRUD. Rails has embraced CRUD as a design technique and as a way to simplify the modeling process. It's no surprise then that this chapter takes an in-depth look at how to do CRUD with Active Record.

Let's build on the blog application you started in Chapter 3. Although your application doesn't do much yet, it's at a stage where it's easy to demonstrate these concepts in a more concrete fashion.

This section uses the console, so keep it open as you work, and feel free to experiment as much as you want. The more experimentation you do, the deeper your understanding will be.

Creating New Records

You start by creating a new article in the database so you have something to work with. There are a few different ways to create new model objects, but they're all variations on the same theme. This section shows how each approach works and explains the often subtle differences among them.

Resetting the Database

Before we begin creating records, we'll reset our database to a clean state. If we had data we cared about keeping, this would be a bad idea! But since we don't, resetting our database will help your output more closely match the output shown in the following examples. From a directory within your Rails project, issue the following command:

```
$ rails db:reset
Dropped database 'db/development.sqlite3'
Dropped database 'db/test.sqlite3'
Created database 'db/development.sqlite3'
Created database 'db/test.sqlite3'
```

This command drops the database, recreates it, loads the schema, and seeds your database with seed data according to your db/seeds.rb file (which is empty at this point).

Using the *new* Constructor

The most basic way to create a new model object is with the new constructor. If you read the crash course section on Ruby classes earlier, you're sure to recognize it. If you didn't, then it's enough that you know new is the usual way to create new objects of any type. Active Record classes are no different. Try it now:

```
>> article = Article.new
=> #<Article id: nil, title: nil, body: nil, published_at: nil, created_at: nil,
updated_at: nil, excerpt: nil, location: nil>
```

All you're doing here is creating a new `Article` object and storing it in the local variable `article`. True to form, the console responds with the return value of the method, which in this case is a *string* representation of the model object. It may look a little funny, but this is what all Ruby objects look like when you inspect them. The response lists the attributes of the `Article` class. Starting here, you could call a few of the `article` variable methods. For example, the `new_record?` method tells you whether this object has been persisted (saved) to the database, and the `attributes` method returns a hash of the attributes that Active Record garnered by reflecting on the columns in the table. Each key of the hash will be the name of a column (`body`, `created_at`, etc.).

```
>> article.new_record?
=> true
>> article.attributes
=> {"id"=>nil, "title"=>nil, "body"=>nil, "published_at"=>nil, "created_
at"=>nil, "updated_at"=>nil, "excerpt"=>nil, "location"=>nil}
```

Here, you're using *reader* methods, which read and return the value of the attribute in question. Because this is a brand-new record and you haven't given it any information, all your attributes are `nil`, which means they have no values. Let's remedy that now using (what else?) *writer* methods:

```
>> article.title = 'RailsConf'
=> "RailsConf"

>> article.body = 'RailsConf is the official gathering for Rails developers..'
=> "'RailsConf is the official gathering for Rails developers.."

>> article.published_at = '2020-01-31'
=> "2020-01-31"
```

Note   A return of `nil` always represents nothing. It's a helpful little object that stands in the place of nothingness. If you ask an object for something and it returns `false`, then false is *something*, so it's not a helpful representation. As a nerdy fact, in logics, false and true are equal and opposite values, but they're values in the end. The same is true of zero (0). The number 0 isn't truly nothing— it's an actual representation of an abstract nothing, but it's still something. That's why in programming you have `nil` (or `null` in other languages).

Now, when you inspect your `Article` object, you can see that it has attributes:

```
>> article
=> #<Article id: nil, title: "RailsConf", body: "RailsConf is the official
 gathering for Rails devel...", published_at: "2020-01-31 00:00:00",
 created_at: nil, updated_at: nil, excerpt: nil, location: nil>
```

You still haven't written a new record. If you were to look at the `articles` table in the database, you wouldn't find a record for the object you're working with. (If you squint really hard at the preceding object-inspection string, notice that no `id` has been assigned yet.) That's because you haven't yet saved the object to the database. Fortunately, saving an Active Record object couldn't be any easier:

```
>> article.save
   (0.1ms)  begin transaction
 Article Create (0.7ms)  INSERT INTO "articles" ("title", "body",
 "published_at", "created_at", "updated_at") VALUES (?, ?, ?, ?, ?)
 [["title", "RailsConf"], ["body", "RailsConfig is the official gathering
 for Rails developers.."], ["published_at", "2020-01-31 00:00:00"],
 ["created_at", "2020-02-01 01:04:01.870579"], ["updated_at", "2020-02-01
 01:04:01.870579"]]
   (5.0ms)  commit transaction
=> true
```

When you save a new record, an SQL INSERT statement is constructed behind the scenes; notice that Rails has displayed the generated SQL for you. If the INSERT is successful, the `save` operation returns `true`; if it fails, `save` returns `false`. You can ask for a count of the number of rows in the table just to be sure that a record was created:

```
>> Article.count
=> 1
```

Sure enough, you have a new article! You've got to admit, that was pretty easy. (You may have created some articles during the scaffolding session. If so, don't be surprised if you have more than one article already.) Additionally, if you ask the article whether it's a `new_record?`, it responds with `false`. Because it's saved, it's not "new" anymore:

```
y
>> article.new_record?
=> false
```

Let's create another article. This time, we'll omit all the chatter from the console so you can get a better sense of how the process plays out. You create a new object and place it in a variable, you set the object's attributes, and finally you save the record. Note that although you're using the local variable `article` to hold your object, it can be anything you want. Usually, you use a variable that indicates the type of object you're creating, like `article` or, if you prefer shorthand, just a:

```
>> article = Article.new
```

```
>> article.title      = "Introduction to SQL"
>> article.body    = "SQL stands for Structured Query Language, .."
>> article.published_at        = Time.zone.now
```

```
>> article.save
```

Note   Although writer methods look like assignments, they're really methods in disguise. `article.title = 'something'` is the functional equivalent of `article.title=('something')`, where `title=()` is the method. Ruby provides a little syntactic sugar to make writers look more natural.

Now you're rolling! You've already created a few articles and haven't had to write a lick of SQL. Given how easy this is, you may be surprised that you can do it in even fewer steps, but you can. Instead of setting each attribute on its own line, you can pass all of them to new at once. Here's how you can rewrite the preceding process of creating a new record in fewer lines of code:

```
>> article = Article.new(title: "Introduction to Active Record",
body: "Active Record is Rails's default ORM..", published_at: Time.zone.now)
>> article.save
```

Not bad, but you can do even better. The new constructor creates a new object, but it's your responsibility to save it. If you forget to save the object, it will never be written to the database. There is another method available that combines the creating and saving steps into one.

Using the *create* Method

When you want to create an object and save it in one fell swoop, you can use the `create` method. Use it now to create another article:

```
>> Article.create(title: "RubyConf 2020", body: "The annual RubyConf will
take place in..", published_at: '2020-01-31')
=> #<Article id: 4, title: "RubyConf 2020", body: "The annual RubyConf will take
place in..", published_at: "2020-01-31 00:00:00", created_at: "2020-01-31
23:17:19", updated_at: "2020-01-31 23:17:19", excerpt: nil, location: nil>
```

Instead of returning `true` or `false`, the `create` method returns the object it created—in this case, an `Article` object. You're actually passing a hash of attributes to the `create` method. Although hashes are normally surrounded by curly braces, *when a hash is the last argument to a Ruby method, the braces are optional.* You can just as easily create the attribute's hash first and then give that to `create`:

```
>> attributes = { title: "Rails Pub Nite", body: "Rails Pub Nite is every
3rd Monday of each month, except in December.", published_at: "2020-01-31"}
=> {:title=>"Rails Pub Nite", :body=>"Rails Pub Nite is every
3rd Monday of each month, except in December.", :published_at=>" 2020-01-31"}
>> Article.create(attributes)
```

```
=> #<Article id: 5, title: "Rails Pub Nite", body: "Rails Pub Nite is every 3rd
Monday of each month, e...", published_at: "2020-01-31 00:00:00",
created_at: "2020-01-31 23:36:07", updated_at: "2020-01-31 23:36:07",
excerpt: nil, location: nil>
```

Let's see how many articles you've created by doing a `count`:

```
>> Article.count
=> 5
```

You're getting the hang of this now. To summarize, when you want to create a new object and save it manually, use the `new` constructor; when you want to create and save in one operation, use `create`. You've already created five new records, which are plenty for now, so let's move on to the next step: finding records.

Reading (Finding) Records

Now that you have a few articles to play with, it's time to practice finding them. Every model class understands the `find` method. It's quite versatile and accepts a number of options that modify its behavior.

Let's start with the basics. `find` is a class method. That means you use it on the model class rather than an object of that class, just as you did the `new` and `create` methods. Like `new` and `create`, a `find` operation, if successful, returns a new object.

You can call `find` four ways:

- `find(:id)`: Finds a single record by its unique `id` or multiple records if `:id` is an array of ids

- `all`: Finds all records in the table

- `first`: Finds the first record

- `last`: Finds the last record

The following sections go through the different ways to call `find` and explain how to use each.

Finding a Single Record Using an ID

The `find`, `first`, and `last` methods mostly return a single record. The `:id` option is specific; you use it when you're looking for a specific record and you know its unique `id`. If you give it a single `id`, it either returns the corresponding record (if there is one) or raises an exception (if there isn't one). If you pass an array of ids—like `[4, 5]`—as the parameter, the method returns an array with all records that match the passed in ids. The `first` method is a little more forgiving; it returns the first record in the table or `nil` if the table is empty, as explained in the next section.

You can find a single record using its unique `id` by using `find(:id)`. Here's how it works:

```
>> Article.find(3)
=> #<Article id: 3, title: "Introduction to Active Record", body: "Active Record
is Rails's default ORM..", published_at: "2020-01-31 04:00:00",
created_at: "2020-01-31 23:15:37", updated_at: "2020-01-31 23:15:37",
excerpt: nil, location: nil>
```

As you can see, you found the article with the `id` of 3. If you want to take a closer look at what was returned, you can store the result in a local variable:

```
>> article = Article.find(3)
=> #<Article id: 3 ...>
>> article.id
=> 3
>> article.title
=> "Introduction to Active Record"
```

Here, you store the object that `find` returned in the local variable `article`. Then, you can interrogate it and ask for its attributes.

All this works because an article with the `id` 3 *actually exists*. If instead you search for a record that you know doesn't exist (say, 1037), Active Record raises an exception:

```
>> Article.find 1037
ActiveRecord::RecordNotFound: (Couldn't find Article with 'id'=1037)
...
```

Active Record raises a `RecordNotFound` exception and tells you it couldn't find any articles with the `id` of 1037. Of course it couldn't. You know that no such record exists. The lesson here is that you use `find(:id)` when you're looking for a specific record that you expect to exist. If the record doesn't exist, it's probably an error you want to know about; therefore, Active Record raises `RecordNotFound`.

RECOVERING FROM RECORDNOTFOUND ERRORS

When you use `find` with a single `id`, you expect the record to exist. Usually we don't want to display Rails error messages directly to the user, but we can make them nicer and customize the verbiage. So how can you recover gracefully from a `RecordNotFound` exception if you need to? You can use Ruby's facility for error handling: `begin` and `rescue`. Here's how this works:

```
begin
  Article.find(1037)
rescue ActiveRecord::RecordNotFound
  puts "We couldn't find that record"
end
```

First, you open a `begin` block. Then, you cause a `RecordNotFound` error by deliberately searching for a record that you know doesn't exist. When the error occurs, Ruby runs the code you put inside the `rescue` part of the body, which prints a friendly message.

You can put anything you like in the rescue block—you might want to render a specific view here, log the error, or even redirect to another location. Error handling works the same way with other error messages also. If you need to rescue from any error at all, you can just use rescue without specifying an error class.

Finding a Single Record Using *first*

You can find the first record that the database returns by using the `first` method. This always returns exactly one item, unless the table is empty, in which case `nil` is returned:

```
>> Article.first
=> #<Article id: 1, title: "RailsConf", body: "RailsConf is the official
 gathering for Rails devel...", published_at: "2020-01-31 00:00:00",
 created_at: "2020-01-31 23:12:09", updated_at: "2020-01-31 23:12:09",
 excerpt: nil, location: nil>
```

Keep in mind that this isn't necessarily the first record in the table. It depends on the database software you're using and the default order in which you want your records to be retrieved. Usually records are ordered by either `created_at` or `updated_at`. If you need to be sure you get the first record you're expecting, you should specify an order. It's the equivalent of saying `SELECT * FROM table LIMIT 1` in SQL. If you need to find a record and don't particularly care which record it is, `first` can come in handy. Note that `first` doesn't raise an exception if the record can't be found.

The `last` method works exactly the same as `first`; however, records are retrieved in the inverse order of `first`. For example, if records from articles are listed in chronological order for `first`, they're retrieved in inverse chronological order for `last`:

```
>> Article.last
=> #<Article id: 5, title: "Rails Pub Nite", body: "Rails Pub Nite is every 3rd
Monday of each month, e...", published_at: "2020-01-31 00:00:00",
created_at: "2020-01-31 23:36:07", updated_at: "2020-01-31 23:36:07",
excerpt: nil, location: nil>
```

Finding All Records

So far, you've looked at finding a single record. In each case, `find`, `first`, or `last` returns a single `Article` object. But what if you want to find more than one article? In your application, you want to display all the articles on the home page.

If you run the `all` method, it returns all records for that class:

```
>> articles = Article.all
=> #<ActiveRecord::Relation [#<Article id: 1,..> #<Article id: 2,..>,
#<Article id: 3,..>,
#<Article id: 4,..> , #<Article id: 5,..>]>
```

Look closely at the response, and you'll see that an instance of ActiveRecord::Relation was returned. Most ActiveRecord query methods return an instance of ActiveRecord::Relation. Why do this instead of simply returning an array of Article instances? By returning an ActiveRecord::Relation, it allows more query methods to be chained together and for the SQL to be executed at the last possible moment. We'll see an example of that soon.

Even though articles at this point is an ActiveRecord::Relation object, it can behave in many cases like an array. Like all Ruby arrays, you can ask for its size:

```
>> articles.size
=> 5
```

Because `articles` acts like an array, you can access the individual elements it contains by using its *index*, which is numeric, starting at 0:

```
>> articles[0]
=> #<Article id: 1, title: "RailsConf", body: "RailsConf is the official
 gathering for Rails devel...", published_at: "2020-01-31 00:00:00",
 created_at: "2020-01-31 23:12:09", updated_at: "2020-01-31 23:12:09",
 excerpt: nil, location: nil>
```

And after you've isolated a single `Article` object, you can find its attributes:

```
>> articles[0].title
=> "RailsConf"
```

What's happening here is that all produces an array, and you access the object at the 0 index and call the title method. You can also use the first method, which all arrays respond to, and get the same result, but with a little more natural syntax:

```
>> articles.first.title
=> "RailsConf"
```

If you want to iterate over the collection, you can use the each method, which, again, works with all arrays. Here, you loop over the array, extract each item into a variable called article, and print its title attribute using the puts command:

```
>> articles.each { |article| puts article.title }
RailsConf
Introduction to SQL
Introduction to Active Record
RubyConf 2020
Rails Pub Nite
=> [#<Article id: 1,..> #<Article id: 2,..>, #<Article id: 3,..>,
#<Article id: 4,..> , #<Article id: 5,..>]
```

Sometimes you want your results ordered. For example, if you're listing all your articles, you might want them listed alphabetically by title. To do so, you can use the order method, which accepts as argument the name of the column or columns. For you SQL heroes, it corresponds to the SQL ORDER clause:

```
>> articles = Article.order(:title)
=> #<ActiveRecord::Relation [#<Article id: 3,..> #<Article id: 2,..>,
#<Article id: 5,..>,
#<Article id: 1,..> , #<Article id: 4,..>]>
>> articles.each {|article| puts article.title }
Introduction to Active Record
Introduction to SQL
Rails Pub Nite
RailsConf
RubyConf 2020
=> [#<Article id: 3,..> #<Article id: 2,..>, #<Article id: 5,..>,
#<Article id: 1,..> , #<Article id: 4,..>]
```

Notice that when you call the `order` method, it returns an `ActiveRecord::Relation` object, as you may have expected. As mentioned earlier, one feature of ActiveRecord::Relation is that it allows you to chain calls to multiple methods before sending the command to the database; so you can call `all`, followed by `order`, and some other methods we'll talk about in Chapter 6, to create more precise database queries. Also, Active Record is smart enough to use *lazy loading*, a practice that only hits the database when necessary—in this example, when you call the each method.

By default, any column is ordered in ascending order (e.g., 1–10 or *a–z*). If you want to reverse this to get descending order, use the `:desc` modifier (similar to how you would in SQL):

```
>> articles = Article.order(published_at: :desc)
=> [#<Article id: 3,..> #<Article id: 2,..>, #<Article id: 1,..>,
#<Article id: 4,..> , #<Article id: 5,..>]
>> articles.each {|article| puts article.title }
Introduction to Active Record
Introduction to SQL
RailsConf
RubyConf 2020
Rails Pub Nite
=> [#<Article id: 3,..> #<Article id: 2,..>, #<Article id: 1,..>,
#<Article id: 4,..> , #<Article id: 5,..>]
```

Finding with Conditions

Although finding a record by its primary key is useful, it requires that you know the `id` to begin with, which isn't always the case. Sometimes you want to find records based on other criteria. This is where conditions come into play. Conditions correspond to the SQL `WHERE` clause. If you want to find a record by its title, you call the `where` method and pass a value that contains either a hash of conditions or an SQL fragment.

Here, you use a hash of conditions to indicate you want the first article with the title RailsConf:

```
>> Article.where(title: 'RailsConf').first
=> #<Article id: 1, title: "RailsConf", body: "RailsConf is the official
 gathering for Rails devel...", published_at: "2020-01-31 00:00:00",
 created_at: "2020-01-31 23:12:09", updated_at: "2020-01-31 23:12:09",
 excerpt: nil, location: nil>
```

Because you use first, you get only one record (the first one in the result set, even if there is more than one result). If you instead use all, you get back a collection, even if the collection has only one item in it:

```
>> Article.where(title: 'RailsConf').all
=> #<ActiveRecord::Relation [#<Article id: 1, title: "RailsConf", body:
"RailsConf is the official  gathering for Rails devel...", published_at:
"2020-01-31 00:00:00",
 created_at: "2020-01-31 23:12:09", updated_at: "2020-01-31 23:12:09",
 excerpt: nil, location: nil>]>
```

Notice the square brackets, and remember that they indicate an array. More often than not, when you're doing an all operation, you expect more than one record in return. But all always produces an array, even if that array is empty:

```
>> Article.where(title: 'Unknown').all
=> #<ActiveRecord::Relation []>
```

Updating Records

Updating a record is a lot like creating a record. You can update attributes one at a time and then save the result, or you can update attributes in one fell swoop. When you update a record, an SQL UPDATE statement is constructed behind the scenes. First, you use a find operation to retrieve the record you want to update; next, you modify its attributes; and finally, you save it back to the database:

```
>> article = Article.first
>> article.title = "Rails 6 is great"
>> article.published_at = Time.zone.now
>> article.save
=> true
```

This should look pretty familiar by now. The only real difference between this process and the process of creating a new record is that instead of creating a brand-new row, you fetch an existing row. You update the attributes the exact same way, and you save the record the same way. Just as when you create a new record, when `save` operates on an existing record, it returns `true` or `false`, depending on whether the operation was successful.

When you want to update an object's attributes and save it in a single operation, you use the `update_attributes` method. Unlike when you create a new record with `create`, because you're updating a record, you need to fetch that record first. That's where the other subtle difference lies. Unlike `create`, which is a class method (it operates on the class, not on an object), `update_attributes` is an instance method. Instance methods work on objects or instances of a class. Here's an example:

```
>> article = Article.first
>> article.update_attributes(title: "RailsConf2020", published_at: 1.day.ago)
=> true
```

Deleting Records

You're finally at the last component of CRUD: delete. When you're working with databases, you inevitably need to delete records. If a user cancels their order or if a book goes out of stock or even if you have an error in a given row, you may want to delete it. Sometimes you need to delete all rows in a table, and sometimes you want to delete only a specific row. Active Record makes deleting rows every bit as easy as creating them.

There are two styles of row deletion: `destroy` and `delete`. The `destroy` style works on the *instance*. It instantiates the object, which means it finds a single row first and then deletes the row from the database. The `delete` style operates on the *class*, which is to say it operates on the table rather than a given row from that table.

Using destroy

The easiest and most common way to remove a record is to use the destroy method, which means the first thing you need to do is find the record you want to destroy:

```
>> article = Article.last
>> article.destroy
=> #<Article id: 5, title: "Rails Pub Nite", body: "Rails Pub Nite is
every 3rd
Monday of each month, e...", published_at: "2020-01-31 00:00:00",
created_at: "2020-01-31 23:36:07", updated_at: "2020-01-31 23:36:07",
excerpt: nil, location: nil>
```

If you're interested, the SQL that Active Record generates in response to the destroy operation is as follows:

```
DELETE FROM articles WHERE id = 5;
```

As a result, the article with the id of 5 is permanently deleted. But you still have the object hanging around in the variable article, so how can it really be gone? The answer is that although the object remains *hydrated* (retains all its attributes), it's *frozen*. You can still access its attributes, but you can't modify them. Let's see what happens if you try to change the location:

```
>> article.location = 'Toronto, ON'
RuntimeError (Can't modify frozen hash)
```

It appears that the deleted article is now frozen. The object remains, but it's read-only, so you can't modify it. Given this fact, if you're going to delete the record, you don't really need to create an explicit Article object after all. You can do the destroy in a one-line operation:

```
>> Article.last.destroy
```

Here, the object instantiation is implicit. You're still calling the destroy instance method, but you're not storing an Article object in a local variable first.

You can still do better. You can use the class method destroy, which does a find automatically. As with find and create, you can use destroy directly on the class (i.e., you don't create an object first). Because it operates on the table and not the row, you need to help it by telling it which row or rows you want to target. Here's how you delete the article with the id 1:

```
>> Article.destroy(1)
=> [#<Article id: 1, title: "RailsConf", body: "RailsConf is the official
 gathering for Rails devel...", published_at: "2020-01-31 00:00:00",
 created_at: "2020-01-31 23:12:09", updated_at: "2020-01-31 23:12:09",
 excerpt: nil, location: nil>]
```

Sometimes you want to destroy more than one record. Just as with `find`, you can give `destroy` an array of primary keys whose rows you want to remove. Use square brackets (`[]`) to indicate that you're passing an array:

```
>> Article.destroy([2,3])
=> [#<Article id: 2, ..>, #<Article id: 3, ..>]
```

Using *delete*

The second style of row deletion is `delete`. Every Active Record class has class methods called `delete` and `delete_all`. The `delete` family of methods differs from `destroy` in that they don't instantiate or perform callbacks on the object they're deleting. They remove the row immediately from the database.

Just like `find` and `create`, you use `delete` and `delete_all` directly on the class (i.e., you don't create an object first). Because the method operates on the table and not the row, you need to help it by telling it which row or rows you want to target:

```
>> Article.delete(4)
=> 1
```

Here you specify a single primary key for the article you want to delete. The operation responds with the number of records removed. Because a primary key uniquely identifies a single record, only one record is deleted.

Just as with `find`, you can give `delete` an array of primary keys whose rows you want to delete. Use square brackets (`[]`) to indicate that you're passing an array:

```
>> Article.delete([5, 6])
=> 0
```

The return of the `delete` method in this case is 0, since we didn't have records with id's 5 and 6 in our database. Zero records were deleted.

> **Note**   Unlike `find`, which is capable of collecting any arguments it receives into an array automatically, `delete` must be supplied with an array object explicitly. So, although `Model.find(1,2,3)` works, `Model.delete(1,2,3)` fails with an argument error (because it's really receiving three arguments). To delete multiple rows by primary key, you must pass an actual array object. The following works, because it's a single array (containing three items) and thus a single argument: `Model.delete([1,2,3])`.

Deleting with Conditions

You can delete all rows that match a given condition with the `delete_by` class method. The following deletes all articles before a certain date:

```
>> Article.delete_by("published_at < '2011-01-01'")
>> 0
```

The return value of `delete_by` is the number of records deleted.

When Good Models Go Bad

So far, you've been nice to your models and have made them happy by providing just the information they need. But in Chapter 3 you provided *validations* that prevented you from saving bad records to the database. Specifically, you told the `Article` model that it should never allow itself to be saved to the database if it isn't given a `title` and `body`. Look at the `Article` model, as shown in Listing 5-1, to recall how validations are specified.

Listing 5-1. The `app/models/article.rb` File

```
class Article < ApplicationRecord
    validates :title, :body, presence: true
end
```

You may have noticed in your generated scaffolding that you use a helper method called `errors.full_messages` to print out a helpful error message. That helper isn't black magic; it's a bit of code that asks the model associated with the form for its list of errors (also referred to as the *errors collection*) and returns a nicely formatted block of HTML to show the user.

Note   You may have noticed that you call methods in Ruby with a dot (`.`). For instance, you say `article.errors` to get the errors collection back. However, Ruby documentation uses the # symbol along with the class name to let the reader know that there is a method it can call on for an instance of that class. For example, on the `Article` class, you can use the method `article.title` as `Article#title`, because it's something that acts on a particular `article` but not the `Article` class itself. You've also seen that you can write the code `Article.count`, because you don't need to know about a particular `@article`, but only `Article` objects in general. Keep this convention in mind when you're reading Ruby documentation.

The secret to this is that every Active Record object has an automatic attribute added to it called `errors`. To get started, create a fresh `Article` object:

```
>> article = Article.new
=> #<Article id: nil, title: nil, body: nil, published_at: nil,
created_at: nil,
updated_at: nil, excerpt: nil, location: nil>
>> article.errors.any?
=> false
```

This seems odd: you know this new article should have errors, because it's invalid—you didn't give it a title or a body. This is because you haven't triggered the validations yet. You can cause them to occur a couple of ways. The most obvious way is to attempt to save the object:

```
>> article.save
=> false
```

Every time you've used `save` before, the model has happily chirped `true` back to you. But this time, `save` returns `false`. This is because before the model allows itself to be saved, it runs through its gauntlet of validations, and one or more of those validations failed.

You would be right to guess that if you tried `article.errors.any?` again, it would return `true`:

```
>> article.errors.any?
=> true
```

Let's interrogate the `errors` collection a little more closely with the `full_messages` method:

```
>> article.errors.full_messages
=> ["Title can't be blank", "Body can't be blank"]
```

Voilà! Look how helpful the model is being. It's passing back an array of error messages.

If there is only one attribute that you care about, you can also ask the `errors` collection for a particular attribute's errors:

```
>> article.errors.messages[:title]
=> "can't be blank"
```

Notice that because you tell it which attribute you're looking for, the message returns a slightly different result than before. What if you ask for an attribute that doesn't exist or doesn't have errors?

```
>> article.errors.messages(:nonexistent)
=> []
```

You get back an empty array, which lets you know that you didn't find anything. Another helpful method is `size`, which, as you saw earlier, works with all arrays:

```
>> article.errors.size
=> 2
```

Saving isn't the only way you can cause validations to run. You can ask a model object if it's `valid?`:

```
>> article.valid?
=> false
```

If you try that on a new object, the `errors` collection magically fills up with your pretty errors.

Summary

In this chapter, you've become familiar with using the console to work with models. You've learned how to create, read, update, and destroy model objects. Also, you've briefly looked into how to see the simple errors caused by the validations you set up on your model in Chapter 3.

The next chapter discusses how to create relationships (called *associations*) among your models, and you begin to see how Active Record helps you work with your data in extremely powerful ways. It also expands on the concept of validations and shows how you can do a lot more with `validates`. You'll see that Rails provides a bevy of prewritten validators and an easy way to write your own customized validators.

CHAPTER 6

Advanced Active Record: Enhancing Your Models

Chapter 5 introduced the basics of Active Record and how to use it. This chapter delves more deeply into Active Record and teaches you how to enhance your models.

Model enhancement is a general term. It refers to endowing your models with attributes and capabilities that go beyond what you get from subclassing `ActiveRecord::Base`. A model contains all the logic that governs its citizenship in the world of your application. In the model, you can define how it interacts with other models, what a model should accept as a minimum amount of information for it to be considered valid, and other abilities and responsibilities.

Models need to relate to one another. In the real world, bank accounts have transactions, books belong to authors, and products have categories. These relationships are referred to as *associations*, and Active Record makes them easy to work with. Models also have requirements. For instance, you can't have a transaction without an amount—it might break your system if someone tried to have an empty transaction. So Active Record gives you easy ways to tell a model what it should expect in order to be saved to the database.

This chapter will teach you how to programmatically enhance your models so they're more than just simple maps of your tables. To demonstrate the concepts, you build on the blog application you started in Chapter 3, so keep it handy if you want to follow along with the examples.

Adding Methods

Let's begin with a brief review of Active Record basics. At the simplest level, Active Record works by automatically wrapping database tables whose names match the plural, underscored version of any classes that inherit from `ActiveRecord::Base`. For example, if you want to wrap the users table, you create a subclass of ApplicationRecord (which is a subclass of ActiveRecord::Base) called User, like this:

```
class User < ApplicationRecord
end
```

That's all you really need to have Active Record map the users table and get all the basic CRUD functionality described in Chapter 5. But few models are actually this bare.

So far, you've left your model classes unchanged. That's a good thing, and it speaks to the power and simplicity of Active Record. However, it leaves something to be desired. Most of the time, your models need to do a lot more than just wrap a table.

Note   If you're familiar with SQL, you're probably feeling that Active Record provides only simple case solutions and can't handle complicated cases. That's entirely untrue. Although SQL is useful for highly customized database queries, most Rails projects rarely need to touch SQL, thanks to some clever tricks in Active Record.

The primary way in which you enhance models is by adding methods to them. This is referred to as adding *domain logic*. With Active Record, all the logic for a particular table is contained in one place: the model. This is why the model is said to *encapsulate* all the domain logic. This logic includes access rules, validations, relationships, and, well, just about anything else you feel like adding.

In addition to all the column-based reader and writer methods you get by wrapping a table, you're free to define your own methods on the class. An Active Record subclass isn't much different from a regular Ruby class; about the only difference is that you need to make sure you don't unintentionally overwrite any of Active Record's methods (e.g., find, save, or destroy). For the most part, though, this isn't a problem.

Let's look at a simple example. You often need to format data, rather than accessing a model attribute in its raw form. In the blog application, you want to be able to produce a formatted, long title that includes the title of the article and its date. To accomplish this, all you need to do is define a new instance method called long_title that performs the concatenation of those attributes and produces a formatted string. Update your copy of app/models/article.rb so that it matches the code shown in Listing 6-1 by adding the long_title method definition.

Listing 6-1. Custom `long_title` Method, in app/models/article.rb:
https://gist.github.com/nicedawg/0355af37c2e0375b004d4e0c12566b4b

```
class Article < ApplicationRecord
  validates :title, :body, presence: true

  def long_title
     "#{title} - #{published_at}"
  end
end
```

You've just created an instance method on the model; that is, you've told the `Article` model that it's now endowed with a new attribute called `long_title`. You can address `long_title` the same way you would any other method on the class. Open an irb session and try this on the console. From the terminal window, make sure you're inside the blog application directory, and then start up the Rails console with the following command:

```
$ rails console
```

This should drop you at a simple irb prompt with two right arrows and a blinking cursor; this may look a bit different based on your environment. From here, you create a new article and use it to call the `long_title` method:

```
>> Article.create title: 'Advanced Active Record', published_at: Date.today,
body: 'Models need to relate to each other. In the real world, ...'
=> #<Article id: 1, title: "Advanced Active Record", ...>
>> Article.last.long_title
=> "Advanced Active Record - 2020-02-03 00:00:00 UTC"
```

There is no difference between the methods Active Record creates and those you define. Here, instead of asking the model for one of the attributes garnered from the database column names, you define your *own* method called `long_title`, which does a bit more than the standard `title` method.

The methods you add to your models can be as simple as returning `true` or `false` or as complicated as doing major calculations and formatting on the object. The full power of Ruby is in your hands to do with as you please.

Don't worry if you don't feel comfortable adding your own methods to models just yet. The important part to note from this section is that Active Record models are regular Ruby classes that can be augmented, modified, played with, poked, and turned inside out with sufficient Ruby-fu. Knowing this is extremely helpful in being able to pull back the curtain and understand the advanced features of Active Record.

FAT MODELS

Some might be nervous by the `long_title` method you just used. They may see it as a violation of the MVC paradigm. They might ask, "Isn't formatting code supposed to be in the view?" In general, the answer is yes. However, it often helps to have models that act as intelligent objects. If you ask a model for some information about itself, it's natural to assume that it can give you a decent answer that doesn't require a large amount of work later on to figure out what it means. So small formatted strings and basic data types that faithfully represent the data in the model are good things to have in your code.

An intelligent model like this is often called *fat*. Instead of performing model-related logic in other places (i.e., in controllers or views), you keep it in the model, thus making it fat. This makes your models easier to work with and helps your code stay DRY.

A basic rule of thumb while trying to stay DRY is that if you find yourself copying and pasting a bit of code, it may be worth your time to take a moment and figure out if there is a better way to approach the problem. For instance, if you had kept the `Article#long_title` formatting outside the model, you might have needed to repeat the same basic string-formatting procedure every time you wanted a human-friendly representation of an article's title. Then again, creating that method is a waste of time if you're going to use it in only one place in the application and never again.

This is where programmer experience comes in. As you learn and mature in your Rails programming, you'll find it easier and easier to figure out where stuff is supposed to go. If you're always aiming for a goal of having the most maintainable and beautiful code you can possibly write, your projects will naturally become easier to maintain.

Next, let's look at another common form of model enhancement: associations. Active Record's associations give you the ability to define in simple terms how models relate to and interact with one another.

Using Associations

It's a lowly application that has only one table. Most applications have many tables, and these tables typically need to relate to one another in one way or another. *Associations* are a common model enhancement that let you relate tables to one another.

Associations are natural constructs that you encounter all the time in the real world: articles have comments, stores have products, magazines have subscriptions, and so on. In a relational database system, you relate tables using a *foreign key reference* in one table to the *primary key* of another table.

Note   The terms *relationship* and *association* can be used pretty much interchangeably. However, when this book refers to *associations*, it generally means the association on the Active Record side, as opposed to the actual foreign key relationships at the database level.

Let's take the example of articles and comments. In a situation where a given article can have any number of comments attached to it, each comment *belongs to* a particular article. Figure 6-1 demonstrates the association from the database's point of view.

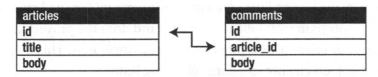

Figure 6-1. *The relationship between the* articles *and* comments *tables*

The example in Figure 6-1 uses a column named article_id in the comments table to identify the related article in the articles table. In database speak, comments holds a *foreign key reference* to articles.

By Rails convention, the foreign key column is the singular, lowercase name of the target class with _id appended. So, for products that belong to a particular store, the foreign key is named store_id; for subscriptions that belong to magazines, the foreign key is named magazine_id; and so on. Here's the pattern:

```
#{singular_name_of_parent_class}_id
```

Table 6-1 shows a few more examples, just to drive this concept home.

Table 6-1. *Sample Foreign Key References*

Model	Table	Foreign Key to Reference This Table
Article	articles	article_id
Person	people	person_id
Friend	friends	friend_id
Category	categories	category_id
Book	books	book_id

Whenever you need one table to reference another table, remember to create the foreign key column in the table doing the referencing. In other words, the model that contains the "belongs_to" needs to have the foreign key column in it. That's all your table needs before you can put Active Record's associations to work.

Declaring Associations

As you've probably come to expect by now, Active Record makes working with associations easy. You don't need to get down to the bare metal of the database very often. As long as you understand the concept of primary and foreign keys and how to create basic relationships in your tables, Active Record does the proverbial heavy lifting, converting foreign key relationships into rich object associations. This means you get to access associated objects cleanly and naturally using Ruby:

```
article.comments
store.products
magazine.subscriptions
```

After the relationships are defined in your database tables, you use a set of macro-like class methods in your models to create associations. They look like this:

- has_one

- has_many

- belongs_to

- has_and_belongs_to_many

Here's a quick example. The `Message` model declares a `has_many` relationship with `Attachment`; `Attachment` returns the favor by declaring that each of its objects belongs to a particular `Message`:

```
class Message < ApplicationRecord
  has_many :attachments
end

class Attachment < ApplicationRecord
  belongs_to :message
end
```

Given these instructions, Active Record expects to find a table called `attachments` that has a field in it called `message_id` (the foreign key reference). It uses this association to let you enter things like `Message.first.attachments` and get an array (or a *collection*) of `Attachment` objects that belongs to the first `Message` in the database. Moreover, you can work with your associations in both directions. So you can enter `Attachment.first.message` to access the `Message` to which the first `Attachment` belongs. It sounds like a mouthful, but when you get the hang of it, it's quite intuitive.

Whenever you declare an association, Active Record automatically adds a set of methods to your model that makes dealing with the association easier. This is a lot like the way in which Active Record creates methods based on your column names. When it notices you've declared an association, it dynamically creates methods that enable you to work with that association. The following sections go through the different types of associations and describe how to work with them. You also learn about the various options you can use to fine-tune associations.

Creating One-to-One Associations

One-to-one associations describe a pattern where a row in one table is related to exactly one row in another table.

Suppose that in your blog application, you have users and profiles, and each user has exactly one profile. Assume you have `User` and `Profile` models, and the corresponding `users` and `profiles` tables have the appropriate columns. You can tell your `User` model that it *has one* `Profile` and your `Profile` model that it *belongs to* a `User`. Active Record takes care of the rest. The `has_one` and `belongs_to` macros are designed to read like regular English, so they sound natural in conversation and are easy to remember. Each represents a different side of the equation, working in tandem to make the association complete.

Note   Part of the Rails philosophy about development is that the gap between programmers and other project stakeholders should be bridged. Using natural language, such as *has one* and *belongs to*, in describing programmatic concepts helps bridge this gap, providing a construct that everyone can understand.

Adding the User and Profile Models

When you started the blog application, you decided to let anyone create new articles. This worked fine when only one person was using the system; but you want this to be a multiple-user application and let different people sign up, sign in, and start writing their own articles separately from one another.

Let's fire up the generator and create the User model:

```
$ rails generate model User email:string password:string
```

Just as you saw in Chapter 3, the model generator creates, among other things, a model file in app/models and a migration in db/migrate. Open db/migrate/20200204011416_create_users.rb, and you should see the now-familiar code in Listing 6-2. (Remember that the timestamp in the migration file will differ.)

Listing 6-2. Migration to Create the users Table, db/migrate/20200204011416_create_users.rb

```
class CreateUsers < ActiveRecord::Migration[6.0]
  def change
    create_table :users do |t|
      t.string :email
      t.string :password

      t.timestamps
    end
  end
end
```

This is standard migration fare. In the change definition, you use the create_table method to create a new users table. The new table object is *yielded* to the block in the variable, t, on which you call the string method to create each column. Along with the standard email field, you specify a password field, which you use for authentication, as explained in the "Reviewing the Updated Models" section later in this chapter. The primary key, id, is created automatically, so there's no need to specify it here.

As you probably noticed, the User model is extremely simple: it only contains information that allows the user to authenticate into the application. Some users may want to add a lot more detail about themselves and would love the ability to enter personal information such as their birthday, a biography, their favorite color, their Twitter account name, and so on. You can create a Profile model to hold such information outside the scope of the User model. Just as you did for the User model, use the generator again:

```
$ rails generate model Profile user:references name:string birthday:date
bio:text color:string twitter:string
```

You also have a migration file for the Profile model in db/migrate/20200204013911_create_profiles.rb—feel free to take a peek. Notice the existence of the foreign key for users in the profiles schema. Also recall that you don't need to specify primary keys in migrations because they're created automatically.

Now, all you need to do is run the migrations and create the new tables using the db:migrate Rails command. Run the migrations with the following command:

```
$ rails db:migrate
```

```
==  CreateUsers: migrating ==============================================
-- create_table(:users)
   -> 0.0019s
==  CreateUsers: migrated (0.0020s) =====================================

==  CreateProfiles: migrating ===========================================
-- create_table(:profiles)
   -> 0.0027s
==  CreateProfiles: migrated (0.0035s) ==================================
```

With the table and foreign keys in place, Listings 6-3 and 6-4 show how to declare the one-to-one association on the User and Profile models, respectively. Please update your User model in app/models/user.rb to match Listing 6-3. However, we won't need to update the Profile model to match Listing 6-4; the *rails generate* command added exactly what we needed!

Listing 6-3. The User Model, app/models/user.rb: https://gist.github. com/nicedawg/b66208334e6be63b24fcdf1d74eebf3b

```
class User < ApplicationRecord
  has_one :profile
end
```

Listing 6-4. The Profile Model, app/models/profile.rb: https://gist. github.com/nicedawg/06e2f87d7159eb1af94a16cde5a9fe06

```
class Profile < ApplicationRecord
  belongs_to :user
end
```

The has_one declaration on the User model tells Active Record that it can expect to find one record in the profiles table that has a user_id matching the primary key of a row in the users table. The Profile model, in turn, declares that each of its records belongs_to a particular User.

Telling the Profile model that it belongs_to :user is saying, in effect, that each Profile object references a particular User. You can even go so far as to say that User is the parent and Profile is the child. The child model is dependent on the parent and therefore references it. Figure 6-2 demonstrates the has_one relationship.

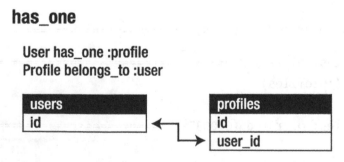

Figure 6-2. *The one-to-one relationship between users and profiles*

Let's get inside a console session (`rails console`) and see how this comes together. If you have a console session opened, run the `reload!` command in the console session to make sure it loads the newly generated models. Follow along to create objects and relate them to one another. First, create a user and a profile as follows:

```
>> reload!
Reloading...
>> user = User.create(email: "user@example.com", password: "secret")
=> #<User id: 1, email: "user@example.com", password: [FILTERED], created_
at: "2020-02-04 01:42:21", updated_at: "2020-02-04 01:42:21">
>> profile = Profile.create(name: "John Doe",
bio: "Ruby developer trying to learn Rails")
=> #<Profile id: nil, user_id: nil, name: "John Doe", birthday: nil, bio:
"Ruby developer trying to learn Rails", color: nil, twitter: nil, created_
at: nil, updated_at: nil>
```

Note   The `reload!` method reloads the Rails application environment within your console session. You need to call it when you make changes to existing code. It's exactly as if you had restarted your console session—all the variables you may have instantiated are lost.

Although you've successfully created a user, look closely and you'll see the profile failed to save! (See how after calling Profile.create, a profile with a nil id was returned?) What happened?

```
>> profile.errors
=> #<ActiveModel::Errors:0x00007ffd53a87958 @base=#<Profile id: nil, user_
id: nil, name: "John Doe", birthday: nil, bio: "Ruby developer trying to
learn Rails", color: nil, twitter: nil, created_at: nil, updated_at: nil>,
@messages={:user=>["must exist"]}, @details={:user=>[{:error=>:blank}]}>
```

The profile failed to save because its user is nil. The belongs_to association also adds a validation to ensure it is present. We could change the Profile class to optionally belong to a user—belongs_to :user, optional: true—but for our purposes, we don't want profiles to exist without a user.

To successfully create the profile so that it is associated with the user, we can just assign it and call save, like this:

```
>> profile.user = user
=> #<User id: 1, email: "user@example.com", password: [FILTERED], created_at:
   "2020-02-04 01:42:21", updated_at: "2020-02-04 01:42:21">
>> profile.save
=> true
```

Assignment is assignment, whether it's a name attribute to which you're assigning the value Joe or an association method to which you're assigning an object. Also notice that the profile's user_id attribute is updated to the value of user.id: This is what bonds both objects together. Now, when you ask the user object for its profile, it happily responds with one:

```
>> user.profile
=> #<Profile id: 1, user_id: 1, name: "John Doe", birthday: nil, bio: "Ruby
developer trying to learn Rails", color: nil, twitter: nil, created_at:
"2020-02-04 01:52:51", updated_at: "2020-02-04 01:52:51">
```

That's all there is to it. Although this is pretty good, you can do a bit better. You can create and save the profile in one shot and have it perform the association automatically, like this:

```
>> user.profile.destroy
=> #<Profile id: 1, user_id: 1, name: "John Doe", birthday: nil, bio: "Ruby
developer trying to learn Rails", color: nil, twitter: nil, created_at:
"2020-02-04 01:52:51", updated_at: "2020-02-04 01:52:51">

>> user.create_profile name: 'Jane Doe', color: 'pink'
=> #<Profile id: 2, user_id: 1, name: "Jane Doe", birthday: nil, bio: nil,
color: "pink", twitter: nil, created_at: "2020-02-04 01:55:23", updated_at:
"2020-02-04 01:55:23">
```

Using the create_profile method to create a new profile initializes the Profile object, sets its foreign key to user.id, and saves it to the database. This works for any has_one association, no matter what it's named. Active Record automatically generates the create_#{association_name} method for you. So if you had an Employee model set up with an association like has_one :address, you would get the create_address method automatically.

These alternatives for doing the same thing may seem confusing, but they're really variations on the same theme. In all cases, you're creating two objects (the parent and the child) and telling each about the other. Whether you choose to do this in a multistep operation or all on one line is entirely up to you.

Earlier, you learned that declaring a has_one association causes Active Record to automatically add a suite of methods to make working with the association easier. Table 6-2 shows a summary of the methods that are added when you declare a has_one and belongs_to relationship between User and Profile, where user is a User instance.

Table 6-2. *Methods Added by the has_one Association in the User/Profile Example*

Method	Description
user.profile	Returns the associated (Profile) object; nil is returned if none is found.
user.profile=(profile)	Assigns the associated (Profile) object, extracts the primary key, and sets it as the foreign key.
user.profile.nil?	Returns true if there is no associated Profile object.
user.build_profile(attributes={})	Returns a new Profile object that has been instantiated with attributes and linked to user through a foreign key but hasn't yet been saved.
user.create_profile(attributes={})	Returns a new Profile object that has been instantiated with attributes and linked to user through a foreign key and that has already been saved.

Although you're using the User.has_one :profile example here, the rules work for any object associated to another using has_one. Here are some examples, along with sample return values:

```
user.profile
#=> #<Profile id: 2, user_id: 1, ...>
user.profile.nil?
#=> false
user.profile.destroy
#=> #<Profile id: 2, user_id: 1, ..,>
```

```
user.build_profile(bio: 'eats leaves')
#=> #<Profile id: nil, user_id: 1, ...>
user.create_profile(bio: 'eats leaves')
#=> #<Profile id: 3, user_id: 1, ...>
```

The has_one declaration can also include an options hash to specialize its behavior if necessary. Table 6-3 lists the most common options. For a complete list of all options, consult the Rails API documentation (https://api.rubyonrails.org/classes/ActiveRecord/Associations/ClassMethods.html#method-i-has_one).

Table 6-3. *Common has_one Options*

Option	Description	Example
:class_name	Specifies the class name of the association. Used when the class name can't be inferred from the association name.	has_one :profile, class_name: 'Account'
:foreign_key	Specifies the foreign key used for the association in the event that it doesn't adhere to the convention of being the lowercase, singular name of the target class with _id appended.	has_one :profile, foreign_key: 'account_id'
:dependent	Specifies that the associated object should be removed when this object is. If set to :destroy, the associated object is deleted using the destroy method. If set to :delete, the associated object is deleted without calling its destroy method. If set to :nullify, the associated object's foreign key is set to NULL.	has_one :profile, dependent: :destroy

Creating One-to-Many Associations

One-to-many associations describe a pattern where a row in one table is related to one or more rows in another table. Examples are an Email that has many Recipients or a Magazine that has many Subscriptions.

Up until now, your articles have been orphaned—they don't belong to anyone. You remedy that now by associating users with articles. In your system, each article belongs to a user, and a user may have many articles. Figure 6-3 illustrates this association.

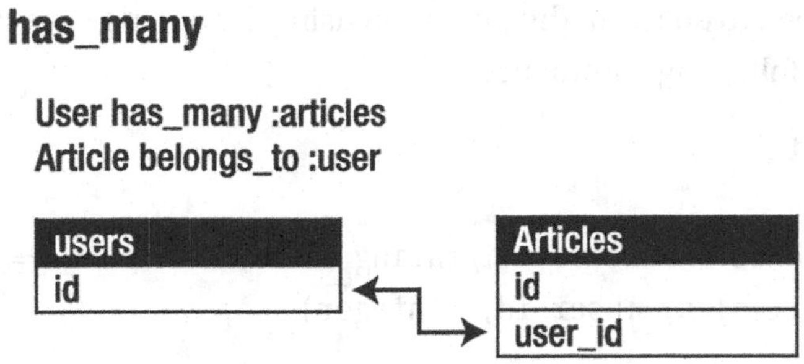

has_many

User has_many :articles
Article belongs_to :user

Figure 6-3. *The one-to-many relationship between users and articles*

Associating User and Article Models

Just as you associated users and profiles, you want to have a similar relationship between users and articles. You need to add a foreign key user_id in the articles table that points to a record in the users table.

Fire up the migration generator:

```
$ rails g migration add_user_reference_to_articles user:references
```

Notice that we used *rails g* instead of *rails generate*. Some of the most commonly used Rails commands have a shortcut—rails **g**enerate, rails **s**erver, rails **c**onsole, rails **t**est, and rails **db**console. We'll generally use the full command in this book, but feel free to use the shortcuts:

Open db/migrate/20200204020148_add_user_reference_to_articles.rb, and update it by removing *null: false* so that it matches the code in Listing 6-5.

Listing 6-5. Migration to Add User to Articles 20200204020148_add_user_reference_to_articles

```
class AddUserReferenceToArticles < ActiveRecord::Migration[6.0]
  def change
    add_reference :articles, :user, foreign_key: true
  end
end
```

We needed to remove *null: false* because our existing articles don't yet have a user_id and our migration would have failed.

Now, all you need to do is run the migration using the db:migrate task. Run the migration with the following command:

```
$ rails db:migrate
```

```
==  AddUserReferenceToArticles: migrating ================================
-- add_column(:articles, :user_id, :integer)
   -> 0.0012s
==  AddUserReferenceToArticles: migrated (0.0015s) =======================
```

With the foreign key in place, Listings 6-6 and 6-7 show how you declare the one-to-many association in your Article and User models, respectively. Add these to the relevant models.

Listing 6-6. The Article Model, belongs_to Declaration in app/models/article.rb: https://gist.github.com/nicedawg/53289dd2be8683975f28283761f06fa0

```ruby
class Article < ApplicationRecord
  validates :title, :body, presence: true

  belongs_to :user

  def long_title
    "#{title} - #{published_at}"
  end
end
```

Listing 6-7. The User Model, has_many Declaration in app/models/user.rb: https://gist.github.com/nicedawg/48f1cdf5917a3322347642e6ada25016

```ruby
class User < ApplicationRecord
  has_one :profile
  has_many :articles
end
```

That's all there is to it. This bit of code has endowed your Article and User models with a lot of functionality.

Note   For has_one and has_many associations, adding a belongs_to on the other side of the association is always recommended. The rule of thumb is that the belongs_to declaration always goes in the class with the foreign key.

Creating a New Associated Object

Your associations are in place; so let's get back into the code to put what you've learned to the test. Do this exercise on the console: either run `rails console` to start a new console session or type `reload!` if you still have a console window open from the previous section.

Let's test whether the association between users and articles is set up correctly. If it is, you should be able to ask the user object for its associated articles, and it should respond with a collection. Even though you haven't created any articles for this user yet, it should still work, returning an empty collection:

```
>> reload!
Reloading...
=> true
>> user = User.first
=> #<User id: 1, email: "user@example.com", password: [FILTERED], created_
at: "2020-02-04 01:42:21", updated_at: "2020-02-04 01:42:21">
>> user.articles
=> #<ActiveRecord::Associations::CollectionProxy []>
```

Great! The has_many association is working correctly, and the User instance now has an articles method, which was created automatically by Active Record when it noticed the has_many declaration.

Let's give this user some articles. Enter the following commands:

```
>> user.articles << Article.first
=> [#<Article id: 1, ..., user_id: 1>]
>> user.articles.size
=> 1
>> user.articles
=> [#<Article id: 1, ..., user_id: 1>]
```

By using the append (<<) operator, you attach `Article.first` onto your `user` object. When you use << with associations, it automatically saves the new association. Some things in Active Record don't happen until you say `save`, but this is one of the examples where that part is done automatically.

What did that do exactly? Let's look into the article and find out:

```
>> Article.first.user_id
=> 1
```

See how this article's `user_id` points to the user with an `id` of 1? This means you've successfully related the two objects. You can even ask an `Article` instance for its `user`:

```
>> Article.first.user
=> #<User id: 1, email: "user@example.com", password: [FILTERED], created_
at: "2020-02-04 01:42:21", updated_at: "2020-02-04 01:42:21">
```

Voilà! Your models can really start to express things now. The `has_many` and `belongs_to` declarations create more methods, as you did earlier with the `long_title` method. Let's look at what else these happy little helpers brought along to the party. Table 6-4 shows a summary of the methods that are added when you declare a `has_many` and `belongs_to` relationship between `User` and `Article` (user represents a `User` instance).

Table 6-4. *Methods Added by the `has_many` Association in the User and Article Models*

Method	Description
user.articles	Returns an array of all the associated articles. An empty array is returned if no articles are found.
user.articles=(articles)	Replaces the `articles` collection with the one supplied.
user.articles << article	Adds the article to the user's articles collection.
user.articles. delete(articles)	Removes one or more articles from the collection by setting their foreign keys to NULL.
user.articles.empty?	Returns `true` if there are no associated `Article` objects for this user.

(continued)

Table 6-4. (*continued*)

Method	Description
user.articles.size	Returns the number of associated Article objects for this user.
user.article_ids	Returns an array of associated article ids.
user.articles.clear	Clears all associated objects from the association by setting their foreign keys to NULL.
user.articles.find	Performs a find that is automatically scoped off the association; that is, it finds only within items that belong to user.
user.articles.build(attributes={})	Returns a new Article object that has been instantiated with attributes and linked to user through a foreign key but hasn't yet been saved. Here's an example: user.articles.build(title: 'Ruby 1.9').
user.articles.create(attributes={})	Returns a new Article object that has been instantiated with attributes and linked to user through a foreign key and has already been saved. Here's an example: user.articles.create(title: 'Hoedown').

You're using the User.has_many :articles example here, but the rules work for any object associated with another using has_many. Here are some examples, along with sample return values:

```
>> user.articles
=> [#<Article id: 1, ...>]
>> user.articles << Article.new(title: 'One-to-many associations',
body: 'One-to-many associations describe a pattern ..')
=> [#<Article id: 1, ...>, #<Article id: 2, ...>]
>> user.article_ids
=> [1, 2]
>> user.articles.first
=> #<Article id: 1, ...>
>> user.articles.clear
=> []
```

```
>> user.articles.count
 => 0
>> Article.count
 => 2
>> user.articles.create title: 'Associations',
body: 'Active Record makes working with associations easy..'
=> #<Article id: 3, ...>
```

You can also pass in options to your association declaration to affect the way you work with those associations. Table 6-5 lists some of the most common options.

Table 6-5. *Common has_many Options*

Option	Description	Example
`:class_name`	Specifies the class name of the association. Used when the class name can't be inferred from the association name.	`has_many :articles, class_name: 'Post'`
`:foreign_key`	Specifies the foreign key used for the association in the event that it doesn't adhere to convention of being the lowercase, singular name of the target class with `_id` appended.	`has_many :articles, foreign_key: 'post_id'`
`:dependent`	Specifies that the associated objects should be removed when this object is. If set to `:destroy`, the associated objects are deleted using the `destroy` method. If set to `:delete`, the associated objects are deleted without calling their `destroy` method. If set to `:nullify`, the associated objects' foreign keys are set to NULL.	`has_many :articles, dependent: :destroy`

There's much more to `has_many` associations than can possibly be covered here, so be sure to check out the Rails API documentation (`https://api.rubyonrails.org/classes/ActiveRecord/Associations/ClassMethods.html#method-i-has_many`) for the full scoop.

Applying Association Options

It's time to apply what you've learned to your domain model. Specifically, you use the :order option to apply a default order to the User.has_many :articles declaration, and you use the :dependent option to make sure when you delete a user, all their articles are deleted as well.

Specifying a Default Order

When you access a user's articles, you want to make sure they come back in the *order* in which they've been published. Specifically, you want the oldest to be at the bottom of the list and the newest to be at the top. You can do this by configuring the has_many association with a default order using the order method in a scope. (We'll explain scopes in detail later in this chapter.) Add a scope block to specify the default order of the has_many :articles declaration, as shown in Listing 6-8.

Listing 6-8. A Default Order Added to has_many: https://gist.github.com/ nicedawg/68b6e0849dd05c1c70cb3cc076724bc4

```
class User < ApplicationRecord
  has_one :profile
  has_many :articles,  -> { order 'published_at DESC' }
end
```

You give the name of the field that you want to order by, and then you say either ASC (ascending) or DESC (descending) to indicate the order in which the results should be returned. Because time moves forward (to bigger numbers), you want to make sure you're going back in time, so you use the DESC keyword here.

Note   ASC and DESC are SQL keywords. You're actually specifying an *SQL fragment* here, as discussed in the "Advanced Finding" section later in this chapter.

You can also specify a secondary order by adding a comma between arguments. Let's say you want to sort by the title of the article *after* you sort by the date. If two articles have been published on the same day, they are ordered first by the date and then by the lexical order of the title. Listing 6-9 shows the article title added to the :order option.

Listing 6-9. Adding the Title to the Default Order for has_many: https://
gist.github.com/nicedawg/d2054b9db2cfbb105c41c60dd9134f4c

```
class User < ApplicationRecord
  has_one :profile
  has_many :articles, -> { order 'published_at DESC, title ASC' }
end
```

Notice that you use ASC for ordering on the title. This is because as letters go up in the alphabet, their value goes up. So, to sort alphabetically, use the ASC keyword.

Specifying Dependencies

Frequently, dependencies exist between models. For instance, in your blog application, if you delete users, you want to make sure they don't have articles in the system. Said another way, an Article is dependent on its User. You can let Active Record take care of this for you automatically by specifying the :dependent option to your association. Listing 6-10 shows all the options to has_many :articles, including the :dependent option.

Listing 6-10. The :dependent Option Added to has_many: https://gist.
github.com/nicedawg/820570d78eefefda528ef502de7f1492

```
class User < ApplicationRecord
  has_one :profile
  has_many :articles, -> { order 'published_at DESC, title ASC' },
                    dependent: :destroy
end
```

By passing in the symbol :destroy, you declare not only that articles are dependent but also that when the owner is deleted, you want to call the destroy method on every related article. This ensures that any *_destroy callbacks on the Article instances are called (callbacks are discussed later, in the "Making Callbacks" section). If you want to skip the callbacks, you can use the :delete option instead of :destroy, which deletes the records directly via SQL.

Let's say you want to set the foreign key column (user_id) to NULL in the articles table, instead of completely destroying the article. Doing so essentially orphans the articles. You can do this by using the :nullify option instead of :destroy. If you don't use the :dependent option and you delete a user with associated articles, you break foreign key references in your articles table. For this application, you want to keep the :nullify option, as per Listing 6-11.

Listing 6-11. The :dependent :Option Set to :nullify: https://gist.github. com/nicedawg/82417ace639cd900d89832a4057362fc

```
class User < ApplicationRecord
  has_one :profile
  has_many :articles, -> { order 'published_at DESC, title ASC' },
                    dependent: :nullify
end
```

Creating Many-to-Many Associations

Sometimes, the relationship between two models is many-to-many. This describes a pattern where two tables are connected to multiple rows on both sides. You use this in the blog application to add categories to articles. If you wanted to allow only one category to be selected for a given article, you could use has_many. But you want to be able to apply multiple categories.

Think about this for a minute: an article can have many categories, and a category can have many articles—where does the belongs_to go in this situation? Neither model belongs to the other in the traditional sense. In Active Record speak, this kind of association is has_and_belongs_to_many (often referred to as habtm for short).

The has_and_belongs_to_many association works by relying on a join table that keeps a reference to the foreign keys involved in the relationship. The join table sits between the tables you want to join: articles and categories. Not surprisingly, then, the join table in this case is called articles_categories. Pay particular attention to the table name. It's formed from the names of each table in alphabetical order, separated by an underscore. In this case, the a in articles comes before the c in categories—hence, articles_categories. Figure 6-4 illustrates this relationship.

has_and_belongs_to_many

Category has_and_belongs_to_many :articles
Article has_and_belongs_to_many :categories

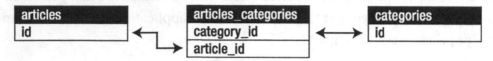

Figure 6-4. *The many-to-many relationship between* articles *and* categories

Let's start by adding the Category model. This is a simple matter of generating the model, consisting of just a name column. Run the following command inside your application root:

```
$ rails generate model Category name:string
```

Look at the generated migration in db/migrate/20200214004535_create_categories.rb; it's pretty familiar territory at this point. You need another migration to create the join table. Do that now by running the following command:

```
$ rails generate migration CreateJoinTableArticlesCategories article category
```

By naming our migration this way and passing the singular names of the models involved, this gave the *rails generate* command a hint that we wanted to create a join table and populated the resulting migration file with the commands we need.

Remember that when you use create_table inside a migration, you don't need to specify the primary key, because it's created automatically. Well, in the case of a join table, you don't want a primary key. This is because the join table isn't a first-class entity in its own right. Creating tables without primary keys is the exception and not the rule, so you need to explicitly tell create_table that you don't want to create an id. It's easy to forget, so Rails has added a new migration method called create_join_table to take care of that for you.

Take a look at Listing 6-12 to see how we'll create a join table for our articles and categories. Uncomment the *t.index* lines so that database indexes will be created which will make related database queries more efficient.

Listing 6-12. The `db/migrate/20200214004646_create_join_table_articles_categories.rb`: File

```
class CreateJoin TableArticlesCategories < ActiveRecord::Migration[6.0]
  def change
    create_join_table :articles, :categories do |t|
      t.index [:article_id, :category_id]
      t.index [:category_id, :article_id]
    end
  end
end
```

This migration will create the articles_categories table with the right fields to support the associations. It also adds indexes to make sure that querying the database for an article's categories (or a category's articles) is fast. Go ahead and run the migrations:

```
$ rails db:migrate
```

```
== 20200214004535 CreateCategories: migrating ============================
-- create_table(:categories)
   -> 0.0061s
== 20200214004535 CreateCategories: migrated (0.0063s) ====================

== 20200214004646 CreateJoinTableArticlesCategories: migrating ===========
-- create_join_table(:articles, :categories)
   -> 0.0051s
== 20200214004646 CreateJoinTableArticlesCategories: migrated (0.0052s)
================
```

With the `Category` model and the join table in place, you're ready to let Active Record in on your association. Open the `Article` and `Category` models and add the `has_and_belongs_to_many` declarations to them, as shown in Listings 6-13 and 6-14, respectively.

Listing 6-13. Adding the has_and_belongs_to_many Declaration in the Article Model app/models/article.rb: https://gist.github.com/nicedawg/ c4ddd9231b23014146f1e06efaee8999

```
class Article < ApplicationRecord
  validates :title, :body, presence: true

  belongs_to :user
  has_and_belongs_to_many :categories

  def long_title
    "#{title} - #{published_at}"
  end
end
```

Listing 6-14. Adding the has_and_belongs_to_many Declaration in Category Model app/models/category.rb:https://gist.github.com/nicedawg/ df770f7673069c0d2ba0b45b3d8cc54f

```
class Category < ApplicationRecord
  has_and_belongs_to_many :articles
end
```

Seeding Data

As part of creating an application skeleton, Rails added a file called db/seeds.rb, which defines some data you always need in your database. The seeds file contains Ruby code, so you can use the classes and methods—including associations—available in your models, such as create and update. Open it and create one user and a few categories so that it looks like Listing 6-15.

Listing 6-15. The db/seeds.rb File: https://gist.github.com/nicedawg/9d4c4 a01b8453cddc58e46150d38c105

```
User.create email: 'mary@example.com', password: 'guessit'

Category.create [
  {name: 'Programming'},
  {name: 'Event'},
```

```
  {name: 'Travel'},
  {name: 'Music'},
  {name: 'TV'}
]
```

That should do nicely. You can load your seed data using the Rails command
db:seed:

```
$ rails db:seed
```

If you need to add more default categories later, you can append them to the seeds
file and reload it. If you want to rerun the seed data, the trick lies in the fact that the
seeds file doesn't know whether the records already in the database have to be cleaned
up; running rake db:seed again adds all records one more time, and you end up with
duplicate user and categories. You should instead call rails db:setup, which recreates
the database and adds the seed data as you may expect.

Let's give this a test run. Get your console ready, reload!, and run the following
commands:

```
>> article = Article.last
=> #<Article id: 3, title: "Associations", ...>
>> category = Category.find_by name: 'Programming'
=> #<Category id: 1, name: "Programming", ..>
>> article.categories << category
=> [#<Category id: 1, name: "Programming", ..>]
>> article.categories.any?
=> true
>> article.categories.size
=> 1
```

Here, you automatically associate a category with an article using the << operator.
You can even do this from the category side of the association. Try the following:

```
>> category.articles.empty?
=> false
>> category.articles.size
=> 1
>> category.articles.first.title
=> "Associations"
```

You just did the opposite of the previous test: `has_and_belongs_to_many` works in both directions, right? So you found your category and asked it for its first article titled "Associations" because that's what you associated in the other direction.

Using `has_and_belongs_to_many` is a very simple way to approach many-to-many associations. However, it has its limitations. Before you're tempted to use it for more than associating categories with articles, note that it has no way of storing additional information on the join. What if you want to know *when* or *why* someone assigns a category to an article? This kind of data fits naturally in the *join table*. Rails includes another type of association called `has_many :through`, which allows you to create rich joins like this.

Creating Rich Many-to-Many Associations

Sometimes, when you're modeling a many-to-many association, you need to put additional data on the join model. But because Active Record's `has_and_belongs_to_many` uses a join table (for which there is no associated model), there's no model on which to operate. For this type of situation, you can create *rich* many-to-many associations using `has_many :through`. This is really a combination of techniques that ends up performing a similar but more robust version of `has_and_belongs_to_many`.

The basic idea is that you build or use a full model to represent the join table. Think about the blog application: articles need to have comments, so you create a `Comment` model and associate it with `Article` in a one-to-many relationship using `has_many` and `belongs_to`. You also want to be able to retrieve all the comments added to users' articles. You could say that users have many comments that belong to their articles or users have many comments through articles. Figure 6-5 illustrates this relationship.

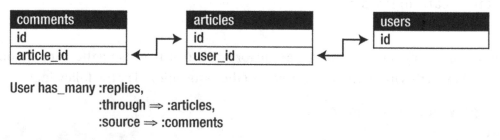

Figure 6-5. *The rich many-to-many relationship between comments and users, through articles*

Let's generate the model and migration for the Comment model:

```
$ rails generate model comment article_id:integer name:string email:string
body:text
```

invoke	active_record
create	db/migrate/20200214010834_create_comments.rb
create	app/models/comment.rb
invoke	test_unit
create	test/unit/comment_test.rb
create	test/fixtures/comments.yml

Migrate by issuing the `rails db:migrate` command:

```
$ rails db:migrate
```

```
== 20200214010834 CreateComments: migrating ==============================
-- create_table(:comments)
   -> 0.0106s
== 20200214010834 CreateComments: migrated (0.0109s) ====================
```

Update your models to reflect the one-to-many association between comments and articles. Listings 6-16 and 6-17 show the updated Comment and Article models, respectively.

Listing 6-16. The Comment Model in app/models/Comment.rb: https://gist. github.com/nicedawg/1704eb1a760eb147d802b92d20d2ad29

```
class Comment < ApplicationRecord
  belongs_to :article
end
```

Listing 6-17. The Article Model in app/models/article.rb: https://gist. github.com/nicedawg/016592081e5ea73a4170af60afa7043a

```
class Article < ApplicationRecord
  validates :title, :body, presence: true
```

```ruby
  belongs_to :user
  has_and_belongs_to_many :categories
  has_many :comments

  def long_title
    "#{title} - #{published_at}"
  end
end
```

Nothing is new here—what you implement is very similar to the users and articles relationship you saw earlier, but instead of a user having many articles, an article has many comments.

Let's get back to the relationship between users and comments. You need to tell your User model that a user has many comments through its articles. Basically, you use the Article model as a join table between users and comments. You achieve the linking using the has_many :through method. Listing 6-18 shows the updated User model.

Listing 6-18. The Updated User Model, has_many :through Declarations in app/ models/user.rb: https://gist.github.com/nicedawg/23d2377fd1ac4d87c992ac c341c6b8ad

```ruby
class User < ApplicationRecord
  has_one :profile
  has_many :articles, -> { order 'published_at DESC, title ASC' },
           dependent: :nullify
  has_many :replies, through: :articles, source: :comments
end
```

Notice that you rework how you name associations. One aspect of the Rails philosophy is that you should always be questioning and refactoring your code to work with best practices. In this incarnation, comments that users receive on their articles are called replies.

As an added benefit, has_many :through allows you to easily have nice names for your associations. The :source option lets you define the source name of the association. In this case, the replies are the articles' comments, so you set the :source option accordingly.

Let's play with this on the console to see how it works—don't forget to `reload!`. You first find the first user, find the user's first article, and create a comment on it. Then, you see that comment directly from the `user` object:

```
>> user = User.first
=> #<User id: 1, email: "user@example.com", ...>
>> user.replies.empty?
=> true
>> article = user.articles.first
=> #<Article id: 3, title: "Associations", ..., user_id: 1>
>> article.comments.create(name:  'Guest',
email: 'guest@example.com', body: 'Great article!')
=> #<Comment id: 1, article_id: 3, name: "Guest", ...>
>> user.replies
=> [#<Comment id: 1, article_id: 3, name: "Guest", ...>]
>> user.replies.size
=> 1
```

Advanced Finding

Chapter 5 covered use of the `find` class method in Active Record. This section expands on different find operations using the `where` method. Building advanced finder methods is one of the most important things you do with your models.

Using the *where* Method

The most basic condition style is the hash syntax. Active Record takes the `Hash` passed to the `where` method and turns the keys into column names and the values into parameters to match. The hash syntax is useful only if you're trying to find an exact match. Run the following command in a console window to try out the hash syntax:

```
>> Article.where(title: 'Advanced Active Record')
=> [#<Article id: 1, title: "Advanced Active Record", ...>]
```

The hash syntax works well for straightforward `where` operations where you use only ANDs to join together the conditions (i.e., all conditions must match). However, sometimes you need more flexibility than exact matches.

Using an SQL Fragment

To specify conditions, you can pass in an SQL fragment as a string that is sent directly to the query. You need to have a pretty decent knowledge of SQL to use this kind of syntax; but it provides a lot of flexibility, and you can create arbitrarily complex SQL fragments if you're an SQL ninja.

Try the same find operation as in the previous section, but use a pure SQL condition fragment:

```
>> Article.where("title = 'Advanced Active Record'")
=> [#<Article id: 1, title: "Advanced Active Record", ...>]
```

Let's try something more complicated that only SQL is able to do:

```
>> Article.where("created_at > '2020-02-04' OR body NOT LIKE '%model%'")
=> [#<Article id: 1, title: "Advanced Active Record", ...>, #<Article
id: 2, title: "One-to-many associations", ...>, #<Article id: 3, title:
"Associations", ...>]
```

Instead of using the = sign, you use the greater-than (>) symbol to make sure the date occurs after February 4, 2020. This is followed by the SQL OR operator, which says "if this first part isn't a match, then try the right-hand side and give it a second chance at matching." Therefore, you check the right-hand side only if the left-hand side fails. If an item fails the created_at match, you check to see if the body is NOT LIKE code. You can think of OR as a more permissive joining operator. It only cares that one of the conditions is a match. OR has a sister named AND, which requires that both conditions are true:

```
>> Article.where("created_at > '2020-02-04' AND body NOT LIKE '%model%'")
=> [#<Article id: 2, title: "One-to-many associations"...>, #<Article id:
3, title: "Associations", ...>]
```

You also use the SQL LIKE (modified using NOT, for negation) operator, which allows you to make partial matches. Normally, when using =, SQL requires that the strings match *perfectly*. However, LIKE is more permissive and allows partial matches when used with the % wildcard. The % symbols are SQL wildcard characters that apply in LIKE clauses. A % at the beginning of a pattern says that the pattern must match at the end of the field (the beginning can be any sequence of characters); a % at the end means that the pattern must match at the beginning, where the end can be any sequence of characters.

Using a % on both sides of the pattern means that it must match anywhere in the field. Using %model% means that the word *model* must occur somewhere (anywhere) in the body of the article. In the previous example, you don't want articles that have the word *model*; therefore, an article with the sentence "I don't have your match" is accepted as a match.

As you can see, this usage has all the flexibility of SQL, but it also has SQL's natural limitations. For instance, you may need to find information based on what the user passes into the application via the request parameters in your application (Chapter 8 covers request parameters). If you aren't careful, those data can be very dangerous to your application, because they are open to SQL injection attacks. In such an attack, a user submits malicious code that tricks your database server into doing far more than you intended. For more information about SQL injection, check out the Wikipedia article at https://en.wikipedia.org/wiki/SQL_injection. Fortunately, Rails gives you a way to avoid such threats by using the array condition syntax, which performs correctly quoted replacements.

Using an Array Condition Syntax

The array condition syntax gives you the ability to specify conditions on your database calls in a safer way than using SQL syntax. Also, you don't need to worry as much about SQL specifics like quoting and other concerns, because it does automatic conversions for you on the inputs you give it. This is how it protects against SQL injection—it ensures that the substituted values are safely quoted, thereby preventing malicious users from injecting arbitrary SQL into your queries.

The following example requires the use of a nice little Ruby method called Time.now. Basically, it returns a Time object that is set to the current time. Let's see if you can find all the articles that were published before today:

```
>> Article.where("published_at < ?", Time.now)
=> [#<Article id: 1, title: "Advanced Active Record", ...>]
```

Instead of writing in the date, you put a ? in the spot where you'd normally write the value you want to find. The where method takes the second element in the array, Time.now, and replaces it where the first ? appears. Additionally, the array syntax automatically takes your time and converts it into something your database likes. You can invoke the to_sql method after the where method to inspect the issued SQL statement:

```
>> Article.where("published_at < ?", Time.now).to_sql
=> "SELECT \"articles\".* FROM \"articles\" WHERE (published_at < '2020-02-14
01:26:23.278875')"
```

You give it a Time object, and it turns the object into the format that pleases your database. If you had passed it a string, it wouldn't have converted. You can even pass some information from another model:

```
>> Article.where("created_at = ?", Article.last.created_at)
=> [#<Article id: 3, title: "Associations", ...>]
```

That condition returns all the articles created at the same moment as the last article. You can pass as many conditions as you want, as long as they occur in the same order as the question marks:

```
>> Article.where("created_at = ? OR body LIKE ?", Article.last.created_at, 'model')
=> [#<Article id: 3, title: "Associations", ...>]
```

MONITORING THE LOGS

You can see the SQL statements issued by your application in the file log/development. log. It's often useful to monitor what the server is doing. You may have already noticed that when you run rails server, it tells you about what is going on in your application. However, different web servers (depending on what you've installed) give different outputs, some more descriptive than others.

Fortunately, Rails prints all of its activities to a log file. If you look in your log directory, you see log/development.log. This is the file where all the activities of your application are output. If you're running in production mode, the log file is log/production.log.

This file is written to live by your server. Sometimes it's useful (especially on a live server) to monitor the events occurring on your server. If you're on a UNIX system, you can run the command tail -f log/development.log to get a live feed from your logs. If you're on a Windows system, you can find several applications that behave like tail with a quick Google search.

During debugging, it can be useful to output messages to the log to see what's going on with your application. Almost anywhere in your application, you can type this:

```
Rails.logger.debug "This will only show in development"
Rails.logger.warn "This will show in all environments"
```

Both of these messages print directly to the log file and can be extremely useful for figuring out what is happening with your server.

The main disadvantage with the array syntax is that it can become confusing to remember the order of the elements you're passing in for the conditions.

Instead of adding a list of things at the end of the array, you can pass in a hash and change the question marks to actual named replacements. This can help you keep the order of your arguments straight:

```
>> Article.where("title LIKE :search OR body LIKE :search",
{search: '%association%'})
=> [#<Article id: 2, title: "One-to-many associations", ...>,
#<Article id: 3, title: "Associations", ...>]
```

As you can see, you can reuse the same term in multiple places in your condition. If you were using the regular array syntax, you'd have to pass the same value `'%association%'` twice. This is especially useful if you have many, many conditions.

Using Association Proxies

Association proxy is a fancy term for the ability to chain together multiple calls to Active Record. You've been using this technique throughout the book, but it hasn't received special mention. Here is a basic example of association proxies:

```
>> User.first.articles.all
=> [#<Article id: 3, title: "Associations", ...>]
```

This code returns all the articles of the first user. The `all` method (off `articles`) is automatically scoped to the user, which is to say it finds articles that belong to that user. If you recall, `articles` is a has_many relationship on the User model.

Scoped finders are also more secure. Imagine a multiple-user system where data owned by one user shouldn't be accessible by another user. Finding an associated object (say, an article) by its `id` doesn't restrict it to articles owned by a particular user.

You could pass in the `article_id` and the `user_id` as conditions, but that's sloppy and prone to error. The correct way to do this is to scope all find operations off the user in question. For example, assuming you have a `User` object stored in the variable `current_user`, `current_user.articles.find(1)` ensures that the article with id `1` is returned only if it belongs to the `current_user`.

Anyone who has done database work will realize that this incredibly simple syntax is far easier than the SQL queries that need to be created to achieve similar results. If you play around with these chains, you can check out the log to see the SQL that's generated—be happy that you didn't have to write it yourself!

This technique doesn't just apply to finding. You can use it to automatically assign ownership with `build` and `create` constructors by setting the appropriate foreign keys. Consider the following example, which creates a new article for the `current_user`. It automatically sets the article's `user_id` to that of the current user:

```
current_user.articles.create(title: 'Private', body: 'Body here..')
```

This is much better than the alternative, which is to go through the `Article` model directly and set the `user_id` as an attribute (`Article.create(user_id: current_user.id)`). As a rule, whenever you need to restrict find operations to an owner or if you're assigning ownership, you should use the power of the association proxy.

Other Finder Methods

Active Record ships with other finder methods that complement the `where` method and can be used on their own as well. Table 6-6 lists some of those methods with a brief description and a quick example.

Table 6-6. Some Active Record Finder Methods

Method	Description	Example
where(conditions)	Specifies the conditions in which the records are returned as a WHERE SQL fragment.	Article.where("title = 'Advanced Active Record'")
order	Specifies the order in which the records are returned as an ORDER BY SQL fragment.	Article.order("published_at DESC")

(continued)

Table 6-6. (*continued*)

Method	Description	Example
limit	Specifies the number of records to be returned as a LIMIT SQL fragment.	Article.limit(1)
joins	Specifies associated tables to be joined in as a JOIN SQL fragment.	Article.joins(:comments)
includes	Specifies associated tables to be joined and loaded as Active Record objects in a JOIN SQL fragment.	Article.includes(:comments)

You've used the where method before. Let's take the rest for a spin:

```
>> Article.all
=> [#<Article id: 1, title: "Advanced Active Record", ...>,
#<Article id: 2, title: "One-to-many associations", ...>,
#<Article id: 3, title: "Associations", ...>]
>> Article.order("title ASC")
=> [#<Article id: 1, title: "Advanced Active Record", ...>,
#<Article id: 3, title: "Associations", ...>,
#<Article id: 2, title: "One-to-many associations", ...>]
>> Article.limit(1)
=> [#<Article id: 1, title: "Advanced Active Record", ...>]
>> Article.order("title DESC").limit(2)
=> [#<Article id: 2, title: "One-to-many associations", ...>,
#<Article id: 3, title: "Associations", ...>]
```

You first retrieve a list of articles with all; then, you retrieve all articles ordered alphabetically by their title using the order method. After that, you retrieve a single article using the limit method. Finally, you chain the limit method to order to retrieve a couple of articles after sorting them. All methods listed in Table 6-6 are chainable; when you chain finder methods to one another, Rails combines their specifics to form a single query to the database.

Default Scope

As you write applications, you may notice that you repeat certain conditions many times throughout your code. For the blog application, it would make sense to display categories in alphabetical order, as the user would expect. Rails provides a technique called *scope* to encapsulate commonly used find operations. Rails doesn't enforce a default order; it lets the database take care of sorting the results, which in most cases is done on the primary key id. Let's look at how your Category records are returned now:

```
>> Category.all
=> [#<Category id: 1, name: "Programming", ...>, #<Category id: 2, name:
"Event", ...>,
#<Category id: 3, name: "Travel", ...>, #<Category id: 4, name: "Music", ..>,
#<Category id: 5, name: "TV", ...>]
```

As you can see, categories are returned according to their primary key id. Let's make sure categories are always listed alphabetically, regardless of the conditions you use for the query. The code in Listing 6-19 tells the Category class that you always want records to be ordered by the name field.

Listing 6-19.   The default_scope Declaration in app/models/category.rb:
https://gist.github.com/nicedawg/f16cbf50672545b569db91995dc1ee6c

```
class Category < ApplicationRecord
  has_and_belongs_to_many :articles

  default_scope { order :name }
end
```

As you may expect, you can pass any finder method to default_scope. Let's see the order in which your categories are retrieved now:

```
>> reload!
Reloading...
>> Category.all
=> [#<Category id: 2, name: "Event", ...>, #<Category id: 4, name: "Music", ...>,
#<Category id: 1, name: "Programming", ...>, #<Category id: 5, name: "TV", ...>,
#<Category id: 3, name: "Travel", ...>]
```

As you can see, your categories are sorted alphabetically by default.

Named Scope

The default scope is useful. But in most cases, the only code you want to have there is default ordering for your application, because adding a condition to `default_scope` would cause that condition to be applied every time. For queries that you run often, you should create named scopes that make your code easier to read and maintain.

Let's create two named scopes: the first one lists all the articles with a `published_at` date and is named `:published`; the second scope lists all the articles without a `published_at` date and is named `:draft`. You create both scopes using the `scope` method, which takes the name of the scope as its first parameter and a finder method call as its second. Listing 6-20 shows the updated `Article` model.

Listing 6-20. Named Scope Declarations in app/models/article.rb: https://gist.github.com/nicedawg/322f265fd4499310098e37b80bc66fef

```ruby
class Article < ApplicationRecord
  validates :title, :body, presence: true

  belongs_to :user
  has_and_belongs_to_many :categories
  has_many :comments

  scope :published, -> { where.not(published_at: nil) }
  scope :draft, -> { where(published_at: nil) }

  def long_title
    "#{title} - #{published_at}"
  end
end
```

As in a regular `where` method, you can use arrays as parameters. In fact, you can chain finder methods with other named scopes. You define the `recent` scope to give you articles recently published: first, you use the `published` named scope, and then you chain to it a `where` call (Listing 6-21).

Listing 6-21. Recent Named Scope Declaration in app/models/article.rb:
https://gist.github.com/nicedawg/aac8a3412e80ea6f3398dfc5817a2f14

```ruby
class Article < ApplicationRecord
  validates :title, :body, presence: true

  belongs_to :user
  has_and_belongs_to_many :categories
  has_many :comments

  scope :published, -> { where.not(published_at: nil) }
  scope :draft, -> { where(published_at: nil) }
  scope :recent, -> { where('articles.published_at > ?', 1.week.ago.to_date) }

  def long_title
    "#{title} - #{published_at}"
  end
end
```

Note   Wondering what the strange -> { } syntax is which we use for scopes? It's a shorthand syntax for generating a lambda—a self-contained standalone method in Ruby, which is executed only when you invoke it. You must use a lambda or some other object that responds to call when defining a scope. By wrapping our code in a lambda, we're assured it will be reevaluated every time the scope is used. Without using a lambda, it would only be evaluated once, meaning, for example, calling Article.draft may end up returning stale data—including some articles which are no longer drafts—and perhaps omitting new draft articles which were created since the first usage of Article.draft.

To make scopes even more useful, you can define scopes that can receive parameters, instead of hardcoding the values you want to query with. You need search functionality that allows the end user to look up articles by title; so let's add another scope called where_title that accepts an argument and searches by it (Listing 6-22).

Listing 6-22. The where_title Named Scope Declaration in app/models/article. rb: https://gist.github.com/nicedawg/271672430205b48c7ffb068582991ca8

```ruby
class Article < ApplicationRecord
  validates :title, :body, presence: true

  belongs_to :user
  has_and_belongs_to_many :categories
  has_many :comments

  scope :published, -> { where.not(published_at: nil) }
  scope :draft, -> { where(published_at: nil) }
  scope :recent, -> { where('articles.published_at > ?', 1.week.ago.to_date) }
  scope :where_title, -> (term) { where("articles.title LIKE ?", "%#{term}%") }

  def long_title
    "#{title} - #{published_at}"
  end
end
```

Now that you've added those scopes, let's see them in action in a console session. When you look at the results of running the methods, you get an English-like syntax that makes the code easy to read and expand. Pay special attention to the line that uses `Article.draft.where_title("one")`, which shows how you chain scopes to get the exact data you want:

```
>> reload!
Reloading...
>> Article.published
=> [#<Article id: 1, title: "Advanced Active Record", ...>]
>> Article.draft
=> [#<Article id: 2, title: "One-to-many associations", ...>,
#<Article id: 3, title: "Associations", ...>]
>> Article.recent
=> [#<Article id: 1, title: "Advanced Active Record", ...>]
>> Article.draft.where_title("one")
=> [#<Article id: 2, title: "One-to-many associations", ...>]
>> Article.where_title("Active")
=> [#<Article id: 1, title: "Advanced Active Record", ...>]
```

Applying Validations

It's probably a safe bet that you don't want every field in your tables to be optional. Certain fields need to be required, terms of service agreements need to be accepted, and passwords need to be confirmed. That's just the way it is when you're building web applications, and Rails understands this. Consider this example of an Account model:

```
class Account < ApplicationRecord
  validates :login, presence: true
  validates :password, confirmation: true
  validates :terms_of_service, acceptance: true
end
```

Like associations, validations are sets of high-level macros that let you selectively apply common validation requirements to your model's attributes. In this section, you create a full set of validations for your blog application, and you see firsthand how easy it is to perform basic validations with Active Record. You start by applying some of the built-in validations, and then you build a couple custom validation methods.

Using Built-in Validations

Rails has myriad built-in validators, all of which are accessible through the `validates` method. Here you will learn about some of the options the `validates` method accepts as you apply them to your blog application. Check the API for details of all the Rails validators (`https://api.rubyonrails.org/classes/ActiveModel/Validations/ClassMethods.html`).

As a reference to get you started, you can pass two common options into any built-in validator. These are described in Table 6-7.

Table 6-7. *Default Options for All Validators*

Option	Description	Example
:message	Specifies the error message shown if validation fails.	message: 'too long'
:on	Specifies when this validation happens. The default is :save. Other options are :create and :update.	on: :create

Validating That a Value Has Been Entered

You can use the :presence option to make sure a user has entered *something* into a field. This is very useful in many cases. You have those validations in the Article model for the title and body fields, as shown in Listing 6-23.

Listing 6-23. The Article Model, Validating Presence in app/models/article.rb
https://gist.github.com/nicedawg/869fe075987f4a8f0d20a1bb1ac1632c

```
class Article < ApplicationRecord
  validates :title, :body, presence: true

  belongs_to :user
  has_and_belongs_to_many :categories
  has_many :comments

  scope :published, -> { where.not(published_at: nil) }
  scope :draft, -> { where(published_at: nil) }
  scope :recent, -> { where('articles.published_at > ?', 1.week.ago.to_
  date) }
  scope :where_title, -> (term) { where("articles.title LIKE ?",
  "%#{term}%") }

  def long_title
    "#{title} - #{published_at}"
  end
end
```

The default message is "can't be blank."

Validating That a Value Is Unique

Often, you want to ensure that a certain field is unique. The :uniqueness option validates whether the value of the specified attribute is unique across the system. You use this method in the User model to make sure each email is unique, as shown in Listing 6-24.

Listing 6-24. The validates_uniqueness_of Method in app/models/user.rb

```
class User < ApplicationRecord
  validates :email, uniqueness: true

  has_one :profile
  has_many :articles, -> { order 'published_at DESC, title ASC' },
           dependent: :nullify
  has_many :replies, through: :articles, source: :comments
end
```

When the record is created, a check is performed to ensure no record exists in the database with the given value for the specified attribute email (that maps to a column). When the record is updated, the same check is made, disregarding the record itself. The default error message is "#{*value*} has already been taken."

The :scope option can also validate whether the value of the specified attributes is unique based on multiple parameters. For example, you can use it to ensure that a teacher is on the schedule only once per semester for a particular class:

```
class Schedule < ApplicationRecord
  valdates :teacher_id, uniqueness: { scope: [:semester_id, :class_id] }
end
```

Validating Length or Size

Sometimes you want to validate the length, or size, of a field entry. You can do this by using the :length option. You use this method in the User model to specify a valid number of characters for an email address, as shown in Listing 6-25. The option for specifying a size range is :within.

Listing 6-25. The validates_length_of Method in app/models/user.rb

```
class User < ApplicationRecord
  validates :email, uniqueness: true
  validates :email, length: { in: 5..50 }
```

```
has_one :profile
has_many :articles, -> { order 'published_at DESC, title ASC' },
         dependent: :nullify
has_many :replies, through: :articles, source: :comments
end
```

If you want to ensure only the minimum or maximum, you can use the `:minimum` or `:maximum` option. Table 6-8 lists the most common `:length` validator's options.

Table 6-8. *Options for Validating :length*

Option	Description
`:minimum`	Specifies the minimum size of the attribute.
`:maximum`	Specifies the maximum size of the attribute.
`:is`	Specifies the exact size of the attribute.
`:in`	Specifies the valid range (as a Ruby Range object) of values acceptable for the attribute.
`:allow_nil`	Specifies that the attribute may be `nil`; if so, the validation is skipped.
`:too_long`	Specifies the error message to add if the attribute exceeds the maximum.
`:too_short`	Specifies the error message to add if the attribute is below the minimum.
`:wrong_length`	Specifies the error message to add if the attribute is of the wrong size.
`:message`	Specifies the error message to add if `:minimum`, `:maximum`, or `:is` is violated.

Validating the Format of an Attribute

The `:format` option checks whether a value is in the correct format. Using this method requires familiarity with regular expressions (regex) or being able to steal other people's regular expressions. The classic example (and the one you need) is email. Update the `validates` method as shown in Listing 6-26.

Listing 6-26. Update validates :format Method in app/models/user.rb:
https://gist.github.com/nicedawg/7814013e0aa05613ea1e8f6a0b6ba89f

```
class User < ApplicationRecord
  validates :email, uniqueness: true
  validates :email, length: { in: 5..50 }
  validates :email, format: { with:  /\A[^@][\w.-]+@[\w.-]+[.][a-z]{2,4}\z/i }

  has_one :profile
  has_many :articles, -> { order 'published_at DESC, title ASC' },
           dependent: :nullify
  has_many :replies, through: :articles, source: :comments
end
```

Don't be put off by how complicated this looks. You pass in the :with option and a regex object to say what patterns you want to match.

Tip   If you want to learn more about using regular expressions, you can find many tutorials and books on the subject. One good reference is Nathan Good's *Regular Expression Recipes* (Apress, 2005).

Validating Confirmation

Whenever a user changes an important piece of data (especially the password), you may want the user to confirm that entry by typing it again. This is the purpose of the :confirmation validation helper. When you use this helper, you create a new virtual attribute called #{*field_name*}_confirmation. Add this to the User model for password confirmation, as shown in Listing 6-27.

Listing 6-27. The validates :confirmation Method in app/models/user.rb:
https://gist.github.com/nicedawg/d5398b7f716bfa919a233e6cb68b6925

```
class User < ApplicationRecord
  validates :email, uniqueness: true
  validates :email, length: { in: 5..50 }
  validates :email, format: { with:  /\A[^@][\w.-]+@[\w.-]+[.][a-z]{2,4}\z/i }
  validates :password, confirmation: true
```

```
has_one :profile
has_many :articles, -> { order 'published_at DESC, title ASC' },
         dependent: :nullify
has_many :replies, through: :articles, source: :comments
end
```

The `password` attribute is a column in the `users` table, but the `password_confirmation` attribute is virtual. It exists only as an in-memory variable for validating the password. This check is performed only if `password_confirmation` isn't `nil` and runs whenever the object is saved.

Other Validations

There is one other important validation helper, `:acceptance`, which validates the acceptance of a Boolean field.

Building Custom Validation Methods

In the blog application, you'd like to make sure no one creates a comment for an article that hasn't been published yet. First, you need to create a method so you can ask an `Article` whether its `published_at` field is null by using the `present?` method, which returns `true` if a value exists and `false` otherwise. This method is useful outside validations, because you may want to indicate on the administration interface later whether an article has been published. Let's add that method now and call it `published?`. Add the code shown in Listing 6-28 to the `Article` model.

Listing 6-28. Adding the `published?` Method in app/models/article.rb: https://gist.github.com/nicedawg/9751e165bf7106c97044f4b133d1e322

```
class Article < ApplicationRecord
  validates :title, :body, presence: true

  belongs_to :user
  has_and_belongs_to_many :categories
  has_many :comments
```

```
scope :published, -> { where.not(published_at: nil) }
scope :draft, -> { where(published_at: nil) }
scope :recent, -> { where('articles.published_at > ?', 1.week.ago.to_date) }
scope :where_title, -> (term) { where("articles.title LIKE ?", "%#{term}%") }

def long_title
  "#{title} - #{published_at}"
end

def published?
  published_at.present?
end
end
```

This gets you a step closer to your goal. When building validations, Active Record gives you nice objects called *errors* to use. Whenever you want to add a validation error to the list of errors, you just type `errors.add(column_name, error_message)`. So let's implement a method called `article_should_be_published` in the Comment class that uses this functionality, as shown in Listing 6-29.

Listing 6-29. Adding the `article_should_be_published` Method in app/models/comment.rb

```
class Comment < ApplicationRecord
  belongs_to :article

  def article_should_be_published
    errors.add(:article_id, 'is not published yet') if article && !article.
    published?
  end
end
```

This checks whether you should apply the error by evaluating the `if` statement. If that `if` statement is `true`, you want to add an error into the `errors` object. Note that before you test whether the article is published, you make sure `article` isn't `nil`. This is so your test doesn't throw an error. If `article` is `nil`, that should be handled by another validator: the `validates_presence_of` method.

How do you tell Active Record that this method should be run before a save? You use the validate class method and pass it a symbol with the name of the method. At the top of your Comment class, add the code shown in Listing 6-30. Note that we also expect comments to have values for name, email, and body; so we add a presence validation call.

Listing 6-30. The validate Method in app/models/comment.rb

```
class Comment < ApplicationRecord
  belongs_to :article

  validates :name, :email, :body, presence: true
  validate :article_should_be_published

  def article_should_be_published
    errors.add(:article_id, 'is not published yet') if article && !article.
    published?
  end
end
```

This advises Active Record to pay attention to your new article_should_be_published method. In Chapter 16, you write tests to make sure this is working. But you can also go to the console—if you have it open already, don't forget to reload!—and try to create an invalid object to see if it reports errors for you. The easiest way to get to errors in an Active Record object is with comment.errors.full_messages, as shown here:

```
>> article = Article.draft.first
=> #<Article id: 2, title: "One-to-many associations", ...>
>> comment = article.comments.create name: 'Dude',
email: 'dude@example.com', body: 'Great article!'
=> #<Comment id: nil, article_id: 2, name: "Dude", email: "dude@example.com",
body: "Great article!", created_at: nil, updated_at: nil>
>> comment.errors.full_messages
=> ["Article is not published yet"]
```

Making Callbacks

You often want to have certain things happen during the lifecycle of the model. Certain actions need to happen during certain events pertaining to a particular model.

167

For instance, what if you want to send an email to your administrator whenever someone cancels an account? Or perhaps you want to make sure to create a new model because some other model was also created. Sometimes, certain actions in the life of a model should execute associated actions.

To implement this, Active Record has *callbacks*. Six callbacks are commonly used in Active Record models:

- `before_create`
- `after_create`
- `before_save`
- `after_save`
- `before_destroy`
- `after_destroy`

As you can see, the names of the Rails callbacks describe their purpose. When you create a method with any of these names in your model, the method is called automatically by the model during the time the name suggests. For instance, if you make a `before_save` method, that method is called right before the model object is saved.

Any callback that starts with `before_` can stop the execution chain if it returns `false`. For instance, if you define `before_create`, you ensure that this model object will *never* be created:

```
def before_create
  false
end
```

This can be a gotcha later if you're doing something like an assignment of `false` to a variable. If you're ever confused why a model won't save, check your `before_` filters.

In the blog application, you'd like to make sure that when a user creates a comment, an email is automatically sent to the article author. Although you don't send an email here, this chapter goes over the steps required to put together code to eventually send the email in Chapter 12. To set this up, you add an `after_create` method to the `Comment` class that will eventually have the code to send an email. Add the method shown in Listing 6-31 to the `Comment` model.

Listing 6-31. Adding `after_create` Method in app/models/comment.rb

```ruby
class Comment < ApplicationRecord
  belongs_to :article

  validates :name, :email, :body, presence: true
  validate :article_should_be_published

  def article_should_be_published
    errors.add(:article_id, "is not published yet") if article
    && !article.published?
  end

  def after_create
    puts "We will notify the author in Chapter 12"
  end
end
```

You use the code you want to be executed directly in the code of the `after_create` method. This is nice and simple, but you should probably use the pattern as you did for `validate` in Listing 6-30, where you pass in a symbol that references the method to run when the validation is performed. This helps keep the code readable and easier to augment in the future, because you can supply an arbitrary number of methods to run on a callback, separated by a comma. Name the method `email_article_author`, and tell Active Record to run it after a record is created, as shown in Listing 6-32.

Listing 6-32. The email_article_author Method Specified as an `after_create` Callback in app/models/comment.rb: https://gist.github.com/nicedawg/03868 d69e4b318cfcd73d87fe495dd23

```ruby
class Comment < ApplicationRecord
  belongs_to :article

  validates :name, :email, :body, presence: true
  validate :article_should_be_published

  after_create :email_article_author

  def article_should_be_published
```

```
    errors.add(:article_id, 'is not published yet') if article && !article.
    published?
  end

  def email_article_author
    puts "We will notify #{article.user.email} in Chapter 12" if article.
    user
  end
end
```

Active Record provides many more callbacks than are mentioned here, but those listed at the beginning of this section are the ones you'll find yourself using often. Some of the others are used in extremely rare cases (for instance, `after_initialize`, which is called after an object is initialized). These callbacks can help you with just about anything you need to do during the lifecycle of a model. They're part of smart models, which know how to deal with their own birth, life, and death. See `https://guides.rubyonrails.org/active_record_callbacks.html` for more information.

Updating the User Model

You still need to do a little work on your User model. You can apply many of the techniques described in this chapter, such as custom methods to allow you to perform user authentication and validation methods to make sure your data stay clean.

When you created the user migration (Listing 6-2), you added a field called `password`. This field stores a plain-text password, which, if you think about it, isn't very secure. It's always a good idea to encrypt any sensitive data so they can't be easily read by would-be intruders. You deal with the encryption in the User model itself, but the first thing you do is rename the field in the database from `password` to `hashed_password`. This is so you can create a custom accessor called `password` with which to set the password while maintaining a field to store the encrypted version in the database. The plain-text password is never saved.

To accomplish this, you create a migration. From the terminal, issue the following command to create the new migration:

```
$ rails generate migration rename_password_to_hashed_password
```

Next, fill in the migration as shown in Listing 6-33.

Listing 6-33. Migration to Rename password to hashed_password in db/migrate/20200214024558_rename_password_to_hashed_password.rb: https://gist.github.com/nicedawg/1b40a825d44fb4a99393fec8884f4043

```
class RenamePasswordToHashedPassword < ActiveRecord::Migration[6.0]
  def change
    rename_column :users, :password, :hashed_password
  end
end
```

Run the migration using the `rails db:migrate` command, as follows:

```
$ rails db:migrate
```

```
== 20200214024558 RenamePasswordToHashedPassword: migrating ===============
-- rename_column(:users, :password, :hashed_password)
   -> 0.0220s
== 20200214024558 RenamePasswordToHashedPassword: migrated (0.0222s)
==========
```

Next, update your User model so it looks like that in Listing 6-34. You program all the user authentication methods you need for allowing users to log in. Let's look at the code first and then see in detail what you've done.

Listing 6-34. Current User Model in app/models/user.rb: https://gist.github.com/nicedawg/fd5a29e943c06b7e93824a0b71cfd16c

```
require 'digest'

class User < ApplicationRecord
  attr_accessor :password

  validates :email, uniqueness: true
  validates :email, length: { in: 5..50 }
  validates :email, format: { with:  /\A[^@][\w.-]+@[\w.-]+[.][a-z]{2,4}\z/i }
  validates :password, confirmation: true, if: :password_required?
  validates :password, length: { in: 4..20 }, if: :password_required?
  validates :password, presence: true, if: :password_required?
```

```ruby
  has_one :profile
  has_many :articles, -> { order 'published_at DESC, title ASC' },
           dependent: :nullify
  has_many :replies, through: :articles, source: :comments

  before_save :encrypt_new_password

  def self.authenticate(email, password)
    user = find_by email: email
    return user if user && user.authenticated?(password)
  end

  def authenticated?(password)
    self.hashed_password == encrypt(password)
  end

  protected

  def encrypt_new_password
    return if password.blank?
    self.hashed_password = encrypt(password)
  end

  def password_required?
    hashed_password.blank? || password.present?
  end

  def encrypt(string)
    Digest::SHA1.hexdigest(string)
  end
end
```

Note   The SHA1 hashing algorithm used in this example is weak and was only used for an example. For production websites, you should take a look at the bcrypt gem (`https://github.com/codahale/bcrypt-ruby`).

Whenever you store something sensitive like a password, you should encrypt it. To encrypt the password in your User model, you use a simple algorithm called a *hash* that creates a random-looking string from the provided input. This hashed output can't be turned back into the original string easily, so even if someone steals your database, they will have a prohibitively difficult time discovering your users' passwords. Ruby has a built-in library called Digest that includes many hashing algorithms.

Let's go through the additions to the User model:

- *require 'digest':* You start by requiring the Digest library you use for encrypting the passwords. This loads the needed library and makes it available to work within your class.

- *attr_accessor :password:* This defines an accessor attribute, password, at the top of the class body. It tells Ruby to create reader and writer methods for password. Because the password column doesn't exist in your table anymore, a password method isn't created automatically by Active Record. Still, you need a way to set the password before it's encrypted, so you make your own attribute to use. This works like any model attribute, except that it isn't persisted to the database when the model is saved.

- *before_save :encrypt_new_password:* This before_save callback tells Active Record to run the encrypt_new_password method before it saves a record. That means it applies to all operations that trigger a save, including create and update.

- *encrypt_new_password:* This method should perform encryption only if the password attribute contains a value, because you don't want it to happen unless a user is changing their password. If the password attribute is blank, you return from the method, and the hash_password value is never set. If the password value isn't blank, you have some work to do. You set the hashed_password attribute to the encrypted version of the password by laundering it through the encrypt method.

- *encrypt:* This method is fairly simple. It uses Ruby's Digest library, which you included on the first line, to create an SHA1 digest of whatever you pass it. Because methods in Ruby always return the last thing evaluated, encrypt returns the encrypted string.

- *password_required?:* When you perform validations, you want to make sure you're validating the presence, length, and confirmation of the password only if validation is required. And it's required only if this is a new record (the hashed_password attribute is blank) or if the password accessor you created has been used to set a new password (password.present?). To make this easy, you create the password_ required? predicate method, which returns true if a password is required or false if it's not. You then apply this method as an :if condition on all your password validators.

- *self.authenticate:* You can tell this is a class method because it's prefixed with self (it's defined on the class *itself*). That means you don't access it via an instance; you access it directly off the class, just as you would find, new, or create (User.authenticate, not @user = User.new; @user.authenticate). The authenticate method accepts an email address and an unencrypted password. It uses a dynamic finder (find_by_email) to fetch the user with a matching email address. If the user is found, the user variable contains a User object; if not, it's nil. Knowing this, you can return the value of user if, and only if, it isn't nil and the authenticated? method returns true for the given password (user && user. authenticated?(password)).

- *authenticated?:* This is a simple predicate method that checks to make sure the stored hashed_password matches the given password after it has been encrypted (via encrypt). If it matches, true is returned.

Let's play with these new methods from the console so you can get a better idea of how this comes together:

```
>> reload!
Reloading...
=> true
>> user = User.first
=> #<User id: 1, email: "user@example.com", ..>
>> user.password = 'secret'
=> "secret"
```

```
>> user.password_confirmation = 'secret'
=> "secret"
>> user.save
=> true
>> user.hashed_password
=> "e5e9fa1ba31ecd1ae84f75caaa474f3a663f05f4"
>> User.authenticate('user@example.com', 'secret')
=> #<User id: 1, email: "user@example.com", ...>
>> User.authenticate('user@example.com', 'secret2')
=> nil
>> second_user = User.last
=> #<User id: 2, email: "mary@example.com", ...>
>> second_user.update(password: 'secret',
password_confirmation: 'secret')
=> true
>> User.authenticate('mary@example.com', 'secret')
=> #<User id: 2, email: "mary@example.com", ...>
```

When you ask the User model to authenticate someone, you pass in the email address and the plain-text password. The authenticate method hashes the given password and then compares it to the stored (hashed) password in the database. If the passwords match, the User object is returned, and authentication was successful. When you try to use an incorrect password, nil is returned. In Chapter 8, you write code in your controller to use these model methods and allow users to log in to the site. For now, you have a properly built and secure backend for the way users authenticate.

With the validation in the User model, the db/seeds.rb file also needs to be updated to make sure it follows the rules expected in the model. While we are at it, we also add some code to create a few articles. Update your db/seeds.rb file so that it looks like Listing 6-35.

Listing 6-35. Current Seeds File in db/seeds.rb: https://gist.github.com/nic edawg/86d1950f400c39eadd23067a3f26bd5e

```ruby
user = User.create email: 'mary@example.com', password: 'guessit',
password_confirmation: 'guessit'

Category.create [
  {name: 'Programming'},
  {name: 'Event'},
  {name: 'Travel'},
  {name: 'Music'},
  {name: 'TV'}
]

user.articles.create([
  {
    title: 'Advanced Active Record',
    body: "Models need to relate to each other. In the real world, ..",
    published_at: Date.today,
  },
  {
    title: 'One-to-many associations',
    body: "One-to-many associations describe a pattern ..",
    published_at: Date.today
  },
  {
    title: 'Associations',
    body: "Active Record makes working with associations easy..",
    published_at: Date.today
  },
])
```

Reviewing the Updated Models

You've made a lot of changes to your models, so let's make sure we're on the same page before you move on. Look at the Article, Category, and Comment models in Listings 6-36, 6-37, and 6-38, respectively, and make sure yours match.

Listing 6-36. Current Article Model in app/models/article.rb

```ruby
class Article < ApplicationRecord
  validates :title, :body, presence: true

  belongs_to :user
  has_and_belongs_to_many :categories
  has_many :comments

  scope :published, -> { where.not(published_at: nil) }
  scope :draft, -> { where(published_at: nil) }
  scope :recent, -> { where('articles.published_at > ?', 1.week.ago.to_date) }
  scope :where_title, -> (term) { where("articles.title LIKE ?", "%#{term}%") }

  def long_title
    "#{title} - #{published_at}"
  end

  def published?
    published_at.present?
  end
end
```

Listing 6-37. Current Category Model in app/models/category.rb

```ruby
class Category < ApplicationRecord
  has_and_belongs_to_many :articles

  default_scope { order :name }
end
```

Listing 6-38. Current Comment Model in app/models/comment.rb

```ruby
class Comment < ApplicationRecord
  belongs_to :article

  validates :name, :email, :body, presence: true
  validate :article_should_be_published

  after_create :email_article_author

  def article_should_be_published
    errors.add(:article_id, 'is not published yet') if article && !article.
    published?
  end

  def email_article_author
    puts "We will notify #{article.user.email} in Chapter 12"
  end
end
```

Summary

After reading this chapter, you should have a complete understanding of Active Record models. The chapter covered associations, conditions, validations, and callbacks at breakneck speed. Now the fun part starts. In the next chapter, you get to use all the groundwork established in this chapter to produce the web interface for the data structures you've created. This is when you get to reap the benefits of your hard work.

## CHAPTER 7

Action Pack: Working with Routes, Controllers, and Views

When you type a URL into your browser's address bar and press Enter, a few things happen behind the scenes. First, the domain name is translated into a unique address by which the server that hosts the application can be identified. The request is then sent to that server, which begins a chain of events that culminates in a response. The response is usually, but not always, in the form of an HTML document, which is essentially a text document full of special code that your browser understands and can render visually on your screen. At this point, the request cycle is complete, and the browser waits for further input from you. If you click a link somewhere on the page or type a new URL in the address bar, the cycle begins all over again: the request is sent, the server processes it, and the server sends back the response.

When you make a request to a Rails application, this request cycle is the responsibility of a component of Rails called Action Pack. The Action Pack library is an integral component of the Rails framework and one that you need to be familiar with if you intend to master Rails.

This chapter begins with an overview of Action Pack. Then, you get to work using it in your sample blog application.

Note If you need to get the code at the exact point where you finished Chapter 6, download the source code zip file from the book's page on `www.apress.com` and extract it on your computer.

179

© Brady Somerville, Adam Gamble, Cloves Carneiro Jr and Rida Al Barazi 2020
B. Somerville et al., *Beginning Rails 6*, https://doi.org/10.1007/978-1-4842-5716-6_7

Action Pack Components

You've been introduced to the MVC pattern, but if you need a refresher, here it is. The *model* is your application's world, most often represented by database objects like articles, comments, and subscribers. The *controller* is the grand orchestrator, dealing with requests and issuing responses. The *view* is the code that contains instructions for rendering visual output for a browser, like HTML.

Armed with this refresher, you may be able to guess what roles are played by Action Pack. This isn't a test, so here's the answer: Action Pack is the controller and the view. The controller performs the logic, and the view renders the template that is given back to the requesting browser. Not surprisingly, two of the modules that make up the Action Pack are named accordingly: Action Controller and Action View.

Action Pack has another important component: Action Dispatch. A typical Rails app has multiple controllers—each of which handles requests for a particular area of concern. (For example, in previous chapters, we built ArticlesController, which returns responses for requests specific to articles.) How does Rails know which controller should handle a particular request? Action Dispatch, among other things, handles *routing*— which decides which controller should handle a given request.

At this point, you may be wondering why the router, view, and controller are wrapped up in a single library, unlike models, which have a library of their own. The answer is subtle and succinct: routes, controllers, and views are very closely related. The sections that follow paint a more complete picture of both the role and the relationship of controllers and views, how they work, and how they work together to create and control the interface of a Rails application.

Action Controller

Controllers orchestrate your application's flow. Every time a user requests a page, submits a form, or clicks a link, that request is handled—in one way or another—by a controller. When you're programming your application, you spend a lot of time building controllers and giving them instructions on how to handle requests.

The concept of controllers can sometimes be difficult for newcomers to grasp. Even if you've built web applications before, say in ASP (Active Server Pages) or PHP (PHP Hypertext Preprocessor), you may not be used to this form of separation, where the mechanics of flow are controlled by a separate entity and not embedded in the pages themselves.

Let's look at the example of the CD player in a car to illustrate the concept of controllers. The player is required to respond to certain events, such as the user pressing the play button, fast-forwarding, or rewinding a track. When you push a button, you expect something to happen—you've made a request, and you wait for the subsequent response.

If your CD player were a Rails application, the instructions for what to do when a certain event takes place, such as pressing the eject button, would be contained in a controller. If you were to sketch it on paper, it might look something like this:

- CD Player

- Play

- Stop

- Fast-forward

- Rewind

- Eject

These events, or actions, describe what the player should be capable of *doing*. Obviously, each of these actions would need to be programmed to do something with the disk inside the player. When someone presses Eject, you would first call on the stop action (if the disk is playing) and then arrange for the player to spit out the disk. You would code all the instructions for dealing with an eject event into the controller— specifically, inside the eject action. The same would apply for play, fast-forward, and rewind.

It's worth noting that this type of logic has nothing to do with the CD itself, nor does it have anything to do with the music on the CD. If this were a Rails application, the CD would be the model. It can be used independently of the player. In fact, it can be used in all sorts of players, not just the one in your car.

The stereo in your car is probably capable of more than just playing CDs. Most stereos have a radio receiver built in as well. The radio would have its own set of events that would likewise need to be handled. These actions might include things like changing stations, setting presets, and switching between AM and FM. To keep things well organized, you would probably want to group these actions inside their own controller, separate from the CD controller. After all, the radio and the CD player do different things.

When you're dealing with a Rails application, it's not much different. You separate the things that you need your application to do with an object from the object itself. Even when you're not dealing directly with an object (adjusting the volume on your car stereo has little to do with either the CD in the player or the station on the radio), you still handle the event inside a controller.

Each controller in Rails is designed as a Ruby class. Without getting too technical, Listing 7-1 shows how the CD player example would look if it were a Ruby class.

Listing 7-1. CDPlayer Class

```
class CDPlayer
  def play
  end

  def stop
  end

  def fast_forward
  end

  def rewind
  end

  def eject
  end
end
```

Inside the CDPlayer class, you define a method for each action, or each thing you want your CD player to be able to do. So, if you were to send the message "play" to an instance of the CDPlayer class, it would know how to handle it (of course, because the play method is empty in this example, nothing would happen). On the other hand, if you sent the message "pause," Ruby would raise an exception and tell you that the method wasn't found. If you wanted CDPlayer objects to respond to that message, you would need to add a method called (you guessed it) pause.

All the methods in this class are public, which means they can be invoked by anyone. You don't need to do anything special to a method to make it public. *Unless otherwise declared, all methods in a Ruby class are public by default.* If you were to mark an action as private, though, it could be used only internally by the class. For example, if the stop method were private, it would raise a NoMethodError if you called it from outside the

CDPlayer class. However, the eject method is free to call on stop, because it does so internally. Although the usefulness of this feature will become apparent as you continue to learn about controllers, consider this: if your CD player needed to display the time remaining for a given track, it might need to perform a few calculations to figure that out. You might create a method for doing these internal calculations, but would you want that method to be accessible from the outside? Would you have a button called Calculate on your player?

It's time for a working definition: *Action Controllers are Ruby classes containing one or more public methods known as actions.* Each action is responsible for responding to a request to perform some task. A typical controller is most often a collection of actions that relates to a specific area of concern. For example, consider the blog application you've been building in the previous chapters. The controller that manages articles has the class name ArticlesController and has action methods for listing, creating, reading, updating, and deleting articles.

The example of the CD player worked well to illustrate the basic concept of controllers, but it won't take you much further when dealing with web applications. If you were really dealing with a CD player, you would press Play, the disc would start playing, and that would be the end of it. But because Rails was specifically designed for building web applications, it makes a fair number of assumptions about what you want your actions to do when they're finished firing. Chief among these is the rendering of a view.

Imagine that you're reading a list of posts on someone's blog. You click the title of a post, and you expect to be taken to a new screen that shows you just that post. You requested an action (show), and in response, you receive a new screen. This happens all the time in the world of web applications: when you click a link, you expect to go to a new page.

In Rails, it's the general case that when actions have completed their work, they respond by rendering a view. The concept of actions rendering views is so common that Rails has internalized it as a convention: *unless otherwise stated, when an action is finished firing, it renders a view.* How does Rails know what view to render if you don't tell it? It looks for a view whose name matches that of the requested action. This should give you some insight as to why Action Controller and Action View are bundled together in Action Pack. Because of the way controller actions relate to views, a few other mechanisms facilitate their communication, all of which are covered shortly.

Action View

The Action View library is another important part of Action Pack. Given that controllers are responsible for handling the request and issuing a response, views are responsible for rendering the output of a response in a way a browser (or any other user agent) can understand. Let's say you request the index action from the ArticlesController. After performing the logic to retrieve a list of articles, the controller hands off to the view, which formats the list of articles to make them look pretty. The controller then collects the results of the render, and the HTML is sent back to the browser, thus completing the request cycle.

Although the controller and the view are separate entities, they need to communicate with each other. The primary mechanism by which they do this is through shared variables. These shared variables are called *instance variables* and are easy to spot in Ruby because they're prefixed with the @ symbol. Keep this in mind as you look at the view example in Listing 7-2, which uses an instance variable called @articles to produce an articles listing.

Listing 7-2. An Example View

```
<html>
  <body>
    <ul>
      <% @articles.each do |article| %>
        <li><%= article.title %></li>
      <% end %>
    <ul>
  </body>
</html>
```

Even without knowing any Ruby, you should be able to guess what this code does: it iterates over the collection of articles stored in the variable @articles and prints the title of each between HTML list item (<li>) tags. If @articles contained three articles whose titles were One, Two, and Three, respectively, the preceding code would be compiled to the following:

```
<html>
  <body>
    <ul>
      <li>One</li>
      <li>Two</li>
      <li>Three</li>
    <ul>
  </body>
</html>
```

You may wonder where the variable @articles came into being. If you guessed in the controller, you would be right. The controller sets up instance variables that the view can access. In this case, the controller created a variable called @articles, and the view was given automatic access to it. Notice that the view doesn't perform any logic to fetch the list of articles; it relies on the controller to have set up the variable and performs the display logic necessary to turn the collection into a browser-ready HTML list.

Embedded Ruby

The code you see mixed into the HTML markup is Ruby. Because templates that are capable of dealing only with static HTML wouldn't be very useful, Action View templates have the benefit of being able to use Embedded Ruby (ERb) to programmatically enhance them.

Using ERb, you can embed Ruby into your templates and give them the ability to deal with data from the controller to produce well-formed HTML representations. ERb is included in the Ruby Standard library, and Rails makes extensive use of it. You trigger ERb by using embeddings such as <% %> and <%= %> in your template files to evaluate or print Ruby code, respectively. If you've ever worked with ASP, JSP (Java Server Page), or PHP, this style of embedding should be familiar to you.

In the example in the preceding section, the loop is constructed within *evaluation embedding* tags (<% %>), and the article's title is printed using *output embedding* tags (<%= %>). Pay close attention to the subtle difference between the two embedding types: output embedding includes an equals sign; regular embedding doesn't. When you use output embedding, you're effectively saying *print the results of the Ruby code when it's evaluated*. Regular embedding doesn't print results; it evaluates whatever is between the tags and goes on its merry way. If you mistakenly omit the equals sign, no errors are raised, but nothing is printed either. You have a set of empty list tags.

Note   Following the Model behavior, Rails is modular and can be used with other templating libraries. A popular alternative is the Haml (`http://haml-lang.com`) template language used by many Rails developers.

Helpers

The terms of the MVC are fairly strict in the way they advocate the separation of components. Controllers really shouldn't concern themselves with the generation of view code, and views shouldn't concern themselves with anything but the simplest of logic. Although it's possible to use ERb to execute arbitrary Ruby code inside a view, and although controllers are certainly capable of generating markup, it's generally considered in violation of the MVC pattern to do so. This is where helpers come in to play.

Action Pack's *helpers* do exactly what their name implies: they help views by providing a convenient location to encapsulate code that would otherwise clutter the view and violate the terms of the MVC. They offer a middle ground between controllers and views and help to keep your application organized and easy to maintain.

If you think about it, ERb tags really aren't the best place for performing complex logic, and templates can quickly become unwieldy when creating markup programmatically. For this reason, Action Pack includes a large suite of built-in helpers for generating all sorts of HTML fragments—from creating forms and formatting dates to making hyperlinks and image tags. And when the built-in helpers aren't enough, you can write your own. Each controller gets its own helper module that's mixed in automatically, ready to lend your templates a hand when they need it.

Routing

All the information pertaining to which controller and action to call on comes in the form of the request URL. Action Pack includes a specialized component called *routing*, which is responsible for dissecting the incoming URL and delegating control to the appropriate controller and action.

Every request that comes into your web application originates in the form of a URL. The routing system allows you to write the rules that govern how each URL is picked apart and handled.

A traditional URL contains the path to a file on the server, relative to the server's home directory. Here's an example:

```
http://example.com/articles/show.asp?id=1037
```

You can tell a lot from this URL. First, you know the server technology being used is Microsoft's ASP. Given that, you also know that this URL resolves to the `show.asp` script, which is inside the `/articles` directory. In this case, there is no URL rewriting going on; the mapping of the URL to the script that handles it is one-to-one.

The problem with this kind of mapping is that you have no control over the URL. The URL is coupled to the script. What if you want to invoke the `show.asp` script but want the URL to read `articles/detail.asp` instead of `show.asp`? Or better yet, what if you don't want to expose the underlying script implementation (ASP) at all and use just `articles/detail`? There's no way. The lack of flexibility in this kind of URL mapping is a problem. If you ever need to change the name of the script being invoked, you instantly break all the URL references. This can be a major pain if you need to update all your code, especially if your pages are indexed by search engines.

Action Pack's routing solves this problem by decoupling the URL from the underlying program implementation. In Rails, the URL is related to the specific resource being requested, and it can be formatted to correctly identify that resource without having to conform to the name of the script that does the handling. When thought of in this way, URLs become part of the interface of an application, unrelated to the files that are ultimately invoked to process a request.

There are myriad reasons why a routing system is a good idea. Here are just a few of them:

- Decoupled URLs can convey meaning, becoming part of the interface.

- Clean, readable URLs are more user-friendly and easier to remember.

- URLs can be changed without affecting the underlying implementation.

Of course, like most things in Rails, the routing system is open to configuration; and one of the great benefits of routes is that because they're decoupled, they can be customized to create meaningful URLs without much effort. This chapter teaches you how to build and customize routes for your application, understand the default routes that Rails creates for you, create named routes, and use routes when creating links and redirects in your code.

RESTful Resources

Rails adapted RESTful design as a convention in Rails 1.2 onward. Representational State Transfer (REST) is a principle used mainly over the HTTP protocol to offer a better interface for client-server operations. This section first discusses the REST concept and then explains how Rails implemented it through RESTful controllers and resources.

The REST principle is based on working with information in the form of *resources*. Each piece of information is dealt with as a *resource*, each resource has a unique interaction point for every *action* that can be performed on it, and each interaction point (action) is normally represented using a URL and a request method.

For example, think of a blog, which is a collection of information resources. Every article is a resource, and every action you perform on it, such as read, edit, or delete, has its own interaction point, mainly identified by a URL and a request method.

HTTP protocol, which is the main web protocol you normally use in browsers, has several request methods. These are the primary ones used in RESTful design:

- POST: Normally used to *submit* forms and create *new* resource data

- GET: Mainly used to request a page to *view* a resource or more

- PATCH/PUT: Used to modify a specific resource

- DELETE: Used to delete a resource

Do those methods remind you of anything? If you're thinking of CRUD, then you're right. Taking the main database operations create, read, update, and delete (CRUD) in REST design and tying them up with HTTP's main methods gives you what's called a *RESTful* web service.

RESTful web services are commonly used in APIs (referred to as REST APIs) by associating every CRUD method with its corresponding HTTP method:

- `POST/Create`: Creates a resource

- `GET/Read`: Requests a specific resource or group of resources

- `PATCH/PUT/Update`: Edits attributes of a resource

- `DELETE/Delete`: Deletes a resource

Rails implemented RESTful design for controllers by introducing the concept of resources. Every model in your application is dealt with via a controller as a resources set, and that RESTful controller has certain methods that handle your regular operations on that model. We'll examine that in depth after you understand the Action Pack request cycle.

Action Pack Request Cycle

The entire request-to-response process is called the Action Pack *request cycle*. The request cycle consists of the following steps:

1. Rails receives a request from the outside world (usually a browser).

2. Routing picks apart the request to determine the controller and action to invoke.

3. A new controller object is instantiated, and an action method is called.

4. The controller interacts with a model (usually performing a CRUD operation in a database with an ActiveRecord model, but not necessarily).

5. A response is sent back to the browser, in the form of either a render or a redirect.

Figure 7-1 illustrates the process.

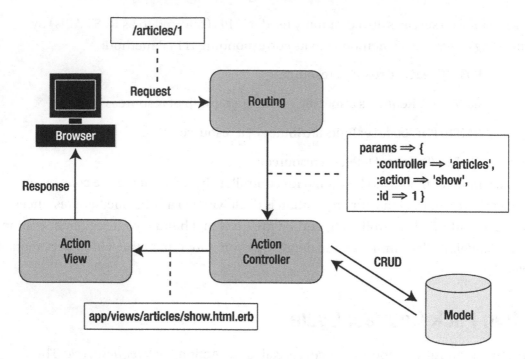

Figure 7-1. *The Action Pack request cycle*

Not long ago (and still today), developers used to construct *server pages*. Such a page had a bunch of code at the top of an otherwise static page, just above the opening HTML tag. The markup was littered with different sorts of code: it wasn't unusual to see the database being accessed, forms being processed, sessions being set, and all manner of logic being performed in line. The web server was responsible for controlling the application—one page redirecting to another, running the code, and then dumping the results to the screen. For example, consider this poorly written PHP code:

```php
<?php
  // articles.php
  require_once("db.inc.php");
  require_once("header.inc.php");

  $result = mysql_query("SELECT * FROM articles") or die(mysql_error());
?>
```

```
<table>
    <tr>
     <th>Title</th>
     <th>Excerpt</th>
      <?php
        if($logged_in) {
          echo "<th>Actions</th>";
        }
      ?>
    </tr>
    <?php
      while($a = mysql_fetch_array($result)) {
        echo "<tr>";
        echo "<td><a href='/article.php?id=".$a['id']."'>" . $a['title'] .
        "</a></td>";
        echo "<td>" . $a['excerpt'] . "</td>";
        if ($logged_in) {
          echo "<td>";
            echo "<td><a href='/edit.php?id=".$a['id']."'>Edit</a></td>";
            echo "<td><a href='/delete.php?id=".$a['id']."'>Delete</a></td>";
          echo "</td>";
        }
        echo "</tr>";
      }
    ?>
</table>

<?php
    require_once("footer.inc.php");
?>
```

This isn't even that bad of an example! We won't get into the multitude of reasons why this is a bad idea, except to say that it presents the problem of coupling. In this scenario, the business logic and the view are mashed together, making the code more difficult to maintain and debug. ASP and PHP pages are notable offenders, and if you're coming from either of these camps, the concept of separating concerns may be foreign at first. Here's a way to think about it that may help. Imagine taking the code and logic from the top of each page and sticking it in one place, leaving only the HTML behind. Then, instead of using the web server to invoke each page as you would with a static site, have the web server call on a single dispatcher, which finds the code you want to execute and calls it. The code it invokes—the file that contains the processing logic extracted from the server page—is called the controller. Instead of logic being divided among pages, it's divided into actions.

The single biggest advantage of this pattern is that the processing logic is decoupled from the view and safely contained in one place. As you can see, it's a lot easier to work this way. The interplay between actions is considerably easier to visualize and understand when it isn't spread out over a host of locations. Your server pages become lightweight views, left to handle only the simplest of instructions, if any.

A Controller Walk-Through

Instead of boring you with more theory about controllers, views, and MVC, let's dig in and start writing some real-world code. You'll continue building your blog application, examining the finer points and the places where convention wins out over configuration. Along the way, this section touches on some of the most essential controller and view concepts. By the end of this walk-through, you should have a complete grasp of how the Rails request cycle works and a working example to refer to and expand on in the subsequent chapters. The purpose of this walk-through isn't to examine each and every aspect of Action Pack in detail, but rather to give you a practical overview of how the components—routes, controllers, helpers, views, layouts, and partials—work together to control your application and construct its interface.

Setting Up Routes

Links and URLs are important in web applications. They serve as the entry point to the application and contain all the information required to route an incoming request to the controller and action that will handle it. Before you get into the meat of understanding controllers and their actions, you need to spend a few minutes learning how to get from request to response. It all starts with routing.

Routing Basics

In Rails, all the rules for mapping URLs to controllers are a matter of configuration. You find the `routes.rb` file in the `config` directory.

Routing priority is based on the order in which routes exist in `routes.rb`, so that the first route defined has the highest priority. If an incoming URL matches the first route defined, the request is sent along, and no other routes are examined.

Here's an example that matches a specific pattern and sets the controller and action in response:

```
get '/teams/home', to: 'teams#index'
```

This route matches a URL like `http://example.com/teams/home` and routes the request to the `index` action on the `teams` controller. The names of the controller and action are separated by the # symbol. You can also set arbitrary parameters when using the route. For example, let's say you want to set a parameter called `query` that you can access and use in your controller:

```
get '/teams/search/:query', to: 'teams#search'
```

This route matches a URL like `http://example.com/teams/search/toronto`, routing the request to the `teams` controller and the `search` action. The third segment in the URL is assigned to the `:query` parameter and passed to the search action, because you specify `:query` as an inline variable.

Routes can be complex, and it's possible to apply conditions and other forms of logic to them. For the most part, though, you can get a lot of mileage from the general cases outlined here. The Rails API documentation (`https://guides.rubyonrails.org/routing.html`) contains details on using the more complex routing features.

Named Routes

One of the coolest things about routing in Rails is a feature known as *named routes*. You can assign a name to a given route to make referring to it in code easier. You still define the route the same way as a regular route, but you need a new hash pair, where the key is `:as` and the value is the name of the route.

For example, let's take the search route defined in the previous section and turn it into a named route:

```
get '/teams/search/:query', to: 'teams#search', as: 'search'
```

With this definition in place, Rails creates helper methods that allow you to reference this particular route using its name: `search_url` and `search_path`. The `*_url` variant returns a full URL including the protocol and hostname (`http://example.com/teams/search`), whereas the `*_path` variant returns just the path (`/teams/search`).

Later in this chapter, we'll cover redirection methods and hyperlink generation helpers. For now, note that you can use them with named routes:

```
link_to "Search", search_path
```

outputs

```
<a href="/teams/search">Search</a>
```

Named routes are shorter, DRYer, and impervious to changes made at the routing level. So if you change the controller name from `teams` to `cities`, you don't need to update links that use the named route; for the unnamed version, you do.

RESTful Routes and Resources

Earlier, we said that RESTful design information is dealt with in the form of resources. Rails makes it easy for you to do that: for every action in your controller, you have an associated named route to call.

Resources are configured in the `routes.rb` file using the `resources` method. If you look at the routes file in your blog application, you see `resources :articles` at the top: it was added when you generated the articles scaffold in Chapter 3. The `resources :articles` method defines the following named routes for the articles controller:

```
article_path => /articles/:id
articles_path => /articles
edit_article_path => /articles/:id/edit
new_article_path => /articles/new
```

The `resources` method generated four named routes for you; but when you open the `ArticlesController`, you have seven actions (Table 7-1). How can you access the remaining actions? Remember that when you learned about REST earlier, you saw that every operation is identified by both a URL *and* a request method. Using different request methods with the generated named routes, Rails routes them to the appropriate controller actions.

Table 7-1. *Articles Named Routes*

Request Method	Named Routes	Parameters	Controller Action
GET	articles_path		index
POST	articles_path	Article attributes	create
GET	new_article_path		new
GET	edit_article_path	ID	edit
GET	article_path	ID	show
PATCH	article_path	ID and article attributes	update
PUT	article_path	ID and article attributes	update
DELETE	article_path	ID	destroy

Note You can list all the available routes in your application by running the *rails routes* command from the terminal. You can also view a list of routes by going to `http://localhost:3000/rails/info` in your browser while you have your Rails server running in development mode.

By following the REST convention, instead of defining a named route for every action, you use the `resources` method in your routes file. To give some examples, if you want to access the `index` action in your articles controller, you go to `/articles` in your browser; the default request method when you type a URL in your browser is GET. What if you want to create a new article? You can do that by submitting a form to `/articles` with the default request method for forms, POST. To get a specific article, type `/articles/:id`, where `:id` is your article id. It's that simple.

Configuring Routes for the Blog Application

Let's configure the routes to be used in your blog application. You haven't built all the controllers and actions yet (you do that next), but that shouldn't stop you from getting the routes in place.

You can handle an empty request for the root of your application's domain using the `root` method. In the blog application, you want the root URL (`http://localhost:3000`)

to connect to the list of articles. To accomplish this, you add a `root` declaration to your routes file and make it the first route. Make sure your `config/routes.rb` file looks like Listing 7-3 (note that all comments have been deleted).

Listing 7-3. The `config/routes.rb` File: `https://gist.github.com/nicedawg/` `3439fa09dc9be1f791271542308878fc`

```
Rails.application.routes.draw do
  root to: "articles#index"
  resources :articles
end
```

Now, visit the root URL of your project (`http://localhost:3000`). You should see the articles listing, just like on `http://localhost:3000/articles`. Now that we have some routes defined, let's move back to the articles controller and try to understand its actions and templates.

Revisiting the Scaffold Generator

You generated a scaffold for your articles in Chapter 3, and this scaffold generated a RESTful controller for the `Article` model in addition to all the required templates. The generator also added the resources declaration to your `route.rb` file. Listing 7-4 shows the `ArticlesController` that your scaffold generated.

Listing 7-4. The `ArticlesController` `app/controllers/articles_controller.rb`

```
class ArticlesController < ApplicationController
  before_action :set_article, only: [:show, :edit, :update, :destroy]

  # GET /articles
  # GET /articles.json
  def index
    @articles = Article.all
  end

  # GET /articles/1
  # GET /articles/1.json
  def show
  end
```

```ruby
# GET /articles/new
def new
  @article = Article.new
end

# GET /articles/1/edit
def edit
end

# POST /articles
# POST /articles.json
def create
  @article = Article.new(article_params)

  respond_to do |format|
    if @article.save
      format.html { redirect_to @article, notice: 'Article was
      successfully created.' }
      format.json { render :show, status: :created, location: @article }
    else
      format.html { render :new }
      format.json { render json: @article.errors, status: :unprocessable_
      entity }
    end
  end
end

# PATCH/PUT /articles/1
# PATCH/PUT /articles/1.json
def update
  respond_to do |format|
    if @article.update(article_params)
      format.html { redirect_to @article, notice: 'Article was
      successfully updated.' }
      format.json { render :show, status: :ok, location: @article }
    else
      format.html { render :edit }
```

```ruby
      format.json { render json: @article.errors, status: :unprocessable_
        entity }
      end
    end
  end

  # DELETE /articles/1
  # DELETE /articles/1.json
  def destroy
    @article.destroy
    respond_to do |format|
      format.html { redirect_to articles_url, notice: 'Article was
      successfully destroyed.' }
      format.json { head :no_content }
    end
  end

  private
    # Use callbacks to share common setup or constraints between actions.
    def set_article
      @article = Article.find(params[:id])
    end

    # Never trust parameters from the scary internet, only allow the white
    list through.
    def article_params
      params.require(:article).permit(:title, :location, :excerpt, :body,
      :published_at)
    end
end
```

This may look like a lot of code to swallow, but in reality it's simple. The scaffold generator creates the articles controller with the default seven actions discussed earlier for RESTful controllers: index, show, new, edit, create, update, and destroy.

Before your action renders a view, you arrange for it to set an instance variable that the view can use. To refresh your memory, an instance variable is a special kind of Ruby variable that is unique to a given instance of a class, serving as a way for an object to maintain its state. Because views are, in essence, extensions of the controller object, they can access its instance variables directly (although not without some behind-the-scenes Ruby magic that Rails takes care of for you). For all intents and purposes, however, you can consider instance variables to be shared between controllers and views.

You can store any Ruby object in an instance variable, including strings, integers, models, hashes, and arrays. If you reexamine each action in the articles controller, notice that it always starts by setting an instance variable to be called later in that action's view. Let's take the index method as an example (Listing 7-5).

Listing 7-5. The Index Action in app/controllers/articles_controller.rb

```
# GET /articles
# GET /articles.json
def index
  @articles = Article.all
end
```

You define and set an instance variable named @articles, which holds the array of all your articles.

Let's step back a bit. When you call the index method by typing the URL (http://localhost:3000/articles) into your browser—don't forget to start your local server using the rails server command—the request goes first to your routes file, where it's forwarded to the controller. Then, the controller responds to this request by setting an instance variable and rendering *something* back to the browser.

What the controller renders is based on what has been requested. Normally, it's an HTML page request, but it can also be an XML or an Ajax request. It's the responsibility of the respond_to method to define how to respond to each of those requests. In the index action, you accept two formats: HTML, where Rails renders the index template using the path (/articles), and JSON (JavaScript Object Notation), where Rails renders the articles in JSON format using the path (/articles.json). In this case, the respond_to method is implicit, which means that since we didn't need to change any options, it will just use the defaults. You will see the respond_to method actually used when we look at later actions.

Try that in the browser. Visit http://localhost:3000/articles to see the list of articles you know and saw earlier, and visit http://localhost:3000/articles.json to see the result shown in Figure 7-2.

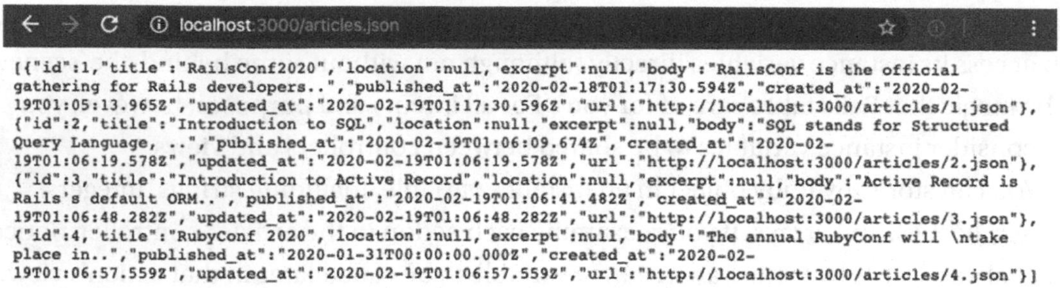

[{"id":1,"title":"RailsConf2020","location":null,"excerpt":null,"body":"RailsConf is the official gathering for Rails developers..","published_at":"2020-02-18T01:17:30.594Z","created_at":"2020-02-19T01:05:13.965Z","updated_at":"2020-02-19T01:17:30.596Z","url":"http://localhost:3000/articles/1.json"},
{"id":2,"title":"Introduction to SQL","location":null,"excerpt":null,"body":"SQL stands for Structured Query Language, ..","published_at":"2020-02-19T01:06:09.674Z","created_at":"2020-02-19T01:06:19.578Z","updated_at":"2020-02-19T01:06:19.578Z","url":"http://localhost:3000/articles/2.json"},
{"id":3,"title":"Introduction to Active Record","location":null,"excerpt":null,"body":"Active Record is Rails's default ORM..","published_at":"2020-02-19T01:06:41.482Z","created_at":"2020-02-19T01:06:48.282Z","updated_at":"2020-02-19T01:06:48.282Z","url":"http://localhost:3000/articles/3.json"},
{"id":4,"title":"RubyConf 2020","location":null,"excerpt":null,"body":"The annual RubyConf will \ntake place in..","published_at":"2020-01-31T00:00:00.000Z","created_at":"2020-02-19T01:06:57.559Z","updated_at":"2020-02-19T01:06:57.559Z","url":"http://localhost:3000/articles/4.json"}]

Figure 7-2. *Output of* `http://localhost:3000/articles.json`

GET AN API FOR FREE

Using RESTful controllers in Rails gives you the ability to have an API for your application. An API is a set of functions that enables other applications to talk to your application. On the Web, this is normally done using JSON, and REST is one of the main architectures used for that.

With Rails and its RESTful controllers, defining your API is a seamless process; basically, you just need to tell your controller to respond to JSON requests, and you have an API. What's neat in Rails is that the scaffold generator adds the JSON part by default to all your controller actions, providing you with an API for free. Rails also supports XML, but JSON is the default.

Rendering Responses

When an action has completed, it attempts to render a template of the same name. That's the case with the index action just discussed: it renders the index.html.erb template by default. The same applies to edit, new, and show actions. But sometimes you want to *render* something else.

If you look at the create and update actions, notice that if the @article.save succeeds, you redirect to the saved @article show page with a friendly message. However, if the save fails, you want to render the new or the edit template. If you didn't explicitly render those templates, the actions would fall through to their default behavior and attempt to render their default create and update templates, which don't exist.

Typically, the first argument to *render* is a string or symbol indicating which template to render (e.g., *render :edit* when the *update* action in our ArticlesController fails to save would cause the articles/edit.html.erb to be rendered). However, the render method offers various ways to render output inline—that is, *without* a template.

For example, *render json: @article.errors* results in the article's errors being sent back to the browser in JSON format, with no template file involved. In addition to *json*, the *render* method supports several other inline-render modes, including :plain, :html, :nothing, :inline, :xml, and :js. For more information on different ways to use the *render* method, visit the following link when you're ready: https://guides.rubyonrails.org/layouts_and_rendering.html#using-render

Redirecting

It may not sound like it, but a redirection is a response. Redirects don't happen on the server side. Instead, a response is sent to your browser that tells it to perform a redirection to another URL. The specifics of issuing a redirect aren't something you need to worry about, though, because Rails provides a specialized method to take care of the internals. That method is called redirect_to, and it's one you'll find yourself using a lot, so it's a good idea to get familiar with it.

The redirect_to method usually takes a URL as a parameter, which in most cases is represented by one of your routes. Let's say that you want to redirect the user to the articles' index page, and the path you use is articles_path—a route added by resources :articles in config/routes.rb; so you execute redirect_to(articles_path). If you look at the destroy action, the user is redirected to articles_url after an article is deleted.

As you can see from the create and update actions, redirect_to can also take an object as a parameter, in which case it redirects to a path that represents that object. This means Rails uses a convention to translate objects to their show action named route. In this case, redirect_to(@article) is a shortcut equivalent to redirect_to(article_path(id: @article)).

WHAT MAKES A CLASS AN ACTION CONTROLLER?

If you're the curious sort (and, of course, you are), you may wonder how ArticlesController, a seemingly normal Ruby class, becomes a full-fledged Action Controller. Well, if you look closely, you'll notice that ArticlesController inherits from another class: ApplicationController. To get a better picture of what's going on, let's take a peek at the ApplicationController class in app/controllers/application_controller.rb:

```
class ApplicationController < ActionController::Base
end
```

The mystery is quickly solved. The simple controller becomes an Action Controller by subclassing the ApplicationController class, itself a subclass of ActionController::Base. This is an example of inheritance and is common in object-oriented programming. When one class subclasses another, it inherits all the behavior and methods of the parent. In the case of the articles controller, it inherits all the capabilities of the ApplicationController. Likewise, ApplicationController inherits all the capabilities of *its* parent, ActionController::Base. The ActionController::Base class effectively endows your articles controller with its special abilities.

ApplicationController is the base from which all the controllers you make inherit. Because it's the parent of all controllers in your application, it's a great place to put methods that you want accessible in every controller.

By looking at the articles controller, you now understand the basic conventions and common concepts of how a RESTful controller normally behaves. You have seven default actions, and in every one of them you do the following:

- Set an instance variable to be used later in the rendered action or template.

- Handle the response using the respond_to method to either do a render or redirect_to another path, depending on the behavior you want to achieve.

Understanding Templates

The next step is to look at the actions' templates. Look in the app/views/articles directory, and you see eight templates:

- _article.json.jbuilder

- _form.html.erb

- edit.html.erb

- index.html.erb

- index.json.jbuilder

- new.html.erb

- show.html.erb

- show.json.jbuilder

The basic convention of Action Pack is as follows: *templates are organized by controller name, and a template with the same name as the action being invoked is rendered automatically.* You don't need to wire up anything. Merely by requesting an action from a controller, Rails renders the corresponding template in that controller's directory inside `app/views/` that has the same name.

Let's try an example. Make sure your local web server is running (`rails server`), and open `http://localhost:3000/articles/` in your browser. You see the articles index page shown in Figure 7-3.

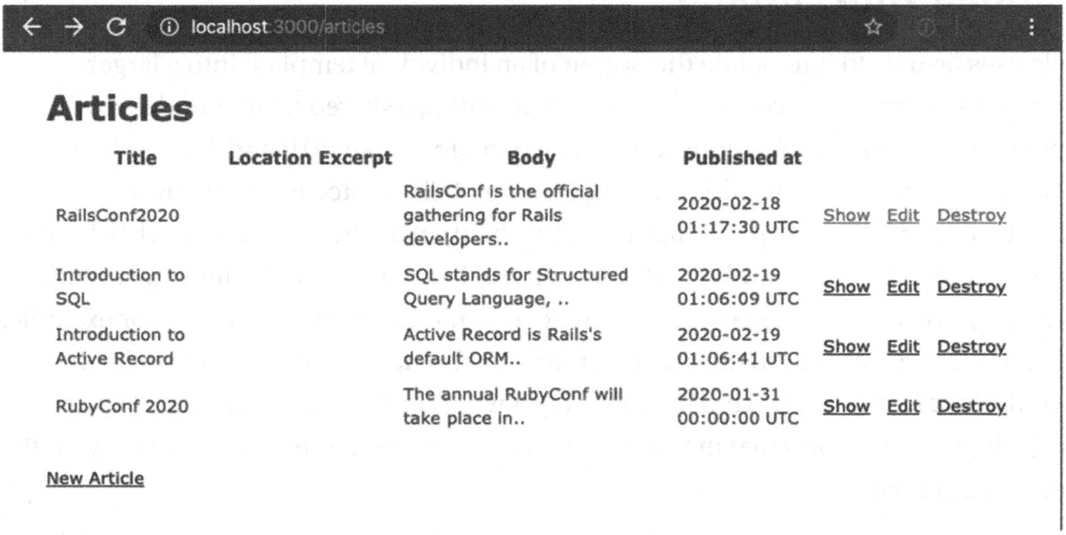

Figure 7-3. *Output of* `http://localhost:3000/articles`

The articles listing is actually rendered from `app/views/articles/index.html.erb`, which follows the convention discussed earlier. It's the articles controller, so it goes to the `articles` directory in `app/views`. After determining which controller to invoke, Rails proceeds to instantiate it and calls its `index` method. Its default response after running the `index` action is to perform a render. Rails looks for a template named `index.html.erb` in the `app/views/articles` directory and loads it. The same applies to the `show` action: the `show.html.erb` template is rendered.

At this point, the request cycle is complete. If you refresh your browser, the cycle begins anew, and the same result is rendered. Notice how all the internals are taken care of for you. All you need to do is create an appropriately named route, controller, action, and view, stick them in the right place, and request the URL in your browser. Rails takes care of making sure everything is knit together properly.

Before you go any further, use your browser's View Source command to see the HTML that was produced. If you know anything about HTML (and chances are you do), you'll quickly realize that some additional HTML code has been rendered around the code in `index.html.erb`; it came from a *layout*. Most web pages have headers, footers, sidebars, and other page elements that, when styled, make the page look pretty. Rails has a built-in facility for dealing with page layouts.

Working with Layouts

Rails uses layouts to interpolate the output of an individual template into a larger whole—a reversal of the common pattern of including a shared header and footer on every page (which, if you've done any work in languages like PHP and ASP, is all too familiar). When you created this blog application, Rails created a default layout file and placed it in `app/views/layouts/application.html.erb`. The `application.html.erb` layout is applied to all controllers. However, if you like your layout to apply to a specific controller, you can create a layout file named after the controller you want. For example, a layout that applies only to the articles controller should be created in `app/views/layouts/articles.html.erb`. That's the way it works in Rails. Just as an action tries to render itself using a view that matches its name, a controller attempts to use a layout that matches its name.

Note   Layouts always default to the most specific declaration. If your controller inherits from `ApplicationController` and doesn't specify a layout directly, Rails will look for a layout named after your controller first. If that layout isn't found, it will look for a layout declaration on `ApplicationController`, and if that isn't found, it will look for a layout named application. In other words, layout declaration follows normal class inheritance.

Open the file app/views/layouts/application.html.erb in your editor. You should see something like the file shown in Listing 7-6.

Listing 7-6. The app/views/layouts/application.html.erb File

```
<!DOCTYPE html>
<html>
  <head>
    <title>Blog</title>
    <%= csrf_meta_tags %>
    <%= csp_meta_tag %>

    <%= stylesheet_link_tag 'application', media: 'all', 'data-turbolinks-
    track': 'reload' %>
    <%= javascript_pack_tag 'application', 'data-turbolinks-track': 'reload' %>
  </head>

  <body>
    <%= yield %>
  </body>
</html>
```

At rendering time, the layout yields the results of the template fragment's execution in place. See the <%= yield %> bit that's highlighted in bold? That's the important part. Wherever you put the yield keyword is where your content goes.

One more thing to note: Rails is all about convention over configuration. Here, the convention is that a layout with the name application.html.erb is automatically applied to all templates unless an alternate is specified. This means that if you change the name of the layout as it stands, it won't be automatically applied. If you want to apply a different layout to a given controller, you can either have a layout named after the controller or specify it in the controller using the class method layout:

```
class ExampleController < ApplicationController
  layout 'my_layout' # Will use a layout in app/views/layouts/my_layout.
  html.erb
end
```

COMMON LAYOUT CONVENTIONS

A few conventions apply to working with layouts:

- A layout named `application.html.erb` is applied automatically unless a more specific candidate exists or is explicitly specified in the controller.

- A layout that matches the name of a controller is automatically applied if present. Controller-specific layouts take precedence over the application-level layout.

- You can use the `layout` directive at the class level in any controller (i.e., not inside an action) to set the layout for the entire controller: `layout 'my_layout'`.

- You can include a layout for a specific action with an explicit call to `render` inside the action: `render layout: 'my_layout'`.

- Sometimes, you want to render an action without a layout. In that case, you can pass `false` in place of the layout name: `render layout: false`.

In practice, you usually use `application.html.erb` and rarely take advantage of the controller-specific layout functionality. On the occasions when you need to use a different layout for a particular controller, use the `layout` directive.

Looking at the Article Form

Let's look at the new template in action. The new action has a single purpose: to initialize and display the form for creating a new article. The actual creation of a new `Article` object is the responsibility of the `Article` model (remember the discussions of the model in Chapters 5 and 6), but it's orchestrated by the controller. Moreover, it needs data (like a title and body), which it must procure from somewhere. The `edit` action isn't any different, except that it finds and displays a form of an existing Article object rather than a new one.

You can extract this information from HTML form elements placed in the view and handled in the controller. Open `new.html.erb` and `edit.html.erb`, which look like Listings 7-7 and 7-8, respectively.

Listing 7-7. Content of app/views/articles/new.html.erb

```
<h1>New Article</h1>
```

<%= render 'form', article: @article %>

```
<%= link_to 'Back', articles_path %>
```

Listing 7-8. Content of app/views/articles/edit.html.erb

```
<h1>Editing Article</h1>
```

<%= render 'form', article: @article %>

```
<%= link_to 'Show', @article %> |
<%= link_to 'Back', articles_path %>
```

Notice the similarity between the templates, especially the render 'form' part highlighted in bold. The render method renders a partial named form in this context. The upcoming section "Staying DRY with Partials" discusses partials in more depth; for now, let's focus on the content of the template in app/views/articles/_form.html.erb (Listing 7-9).

Listing 7-9. Content of app/views/articles/_form.html.erb

```
<%= form_with(model: article, local: true) do |form| %>
  <% if article.errors.any? %>
    <div id="error_explanation">
      <h2><%= pluralize(article.errors.count, "error") %> prohibited this
      article from being saved:</h2>

      <ul>
        <% article.errors.full_messages.each do |message| %>
          <li><%= message %></li>
        <% end %>
      </ul>
    </div>
  <% end %>
```

```
  <div class="field">
    <%= form.label :title %>
    <%= form.text_field :title %>
  </div>

  <div class="field">
    <%= form.label :location %>
    <%= form.text_field :location %>
  </div>

  <div class="field">
    <%= form.label :excerpt %>
    <%= form.text_field :excerpt %>
  </div>

  <div class="field">
    <%= form.label :body %>
    <%= form.text_area :body %>
  </div>

  <div class="field">
    <%= form.label :published_at %>
    <%= form.datetime_select :published_at %>
  </div>

  <div class="actions">
    <%= form.submit %>
  </div>
<% end %>
```

Notice how instead of including the actual markup for form fields (like <input> or <select> tags), you use form helpers for each of your fields. Visit the article's new page at http://localhost:3000/articles/new in your browser, and you'll see that the helpers function to produce a nicely formatted HTML form. Use your browser's View Source command to look at the HTML that was generated. Here's part of the generated HTML:

```
<h1>New Article</h1>

<form action="/articles" accept-charset="UTF-8" method="post"><input
type="hidden" name="authenticity_token" value="Yc+IOEOM4OdEefg/+BFZErrmAcRV
WbZfNuTwG6a4MAFbIvJJlc9Xni51jjXYLlqYqYLrD+/K/vNvWZV+CfGxXA==" />

  <div class="field">
    <label for="article_title">Title</label>
    <input type="text" name="article[title]" id="article_title" />
  </div>

  <div class="field">
    <label for="article_location">Location</label>
    <input type="text" name="article[location]" id="article_location" />
  </div>

  <div class="field">
    <label for="article_excerpt">Excerpt</label>
    <input type="text" name="article[excerpt]" id="article_excerpt" />
  </div>

  <div class="field">
    <label for="article_body">Body</label>
    <textarea name="article[body]" id="article_body"></textarea>
  </div>
  ...
    <div class="actions">
    <input type="submit" name="commit" value="Create Article" data-disable-
    with="Create Article" />
  </div>
</form>
```

Note the way in which Rails formats the name attribute of each form element:
model[*attribute*]. This helps when it comes to parsing the parameters from the form,
as you'll see shortly. If you manually create your form elements (which you need to do
sometimes), you can use this naming convention to make sure your form values are easy

to parse in the controller. Most of the time, though, you use form helpers when working with forms, especially when you're dealing with Active Record objects. Let's spend some time discussing form helpers.

Using Form Helpers

One of the best things about working with templates in Rails is the presence of helpers. Rails comes with a bunch of helper methods that take the tedium out of generating the bits of HTML that your views need. Let's face it, nothing is more of a drag to build than HTML forms. Fortunately, Rails understands the plight of the web developer all too well and provides a suite of easy ways to build forms.

Two basic varieties of form helpers are available:

- *FormHelper:* Active Record–aware tag helpers for creating forms that hook into models.

- *FormTagHelper:* Helpers that output tags. They aren't integrated with Active Record. The names of these helpers are suffixed with _tag.

The FormHelper type is aware of Active Record objects assigned to the template; the FormTagHelper (note the Tag) type isn't. The advantage of the Active Record–aware, FormHelper, helpers is that they know how to populate themselves with data and can automatically be highlighted in the event of validation errors from the model. But not every form element you make corresponds directly to a model attribute. That's where the FormTagHelper group comes in handy. These have no special relationship with Active Record; they just output form tags.

In your article's form template (Listing 7-9), you use six helpers: form_with, label, text_field, text_area, datetime_select, and submit.

The form_with helper is of the FormHelper variety. It creates an HTML form tag using its parameters (*model: article, local: true*, in this case) and places everything in the do..end block inside the resulting form. It also produces and sets a *form local variable* to the form block. The form local variable, in this case called f, is aware of the *Article* object and uses its attributes' names and values when calling the other form helpers: label, text_field, text_area, datetime_select, and submit.

By default, forms use the HTTP POST method. If you want to use a different method, you need to specify it manually using the :method option (e.g., method: "get"). If you recall, POST is the request method you used for the create action in your RESTful-designed controller.

HTTP VERBS

The HTTP protocol defines several request methods, the most popular of which are GET and POST. Both are methods for requesting a web page; the difference is in how the request is sent. GET is the simpler of the two. It includes all the information about the request as part of the URL. POST sends information invisibly, which is to say as part of the request header and not part of the URL. So you can't type a POST request into your browser's location bar. Every time you request a web page via the location bar in your browser, you're using GET. When you submit a form, say, to register on a website, the form is usually submitted via a POST.

How do you know when to use each? The best way to think of this is to consider GET a read method. It should never do anything destructive, such as modifying a database record. POST, on the other hand, can be thought of as a write method. When you need to create data, use POST. PATCH is used when you need to update a record partially, for instance, only changing your email address. PUT is used to update a record completely. There has been a lot of controversy over these verbs on the Internet, but they are effectively used interchangeably in Rails. The DELETE verb is used to destroy a record.

A small note: Most browsers only support the GET and POST verbs. Rails gets around this by using an actual POST request but inserting hidden form fields specifying which actual verb to use. Rails automatically removes this field and converts the request into the specified type. Once the request has reached the controller, it will appear as the intended verb.

Remember that you should never put a state-changing action behind a GET request. For more information, see www.w3.org/2001/tag/doc/whenToUseGet.html.

The label helper is a FormHelper method that outputs an HTML label tag for the provided attribute. Here's an example of the output for :title:

```
<label for="article_title">Title</label>
```

The text_field helper is of the FormHelper variety, meaning that it corresponds to Active Record objects. It creates an HTML input tag whose type is set to "text" and assigns it a name and an ID that match the given object and method (title in this case). Here's what the rendered output looks like:

```
<input type="text" name="article[title]" id="article_title" />
```

The text_area helper is also of the FormHelper variety. It's similar to text_field, except it returns a text area instead of a text input. Here's what the HTML output looks like for the body field:

```
<textarea name="article[body]" id="article_body"></textarea>
```

The datetime_select helper is a FormHelper that outputs a set of HTML select tags to input a date and time value.

The submit helper is a FormHelper that creates an input element whose type is set to "submit". It accepts the name of the submit button as its first argument. If you don't provide a name to the submit method, it generates a name based on the @article object. For example, in the New Article form, the generated name is Create Article, whereas in the Edit Article form, the name is Update Article. Here's the HTML output from the example:

```
<input type="submit" name="commit" value="Create Article" data-disable-
with="Create Article" />
```

All these helpers (and, to be sure, most helpers in Rails) accept a hash of options as their last argument to customize the resulting HTML. For example, to give your title field a class of large, you type f.text_field :title, class: 'large', which adds the class attribute to the output:

```
<input class="large" type="text" name="article[title]" id="article_title" />
```

You can pass arbitrary options in this way, all of which end up as attributes on the resulting tag. For example, to apply an inline style attribute, you can use style: 'background: #fab444'. Here's a list of some of the most common FormHelper helpers:

- text_field
- hidden_field
- password_field
- file_field
- text_area

- `check_box`

- `radio_button`

All these methods can be suffixed with `_tag` to create standard HTML tags (with no Active Record integration).

For a full list of `FormHelper` and `FormTagHelper` methods, consult the Rails API, where you can find a complete reference along with usage examples:

- `https://api.rubyonrails.org/classes/ActionView/Helpers/`
  `FormHelper.html`

- `https://api.rubyonrails.org/classes/ActionView/Helpers/`
  `FormTagHelper.html`

Now, back to your form. Let's see what happens when you submit it. (Make sure your server is still running.) Click the Create Article button, and you see the screen shown in Figure 7-4.

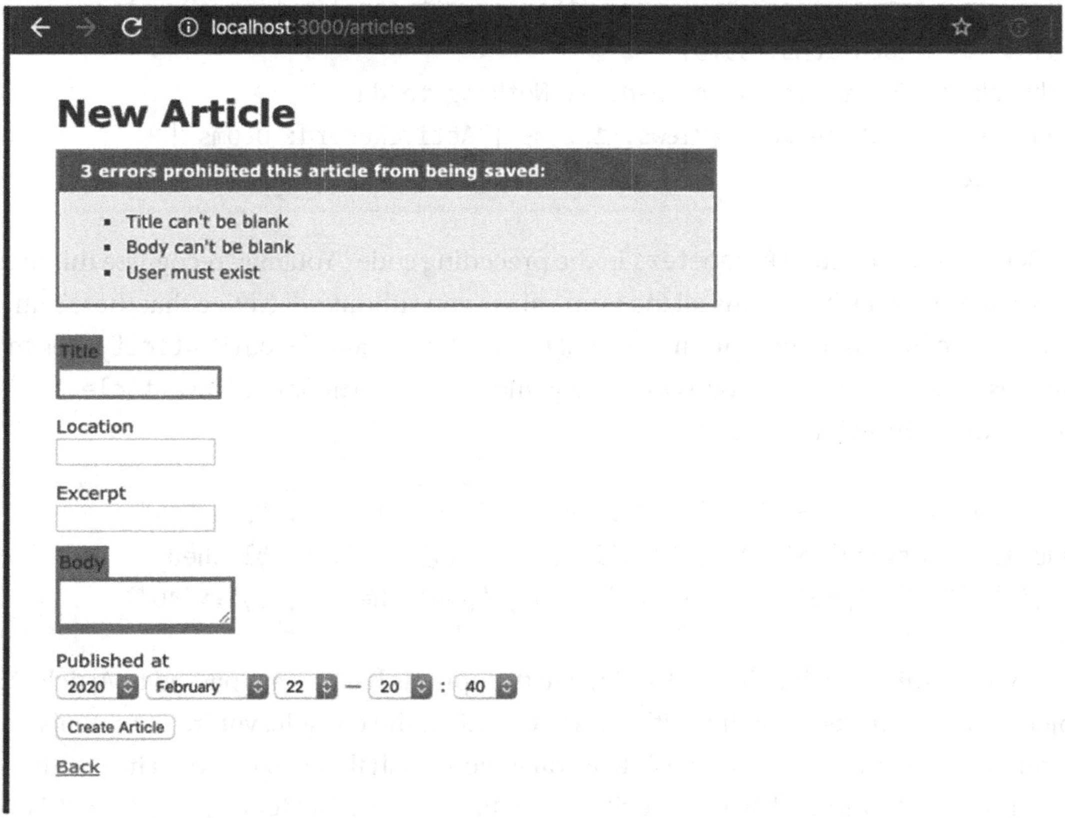

Figure 7-4. *New article form with validation errors*

What happened? Well, as the message says, Rails couldn't create an `article` for you. Of course it couldn't—you set validation rules in your `Article` model to prevent the creation of a new Article object with an empty `title` or body field. But let's look at the output from the server running in the command prompt and see what happened:

```
Started POST "/articles" for ::1 at 2020-02-22 14:40:13 -0600
Processing by ArticlesController#create as HTML
  Parameters: {"authenticity_token"=>"UzFLTMzE6SOnFXLUbbpUlSwAxJ2
  tJeAVkFRmSunZXEbKH4f/IQOVhxyGnUBNkcCrDrqJClaFpzLi4o7U3nb3Yg==",
  "article"=>{"title"=>"", "location"=>"", "excerpt"=>"", "body"=>"",
  "published_at(1i)"=>"2020", "published_at(2i)"=>"2", "published_
  at(3i)"=>"22", "published_at(4i)"=>"20", "published_at(5i)"=>"40"},
  "commit"=>"Create Article"}
  Rendering articles/new.html.erb within layouts/application
  Rendered articles/_form.html.erb (Duration: 5.2ms | Allocations: 3887)
  Rendered articles/new.html.erb within layouts/application (Duration:
  5.6ms | Allocations: 3979)
[Webpacker] Everything's up-to-date. Nothing to do
Completed 200 OK in 28ms (Views: 12.4ms | ActiveRecord: 0.0ms |
Allocations: 10155)
```

See the section titled `Parameters` in the preceding code? You may recognize this as a Ruby hash. This hash contains all the form values you submitted. Notice that there's an entry for the button name (commit), called Create Article, and for `authenticity_token`, which is used for security in Rails to prevent anonymous form posts. The `article` portion of the hash looks like this:

```
"article"=>{"title"=>"", "location"=>"", "excerpt"=>"", "body"=>"",
"published_at(1i)"=>"2020", "published_at(2i)"=>"2", "published_
at(3i)"=>"22", "published_at(4i)"=>"20", "published_at(5i)"=>"40"}
```

If you're thinking that this looks a lot like the options hashes you passed to Article objects when you were working with Active Record on the console, you're right. Rails automatically turns form elements into a convenient hash that you can pass into your models to create and update their attributes. In the sections that follow, you'll put this feature to use in the next action, `create`. First, let's take a deeper look at `params`.

Processing Request Parameters

Request parameters—whether they originate from requests of the GET or POST variety—are accessible via the params hash. To be specific, params is a method that returns a Hash-like ActionController::Parameters object so you can access it using hash semantics. Hashes in Ruby are similar to arrays but are indexed by arbitrary keys—unlike arrays, which are indexed by number. (If you need a quick review of the Hash object, flip to Chapter 4 for a Ruby primer.)

The value of any request variable can be retrieved by its symbolized key. So, if there's a variable called id in the request parameters, you can access it with params[:id]. Just to drive this concept home, let's look at a sample URL and display the params hash that it populates. Point your browser to http://localhost:3000/articles?title=rails&body=great and check the server output. You should see something similar to this:

```
Parameters: {"title"=>"rails", "body"=>"great"}
```

Revisiting the Controller

With an understanding of params under your belt, let's go back to your controller. The create action is the target of the form submission. The method code shown in Listing 7-10 is from the articles controller, just under the new method.

Listing 7-10. The Create Action in app/controllers/articles_controller.rb

```
# POST /articles
# POST /articles.json
def create
  @article = Article.new(article_params)

  respond_to do |format|
    if @article.save
      format.html { redirect_to @article, notice: 'Article was successfully
      created.' }
      format.json { render :show, status: :created, location: @article }
    else
      format.html { render :new }
```

```
    format.json { render json: @article.errors, status: :unprocessable_
    entity }
  end
 end
end
```

Let's walk through this. First, you initialize a new `Article` object with whatever attributes come in via the `article_params` method. You can imagine that taking raw input from the user and putting it directly into your model without filtering it could be dangerous. Imagine that you were letting users sign up using the `User#create` action. If you had an attribute on the User model called `admin` that determined whether or not the user had admin access to the system, a user could just add that parameter in themselves and make themselves an admin. You can see how vital it is that we filter the parameters now! Let's take a look at the `article_params` method:

```
# Never trust parameters from the scary internet, only allow the white list
through.
def article_params
  params.require(:article).permit(:title, :location, :excerpt, :body,
  :published_at)
end
```

The syntax for this is simple. We are telling Rails that we require the `article` param and permit `title`, `location`, `excerpt`, `body`, and `published at`. Any other params will be filtered out before they get to the model. If you try to just pass `params[:article]` to the new or `create` method, an error will be returned. This feature is called "strong parameters."

After we pass the filtered params to the new method, we attempt to save the model. If the save is successful, you use a facility that Rails provides called the *flash* to set a message—by passing the `:notice` option to `redirect_to`—before redirecting to the `show` action on the same `articles` controller. The flash is a special kind of storage mechanism provided by Rails for convenience. It encapsulates the pattern of wanting to set a message on one action and have that message persist to the next, only to disappear after that action is rendered. This is useful for providing user feedback, as you do here to say "Article was successfully created." If you look at the show article file in `app/views/articles/show. html.erb`, you have access to the `notice` variable, allowing the message to be displayed:

```
<p class="notice"><%= notice %></p>
```

The flash message you set is available to the controller and action you redirect to (the show action on the articles controller). There are two special flash cases, notice and alert, which you can use just as you did in the previous example by passing them as arguments to redirect_to.

Note   When you pass notice: "Article was successfully created" to redirect_to, it's identical to calling flash[:notice] = "Article was successfully created" in a separate line. Also, when you retrieve, in any view template, the message using notice, you could as well use flash[:notice]. So you can use any named key when calling flash because it's implemented as a Ruby hash. You store values in it based on a key. The key can be anything you like: you can use any symbol, such as flash[:warning] =, in your controller and later retrieve it in your views using the same flash[:warning] call.

If the save fails, you render the new action again so that any errors can be corrected.

Displaying Error Messages in Templates

Let's try submitting the form empty one more time to explore it again. Sure enough, the form doesn't save. Notice that you're still on the same screen and that the form elements are highlighted in red, as shown in Figure 7-4.

If you look at the HTML source, you see that the input and label tags are surrounded by div elements with the class name field_with_errors:

```
<div class="field_with_errors">
    <label for="article_title">Title</label>
</div>
<div class="field_with_errors">
    <input type="text" value="" name="article[title]" id="article_title">
</div>
```

Rails does this automatically for any fields that fail validation. You can use these classes to style invalid elements.

> **Note**   The style rules that turn the invalid fields red are generated by the scaffold generator and are in app/assets/stylesheets/scaffolds.scss.

The formatted list of errors that appears at the top of the page is rendered using the following code snippet, which is a part of app/views/articles/_form.html.erb:

```erb
<% if article.errors.any? %>
  <div id="error_explanation">
    <h2><%= pluralize(article.errors.count, "error") %> prohibited this
    article from being saved:</h2>

    <ul>
      <% article.errors.full_messages.each do |message| %>
        <li><%= message %></li>
      <% end %>
    </ul>
  </div>
<% end %>
```

Now that you understand this, let's submit the form with valid data. If all goes according to plan, the new article should be created, and you're redirected to that article's show action, where you see the friendly notice message you set. Notice that if you refresh the page using your browser's Refresh button, the notice message disappears.

The *edit* and *update* Actions

The edit and update actions look almost identical to the new and create actions. The main difference is that instead of instantiating a new Article object, you fetch an existing one. This happens with a callback called before_action. This is similar to the Active Record callbacks we looked at in Chapter 6. In this case, the set_article method is called before the show, edit, update, and destroy actions are run. The set_article method loads the article using the id passed in params. This allows your code to stay DRY by keeping you from typing that line multiple times throughout the controller. It works exactly as if the code from the set_article method were typed at the very beginning of your action.

Looking at our action again, we used Active Record's update method to update all the Article attributes with those from the article_params method. If the update fails, update returns false, and your if statement takes the else path (Listing 7-11).

Listing 7-11. The Update Action in app/controllers/articles_controller.rb

```ruby
# PATCH/PUT /articles/1
# PATCH/PUT /articles/1.json
def update
  respond_to do |format|
    if @article.update(article_params)
      format.html { redirect_to @article, notice: 'Article was successfully
      updated.' }
      format.json { render :show, status: :ok, location: @article }
    else
      format.html { render :edit }
      format.json { render json: @article.errors, status: :unprocessable_
      entity }
    end
  end
end
```

Revisiting the Views

Let's get back to the views. If you look at the new and edit templates, you can't help but notice they render almost the same HTML: only the header and navigation are slightly different. Remember from the RESTful discussion that the HTTP request methods for create and update should be POST and PUT, respectively. Rails once more takes care of that for you. You're rendering the same app/view/articles/_form.html.erb partial, but Rails knows the request method to use based on the @article variable passed to the form_with helper.

Try editing one of the articles. The URL should be something like http:// localhost:3000/articles/1/edit; it looks similar to the new form, but with the record information already populated (Figure 7-5).

Figure 7-5. *Editing an existing article*

Thanks to the form_with helper, the form fields are populated with their respective
@article attributes. If you try to submit this form and look at the output from the server
running on the command prompt, you'll see the following:

```
Started PATCH "/articles/1" for ::1 at 2020-02-22 15:10:55 -0600
Processing by ArticlesController#update as HTML
  Parameters: {"authenticity_token"=>"QDD9QBMIUikwWl6NgIqpl2kjuRHOwcZiMqL+
  ltl/bTcK3MQC/SnjANdOMlLIrHAhPFwDgVyYtX7ZYgCvqqYpWw==", "article"=>
  {"title"=>"RailsConf2020", "location"=>"", "excerpt"=>"", "body"=>
  "RailsConf is the official gathering for Rails developers..", "published_
  at(1i)"=>"2020", "published_at(2i)"=>"2", "published_at(3i)"=>"18",
  "published_at(4i)"=>"01", "published_at(5i)"=>"17"}, "commit"=>
  "Update Article", "id"=>"1"}
  Article Load (0.3ms)  SELECT "articles".* FROM "articles" WHERE
  "articles"."id" = ? LIMIT ?  [["id", 1], ["LIMIT", 1]]
  ↳ app/controllers/articles_controller.rb:67:in `set_article'
   (0.1ms)  begin transaction
  ↳ app/controllers/articles_controller.rb:44:in `block in update'
```

```
Article Update (0.6ms)  UPDATE "articles" SET "location" = ?, "excerpt" = ?,
  "published_at" = ?, "updated_at" = ? WHERE "articles"."id" =
? [["location", ""], ["excerpt", ""], ["published_at", "2020-02-18
  01:17:00"], ["updated_at", "2020-02-22 21:10:55.483973"], ["id", 1]]
↳ app/controllers/articles_controller.rb:44:in `block in update'
  (3.5ms)  commit transaction
↳ app/controllers/articles_controller.rb:44:in `block in update'
Redirected to http://localhost:3000/articles/1
Completed 302 Found in 12ms (ActiveRecord: 4.4ms | Allocations: 3742)
```

Notice the bold line: the update action of the articles controller was called as expected. Rails recognized that the article variable passed to form_with wasn't a new record; therefore, it called the update action for you. This is yet another example of convention over configuration in Rails.

Staying DRY with Partials

A typical web application is rife with view code and often suffers from a lot of needless duplication. The HTML forms for adding and modifying articles are good examples of forms that are very similar. Wouldn't it be nice if there were a way to reuse the common elements from one form in more than one place? That's where partial templates come in.

Partial templates, usually referred to as *partials*, are similar to regular templates, but they have a more refined set of capabilities. Partials are used quite often in a typical Rails application, because they help cut down on duplication and keep the code well organized. They follow the naming convention of being prefixed with an underscore, thus distinguishing them from standard templates (which are meant to be rendered on their own).

Rather than creating two separate forms, Rails keeps your code DRY by using a single partial and including it from both the new and edit templates. Let's look at the code from new.html.erb and edit.html.erb, shown in Listings 7-12 and 7-13, respectively.

Listing 7-12. The app/views/articles/new.html.erb File

```
<h1>New Article</h1>
<%= render 'form', article: @article %>
<%= link_to 'Back', articles_path %>
```

221

Listing 7-13. The app/views/users/edit.html.erb File

```
<h1>Editing Article</h1>

<%= render 'form', article: @article %>

<%= link_to 'Show', @article %> |
<%= link_to 'Back', articles_path %>
```

Let's take a closer look at the render method. When referencing the partial in the render method, you don't include the leading underscore:

```
<%= render 'form', article: @article %>
```

We see that two arguments are passed to the render method. The first argument is a string, and the second argument is a hash. (Have you noticed that Rails is a big fan of the options hash?)

The first argument is the partial's name. Upon seeing this, the render method searches the current directory for a file named _form.html.erb. Notice that you don't need to include the leading underscore or the file extension when specifying the partial's name; Rails knows to look for a file in the same directory as the calling template with a leading underscore.

The second argument, *article: @article*, assigns the value of @article to a local variable in the partial named *article*. This isn't strictly necessary—the form partial could have referenced @article directly instead of the *article* local variable. However, the scaffold generator chose to populate local variables in the template because many consider this a best practice; doing so minimizes the scope of the @article instance variable and arguably makes the partial more reusable. The next section explains in more detail.

Local Variable Assignment in Partials

The render method accepts a hash of local variables as part of the options hash. This is an example of what a render partial with local variables looks like:

```
<%= render 'header', title: 'My Blog' %>
```

Any number of local variables can be assigned this way, and any object can be set as the value. In the preceding example, the partial has access to the local variable title.

Rendering an Object Partial

Following the same convention of local variable assignment in partials, Rails makes it easier to render a partial that represents a specific object. For example, suppose you have the following render call in your code:

```
<%= render @article %>
```

Rails looks for a partial in `app/views/articles/_article.html.erb` and automatically assigns a local variable called `article`. It's a shortcut for

```
<%= render 'articles/article', article: @article %>
```

Rendering a Collection of Partials

Another common pattern of rendering partials renders a collection of objects. Rails has a convention for rendering collections where you pass the collection as the first argument of the render method; Rails automatically loops across this collection and renders the partial of every object inside that array accordingly. Here's an example:

```
<%= render @articles %>
```

This behaves exactly like the previous call, but it performs more magic under the hood. For example, if the `@articles` array contains different Active Record objects, such as two articles and two comments, the render call renders the right partial template for each of those objects. It renders `/app/views/comments/_comment.html.erb` for the comment objects and `/app/views/articles/_article.html.erb` for the Article objects. It is roughly equivalent to (but more performant than) the following:

```
<% @articles.each do |object| %>
  <%= render object %>
<% end %>
```

Summary

This chapter covered a lot of ground. It began with a general introduction to the components that compose Action Pack, the Rails library responsible for the controller and the view. Then, it launched into a controller walk-through, where you visited your scaffold-generated controller. In doing so, you learned about routes, what happens when you generate a scaffold, how actions relate to views, and how to work with layouts. You were introduced to Rails' form helpers, and you learned how easily forms integrate with Active Record objects. The chapter also introduced partials, and you learned how to keep your templates DRY and easy to maintain.

This chapter gave you your first taste of Rails outside the model. You now have a complete understanding of how Rails divides its concerns and a firsthand look at MVC in action. You started by modeling your domain in Chapters 5 and 6, and now you've completed the first iteration of building a web application around your domain.

You should be proud of yourself. At this stage, you know a lot about Rails. The next chapter builds on this knowledge, starting with more advanced topics like building a controller from scratch, sessions, and state and sprucing up the application with some CSS.

CHAPTER 8

Advanced Action Pack

Now that you have a very good understanding of how the components of Action Pack work, it's time to dig a little deeper. You start by generating the users controller from scratch, writing its actions, and creating its templates. Then you'll add some functionality to the blog application: you allow users to leave comments when reading an article and make sure only logged-in users have access to adding and editing content. Finally, you give your application some styling so it looks better and more like a real application.

Note   If you need to get the code at the exact point where you finished Chapter 7, download the source code zip file from the book's page on `www.apress.com` and extract it on your computer.

Generating a Controller

It's time to create your first controller from scratch. If you haven't noticed already, Rails ships with generators for most common tasks, and controllers are no exception. The syntax for the controller generator is as follows:

```
$ rails g controller ControllerName [actions] [options]
```

As a minimum, the controller generator takes the name of the controller as an argument, which you can specify using either CamelCase (sometimes called MixedCase) or snake_case. The generator also takes an optional list of actions to generate. For every action you specify, you'll get an empty method stub in the controller and a template in `app/views/#{controller_name}`. To see a list of all available options, you can run the `rails g controller` command without arguments.

225

Tip The help output for the controller generator contains sample usage and options that you're sure to find interesting. All of the generators (and most UNIX commands, for that matter) respond to the `--help` argument (or variations thereof), so you're encouraged to try it whenever you're issuing a system command.

Generate the users controller using the following command:

```
$ rails g controller users
```

```
      create    app/controllers/users_controller.rb
      invoke    erb
      create      app/views/users
      invoke    test_unit
      create      test/controllers/users_controller_test.rb
      invoke    helper
      create      app/helpers/users_helper.rb
      invoke      test_unit
      invoke    assets
      invoke      scss
      create        app/assets/stylesheets/users.scss
```

Let's talk about the controller name we provided to the generator—*users*. The controller generator accepts this name in either "CamelCased" or "under_scored" format. In this case, "users" or "Users" would have resulted in the UsersController being generated. If we wanted to generate a controller that dealt with resources with a compound name, like UserFavoritesController, we would pass either "UserFavorites" or "user_favorites" to the generator.

Take the time to read the output of the generator so you get a sense of all the files that were just created. Notice where the templates are located: in the `app/views` directory, inside a subdirectory named after the controller. In this case, because your controller is called `users`, your templates go in `app/views/users`. Open the newly minted controller file in `app/controllers/users_controller.rb` and take a look (Listing 8-1).

Listing 8-1. Users Controller in app/controllers/users_controller.rb

```
class UsersController < ApplicationController
end
```

Tip   Most of the time, our controllers handle interactions with a collection of things, so we reflect that by using a plural name. However, sometimes our controller handles interactions with a *singleton* resource—like the SessionController we'll add later in this chapter—and is named with a singular name to reflect. Take care to name things appropriately!

As you can see, all the generator gives you is an empty stub. If you want your users controller to do anything useful, you'll need to add a few actions and give it something to do. Let's add the actions you need to the controller now. Edit users_controller.rb so that it looks like the code in Listing 8-2.

Listing 8-2. Updated app/controllers/users_controller.rb: https://gist. github.com/nicedawg/d7074c119699fa9e274321ce9b406424

```
class UsersController < ApplicationController
  before_action :set_user, only: [:show, :edit, :update, :destroy]

  def new
    @user = User.new
  end

  def create
    @user = User.new(user_params)
    if @user.save
      redirect_to articles_path, notice: 'User successfully added.'
    else
      render action: :new
    end
  end

  def edit
  end
```

```ruby
def update
  if @user.update(user_params)
    redirect_to articles_path, notice: 'Updated user information
    successfully.'
  else
    render action: 'edit'
  end
end

private
def set_user
  @user = User.find(params[:id])
end

def user_params
  params
end
end
```

You add four actions: new, create, edit, and update. The actions you add look very similar to the ones you saw in the articles controller in Chapter 7. The main difference is that you aren't using the respond_to block; therefore, Rails directly renders the default erb templates. Let's create those templates: Listings 8-3 and 8-4 show the new and edit templates, respectively.

Listing 8-3. New User Template in app/views/users/new.html.erb: https://gist.github.com/nicedawg/67735ea8d8b9f91373e8ff25785b6f29

```erb
<h1>New User</h1>

<%= render 'form', user: @user %>

<%= link_to 'Back', articles_path %>
```

Listing 8-4. Edit User Template in app/views/users/new.html.erb: https://
gist.github.com/nicedawg/c6aec25865a2b91395b6b4917a0282c9

```
<h1>Editing User</h1>

<%= render 'form', user: @user %>

<%= link_to 'Back', articles_path %>
```

In both the new and edit templates, you render a form partial, which is expected to
be in app/views/users/_form.html.erb. Create the form partial and make sure it looks
like the code in Listing 8-5.

Listing 8-5. User Form Partial in app/views/users/new.html.erb: https://
gist.github.com/nicedawg/3bbe6f0f25443bcf8bc86dd03d30ef39

```
<%= form_with(model: user, local: true) do |form| %>
  <% if user.errors.any? %>
    <div id="error_explanation">
      <h2><%= pluralize(user.errors.count, "error") %> prohibited this user
      from being saved:</h2>

      <ul>
        <% user.errors.full_messages.each do |message| %>
          <li><%= message %></li>
        <% end %>
      </ul>
    </div>
  <% end %>

  <div class="field">
    <%= form.label :email %>
    <%= form.text_field :email %>
  </div>
```

```
<div class="field">
  <%= form.label :password %>
  <%= form.password_field :password %>
</div>

<div class="field">
  <%= form.label :password_confirmation %>
  <%= form.password_field :password_confirmation %>
</div>

<div class="actions">
  <%= form.submit %>
</div>
<% end %>
```

You use the same form helpers discussed in Chapter 7: `text_field` for text input and `password_field` for password inputs. Before you go to the browser to try what you've created, you need to add users as a resource in your routes file. Edit `config/routes.rb` so it looks like the code in Listing 8-6.

Listing 8-6. Adding Users to `routes.rb` in `config/routes.rb`: `https://gist.github.com/nicedawg/22aac8a5ceca489fb82e7df4c00abb98`

```
Rails.application.routes.draw do
  root to: "articles#index"
  resources :articles
  resources :users
end
```

To see it all in action, try adding a new user by visiting `http://localhost:3000/users/new`. The form should look like Figure 8-1.

← → C   ⓘ localhost:3000/users/new

New User

Email

Password

Password confirmation

[Create User]

Back

Figure 8-1. *Adding a new user*

When you try to actually create a user, you should receive an error message `Active Model::ForbiddenAttributesError`. It helpfully highlights the line in the code where the error occurred. Line 9 is where the params actually are added to the user. What happened? If you recall back in Chapter 7, when the scaffold generated the articles controller for us, it was very specific about what params should and shouldn't be sent. In our controller, we're just passing params into it. We need to specify which parameters are acceptable so nefarious users can't hack our system. Modify the `user_params` method to look like this:

UsersController in app/controllers/users_controller.rb

```
def user_params
  params.require(:user).permit(:email, :password, :password_confirmation)
end
```

Run the server again, and retry the user creation. Now you can create a new user, and you can also edit that user if you have the user's ID. In fact, right now anyone can create and edit users; but shortly, you'll change the `edit` and `update` actions' implementation to make sure only users can edit their own profile.

Nested Resources

You added support for comments earlier, but only at the model level. You didn't implement a controller or view for the Comment model, and that's what you'll do now.

Comments are interesting because they're a little different from our other models so far. Comments depend on a particular article; they never exist on their own because they're conceptually meaningless if they're not tied to an article. If we created routes for comments just like we did for articles and users, we would need to take extra steps to ensure that an article id was present for every type of article URL. We *could* do that, but Rails gives us an easier way.

Instead of defining comments as standalone resources, as we did for articles, we'll define them as nested resources of articles. Go to the routes file and update the resources :article call to look like the code in Listing 8-7.

Listing 8-7. Adding Comments to routes.rb in config/routes.rb: https://gist.github.com/nicedawg/5fba18cfbb76e40c21b915b5ae7323e2

```
Rails.application.routes.draw do
    root to: "articles#index"
    resources :articles do
        resources :comments
    end
    resources :users
end
```

To define a nested resource, you use the resources method passed inside a block to the parent resource. Notice how *resources :comments* is passed as a block to the *resources :articles* call; therefore, comments become a nested resource of articles. The named routes for nested resources are different from standalone ones; they're built on top of a singular articles named route, requiring an article ID every time they're called. Table 8-1 lists the generated named routes for comments.

Table 8-1. *Comments' Named Routes*

Request Method	Nested Named Routes	Parameters	Controller Action
GET	article_comments_path	Article ID	index
POST	article_comments_path	Article ID, record hash	create
GET	new_article_comment_path	Article ID	new
GET	edit_article_comment_path	ID, article ID	edit
GET	article_comment_path	ID, article ID	Show
PUT/PATCH	article_comment_path	ID, article ID, and record hash	update
DELETE	article_comment_path	ID, article ID	destroy

Every time you call comment named routes, you must provide an article ID. Let's generate the comments controller and see how you take care of that:

```
$ rails g controller comments
```

```
      create  app/controllers/comments_controller.rb
      invoke  erb
      create    app/views/comments
      invoke  test_unit
      create    test/controllers/comments_controller_test.rb
      invoke  helper
      create    app/helpers/comments_helper.rb
      invoke    test_unit
      invoke  assets
      invoke    scss
      create      app/assets/stylesheets/comments.scss
```

Of the default seven actions for which Rails generates named routes, you need only two for comments: create and destroy. You don't need index, new, and show actions because comments are listed, shown, and added from the article's show page. You don't want to support editing or updating a comment, so you don't need edit or update either. Listing 8-8 shows how the comments controller looks with only those two actions.

Listing 8-8. Comments Controller in app/controllers/comments_controller. rb: https://gist.github.com/nicedawg/3c7aa2c1f8c4c4e37f8398360989b06f

```ruby
class CommentsController < ApplicationController
  before_action :load_article

  def create
    @comment = @article.comments.new(comment_params)
    if @comment.save
      redirect_to @article, notice: 'Thanks for your comment'
    else
      redirect_to @article, alert: 'Unable to add comment'
    end
  end

  def destroy
    @comment = @article.comments.find(params[:id])
    @comment.destroy
    redirect_to @article, notice: 'Comment deleted'
  end

  private

  def load_article
    @article = Article.find(params[:article_id])
  end

  def comment_params
    params.require(:comment).permit(:name, :email, :body)
  end
end
```

Notice the before_action call at the beginning of the controller; it runs the method load_article before all the actions in your comments controller. That's all you'll need to know for now. We'll explain more about controller callbacks shortly.

The `load_article` method does a simple task: it finds the article from the passed `article_id` and assigns it to the `@article` instance variable. Remember that you always have the `article_id` in your parameters because it's always included in your nested named routes. With `load_article` in `before_action`, you'll always have `@article` loaded and accessible in your comments controller's actions and templates.

Also notice how you find and assign `@comment`: you do so using `@article.comments`. This way, you'll make sure you're dealing only with `@article` comments and you don't create or delete comments from another article.

Now let's update the views and create some templates. As mentioned earlier, you *list*, *show*, and add *new* comments from the article's show page; so let's update the article show page, make it a little nicer, and then add new code to display comments. Listing 8-9 shows how `app/views/articles/show.html.erb` looks after the update.

Listing 8-9. Updated Article Show Template in `app/views/articles/show.html.erb`: https://gist.github.com/nicedawg/d344d9d0dca5f16021189c36ecbff1ac

```erb
<%= render @article %>

<h3>Comments</h3>
<div id="comments">
  <%= render @article.comments %>
</div>

<%= render 'comments/new' %>
```

That's a lot of cleaning. First, you extract the displaying attributes into a partial named `app/views/articles/_article.html.erb`, which you call using `render @article`. One of the benefits of creating a partial is that you can use it in other pages, such as the articles' index page, which you'll implement shortly.

Notice that the flash notice is removed from the article show template. To make sure the flash message shows in any view template, you move it to the application layout in `app/views/layouts/application.html.erb` (Listing 8-10).

Listing 8-10. Updated Application Layout Template in app/views/layouts/ application.html.erb: https://gist.github.com/nicedawg/529d79051a3c480 741a78284b092c5dd

```
<!DOCTYPE html>
<html>
  <head>
    <title>Blog</title>
    <%= csrf_meta_tags %>
    <%= csp_meta_tag %>

    <%= stylesheet_link_tag 'application', media: 'all', 'data-turbolinks-
    track': 'reload' %>
    <%= javascript_pack_tag 'application', 'data-turbolinks-track':
    'reload' %>
  </head>

  <body>
    <%= content_tag :p, notice, class: 'notice' if notice.present? %>
    <%= content_tag :p, alert, class: 'alert' if alert.present? %>

    <%= yield %>
  </body>
</html>
```

Then you list comments using the collection render on @article.comments. To refresh your memory, this loops through the article comments, rendering the app/ views/comments/_comment.html.erb partial for every comment.

Finally, you render the app/views/comments/new.html.erb template.

None of the files mentioned have been created yet. Let's do that now. Create app/ views/articles/_article.html.erb, app/views/comments/_comment.html.erb, and app/views/comments/_new.html.erb, as shown in Listings 8-11, 8-12, and 8-13, respectively.

Listing 8-11. Article Partial in app/views/articles/_article.html.erb:
https://gist.github.com/nicedawg/46a0343e2d0d3625741738ab5c3dbbbd

```
<div class="article">
  <h3>
    <%= link_to article.title, article %>
    <span class="actions">
      <%= link_to 'Edit', edit_article_path(article) %>
      <%= link_to 'Delete', article, confirm: 'Are you sure?', method:
      :delete %>
    </span>
  </h3>
  <%= article.body %>
</div>
```

Listing 8-12. Comment Partial in app/views/comments/_comment.html.erb:
https://gist.github.com/nicedawg/88cc01d2470fff4bd968c876de8af76c

```
<div class="comment">
  <h3>
    <%= comment.name %> <<%= comment.email %>> said:
    <span class="actions">
      <%= link_to 'Delete', article_comment_path(article_id: @article, id:
      comment), confirm: 'Are you sure?', method: :delete %>
    </span>
  </h3>
  <%= comment.body %>
</div>
```

Listing 8-13. New Comment Template in app/views/comments/_new.html.erb:
https://gist.github.com/nicedawg/5fb70bd189c6fa14257539898abbd8e6

```
<%= form_with(model: @article.comments.new, url: article_comments_path
(@article), local: true) do |form| %>
  <div class="field">
    <%= form.label :name %><br />
    <%= form.text_field :name %>
  </div>
  <div class="field">
    <%= form.label :email %><br />
    <%= form.text_field :email %>
  </div>
  <div class="field">
    <%= form.label :body %><br />
    <%= form.text_area :body %>
  </div>
  <div class="actions">
    <%= form.submit 'Add' %>
  </div>
<% end %>
```

The article and comment partials are pretty straightforward; aside from the markup, you display the attributes and link to actions.

The new comment form calls form_with and passes a new comment object as the model, configures the form action to send its values to the path to create a comment, and sets *local: true* so that this form isn't sent via Ajax. (We'll change this in the next chapter and explain further.)

Now that you've created the missing templates and added the required code to the controller, let's go to the browser and see how it looks in the article show page. Run your server, go to your browser, and click your way through to an article; you should see something very similar to Figure 8-2.

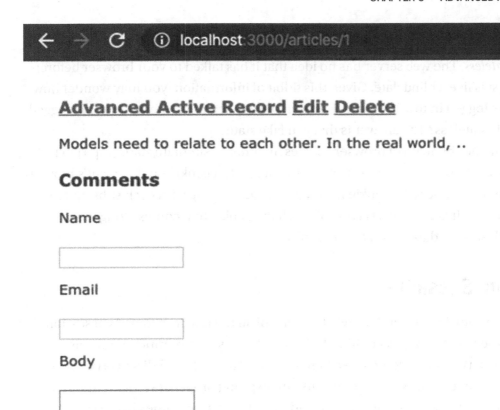

Figure 8-2. *Article show page with a new comment form*

Try adding a few comments and see how the form behaves. Congratulations! You just added comment support to your blog application using nested resources. Now that you have comments and users in the system, let's add some authorization logic to make sure only logged-in users can create and update articles.

Sessions and the Login/Logout Logic

The whole point of having users in your blog application is to allow them to create their *own* articles. But you also need to be able to recognize them when they create an article. Web applications normally do that by using *sessions*. Let's talk a little more about that before you implement it in your application.

Lying in State

HTTP is *stateless*. The web server has no idea that it has talked to your browser before; each request is like a blind date. Given this tidbit of information, you may wonder how you can stay logged in to a given site. How can the application remember you're logged in if HTTP is stateless? The answer is that you fake state.

You've no doubt heard of browser cookies. In order to simulate state atop HTTP, Rails uses cookies. When the first request comes in, Rails sets a cookie on the client's browser. The browser remembers the cookie locally and sends it along with each subsequent request. The result is that Rails is able to match the cookie that comes along in the request with session data stored on the server.

Using the Session

Secure in the knowledge that Rails will take care of all the low-level details of sessions for you, using the session object couldn't be easier. The session is implemented as a hash, just like flash. We should come clean here—flash is a session in disguise (you can think of it as a specialized session due to its autoexpiring properties). Not surprisingly then, the flash and session interfaces are identical. You store values in the session according to a key:

```
session[:account_id] = @account.id
session[:account_id] # => 1

session['message'] = "Hello world!"
session['message'] # => "Hello world!"
```

Session As a Resource

Now that you understand sessions, you can go back to your main task: allowing users to log in and log out. You create a session when the user logs in and clear (destroy) it when they're done. Of course, you do that in a RESTful way, by treating the session as a resource:

Start by generating a sessions controller:

```
$ rails g controller sessions
```

```
      create  app/controllers/sessions_controller.rb
      invoke  erb
      create    app/views/sessions
      invoke  test_unit
      create    test/controllers/sessions_controller_test.rb
      invoke  helper
      create    app/helpers/sessions_helper.rb
      invoke    test_unit
      invoke  assets
      invoke    scss
      create      app/assets/stylesheets/sessions.scss
```

Now define this as a resource in your routes file in config/routes.rb, as shown in Listing 8-14.

Listing 8-14. Adding session to routes.rb in config/routes.rb: https:// gist.github.com/nicedawg/da300c005c68dcd19a0f749b37c01db5

```
Rails.application.routes.draw do
  root to: "articles#index"
  resources :articles do
    resources :comments
  end
  resources :users
  resource :session
end
```

Notice that you define session as a resource and not resources, because you never deal with a set of sessions at once. You never list sessions in an index or anything like that—you just need to create or destroy a *single* session at a time.

Let's step back and try to explain the difference between resource and resources definitions. The main benefit you get from defining resources in your routes file is the named routes that are generated for you. In the case of a single resource definition, you get different named routes: none of them are pluralized, all are singular, and there's no index action. Rails maps six actions instead of the seven in a resources definition. Table 8-2 provides a quick comparison between resources named routes and resource named routes.

Table 8-2. *Named Routes:* resources *vs.* resource

Request Method	resources Named Routes	resource Named Routes	Controller Action
GET	articles_path	Not available	index
POST	articles_path	session_path	create
GET	article_path	session_path	show
PATCH/PUT	article_path	session_path	update
DELETE	article_path	session_path	destroy
GET	edit_article_path	edit_session_path	edit
GET	new_article_path	new_session_path	new

Note   Although a singular name is used for the resource, the controller name is still taken from the plural name, so sessions_controller is the controller for the session resource in this case.

To avoid confusion, let's map this in your mind; to log in, you need to create a session; to log out, you clear that session. You use new_session_path as your login path, and the new template is your login page. POSTing the form in the new session page to session_path *creates* the session. Finally, submitting a DELETE request to session_path *clears* that session, performing a logout. Now, let's map it in the routes file, as shown in Listing 8-15.

Listing 8-15. Adding session to routes.rb in config/routes.rb: https://gist.github.com/nicedawg/2da8a9c657f646e5d74a0a9a69ab34a4

```
Rails.application.routes.draw do
  root to: "articles#index"
  resources :articles do
    resources :comments
  end
```

```
  resources :users
  resource :session
  get "/login", to: "sessions#new", as: "login"
  get "/logout", to: "sessions#destroy", as: "logout"
end
```

You basically define two named routes, login_path and logout_path, which are more meaningful than new_session_path and session_path when referring to those actions.

Logging In a User

As you did for Active Record resources, in the create action, you first check the validity of the resource—in this case through authentication—and you save the state if all is good. If the validity check fails, you return the user to the login page with an error message. In this controller, you never save a record to the database—you save a session object. Listing 8-16 shows the create action.

Listing 8-16. The create Method in app/controllers/sessions_controller. rb: https://gist.github.com/nicedawg/430d678348add4c767c5910fe2f41664

```
class SessionsController < ApplicationController
  def create
    if user = User.authenticate(params[:email], params[:password])
      session[:user_id] = user.id
      redirect_to root_path, notice: "Logged in successfully"
    else
      flash.now[:alert] = "Invalid login/password combination"
      render :new
    end
  end
end
```

First, you use the authenticate class method from the User model to attempt a login (see Listing 6-37 in Chapter 6). Remember that authenticate returns a User object if the authentication succeeds; otherwise, it returns nil. Therefore, you can perform your conditional and your assignment in one shot using `if user = User.authenticate(params[:email], params[:password])`. If the assignment takes place, you want to store a reference to this user so you can keep the user logged in—a perfect job for the session:

```
session[:user_id] = user.id
```

Notice that you don't need to store the entire User object in `session`. You store just a reference to the user's ID. Why not store the entire User object? Well, think about this for a minute: what if the user is stored in `session` and later changes their login? The old login would remain in the session and would therefore be *stale*. This can cause problems if the underlying User model changes. Your entire object could become stale, potentially causing a NoMethodError when accessing attributes that didn't exist on the model at the time it was placed in `session`. The best bet is to just store the `id`.

With a reference to the logged-in user safely stored in `session`, you can redirect to the root path, corresponding to the `articles` controller.

If the assignment doesn't take place and the `User.authenticate` method returns `nil`, you know the provided login and password are invalid, and you return to the login page with an alert message using `flash.now`. RESTfully speaking, the login page is where you enter the *new* session information, so it's basically the new action.

Note   `flash.now` differs from the regular `flash` call by setting a flash message that is only available to the current action. If you recall, regular `flash` makes messages available after a redirect.

But wait: you don't have a new action yet. Don't you need to define it first? The truth is you don't need to initialize anything there—all you need is its template. By having the template, Rails automatically renders that template when it doesn't find the action definition. Let's create the new template, as shown in Listing 8-17.

Listing 8-17. The new Session Template in app/views/sessions/new.html.erb: https://gist.github.com/nicedawg/90549294bbafab30319a0bbf8f993994

```
<h1>Login</h1>

<%= form_with(url: session_path, local: true) do |form| %>
  <div class="field">
    <%= form.label :email %>
    <%= form.text_field :email %>
  </div>
  <div class="field">
    <%= form.label :password %>
    <%= form.password_field :password %>
  </div>
  <div class="actions">
    <%= form.submit "Login" %>
  </div>
<% end %>
```

Notice that we didn't pass a model to form_with as we did earlier with Active Record objects; that's because session isn't an Active Record object. You also submit to session_path because it's a resource, not resources, as explained earlier.

Logging Out a User

The user is logged in when a session is created, so in order to log out the user, you need to clear that session. You do so in the destroy action. The destroy action is fairly straightforward. You clear the session by using the reset_session method that comes with Rails, which does exactly as it says: it resets the session by clearing all the values in it. After you clear the session, you redirect back to the login_path, which is your login screen.

Another way to do this is to specifically clear the user_id key from the session hash, but it's safer for the logout in particular to clear all the session values. Listing 8-18 shows how the sessions controller looks after you add the destroy method.

Listing 8-18. Updated Sessions Controller in app/controllers/sessions_
controller.rb: https://gist.github.com/nicedawg/7393e33a4850121b04ceb7
4a58f11203

```
class SessionsController < ApplicationController
  def create
    if user = User.authenticate(params[:email], params[:password])
      session[:user_id] = user.id
      redirect_to root_path, notice: "Logged in successfully"
    else
      flash.now[:alert] = "Invalid login/password combination"
      render :new
    end
  end

  def destroy
    reset_session
    redirect_to root_path, notice: "You successfully logged out"
  end
end
```

Go ahead and try it. Create a user by going to http://localhost:3000/users/new.
Then log in by visiting the login path at http://localhost:3000/login (Figure 8-3).
Finally, if you want to log out, go to http://localhost:3000/logout.

Figure 8-3. *Login page*

Don't worry about remembering all the URLs. You can link to them when you update
your application layout.

Improving Controllers and Templates

Chapter 7 and earlier parts of this chapter covered generating controllers, creating templates and layouts, and DRYing up with partials. Let's take this a step forward: first, you update article views, and then you add callbacks to some of your controllers, making sure some actions require authorization.

Cleaning Up the Articles Index Page

The current articles' index page uses a table markup to list articles. If you've ever visited a blog, you know you've never seen one like that; so let's change the table markup and loop to a friendlier markup that uses the article's partial in app/views/articles/_article.html.erb. Listing 8-19 shows the updated articles index.

Listing 8-19. Updated Articles Index in app/views/articles/index.html.erb: https://gist.github.com/nicedawg/88db1b679cdfb2b87801d92ebe60adce

```
<h1>Articles</h1>

<div id="articles">
  <%= render @articles %>
</div>

<br>

<%= link_to 'New Article', new_article_path %>
```

Caution   Be careful with reusing partials. In some cases, you may prefer to keep separate files. You reuse the article partial here just to simplify things.

Visit your root path at http://localhost:3000. If all goes right, you should see something similar to Figure 8-4. That looks like a real blog!

Articles

Advanced Active Record Edit Delete

Models need to relate to each other. In the real world, ..

One-to-many associations Edit Delete

One-to-many associations describe a pattern ..

Associations Edit Delete

Active Record makes working with associations easy..

New Article

Figure 8-4. *Blog-like home page*

Adding Categories to the Article Form

In Chapter 6, you added categories to the Article model, but neither your controller nor your templates know about this yet. Let's remedy that now, starting with the article form. Add the code shown in bold in Listing 8-20 to the form partial in app/views/articles/_ form.html.erb.

Listing 8-20. Modified app/views/articles/_form.html.erb: https://gist. github.com/nicedawg/266fab84c1ab59ff72713267d129cd7f

```
<%= form_with(model: article, local: true) do |form| %>
  <% if article.errors.any? %>
    <div id="error_explanation">
      <h2><%= pluralize(article.errors.count, "error") %> prohibited this
      article from being saved:</h2>

      <ul>
        <% article.errors.full_messages.each do |message| %>
          <li><%= message %></li>
        <% end %>
      </ul>
```

```erb
    </div>
  <% end %>

  <div class="field">
    <%= form.label :title %>
    <%= form.text_field :title %>
  </div>

  <div class="field">
    <%= form.label :location %>
    <%= form.text_field :location %>
  </div>

  <div class="field">
    <%= form.collection_check_boxes(:category_ids, Category.all, :id,
    :name) do |b| %>
      <% b.label { b.check_box + b.text } %>
    <% end %>
  </div>

  <div class="field">
    <%= form.label :excerpt %>
    <%= form.text_field :excerpt %>
  </div>

  <div class="field">
    <%= form.label :body %>
    <%= form.text_area :body %>
  </div>

  <div class="field">
    <%= form.label :published_at %>
    <%= form.datetime_select :published_at %>
  </div>

  <div class="actions">
    <%= form.submit %>
  </div>
<% end %>
```

To offer articles the chance to be part of one or more categories, you show all the categories as checkboxes. But how do you associate those checkboxes with the article?

Remember that Chapter 6 talked about the methods that each association adds to your model when you use them. In the case of the `Article` model, the `has_and_belong_to_many :categories` association adds the `category_ids` method, which returns an array of the associated category IDs; it also adds the `category_ids=(category_ids)` method, which replaces the current associated categories with the ones supplied.

Knowing that, look back at the new code added to the form: we use the form helper method *collection_check_boxes*, which takes a few arguments and a block, which we'll now explain.

The first argument, :category_ids, is the attribute on the Article object which we ultimately want to set.

The second argument declares all possible values, so we use Category.all to get the list of all categories known to our app.

The third argument controls how to find the value from a category object in order to store in the article. We use :id, because we want to store the category id.

The last argument declares how to find the text we want to use as a label for a particular checkbox. In this case, we use :name, because the Category model has a name attribute which would be helpful here.

Lastly, this method takes a block which lets us customize how each checkbox is rendered. We want to wrap each checkbox inside a label and add descriptive text, both for aesthetics and usability, so we supply a block which receives a special builder object, and we indicate we want a label tag whose contents are the checkbox and the textual description of the option.

Whew! That's a lot to remember. But don't worry about remembering all of this. Just knowing that helper methods like this exist is good enough; when the need arises, you can find the documentation.

The only thing left to do is go back to the `articles` controller and make sure Rails knows that you want to allow categories to be saved to the article. Otherwise, it would just discard this information and never save it to the article.

Listing 8-21. Modified app/controllers/articles_controller.rb

```
...
# Never trust parameters from the scary internet, only allow the white
list through.
def article_params
  params.require(:article).permit(:title, :location, :excerpt, :body,
  :published_at, category_ids: [])
end
...
```

That's it! Now that you have category integration for articles, try adding a new article; you should see a form similar to that in Figure 8-5.

Figure 8-5. *Updated article form with category checkboxes*

Fill in the mandatory fields, select a couple of categories, and submit the form. Check the parameters output in your `rails server` window. You should see something similar to the following output, depending on the values you entered—pay attention to the category array:

```
Parameters: {"authenticity_token"=>"gjav8j17XIaz5jItg6hJ5wPWSBJ
HLexXuotWEjtEA9JFdEcXHR+ql5JoW2/F5mp1Nm5eUlmBqY/xW7Q1Lu3g4w==",
"article"=>{"title"=>"Advanced Active Record", "location"=>"",
"category_ids"=>["", "2", "1"], "excerpt"=>"", "body"=>"Models
need to relate to each other. In the real world, ..", "published_
at(1i)"=>"2020", "published_at(2i)"=>"2", "published_at(3i)"=>"24",
"published_at(4i)"=>"00", "published_at(5i)"=>"00"}, "commit"=>"Update
Article", "id"=>"1"}
```

If you try to edit the article you just created, you'll see that your categories are selected, and you can modify them like any other article attribute. The `category_ids=` method that the `has_and_belong_to_many` association added for you does all the magic behind the scenes.

Using Filters

Filters provide a way for you to perform operations either before or after an action is invoked. There's even an `around` filter that can wrap the execution of an action. Of the three, the `before` action is the most commonly used, so this section focuses on it.

All the code you place in `before_action` is run before the action in question is called. Pretty simple, really. But there's a catch: if `before_action` returns `false`, the action isn't executed. We often use this to protect certain actions that require a login. If you have an `events` controller and you want the `new` and `create` actions to remain open (anyone can access them), but you want to restrict all other actions to logged-in users, you can do so using filters:

```
class EventsController < ApplicationController
  before_action :authenticate, except: [:new, :create]
end
```

This causes the `authenticate` method to be run before every action except those listed. Assume the `authenticate` method is defined in the `application_controller` controller and is therefore available to every other controller in the system. If the `authenticate` method returns `false`, the requested action isn't executed, thereby protecting it from unauthorized visitors.

You can also use the :only modifier to specify that the filter is to run for *only* the given actions. You can write the preceding example more concisely as follows:

```
before_action :authenticate, only: :destroy
```

Without the :only or :except modifier, the filter runs for all actions.

Controller inheritance hierarchies share filters downward, but subclasses can also add or skip filters without affecting the superclass. Let's say you apply a global filter to the application_controller, but you have a particular controller that you want to be exempt from filtration. You can use skip_before_action, like this:

```
class ApplicationController < ActionController::Base
  before_action :authenticate_with_token
end

class PublicController < ApplicationController
  # We don't want to check for a token on this controller
  skip_before_action :authenticate_with_token
end
```

Filters are a fairly involved topic, and we've only scratched the surface here. Still, you've seen the most common usage pattern: protecting actions. For more information about filters, including usage examples, check out the Rails guide at https://guides.rubyonrails.org/action_controller_overview.html#filters.

Requiring Authentication with Filters

In your blog application, you want to protect blog creation and modification, restricting access to registered users. To do this, you use callbacks that call specific methods and check for the user_id session you set on user login. Recall that any methods you add to the application_controller are available to all other controllers (because it's the superclass of all controllers).

Open the application_controller in app/controllers/application_controller.rb and add the protected methods that enforce your authentication requirement, as shown in Listing 8-22.

Listing 8-22. Modified app/controllers/application_controller.rb:
https://gist.github.com/nicedawg/5f003af093d7db2c9829b85a8a7a4bc5

```ruby
class ApplicationController < ActionController::Base
  helper_method :current_user, :logged_in?

  def current_user
    return unless session[:user_id]
    @current_user ||= User.find_by(id: session[:user_id])
  end

  def authenticate
    logged_in? || access_denied
  end

  def logged_in?
    current_user.present?
  end

  def access_denied
    redirect_to(login_path, notice: "Please log in to continue") and return
    false
  end
end
```

First, we call the *helper_method* method and pass two symbolized names of
methods. This allows view templates to use the *current_user* and *logged_in?* methods in
addition to other subclasses of ApplicationController. You can use this to show or hide
administrative controls (such as adding or editing a given article). Having current_user
around also proves useful in templates, allowing you to access information about users,
such as their email addresses.

The current_user method acts like an *accessor* for the currently logged-in user.
Because it returns a User object, you can call instance methods of User on it, such as
current_user.email. The authenticate method is your filter method (the one you call
from individual controllers). It checks whether there is a currently logged-in user via
logged_in? (which, in turn, checks that there is actually a User returned by current_
user) and calls access_denied if there isn't; access_denied redirects to the login_path
in the sessions controller with a notice message in the flash.

Let's apply the filter to the `articles` controller now. You also apply a filter to the `users` controller to restrict who can edit user profiles.

Applying Filters to Controllers

You apply filters using a declarative syntax. In this case, you'll want to check that a user is authenticated *before* you process a protected action, so you use `before_filter`. Add the filter to the `articles` controller, just inside the class body, as shown in Listing 8-23.

Listing 8-23. Before Filter Added in `app/controllers/articles_controller.rb`: https://gist.github.com/nicedawg/c386e3c50471bb719219aaaae3eda463

```
class ArticlesController < ApplicationController
  before_action :authenticate, except: [:index, :show]
  #...
end
```

Notice how you're able to selectively apply the filter to specific actions. Here, you want every action to be protected *except* `index` and `show`. The `:except` modifier accepts either a single value or an array. You'll use an array here. If you want to protect only a few actions, you can use the `:only` modifier, which, as you would expect, behaves the opposite of `:except`.

You'll also want to use a filter in the `users` controller. Right now, anyone can edit a user as long as they know the user's ID. This would be risky in the real world. Ideally, you want the `edit` and `update` actions to respond only to the currently logged-in user, allowing that user to edit their profile. To do this, instead of retrieving `User.find(params[:id])`, you retrieve `current_user` and apply a filter to protect the `edit` and `update` actions. Listing 8-24 shows the latest version of the `users` controller.

Listing 8-24. Before Filter Added in `app/controllers/users_controller.rb`: https://gist.github.com/nicedawg/0f9ce611a62054eadc97e621ca694ffc

```
class UsersController < ApplicationController
  before_action :authenticate, only: [:edit, :update]
  before_action :set_user, only: [:show, :edit, :update, :destroy]
```

```ruby
def new
  @user = User.new
end

def create
  @user = User.new(user_params)
  if @user.save
    redirect_to articles_path, notice: 'User successfully added.'
  else
    render :new
  end
end

def update
  if @user.update(user_params)
    redirect_to articles_path, notice: 'Updated user information
    successfully.'
  else
    render :edit
  end
end

private

def set_user
  @user = current_user
end

def user_params
  params.require(:user).permit(:email, :password, :password_confirmation)
end
end
```

Try it. If you attempt to add, edit, or delete an article, you're asked to log in (Figure 8-6).

Please log in to continue

Login

Email

Password

[Login]

Figure 8-6. *Authentication required*

We probably don't want to allow any visitor to our blog to delete comments; therefore, authorization code is required in the comments controller. First, you add a `before_action` to authorize users before calling the destroy action. Next, in the destroy action, you find the article, making sure it belongs to the current user by using `current_user.articles.find`. Then, you find the comment on that article; and finally, you destroy it. Listing 8-25 shows the updated code, in bold, for the comments controller.

Listing 8-25. Authorization Before Deleting a Comment in `app/controllers/comments_controller.rb`: https://gist.github.com/nicedawg/b0eb7eaded453697002741b7a7d2ece3

```
class CommentsController < ApplicationController
  before_action :load_article, except: :destroy
  before_action :authenticate, only: :destroy

  def create
    @comment = @article.comments.new(comment_params)
    if @comment.save
      redirect_to @article, notice: 'Thanks for your comment'
    else
      redirect_to @article, alert: 'Unable to add comment'
    end
  end
```

```
def destroy
  @article = current_user.articles.find(params[:article_id])
  @comment = @article.comments.find(params[:id])
  @comment.destroy
  redirect_to @article, notice: 'Comment deleted'
end

private

def load_article
  @article = Article.find(params[:article_id])
end

def comment_params
  params.require(:comment).permit(:name, :email, :body)
end
end
```

Adding Finishing Touches

You're almost finished with your work in this chapter. Only a few tasks remain. You need to spruce up your templates a bit and make them a little cleaner. You also need to make it possible for article owners to edit and delete their articles. Finally, you want to update the layout and apply some CSS styles to make things look pretty. Ready? Let's get started!

Using Action View Helpers

One of the ways you can clean up your templates is with helpers. Rails ships with a bevy of formatting helpers to assist in displaying numbers, dates, tags, and text in your templates. Here's a quick summary:

- *Number helpers:* The NumberHelper module provides methods for converting numbers into formatted strings. Methods are provided for phone numbers, currency, percentages, precision, positional notation, and file size. See https://api.rubyonrails.org/classes/ActionView/Helpers/NumberHelper.html for more information.

- *Text helpers:* The `TextHelper` module provides a set of methods for filtering, formatting, and transforming strings that can reduce the amount of inline Ruby code in your views. See `https://api.rubyonrails.org/classes/ActionView/Helpers/TextHelper.html` for more information.

- *URL helpers:* Rails provides a set of URL helpers that makes constructing links that depend on the controller and action (or other parameters) ridiculously easy. For more information, see `https://api.rubyonrails.org/classes/ActionView/Helpers/UrlHelper.html` and `https://api.rubyonrails.org/classes/ActionController/Base.html`.

A very handy URL helper is `link_to`, which you've used several times already. It creates a hyperlink tag of the given name using a URL constructed according to the options hash given. It's possible to pass a string instead of an options hash to get a link tag that points to any URL. Additionally, if `nil` is passed as a name, the link itself becomes the name. Here's the fine print:

```
link_to(name, options={}, html_options={})
```

This generates an HTML anchor tag using the following parameters:

- The first argument is the link's name.

- The second argument is the URL to link to, given as a string, a named route, or a hash of options used to generate the URL. It can also be an object, in which case Rails replaces it with its `show` action named route.

- The third argument is a hash of HTML options for the resulting tag.

In Ruby, if the last argument to a method is a hash, the curly braces are optional. Most `link_to` helpers therefore look like this:

```
link_to 'New', new_article_path, id: 'new_article_link'
```

If you use all three arguments and pass in options for HTML (like a class or id attribute), you need to disambiguate them. Consider the following example, which uses two hashes—one for the URL generation and another for the HTML options:

```
link_to 'New', {controller: 'articles', action: 'new'}, class: 'large'
```

Notice that you need to use the curly braces for at least the first hash to inform Ruby that there are three arguments. Using braces on the last hash of options is still optional, and you can just as easily include them:

```
link_to 'New', {controller: 'articles', action: 'new'}, {class: 'large'}
```

Escaping HTML in Templates

You should always escape any HTML before displaying it in your views to prevent malicious users from injecting arbitrary HTML into your pages (which is how cross-site scripting attacks are often carried out). The rule of thumb is that whenever you have data that are provided by the user, you can't trust them blindly. You need to escape it. This includes model attributes as well as parameters. Fortunately, Rails escapes all rendered strings for you.

Try adding a new article with some HTML markup in the body, saving, and visiting the show page. If you enter an anchor HTML tag, for example, you see something like the screen shown in Figure 8-7. As you can see, Rails escapes the HTML entered in the body field.

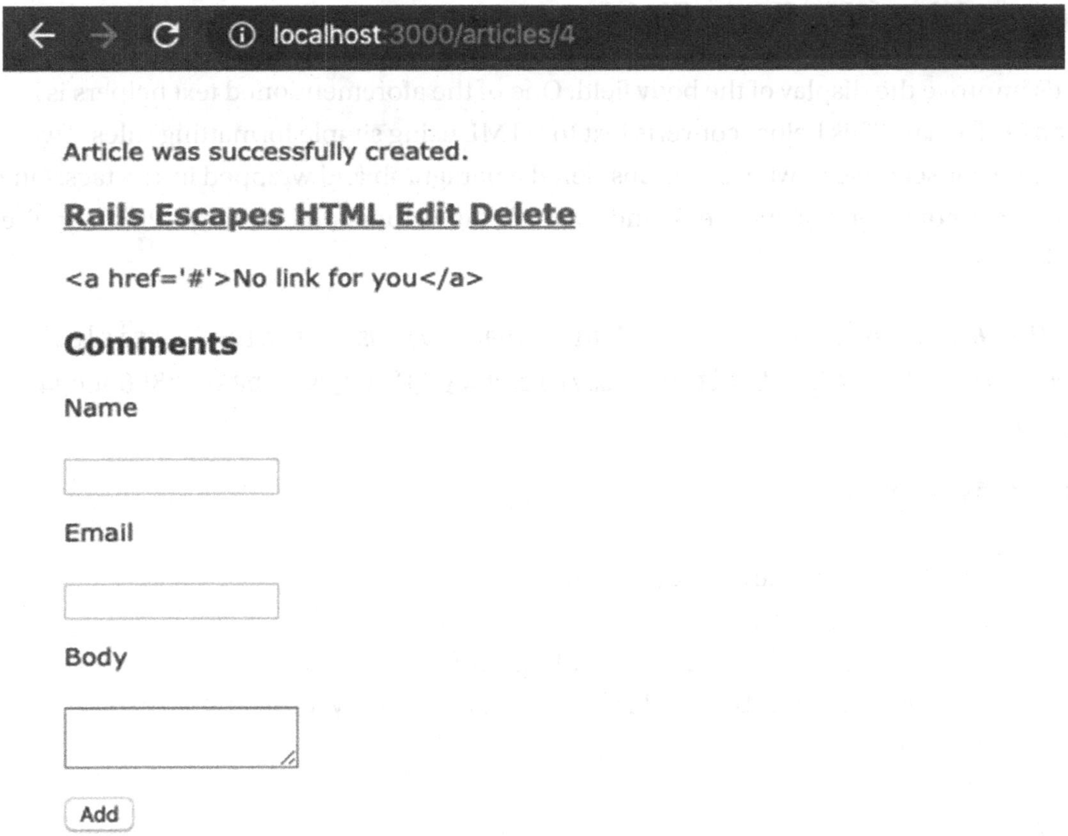

Article was successfully created.

Rails Escapes HTML **Edit** **Delete**

<a href='#'>No link for you</a>

Comments

Name

Email

Body

[Add]

Figure 8-7. *Escaped HTML in the article page*

If you check the source code, you'll see that the characters you entered have been escaped:

```
<a href=&#39;#&#39;>No link for you</a>
```

Sometimes, you may want to display the strings entered by users without escaping them. To do that, Rails provides a method on strings named html_safe that skips the HTML escaping process. To display the article's body in its raw format, which you'll do shortly, you can call article.body.html_safe instead of article.body in the article partial in app/views/articles/_article.html.erb.

Formatting the Body Field

Let's improve the display of the body field. One of the aforementioned text helpers is `simple_format`. This helper converts text to HTML using simple formatting rules. Two or more consecutive newlines are considered a paragraph and wrapped in `<p>` tags. One newline is considered a line break, and a `<br />` tag is appended. Listing 8-26 shows the additions.

Listing 8-26. Formatting Helpers Added in app/views/articles/_article. html.erb: https://gist.github.com/nicedawg/9f00b38de1b439fb856bcb94f3 2fc173

```
<div class="article">
  <h3>
    <%= link_to article.title, article %>
    <span class="actions">
      <%= link_to 'Edit', edit_article_path(article) %>
      <%= link_to 'Delete', article, confirm: 'Are you sure?', method:
      :delete %>
    </span>
  </h3>
  <%= simple_format article.body %>
</div>
```

Adding Edit Controls

You've applied authentication filters, but you still don't have a way to prevent users from editing or deleting articles that belong to other users. To do this, you add a method to the `Article` model that can tell you whether the article in question is owned by the user you pass in. Open the `Article` model and add the `owned_by?` method, as highlighted in bold in Listing 8-27.

Listing 8-27. Updated app/models/article.rb: https://gist.github.com/ nicedawg/c7af0e45492bdc6b0dfc636bc84cdbd9

```
class Article < ApplicationRecord
  validates :title, :body, presence: true
```

```
belongs_to :user
has_and_belongs_to_many :categories
has_many :comments

scope :published, -> { where.not(published_at: nil) }
scope :draft, -> { where(published_at: nil) }
scope :recent, -> { where('articles.published_at > ?', 1.week.ago.to_
date) }
scope :where_title, -> (term) { where("articles.title LIKE ?",
"%#{term}%") }

def long_title
  "#{title} - #{published_at}"
end

def published?
  published_at.present?
end

def owned_by?(owner)
  return false unless owner.is_a?(User)
  user == owner
end
end
```

Now, let's use this method in the article and comment partials in app/views/ articles/_article.html.erb and app/views/comments/_comment.html.erb, respectively, by adding links to edit or delete *only* if the article is owned by the currently logged-in user, as shown in Listings 8-28 and 8-29.

Listing 8-28. Edit Controls for Article in app/views/articles/_article.html. erb: https://gist.github.com/nicedawg/6ba53fc518daf0d4e24c765c106548c8

```
<div class="article">
  <h3>
    <%= link_to article.title, article %>
    <% if article.owned_by? current_user %>
      <span class="actions">
```

```
      <%= link_to 'Edit', edit_article_path(article) %>
      <%= link_to 'Delete', article, confirm: 'Are you sure?', method:
      :delete %>
    </span>
  <% end %>
 </h3>
 <%= simple_format article.body %>
</div>
```

Listing 8-29. Edit Controls for Comment in app/views/comments/_
comment.html.erb: https://gist.github.com/nicedawg/
d2b52b2ef0700dfbdc460f1e9dd7f414

```
<div class="comment">
  <h3>
    <%= comment.name %> <<%= comment.email %>> said:
    <% if @article.owned_by? current_user %>
      <span class="actions">
        <%= link_to 'Delete', article_comment_path(article_id: @article,
        id: comment), confirm: 'Are you sure?', method: :delete %>
      </span>
    <% end %>
  </h3>
  <%= comment.body %>
</div>
```

Note   When you try this in your browser, you may not see the edit and delete links for any of the articles because their user_id field is nil. This is great console practice for you. Start your console with rails console, find your own user record using user = User.find_by_email('email@example.com'), and update all articles in the system using Article.update_all(["user_id = ?", user.id]).

Making Sure Articles Have Owners

You need to make sure that when you add an article, a user is assigned. To do that, you update the create method in the articles controller to use the association between User and Article. When creating the @article variable, instead of using Article.new, you use current_user.articles.new: it instantiates an Article object with the user_id field set to the ID of current_user. That's exactly what you need.

Applying the same logic, you can change the edit, update, and destroy actions to retrieve only articles belonging to the logged-in user. In code parlance, you'll use current_user.articles.find wherever you were using Article.find. Since a few actions no longer need the *:set_article* before_action, we remove them from the list. Listing 8-30 shows the changes to make in app/controllers/articles_controller.rb.

Listing 8-30. Updated app/controllers/articles_controller.rb: https://gist.github.com/nicedawg/40203f4a67681af6d876a89c21e3f576

```
class ArticlesController < ApplicationController
  before_action :authenticate, except: [:index, :show]
  before_action :set_article, only: [:show]

  # GET /articles
  # GET /articles.json
  def index
    @articles = Article.all
  end

  # GET /articles/1
  # GET /articles/1.json
  def show
  end

  # GET /articles/new
  def new
    @article = Article.new
  end
```

```ruby
# GET /articles/1/edit
def edit
  @article = current_user.articles.find(params[:id])
end

# POST /articles
# POST /articles.json
def create
  @article = current_user.articles.new(article_params)

  respond_to do |format|
    if @article.save
      format.html { redirect_to @article, notice: 'Article was
      successfully created.' }
      format.json { render :show, status: :created, location: @article }
    else
      format.html { render :new }
      format.json { render json: @article.errors, status: :unprocessable_
      entity }
    end
  end
end

# PATCH/PUT /articles/1
# PATCH/PUT /articles/1.json
def update
  @article = current_user.articles.find(params[:id])
  respond_to do |format|
    if @article.update(article_params)
      format.html { redirect_to @article, notice: 'Article was
      successfully updated.' }
      format.json { render :show, status: :ok, location: @article }
    else
      format.html { render :edit }
      format.json { render json: @article.errors, status: :unprocessable_
      entity }
    end
  end
```

```
    end
  end

  # DELETE /articles/1
  # DELETE /articles/1.json
  def destroy
    @article = current_user.articles.find(params[:id])
    @article.destroy
    respond_to do |format|
      format.html { redirect_to articles_url, notice: 'Article was
      successfully destroyed.' }
      format.json { head :no_content }
    end
  end

  private
    # Use callbacks to share common setup or constraints between actions.
    def set_article
      @article = Article.find(params[:id])
    end

    # Never trust parameters from the scary internet, only allow the white
    list through.
    def article_params
      params.require(:article).permit(:title, :location, :excerpt, :body,
      :published_at, category_ids: [])
    end
end
```

Adding Custom Helpers

Your blog application is looking pretty good, but let's make it a bit more user-friendly. One thing you can do is add a helpful cancel link beside each submit button on the forms, so users can back out of editing. You could do this by adding a link_to helper beside each button, but you'd need to do this for every form. Because you probably want to repeat this pattern throughout the application, this could end up being a lot of duplication. Why not create a custom helper to do this for you? Listing 8-31 shows the method submit_or_cancel added to the application_helper.

Listing 8-31. The submit_or_cancel Method in app/helpers/ application_helper.rb: https://gist.github.com/nicedawg/ cd8158c477a1974b648da1ab8ff1b5de

```
module ApplicationHelper
  def submit_or_cancel(form, name = "Cancel")
    form.submit + " or " + link_to(name, 'javascript:history.go(-1);',
    class: 'cancel')
  end
end
```

Now, let's use this helper on your forms. Open both the user and the article form partials in app/views/users/_form.html.erb and app/views/articles/_form.html. erb, and update them so they look like Listings 8-32 and 8-33, respectively.

Listing 8-32. Updated app/views/users/_form.html.erb: https://gist. github.com/nicedawg/7f4ede7a53cd8482456dec5191af2253

```
<%= form_with(model: user, local: true) do |form| %>
  <% if user.errors.any? %>
    <div id="error_explanation">
      <h2><%= pluralize(user.errors.count, "error") %> prohibited this user
      from being saved:</h2>

      <ul>
        <% user.errors.full_messages.each do |message| %>
          <li><%= message %></li>
        <% end %>
      </ul>
    </div>
  <% end %>

  <div class="field">
    <%= form.label :email %>
    <%= form.text_field :email %>
  </div>
```

```erb
<div class="field">
  <%= form.label :password %>
  <%= form.password_field :password %>
</div>

<div class="field">
  <%= form.label :password_confirmation %>
  <%= form.password_field :password_confirmation %>
</div>

<div class="actions">
  <%= submit_or_cancel(form) %>
</div>
<% end %>
```

Listing 8-33. Updated app/views/articles/_form.html.erb: https://gist. github.com/nicedawg/fe196bcf0330ebc1b925b4d603877417

```erb
<%= form_with(model: article, local: true) do |form| %>
  <% if article.errors.any? %>
    <div id="error_explanation">
      <h2><%= pluralize(article.errors.count, "error") %> prohibited this
      article from being saved:</h2>

      <ul>
        <% article.errors.full_messages.each do |message| %>
          <li><%= message %></li>
        <% end %>
      </ul>
    </div>
  <% end %>

  <div class="field">
    <%= form.label :title %>
    <%= form.text_field :title %>
  </div>
```

```
<div class="field">
  <%= form.label :location %>
  <%= form.text_field :location %>
</div>

<div class="field">
  <%= form.collection_check_boxes(:category_ids, Category.all, :id,
  :name) do |b| %>
    <% b.label { b.check_box + b.text } %>
  <% end %>
</div>

<div class="field">
  <%= form.label :excerpt %>
  <%= form.text_field :excerpt %>
</div>

<div class="field">
  <%= form.label :body %>
  <%= form.text_area :body %>
</div>

<div class="field">
  <%= form.label :published_at %>
  <%= form.datetime_select :published_at %>
</div>

<div class="actions">
  <%= submit_or_cancel(form) %>
</div>
<% end %>
```

As in the earlier examples, every time you copy and paste view code in more than one template, it means that you very likely can extract it into a helper method.

Giving It Some Style

Your blog application could use a little varnish. Let's update the layout and apply a style sheet.

Updating the Layout

Let's update the main layout and add some style hooks that you can target via CSS. You also add some pieces to allow the user to log in, log out, edit their password, and add a new article. The final result looks like the code in Listing 8-34, with changes in bold.

Listing 8-34. Updated app/views/layouts/application.html.erb: https://gist.github.com/nicedawg/fc953bf06cae995032f8c40590b7f4bb

```
<!DOCTYPE html>
<html>
  <head>
    <title>Blog</title>
    <%= csrf_meta_tags %>
    <%= csp_meta_tag %>

    <%= stylesheet_link_tag 'application', media: 'all', 'data-turbolinks-
    track': 'reload' %>
    <%= javascript_pack_tag 'application', 'data-turbolinks-track':
    'reload' %>
  </head>

  <body>
    <div id="header">
      <h1><%= link_to "Blog", root_path %></h1>
      <div id="user_bar">
        <% if logged_in? %>
          <%= link_to "New Article", new_article_path %> |
          <%= link_to "Edit Password", edit_user_path(current_user) %> |
          <%= link_to "Logout", logout_path %>
        <% else %>
          <%= link_to "Login", login_path %>
        <% end %>
      </div>
    </div>
    <div id="main">
      <%= content_tag :p, notice, class: 'notice' if notice.present? %>
```

```
    <%= content_tag :p, alert, class: 'alert' if alert.present? %>
    <%= yield %>
  </div>
  <div id="footer">
    A simple blog built for the book Beginning Rails 6
  </div>
</body>
</html>
```

We just now added a link to add a new article in the application layout; therefore, we no longer need that link on the articles' index page. Update the app/views/articles/index.html.erb file to remove the new article link. It should look like the code in Listing 8-35.

Listing 8-35. Remove New Article Link from app/views/articles/index.html.erb: https://gist.github.com/nicedawg/b55540aedc034de3851f2e5b1f29eaf9

```
<h1>Articles</h1>

<div id="articles">
  <%= render @articles %>
</div>
```

Applying a Style Sheet

We've prepared a simple CSS that you can apply to make the application look pretty. Listing 8-36 shows the resulting app/assets/stylesheets/application.css file after we've added our custom rules. We're no longer using the app/assets/stylesheets/scaffolds.scss file; remove it to avoid any styling conflicts.

Listing 8-36. The app/assets/stylesheets/application.css File: https://gist.github.com/nicedawg/b8f6e3af51ef7db3bd3f4eda2841558e

```
/*
 * This is a manifest file that'll be compiled into application.css, which
   will include all the files
 * listed below.
 *
```

```
* Any CSS and SCSS file within this directory, lib/assets/stylesheets, or
  any plugin's
* vendor/assets/stylesheets directory can be referenced here using a
  relative path.
*
* You're free to add application-wide styles to this file and they'll
  appear at the bottom of the
* compiled file so the styles you add here take precedence over styles
  defined in any other CSS/SCSS
* files in this directory. Styles in this file should be added after the
  last require_* statement.
* It is generally better to create a new file per style scope.
*
*= require_tree .
*= require_self
*/

* {
  margin: 0 auto;
}

body {
  background-color: #fff;
  color: #333;
}

body, p, ol, ul, td {
  font-family: verdana, arial, helvetica, sans-serif;
  font-size:   13px;
  line-height: 18px;
}

pre {
  background-color: #eee;
  padding: 10px;
  font-size: 11px;
}
```

```
p {
  padding: 5px;
}
a {
  color:#D95E16;
  padding:0 2px;
  text-decoration:none;
}
a:hover {
  background-color:#FF813C;
  color:#FFFFFF;
}
.notice { color: green; }
.alert  { color: red; }
#header, #main, #footer {
  max-width: 800px;
}
#header {
  font-family:"Myriad Web Pro",Helvetica,Arial,sans-serif;
  letter-spacing: 1px;
  border-bottom: 5px solid #333333;
  color:#333333;
  padding: 15px 0;
  height: 35px;
}
#header #user_bar {
  float: right;
  font-size: 10px;
}
#footer {
  border-top: 5px solid #C1C1C1;
  margin-top: 10px;
```

```css
  clear:both;
  padding: 10px 0;
  text-align: center;
  font-size: 11px;
}

#header h1 {
  padding-top: 14px;
  float: left;
  font-size: 30px;
}

#header h1 a{
  color: black;
}

#header h1 a:hover {
  background-color: white;
  color: black;
  border-bottom: 4px solid #ccc;
}

#header p {
  float: right;
}

#main h1 {
  font-size: 16px;
  padding: 10px 0;
  border-bottom: 1px solid #bbb;
  margin-bottom: 10px;
}

#main table{
  margin: 0;
}
```

```css
#main form{
  text-align: left;
}

#main form br{
  display: none;
  float: left;
}

#main form label {
  width: 150px;
  display: block;
  text-align: right;
  padding-right: 10px;
  float: left;
  line-height: 21px;
  vertical-align: center;
  background-color: #F0F0F0;
  border: 2px solid #ccc;
  margin-right: 10px;
}

#main form label.check_box_label {
  width: auto;
  display: inline;
  text-align: right;
  padding-right: 10px;
  line-height: 21px;
  vertical-align: center;
  background-color: #FFF;
  border: none;
}

#main form .field, #main form .actions {
  padding-top: 10px;
  clear: both;
}
```

```css
#main form input[type=text], #main form input[type=password], #main form
textarea {
  float: left;
  font-size: 14px;
  width: 250px;
  padding: 2px;
  border: 2px solid #ccc;
}

#main form input[type=checkbox] {
  margin: 4px;
  float: left;
}

#main form textarea {
  height: 150px;
}

#main form input[type=submit] {
  margin-left: 175px;
  float:left;
  margin-right: 10px;
  margin-bottom: 10px;
}

#main h3 {
  padding-top: 10px;
  height: 20px;
}

#main h3 .actions{
  display:none;
  font-weight: normal;
  font-size: 10px;
}
```

```
#main h3:hover .actions{
  display: inline;
}

.field_with_errors {
  display:table;
  float:left;
  margin:0;
  width:100px;
  margin-right: 10px;
}

#main form .field_with_errors label{
  border: 2px solid red;
  margin-right: 0px;
}

#main form .field_with_errors input, #main form .field_with_
errors  textarea{
  width: 250px;
  border: 2px solid red;
}

#error_explanation {
  width: 413px;
  border: 2px solid red;
  padding: 7px;
  padding-bottom: 12px;
  margin-bottom: 20px;
  background-color: #f0f0f0;
  margin: 0;
}

#error_explanation h2 {
  text-align: left;
  font-weight: bold;
  padding: 5px 5px 5px 15px;
  font-size: 12px;
```

```
  margin: -7px;
  background-color: #c00;
  color: #fff;
}

#error_explanation p {
  color: #333;
  margin-bottom: 0;
  padding: 5px;
  margin: 0;
}

#error_explanation ul li {
  font-size: 12px;
  list-style: square;
}
```

Yikes! That's a lot of CSS! Don't worry, though. Like all the other listings in the book, you can get the code from the gist URL in the listing caption. The code is also available on the book's website (http://www.apress.com) so you can download it and copy it into your project. We certainly don't expect you to type it all in.

With the CSS in place, your application is starting to look nice. If you've done everything correctly, it should look a lot like Figure 8-8.

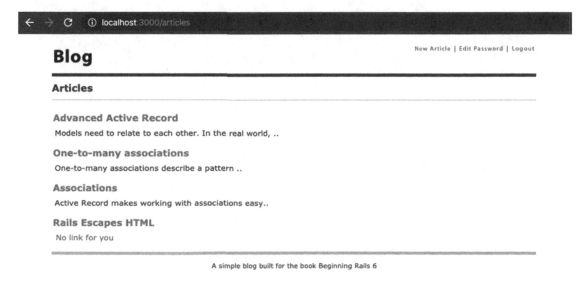

Figure 8-8. Final layout with CSS

Summary

This chapter discussed a fair number of advanced topics, including nested resources, sessions and state, and how to protect actions using filters. But we didn't stop there. You also learned how to sanitize HTML to protect your application from defacement by malicious users, and how to create your own helpers to improve your interface. You even took the time to make your application look pretty, sprucing up the layout and adding some CSS.

The next chapters build on this knowledge, and we'll start by going over how Rails handles JavaScript and CSS.

CHAPTER 9

JavaScript and CSS

JavaScript and CSS (Cascading Style Sheets) have evolved over the years from being nice embellishments on a web page to critical aspects of a web application's user interface. It should be no surprise that Rails, by convention over configuration, makes including modern JavaScript and CSS both easy to incorporate into your web application and flexible to modify for advanced use cases.

Rails 6 introduces the inclusion of the *webpacker* gem by default. The *webpacker* gem (with its default configuration) causes your javascript to be preprocessed and bundled with the popular JavaScript bundler *webpack*. Though *webpack* is capable of also handling CSS, images, fonts, and more, at this point Rails' default configuration only uses *webpack* for JavaScript. To keep things simple, we'll stick with only using *webpack* for JavaScript in this book.

For CSS, images, and fonts, Rails still uses the *Asset Pipeline*, a component of Rails which handles preprocessing and bundling.

Why do we need our JavaScript, CSS, and other assets to be preprocessed and bundled? What does that even mean? We'll give a brief overview of some of the benefits before we apply our knowledge to the blog application we're building.

Note If you need to get the code at the exact point where you finished Chapter 8, download the source code zip file from the book's page on `www.apress.com` and extract it onto your computer.

Benefits of Preprocessing Assets

Why bother preprocessing and bundling your assets? We've been serving JavaScript, CSS, images, and more on our websites for years just fine, right? In the last several years, JavaScript and CSS have exploded in new features and capabilities and have quickly

© Brady Somerville, Adam Gamble, Cloves Carneiro Jr and Rida Al Barazi 2020
B. Somerville et al., *Beginning Rails 6*, https://doi.org/10.1007/978-1-4842-5716-6_9

become integral parts of our web applications, whereas previously they might have just been a nice enhancement.

As our web applications now include more JavaScript and CSS than they used to, we must be concerned with how quickly our users can download our assets. Traditional approaches to optimizing the sizes of our assets required tedious work, or custom scripts.

Also, in recent years, JavaScript and CSS have spawned new languages—such as TypeScript and SASS—which seek to add features that make authoring JavaScript and CSS easier and more featureful. But browsers need JavaScript and CSS, not TypeScript or SASS. Wouldn't it be nice to choose to author our JavaScript and CSS in the language we desire and have it converted automatically to what the browser needs?

In the next few sections, we'll discuss some of these benefits of preprocessing assets in more detail.

Asset Concatenation and Compression

Applications that have a lot of JavaScript and CSS can have hundreds of individual .js and .css files. If a browser has to download all of these files, it causes a lot of overhead just starting and stopping the transfer of files. The Asset Pipeline concatenates both your JavaScript and CSS into files so that a browser only has to download one or two files instead of hundreds. It can also minify and compress the files. This removes things like comments, whitespace, and long variable names from the final output. The final product is functionally equivalent, but usually much smaller. Both of these features combine to make web applications load much faster and are transparent to the user.

Secondary Languages

Browsers have very strong support for both JavaScript and CSS, but if you want to use another language on the frontend or even if you use newer JavaScript features that aren't available in slightly older browsers, you'd be out of luck. The browser would at best ignore it and at worse throw errors all over the screen. webpack and the Asset Pipeline allow you to use other languages that compile down to code that browsers understand. For example, *webpack* (with *babel*) allows you to write modern JavaScript— ES6—which is then transpiled (converted) into older JavaScript which more browsers can understand. The Asset Pipeline allows you to create your app's styles in the SASS language and converts it into standard CSS which browsers understand.

Detailed description of ES6 and SASS is out of the scope of this book, but you should know what they are if you encounter them. For more information on ES6, visit `https://developer.mozilla.org/en-US/docs/Web/JavaScript`, and for more information on SASS, visit `https://sass-lang.com/`.

Asset Locations

Rails allows you to place files in several different locations, depending on whether you want them to be processed by *webpack* or the Asset Pipeline. The following table describes these locations (Table 9-1).

Table 9-1. *Locations for Assets*

Preprocessor	File Location	Description
Asset Pipeline	`app/assets`	This is for assets that are owned by the application. You can include images, style sheets, and JavaScript.
Asset Pipeline	`lib/assets`	This location is for assets that are shared across applications but are owned by you. These assets don't really fit into the scope of this specific application but are used by it.
Asset Pipeline	`vendor/assets`	This location is for assets that are from an outside vendor, like JavaScript or CSS frameworks.
webpack	`app/javascript/packs/`	This location is where you create *packs*—JavaScript files that import *other* Javascript files, meant to be served as a bundle. By default, application.js is installed. You can add to it or create a separate pack when you want a substantially different group of JavaScript files (e.g., admin.js).
webpack	`app/javascript`	This location is where you add smaller JavaScript files which will be imported by pack files, as described in the preceding text.

In general, webpack and the Asset Pipeline stay out of the way, but they empower you to do impressive things with your assets with the default configuration and can be configured to do even more. For more information on the Asset Pipeline, visit `https://guides.rubyonrails.org/asset_pipeline.html`. For more information on *Webpacker*, see `https://github.com/rails/webpacker`.

Turbolinks

Since version 4, Rails has included the Turbolinks gem by default. This gem (and the accompanying JavaScript) aims to speed up your application by using Ajax to request pages instead of the more traditional page requests. It tracks files that are commonly shared across requests, like JavaScript and style sheets, and only reloads the information that changes. It attaches itself to links on your page instead of making those requests the traditional way. It makes an Ajax request and replaces the body tag of your document. Turbolinks also keeps track of the URL and manages the back and forward buttons. It's designed to be transparent to both users and developers.

Turbolinks is turned on by default since Rails 4. It is included in the default JavaScript pack. If you needed to remove Turbolinks for some reason, you could do so, but we'll leave it on for our blog application we're building.

By default, Turbolinks attaches itself to every link on the page, but you can disable it for specific links by attaching a *data-turbolinks="false"* attribute to the link, as shown in Listing 9-1. This causes the link to behave in a traditional fashion.

Listing 9-1. Rails `link_to` Helper with a No-Turbolinks Attribute Attached

```
link_to "Some Link", "/some-location", data: { turbolinks: false }
```

Note   Some JavaScript libraries aren't compatible with Turbolinks. Listing these is out of the scope of this book, but you can find more information at `https://github.com/turbolinks/turbolinks`. If you continue to have problems, you can always disable Turbolinks.

Let's Build Something!

We've talked about the features of Rails that support JavaScript and CSS, but let's actually put JavaScript to work. We've added our style sheets in Chapter 8, but this chapter will focus on making our application use Ajax to load and submit forms.

Ajax and Rails

Ajax is a combination of technologies centered around the XMLHttpRequest object, a JavaScript API originally developed by Microsoft but now supported in all modern browsers. Of course, you could interface with the XMLHttpRequest API directly, but it wouldn't be fun. A far better idea is to use one of several libraries that abstracts the low-level details and makes cross-browser support possible.

Rails makes Ajax easier for web developers to use. Toward that end, it implements a set of conventions that enable you to implement even the most advanced techniques with relative ease.

Most of the Ajax features you implement in Rails applications are coded using JavaScript; so familiarity with JavaScript code always helps and is pretty important for today's web developers.

JavaScript and the DOM

The Document Object Model (DOM) provides a way to interact programmatically with a web page in your browser with JavaScript. Using the DOM, you can add, update, and remove elements from the web page without having to ask the server for a new page.

In the past, different browsers did not provide consistent APIs for interacting with the DOM. Developers were forced to write different JavaScript for different browsers. Eventually, JavaScript frameworks like jQuery emerged to simplify the process of writing code compatible with different browsers.

However, things have changed considerably. Different browsers now provide a more consistent interface (not perfectly consistent, but better!). So while tools like jQuery were considered essential in the not-so-distant past, developers no longer need such frameworks to achieve cross-browser compatibility.

Tip   Wikipedia defines DOM as follows: "The Document Object Model (DOM) is a cross-platform and language-independent convention for representing and interacting with objects in HTML, XHTML, and XML documents" (https:// en.wikipedia.org/wiki/Document_Object_Model).

Working with the DOM is a deep subject; we'll only scratch the surface in this book. But we'll learn enough to add some nice touches to our application. See `https://developer.mozilla.org/en-US/docs/Web/API/Document_Object_Model` for more information.

First, we'll show you a few different ways to select elements from the DOM in the following table (Table 9-2).

Table 9-2. *Selecting Elements from the DOM*

Function	Description
`document.querySelector('#article_123')`	Returns the element matching the given ID `article_123`.
`document.querySelectorAll('.comment')`	Returns a list of elements with the class name `comment`.
`document.querySelectorAll('div.article')`	Returns a list of `div` elements with the class name `article`.

Table 9-2 used some of the most commonly used CSS selectors. For a complete list, see `https://developer.mozilla.org/en-US/docs/Web/CSS/CSS_Selectors`. Also, notice that when we expected a unique element (e.g., with a given id), we used *querySelector*, whereas when we expected any number of elements, we used *querySelectorAll*.

Moving to Practice

Now that you know what Ajax is, how it works, and how to select elements from the DOM, we can apply some of this knowledge to enhance the usability of our application. Mainly, one would use Ajax in their application when they think a snappier interaction is possible and recommended. Let's begin Ajaxifying our blog application in the article page.

Not All Users Comment

If you look at the article page, you quickly notice that every time users read a post, they're presented with a form for entering comments. Although reader participation is paramount, most users are only interested in reading the content. You can modify the article page to not load the comment form automatically; instead, it will load the form only after a user clicks the new comment link.

Loading a Template via Ajax

One of the rules of good interface design is to make things snappy. That is to say, the interface should be responsive and quick to load. A good way to achieve this is to load elements (like forms or content areas) onto the page whenever the user requests them. Modify the article's show template, as shown in Listing 9-2.

Listing 9-2. The Article Partial in app/views/articles/show.html.erb: https://gist.github.com/nicedawg/5e13311132f323e425be2488c7b2f5d4

```
<%= render @article %>

<h3>Comments</h3>

<div id="comments">
  <%= render @article.comments %>
</div>

<%= link_to "new comment", new_article_comment_path(@article), remote:
true, id: 'new_comment_link' %>
```

The template hasn't changed a lot: you no longer directly render the comment form, and you add a link called new comment. The new link still uses the well-known link_to helper to generate a link; however, you pass in the *remote: true* option, which tells Rails that you want the request triggered by this link to hit the server using Ajax.

There are a couple of things to note in the use of link_to in Listing 9-2. First, you send the request to a URL that already exists; the *new_article_comment_path* route identifies a path to a new comment. Second, you use the *id: 'new_comment_link'* option to give the rendered HTML element an ID that you can refer to later.

On the server side, you don't need to make any changes to the comments controller. As currently implemented, you don't explicitly implement a new action; the default behavior in this case is to render the new partial template in app/views/comments/_new. html.erb. But that file doesn't exist, and that isn't really what we want. We want to execute some JavaScript in this case—not just receive some HTML. Instead, we want a separate JavaScript template to be used as a response for this action.

Responding to Requests with JavaScript

When a browser makes a request, it indicates what type of content it hopes to receive. When we add *remote: true* to the preceding link, Rails will now cause the browser to request a JavaScript response, instead of the typical HTML response. To make sure you send a response that includes JavaScript code, you must create a template with the `.js.erb` template extension. Create the `app/views/comments/new.js.erb` template as per Listing 9-3. The following text explains all the lines in the template to make sure you know what's happening.

Listing 9-3. The .js.erb New Comment Template in `app/views/comments/new.js.erb`: https://gist.github.com/nicedawg/944c9b741caa5437101687103e292a94

```
document.querySelector("#comments").insertAdjacentHTML("afterend",
"<%= escape_javascript render partial: 'new' %>");

document.querySelector("#new_comment_link").style.display = 'none';
```

The first line selects the element with id *comments* and inserts after it the rendered output of the `app/views/comments/_new.html.erb` partial. Table 9-3 lists similar DOM methods that you can use to add HTML content to a page with JavaScript.

Table 9-3. *DOM Element Methods for Inserting HTML into a Page*

Method	Description
`insertAdjacentHTML( position, text)`	Inserts the provided text adjacent to the current element, according to position, which can be 'beforebegin', 'afterbegin', 'beforeend', or 'afterend'
`insertAdjacentElement( position, element)`	Inserts the provided element adjacent to the current element, according to the provided position, as in the preceding text
`insertAdjacentText( position, text)`	Inserts the provided text adjacent to the current element, according to the provided position, as in the preceding text. This is recommended when you expect the content to be plain text.

Going back to Listing 9-3, the last line hides the new_comment_element, which contains the link to add a new comment, by setting its style's display attribute to "none." Because you already have the comment form in your page, it makes little sense to keep that link around.

Note   In a similar fashion, you can display a hidden element by setting its style. display attribute to "block," "inline," or other values, depending on the element's intended usage.

Let's see what you built in practice. Open your browser to any existing article, such as http://localhost:3000/articles/2, and notice that the comment form is no longer there (Figure 9-1).

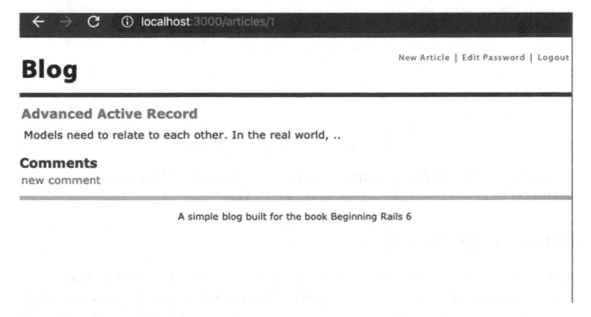

Figure 9-1.   *The article page without the comment form*

As soon as you click the new comment link, the comment form pops into place, and you can add comments (Figure 9-2). You achieved your goal of keeping the user interface cleaner while allowing users to quickly access functionality without having to move to a new page. That's a good start.

Figure 9-2. *The article page with the comment form and without the new comment link*

Making a Grand Entrance

In the previous section, you added an element to the screen via Ajax—the comment form. It's a pretty big form. It's a very obvious inclusion on the page and your users won't miss it; however, sometimes you may want to add just an extra link or highlight some text on a page. To help draw attention to the new content, let's have it fade in.

We'll add some JavaScript to fade in the comment form. Modify your app/views/comments/new.js.erb so it looks like the code in Listing 9-4.

Listing 9-4. The Updated New Comment Template in `app/views/comments/new.js.erb`: https://gist.github.com/nicedawg/1a94805ef8141b48b16a0b2faf8d659b

```
document.querySelector("#comments").insertAdjacentHTML("afterend",
"<%= escape_javascript render partial: 'new' %>");

var comment_form = document.querySelector("#main form");
comment_form.style.opacity = 0;
setTimeout(function() {
  comment_form.style.transition = 'opacity 1s';
  comment_form.style.opacity = 1;
}, 10);

document.querySelector("#new_comment_link").style.display = 'none';
```

We added a few lines that could use some explanation. First, we select the form we just added and store it in the variable *comment_form*. Then, we immediately set the form's opacity to 0, to make it completely transparent. Then, we use the *setTimeout* method to delay the execution of the next steps by 10 milliseconds. (Apparently, newly added content needs a few milliseconds before they're ready to consistently work with CSS transitions.) Lastly, we tell the element that any future changes to its opacity attribute should gradually take place over 1 second, and then we set its opacity to 1—full visibility—and the element begins to fade in.

Arguably, there are better ways of making an element fade in. Perhaps we should have written some CSS rules to handle the transition in combination with JavaScript and made a more reusable solution for fading the element in. We also should make the JavaScript code we added more robust—but for now, this is the simplest way to get what we want, and that's okay!

Open your browser at any article page and look at the shiny effect that is being applied.

Note   You very likely want to learn more about all the various style properties you can change with CSS and JS. For more info, see `https://developer.mozilla.org/en-US/docs/Web/API/ElementCSSInlineStyle/style`.

Using Ajax for Forms

Another user interaction improvement is to not refresh the page after a user adds a new record. In quite a few applications, users may be required to enter a considerable amount of data in forms; so this technique is important to grasp.

In the same way that you made a link submit data via Ajax, we can make forms submit data via Ajax by making sure the *data-remote="true"* attribute is on the form's HTML element. When using the *form_with* helper, as we did with the comment form, that happens automatically! However, we added *local: true* to keep that from happening earlier to help illustrate this point. We can simplify our comment form a bit by removing some parameters we no longer need (Listing 9-5).

Listing 9-5. The Updated Comment Form in app/views/comments/_new.html.erb: https://gist.github.com/nicedawg/5dd35d1922270369b41f52815b57b224

```erb
<%= form_with(model: @article.comments.new, url: article_comments_path
(@article)) do |form| %>
  <div class="field">
    <%= form.label :name %><br />
    <%= form.text_field :name %>
  </div>
  <div class="field">
    <%= form.label :email %><br />
    <%= form.text_field :email %>
  </div>
  <div class="field">
    <%= form.label :body %><br />
    <%= form.text_area :body %>
  </div>
  <div class="actions">
    <%= form.submit 'Add' %>
  </div>
<% end %>
```

Although the changes in the view are minimal, you have to make a few more changes in your controller layer. You want to respond to JavaScript and HTML requests in different ways. Change the create method in your comments controller to look like the code in Listing 9-6.

Listing 9-6. The Updated Comments Controller in app/controllers/comments_ controller.rb: https://gist.github.com/nicedawg/db9226972a7cbc652513d3e 657b959b7

```ruby
class CommentsController < ApplicationController
  before_action :load_article, except: :destroy
  before_action :authenticate, only: :destroy

  def create
    @comment = @article.comments.new(comment_params)
    if @comment.save
      respond_to do |format|
        format.html { redirect_to @article, notice: 'Thanks for your
        comment' }
        format.js
      end
    else
      respond_to do |format|
        format.html { redirect_to @article, notice: 'Unable to add comment' }
        format.js { render :fail_create }
      end
    end
  end

  def destroy
    @article = current_user.articles.find(params[:article_id])
    @comment = @article.comments.find(params[:id])
    @comment.destroy
    redirect_to @article, notice: 'Comment deleted'
  end
```

```ruby
  private

  def load_article
    @article = Article.find(params[:article_id])
  end

  def comment_params
    params.require(:comment).permit(:name, :email, :body)
  end
end
```

The main method in this code is the respond_to helper. By using respond_to, you can have some code in the format.html block that's called when you receive a regular request and some code in the format.js block that's called when a JavaScript request is received. Hang on! There is no code in format.js! When no code is added to a format block, Rails looks for a template named after the view, just like regular views, which means it looks for create.js.erb. When a submitted comment fails validation, you also want to warn the user by displaying error messages; for that, you use format.js { render :fail_create } to render a template named fail_create.js.erb.

The new apps/views/comments/create.js.erb and app/views/comments/fail_create.js.erb templates are shown in Listings 9-7 and 9-8, respectively.

Listing 9-7. The Template in app/views/comments/create.js.erb: https://gist.github.com/nicedawg/cae8f8be678155859b6730b144738599

```javascript
document.querySelector("#comments").insertAdjacentHTML("beforeend",
"<%= escape_javascript render @comment %>");

document.querySelector("#main form").reset();
```

Listing 9-8. The Template in app/views/comments/fail_create.js.erb: https://gist.github.com/nicedawg/0cb4848e5553d60b366d0ecd8f2a1d4d

```javascript
alert("<%= @comment.errors.full_messages.to_sentence.html_safe %>");
```

In the create.js.erb template, you run a couple of JavaScript commands. First, you render the template for a new comment—using *render @comment*—and insert that HTML at the bottom of the comments div, similar to what we've done before.

The *document.querySelector("#main form").reset();* line is a simple call to reset all the elements of the new comment form, which is blank and ready to accept another comment from your user.

In the `fail_create.js.erb` template, you use the `alert` JavaScript function to display a dialog box with the validation error message, as shown in Figure 9-3.

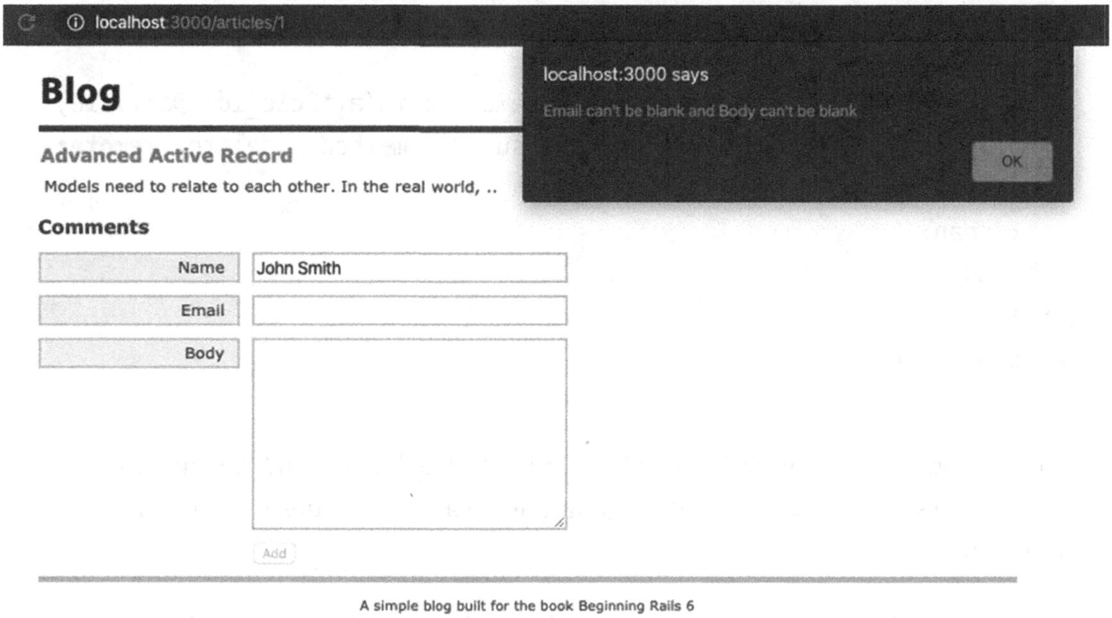

Figure 9-3. *Displaying an error message*

Give it a try: point your browser to an existing article, for example, http://localhost:3000/articles/2, and enter a few—or lots of—comments. As you can see, you can interact with the page in a much more efficient way: there's no need to wait until a full page reload happens.

Deleting Records with Ajax

To complete the "making things snappy" section, you may want to delete some of the comments that are added by users. You can combine the techniques you've learned in this chapter to let users delete comments without delay.

You already have a link to delete comments in the comment template at app/views/comments/_comment.html.erb. To use Ajax with that link, you again need to add the *remote: true* option to the method call. We're also going to add a unique id to each comment so that later, we know which comment to delete (Listing 9-9).

Listing 9-9. The Template in app/views/comments/_comment.html.erb: https://gist.github.com/nicedawg/3710992814a2d9328dd86dd8cd081df5

```erb
<div class="comment" id="comment-<%= comment.id %>">
  <h3>
    <%= comment.name %> <<%= comment.email %>> said:
    <% if @article.owned_by? current_user %>
      <span class="actions">
        <%= link_to 'Delete', article_comment_path(article_id: @article,
        id: comment), confirm: 'Are you sure?', method: :delete, remote:
        true %>
      </span>
    <% end %>
  </h3>
  <%= comment.body %>
</div>
```

The changes in the controller are also minimal. Use the `respond_to` and `format` block to make sure you support both regular and JavaScript requests, as shown in Listing 9-10.

Listing 9-10. The Comments Controller in app/controllers/comments_controller.rb: https://gist.github.com/nicedawg/0d6b6c3907175ed645cd6c1ebb2965c4

```ruby
class CommentsController < ApplicationController
  before_action :load_article, except: :destroy
  before_action :authenticate, only: :destroy

  def create
    @comment = @article.comments.new(comment_params)
    if @comment.save
      respond_to do |format|
        format.html { redirect_to @article, notice: 'Thanks for your
        comment' }
        format.js
      end
```

```ruby
    else
      respond_to do |format|
        format.html { redirect_to @article, notice: 'Unable to add comment' }
        format.js { render :fail_create }
      end
    end
  end

  def destroy
    @article = current_user.articles.find(params[:article_id])
    @comment = @article.comments.find(params[:id])
    @comment.destroy
    respond_to do |format|
      format.html { redirect_to @article, notice: 'Comment deleted' }
      format.js
    end
  end

  private

  def load_article
    @article = Article.find(params[:article_id])
  end

  def comment_params
    params.require(:comment).permit(:name, :email, :body)
  end
end
```

You wire up the delete link in the comment partial to send an Ajax request to the controller. The controller responds to those Ajax requests with the default action, which is to render the app/views/comments/destroy.js.erb file (Listing 9-11).

Listing 9-11. The app/views/comments/destroy.js.erb File: https://gist. github.com/nicedawg/b30f595ec078927ff93ab37f3bb94f14

```javascript
var comments = document.querySelector("#comments");
comments.removeChild(document.querySelector("#comment-<%= @comment.id %>"));
```

In the preceding JavaScript, we select the comments container and then call *removeChild*, passing it the comment element we wish to delete. Removing an element seems a little complicated. Most modern browsers support simply calling *.remove()* on the element you want to remove, but IE doesn't support that feature. We could have added a *polyfill*—a JavaScript library which adds specific features to browsers which don't implement them—but that's out of the scope of this book.

Open your browser to an article page—make sure you are logged in as the article owner—with some comments you want to delete or add lots of spam-like comments. See how quickly you can get rid of comments now? It's a lot better than waiting for page reloads.

Summary

To be sure, JavaScript is a large topic. Entire books, conferences, and technology are devoted to the language, so it goes without saying that this chapter only scratches the surface. Still, in short order, you've learned the basics of implementing Ajax in Rails applications, and you know where to go when you need to dig deeper.

You learned how to make remote Ajax calls using the `remote: true` option for links and forms. You also used a simple visual effect to show new elements on the page, thanks to JavaScript's ability to interact with the DOM.

Finally, you learned about using JavaScript templates—which have the `.js.erb` extension—to produce responses to Ajax requests using JavaScript code. At this stage, you have a solid grasp of the Action Pack side of web development with Rails.

## CHAPTER 10

Active Storage

With version 5.2, Rails introduced a system to make it easy to handle files attached to your application's models. Web applications often need to perform tasks such as saving user-uploaded files, creating thumbnail versions of images, and validating file types. Previously, developers depended on other gems to handle this functionality, but now we have the option to use a system that's a full-fledged part of Rails.

In this chapter, we'll enhance our blog application by adding the ability for users to upload an image to an article, showing a thumbnail version of the image in the list of articles and another version on an individual article's page.

ImageMagick

Since we plan on resizing uploaded images, we need to install ImageMagick—a command-line tool which can perform a wide variety of operations on images, such as resizing, converting formats, cropping, adding borders, watermarking, and more.

Installing on MacOS Catalina

We can use *Homebrew* to install ImageMagick:

```
> brew install imagemagick
```

ImageMagick has several dependencies, so this may take a few minutes. To verify installation, run the following command:

```
> convert -version
```

If you see output like "Version: ImageMagick 7.0.9-26..." (ignoring any major differences in version number), then we are ready to go.

© Brady Somerville, Adam Gamble, Cloves Carneiro Jr and Rida Al Barazi 2020
B. Somerville et al., *Beginning Rails 6*, https://doi.org/10.1007/978-1-4842-5716-6_10

Installing on Windows

Visit `https://imagemagick.org/script/download.php#windows` and download the appropriate ImageMagick-*.exe for your system. For most, the topmost link is suitable. Developers with older systems may need to look for the 32-bit version on the page.

After downloading the ImageMagick exe file, open it to run the installer. We can just accept the defaults. When installation finishes, run the following command in a fresh command prompt to verify installation was successful:

```
> magick --version
```

Ignoring any minor version differences, you should see output that includes something like "Version: ImageMagick 7.0.9-26". If so, we are ready to go!

Installing on Linux

On Ubuntu Linux, we'll run the following command. (If using another distribution of Linux, use your system's package manager to install the imagemagick package.) If prompted, accept the

```
> sudo apt-get install imagemagick
```

To verify installation, run the following command:

```
> convert -v
```

Look for text that says something like "Version: ImageMagick..." If you do, then we're ready to go!

Configuration

Next, we need to generate the database tables needed to store information about our uploaded files. Run the following commands to generate and run the necessary migration:

```
> rails active_storage:install
> rails db:migrate
```

We won't need to change any of Active Storage's default configuration for our sample blog application. But if we wanted to, for example, configure Active Storage to store files in Amazon S3, we would define a new service in config/storage.yml and edit the various config/environments/*.rb files to choose which storage service should be used in a given Rails environment. For more information on configuration options, see `https://edgeguides.rubyonrails.org/active_storage_overview.html`.

Next, since we plan on processing the images we're going to add to our blog, we need to install the *image_processing* gem. The following line is already in our Gemfile—but it's commented out because we didn't need it yet. Uncomment the following line in your Gemfile, save it, and then run *bundle install*:

```
gem "image_processing", "~> 1.2"
```

That's it! We're ready to start enhancing our blog with images.

Saving Uploaded Images

First, we'll update our Article model to declare that it has an attached image. Update your app/models/article.rb so it matches the code in Listing 10-1.

Listing 10-1. Attaching an Image to the Article Model
`https://gist.github.com/nicedawg/0c3a7645b269b5a48bd091fd8feb5754`

```
class Article < ApplicationRecord
  validates :title, :body, presence: true

  belongs_to :user
  has_and_belongs_to_many :categories
  has_many :comments
  has_one_attached :cover_image

  scope :published, -> { where.not(published_at: nil) }
  scope :draft, -> { where(published_at: nil) }
  scope :recent, -> { where('articles.published_at > ?', 1.week.ago.to_
date) }
  scope :where_title, -> (term) { where("articles.title LIKE ?",
"%#{term}%") }
```

```
  def long_title
    "#{title} - #{published_at}"
  end

  def published?
    published_at.present?
  end

  def owned_by?(owner)
    return false unless owner.is_a?(User)
    user == owner
  end
end
```

Adding *has_one_attached :cover_image* to Article allows us to use *article.cover_image* to access the article's cover image file and perhaps perform operations on it. You may have noticed we didn't create any database storage specifically for article cover images. When we generated and ran migrations earlier, we created a *polymorphic* table to store information about attached files. This table stores not only the *id* of the record which owns the attached file but also its *class name* (e.g., "Article"). This allows us to add attachments to any model without needing separate storage for each type.

Now that our database and Article model are prepared to handle cover images, let's add the ability to upload a cover image while creating or updating an article. First, let's edit our article form, found in app/views/articles/_form.html.erb, to match Listing 10-2.

Listing 10-2. Adding Cover Image File Upload Field in the Article Form
https://gist.github.com/nicedawg/74e6d30f99b82da66efc8ea0ee816278

```
<%= form_with(model: article, local: true) do |form| %>
  <% if article.errors.any? %>
    <div id="error_explanation">
      <h2><%= pluralize(article.errors.count, "error") %> prohibited this
      article from being saved:</h2>

      <ul>
        <% article.errors.full_messages.each do |message| %>
          <li><%= message %></li>
        <% end %>
```

```
    </ul>
  </div>
<% end %>

<div class="field">
  <%= form.label :title %>
  <%= form.text_field :title %>
</div>

<div class="field">
  <%= form.label :cover_image %>
  <%= form.file_field :cover_image %>
</div>

<div class="field">
  <%= form.label :location %>
  <%= form.text_field :location %>
</div>

  <%# ... code omitted for brevity ... %>
<% end %>
```

Now that our article form will submit the uploaded cover image, we need to update our ArticlesController to *permit* the cover image to be uploaded. Update your app/controllers/articles_controller.rb to match Listing 10-3.

Listing 10-3. Permitting cover_image Param in ArticlesController
https://gist.github.com/nicedawg/2a59c8b763831130042186ef8e64990c

```
class ArticlesController < ApplicationController
  before_action :authenticate, except: [:index, :show]
  before_action :set_article, only: [:show]

  # ... code omitted for brevity ...

  private
    # Use callbacks to share common setup or constraints between actions.
    def set_article
      @article = Article.find(params[:id])
    end
```

```
    # Never trust parameters from the scary internet, only allow the white
    list through.
    def article_params
      params.require(:article).permit(:title, :cover_image, :location,
      :excerpt, :body, :published_at, category_ids: [])
    end
end
```

Next, we'll display this image in the article partial template (Listing 10-4) so that it appears on the articles index and show pages.

Displaying Uploaded Images

Listing 10-4. Displaying Article Cover Image in the Article Partial `https://gist.github.com/nicedawg/7af1ba628cfeddebf1bac7c51faba0e9`

```
<div class="article">
  <h3>
    <%= link_to article.title, article %>
    <% if article.owned_by? current_user %>
      <span class="actions">
        <%= link_to 'Edit', edit_article_path(article) %>
        <%= link_to 'Delete', article, confirm: 'Are you sure?', method:
        :delete %>
      </span>
    <% end %>
  </h3>
  <hr>
  <% if article.cover_image.attached? %>
    <%= image_tag article.cover_image.variant(resize_to_limit: local_
    assigns.fetch(:cover_image_options, [200, 200])) %>
  <% end %>
  <hr>
  <%= simple_format article.body %>
</div>
```

There's a bit going on there, so let's explain! First, we call *.attached?* to see if this article actually has a cover image. If it does, then we want to display the image, so we use the *image_tag* helper and give a variant of the cover image as the source of the image.

We call *.variant()* to indicate we don't want the original version of the attached image—it could be huge! So we pass *resize_to_limit* with an array of the width and height we desire, which will resize the image while preserving the aspect ratio to fit inside the dimensions requested, as long as it exceeds the dimensions.

However, this is a shared partial—both articles/index and articles/show use it—and we want to use different dimensions for the cover image in those two scenarios. So we use Ruby's *fetch* method on the special *local_assigns* hash, which is populated with any local variables passed into the template, if any. So *local_assigns.fetch(:cover_image_options, [200, 200])* effectively says "if :cover_image_options was passed into this template as a local variable, then use those options. However, if :cover_image_options was *not* passed in, then use [200, 200] as the default."

That was a mouthful to explain, but I'm sure you can see how this is a helpful way to allow a shared partial to function differently in different scenarios. Be careful, though—relying on too many local variables in partials can become unwieldy. At some point, it may be more beneficial to create separate partials.

Next, we'll update app/views/articles/show.html.erb (Listing 10-5) to show a larger variant of the cover image than what is shown on the articles' index page. This will make use of the *local_assigns* code we added in the previous listing.

Listing 10-5. Displaying Larger Cover Image in the Article Show Page https://gist.github.com/nicedawg/6f476ebe496fc6b03c4c3591e97d96d6

```
<%= render partial: @article, locals: { cover_image_options: [500, 500] } %>

<h3>Comments</h3>

<div id="comments">
  <%= render @article.comments %>
</div>

<%= link_to "new comment", new_article_comment_path(@article), remote:
true, id: 'new_comment_link' %>
```

Try it out! Edit an article or create a new one, and upload a web-compatible image, such as a .jpg, .png, or .gif file. Your uploaded file should now be shown on the articles index and show pages, in different sizes.

Removing Uploaded Images

Now that we've added images to articles, we realize we'd like to be able to *remove* images from articles. Currently, we can only add or replace images. To allow the editor to remove cover images, we'll need to update our article form and our articles controller.

First, let's improve our article form by showing a small thumbnail of the cover image and a checkbox that allows the editor to remove the image by editing app/views/articles/_form.html.erb to look something like Listing 10-6.

Listing 10-6. Displaying Cover Image and Removal Checkbox in the Article Form
https://gist.github.com/nicedawg/65148223ee3416242d68a7a370ccc4fb

```
<%= form_with(model: article, local: true) do |form| %>
  <% if article.errors.any? %>
    <div id="error_explanation">
      <h2><%= pluralize(article.errors.count, "error") %> prohibited this
      article from being saved:</h2>

      <ul>
        <% article.errors.full_messages.each do |message| %>
          <li><%= message %></li>
        <% end %>
      </ul>
    </div>
  <% end %>

  <div class="field">
    <%= form.label :title %>
    <%= form.text_field :title %>
  </div>
```

```erb
<div class="field">
  <%= form.label :cover_image %>
  <%= form.file_field :cover_image %>

  <% if article.cover_image.attached? %>
    <p>
      <%= image_tag article.cover_image.variant(resize_to_limit:
      [50, 50]) %>
      <br>
      <%= form.label :remove_cover_image do %>
        <%= form.check_box :remove_cover_image %> Remove this image
      <% end %>
    </p>
  <% end %>
</div>

<div class="field">
  <%= form.label :location %>
  <%= form.text_field :location %>
</div>

<div class="field">
  <%= form.collection_check_boxes(:category_ids, Category.all, :id,
  :name) do |b| %>
    <% b.label { b.check_box + b.text } %>
  <% end %>
</div>

<div class="field">
  <%= form.label :excerpt %>
  <%= form.text_field :excerpt %>
</div>

<div class="field">
  <%= form.label :body %>
  <%= form.text_area :body %>
</div>
```

```
  <div class="field">
    <%= form.label :published_at %>
    <%= form.datetime_select :published_at %>
  </div>

  <div class="actions">
    <%= submit_or_cancel(form) %>
  </div>
<% end %>
```

Next, we'll update our articles controller to allow the *remove_cover_image* value to be passed through the update action into our call to update the Article object, as seen in Listing 10-7.

Listing 10-7. Allowing remove_cover_image in the Articles Controller
https://gist.github.com/nicedawg/52fe5730332e638965f02b8c9b785ca4

```
class ArticlesController < ApplicationController
  before_action :authenticate, except: [:index, :show]
  before_action :set_article, only: [:show]

  # GET /articles
  # GET /articles.json
  def index
    @articles = Article.all
  end

  # GET /articles/1
  # GET /articles/1.json
  def show
  end

  # GET /articles/new
  def new
    @article = Article.new
  end

  # GET /articles/1/edit
  def edit
```

```ruby
    @article = current_user.articles.find(params[:id])
  end

  # POST /articles
  # POST /articles.json
  def create
    @article = current_user.articles.new(article_params)

    respond_to do |format|
      if @article.save
        format.html { redirect_to @article, notice: 'Article was
        successfully created.' }
        format.json { render :show, status: :created, location: @article }
      else
        format.html { render :new }
        format.json { render json: @article.errors, status: :unprocessable_
        entity }
      end
    end
  end

  # PATCH/PUT /articles/1
  # PATCH/PUT /articles/1.json
  def update
    @article = current_user.articles.find(params[:id])
    respond_to do |format|
      if @article.update(article_params)
        format.html { redirect_to @article, notice: 'Article was
        successfully updated.' }
        format.json { render :show, status: :ok, location: @article }
      else
        format.html { render :edit }
        aformat.json { render json: @article.errors, status:
        :unprocessable_entity }
      end
    end
  end
```

```
# DELETE /articles/1
# DELETE /articles/1.json
def destroy
  @article = current_user.articles.find(params[:id])
  @article.destroy
  respond_to do |format|
    format.html { redirect_to articles_url, notice: 'Article was
    successfully destroyed.' }
    format.json { head :no_content }
  end
end

private
  # Use callbacks to share common setup or constraints between actions.
  def set_article
    @article = Article.find(params[:id])
  end

  # Never trust parameters from the scary internet, only allow the white
  list through.
  def article_params
    params.require(:article).permit(:title, :cover_image, :remove_cover_
    image, :location, :excerpt, :body, :published_at, category_ids: [])
  end
end
```

Lastly, we make a small change to our Article model to receive the *remove_cover_image* value and to remove its cover image if that value is "1" whenever the article is saved, as seen in Listing 10-8.

Listing 10-8. Deleting the Attachment When the Article Is Saved
https://gist.github.com/nicedawg/26288ce37ad9f7ad212f827176a665cb

```
class Article < ApplicationRecord
  validates :title, :body, presence: true
```

```
belongs_to :user
has_and_belongs_to_many :categories
has_many :comments

has_one_attached :cover_image
attr_accessor :remove_cover_image
after_save { cover_image.purge if remove_cover_image == '1' }

scope :published, -> { where.not(published_at: nil) }
scope :draft, -> { where(published_at: nil) }
scope :recent, -> { where('articles.published_at > ?', 1.week.ago.to_
date) }
scope :where_title, -> (term) { where("articles.title LIKE ?",
"%#{term}%") }

def long_title
  "#{title} - #{published_at}"
end

def published?
  published_at.present?
end

def owned_by?(owner)
  return false unless owner.is_a?(User)
  user == owner
end
end
```

We used *attr_accessor* to add a getter and setter for an attribute called *remove_cover_image,* which matches the checkbox name we added to the form and permitted in the controller. We then add an *after_save* callback which will call *.purge* on the attached file to delete it if the value of *remove_cover_image* is "1"—the default value of a checked checkbox in Rails.

Try it out! You should be able to edit an article and remove its cover image by checking the "Remove this image" checkbox and clicking "Update Article."

Summary

In this chapter, we installed some prerequisites for processing images, added support for Active Storage to our app, and then added the ability to manage cover images for articles to our app.

There is certainly more to Active Storage than what we covered here. To learn more about Active Storage, read the Rails guide at `https://edgeguides.rubyonrails.org/active_storage_overview.html`.

Also, be aware that Active Storage is not the only solution for handling file attachments. Other gems like CarrierWave and Shrine offer robust alternatives to Active Storage.

CHAPTER 11

Action Text

With version 6, Rails introduced a system to make it easy to enhance text areas with WYSIWYG (What You See Is What You Get) editors. Often, developers need to allow users—who may not be HTML-savvy—to edit HTML content. Rails developers have previously needed to choose from a variety of JavaScript-based WYSIWYG editors, integrate the assets into the Asset Pipeline, and connect them with the desired text area inputs. While Rails developers still have the freedom to do this if we desire, Action Text gives us first-class option.

In this chapter, we'll cover the steps necessary to allow the users in our blog application to easily use HTML when editing their articles' body fields.

Installation

To add support for using Action Text, we'll need to do a few things. First, Action Text stores its data in a separate table (similar to Active Storage, as we saw in the previous chapter). Thankfully, Rails gives us a simple way to generate the needed database migrations. Next, we'll need to include Action Text's JavaScript and CSS in our application.

The first step is to run the `action_text:install` command, as shown in the following with the output:

```
> rails action_text:install
Copying actiontext.scss to app/assets/stylesheets
      create  app/assets/stylesheets/actiontext.scss
Copying fixtures to test/fixtures/action_text/rich_texts.yml
      create  test/fixtures/action_text/rich_texts.yml
Copying blob rendering partial to app/views/active_storage/blobs/_blob.
html.erb
      create  app/views/active_storage/blobs/_blob.html.erb
```

© Brady Somerville, Adam Gamble, Cloves Carneiro Jr and Rida Al Barazi 2020
B. Somerville et al., *Beginning Rails 6*, https://doi.org/10.1007/978-1-4842-5716-6_11

```
Installing JavaScript dependencies
         run  yarn add trix@^1.0.0 @rails/actiontext@^6.0.2-1 from "."
yarn add v1.21.0
[1/4]   Resolving packages...
[2/4]   Fetching packages...
[3/4]   Linking dependencies...
[4/4]   Building fresh packages...
success Saved lockfile.
success Saved 2 new dependencies.
info Direct dependencies
├─ @rails/actiontext@6.0.2-1
└─ trix@1.2.2
info All dependencies
├─ @rails/actiontext@6.0.2-1
└─ trix@1.2.2
✦ Done in 4.81s.
Adding trix to app/javascript/packs/application.js
     append  app/javascript/packs/application.js
Adding @rails/actiontext to app/javascript/packs/application.js
     append  app/javascript/packs/application.js
Copied migration 20200304234710_create_action_text_tables.action_text.rb
from action_text
```

Your output may differ slightly, but take note of some of the things this simple
command did:

- Added Action Text's CSS to our app

- Added Action Text's JavaScript dependencies to our package.json and
  yarn.lock files

- Installed Action Text's JavaScript dependencies into our node_
  modules directory

- Added Action Text's JavaScript to our app's JavaScript pack

- Created the database migration we need to store Action Text data

The only thing left for us to do is to run our database migrations:

```
> rails db:migrate
== 20200304234710 CreateActionTextTables: migrating ===============
-- create_table(:action_text_rich_texts)
   -> 0.0048s
== 20200304234710 CreateActionTextTables: migrated (0.0049s) =======
```

Next we'll describe each of the changes that just happened in a little more detail. We could just skip ahead to enhancing a blog, but we can learn a little bit by paying closer attention to these details.

Action Text CSS

The *action_text:install* command we ran magically added Action Text's CSS to our application, so that the Trix editor (Action Text's WYSIWYG editor of choice) has the styles it needs to look good.

But how did it do this? It simply added the file app/assets/stylesheets/actiontext.css. Don't we need to explicitly load that style sheet somewhere? By default, we don't need to. Listing 11-1 shows an excerpt from our main style sheet.

Listing 11-1. Excerpt from app/assets/stylesheets/application.css
https://gist.github.com/nicedawg/92ed0bf488b5b4aee1eef85982f8383a

```
/*
 * This is a manifest file that'll be compiled into application.css, which
   will include all the files
 * listed below.
 *
 * Any CSS and SCSS file within this directory, lib/assets/stylesheets, or
   any plugin's
 * vendor/assets/stylesheets directory can be referenced here using a
   relative path.
 *
 * You're free to add application-wide styles to this file and they'll
   appear at the bottom of the
```

```
* compiled file so the styles you add here take precedence over styles
  defined in any other CSS/SCSS
* files in this directory. Styles in this file should be added after the
  last require_* statement.
* It is generally better to create a new file per style scope.
*
*= require_tree .
*= require_self
*/
...
```

The comments are helpful here, so read them closely. Essentially, they're saying you could add a special comment line like /*= require 'shiny' */ and Rails will look for a CSS file named "shiny.scss" or "shiny.css" in a few of your application's directories. If it finds one, it will include it in your application.css file. If it doesn't find one in your app's directories, it will then start looking in your included *gems* for a style sheet with the given name.

This is good to know, but it doesn't answer our question—how did Action Text's CSS actually get added to our application.css? The answer is in the bolded line—the "= *require_tree* ." directive in our comment says "look for any style sheets in this directory and any subdirectories and include them." Since the *action_text:install* command added app/assets/stylesheets/actiontext.scss, the *require_tree* directive included that style sheet automatically.

This is a great example of how Rails again uses convention over configuration to simplify the process of adding a style sheet. However, there may be times when *require_tree* is undesirable. Perhaps you need to control the order of style sheet inclusion, or maybe you need to exclude certain style sheets from being included. In those cases, you may need to use the *require* directive to explicitly list the style sheets you wish to include. We won't need to do that for our application, but it's good to know this exists. For more information on these directives (like *require_tree* and *require)*, see https://guides.rubyonrails.org/asset_pipeline.html#manifest-files-and-directives.

Let's take a quick look at the actiontext.scss file which our *action_text:install* command added in Listing 11-2.

Listing 11-2. app/assets/stylesheets/actiontext.scss

https://gist.github.com/nicedawg/aa815191362c98adb5e445c4e803ea82

```scss
//
// Provides a drop-in pointer for the default Trix stylesheet that will
format the toolbar and
// the trix-editor content (whether displayed or under editing). Feel free
to incorporate this
// inclusion directly in any other asset bundle and remove this file.
//
//= require trix/dist/trix

// We need to override trix.css's image gallery styles to accommodate the
// <action-text-attachment> element we wrap around attachments. Otherwise,
// images in galleries will be squished by the max-width: 33%; rule.
.trix-content {
  .attachment-gallery {
    > action-text-attachment,
    > .attachment {
      flex: 1 0 33%;
      padding: 0 0.5em;
      max-width: 33%;
    }

    &.attachment-gallery--2,
    &.attachment-gallery--4 {
      > action-text-attachment,
      > .attachment {
        flex-basis: 50%;
        max-width: 50%;
      }
    }
  }

  action-text-attachment {
    .attachment {
      padding: 0 !important;
```

```
    max-width: 100% !important;
  }
 }
}
```

This style sheet is included in our main style sheet. Notice the bolded text. *This* style sheet includes another style sheet—trix/dist/trix. Where does that come from? We didn't notice that getting added to our application. The *require* directive also loads from our *node_modules* directory. If you look in *node_modules/trix/dist*, you'll see a *trix.css* file. Apparently, Trix's default CSS needed just a bit of tweaking to work with Action Text, so our *actiontext.scss* adds some overrides.

Action Text JavaScript

We just learned how Action Text integrated its CSS into our app; now, we'll take a look at how Action Text integrated its JavaScript into our app.

In the output of `action_text:install`, we see that it ran the command "`yarn add trix@^1.0.0 @rails/actiontext@^6.0.2-1 from "."`" Several things happened here:

- An entry was added to package.json which listed *trix* as a JavaScript dependency, requiring the version number to begin with 1.

- An entry was added to package.json which listed *@rails/actiontext* as a JavaScript dependency, requiring the version number to begin with 6.

- The latest versions of those JavaScript libraries (which satisfied the version requirements) were downloaded into our app's *node_ modules* directory.

- The *exact* versions of these two JavaScript libraries (and *their* dependencies) were added to yarn.lock, to ensure that future installations of these libraries for our app will receive the exact same versions.

Then, the *action_text:install* command appended a couple of lines to our app/ javascript/packs/application.js file, as shown in Listing 11-3.

Listing 11-3. app/javascripts/packs/application.js
https://gist.github.com/nicedawg/b647350cce50f921b2e8ab666474b841

```
// This file is automatically compiled by Webpack, along with any other files
// present in this directory. You're encouraged to place your actual application logic in
// a relevant structure within app/javascript and only use these pack files to reference
// that code so it'll be compiled.

require("@rails/ujs").start()
require("turbolinks").start()
require("@rails/activestorage").start()
require("channels")

// Uncomment to copy all static images under ../images to the output folder and reference
// them with the image_pack_tag helper in views (e.g <%= image_pack_tag 'rails.png' %>)
// or the `imagePath` JavaScript helper below.
//
// const images = require.context('../images', true)
// const imagePath = (name) => images(name, true)
```

require("trix")
require("@rails/actiontext")

Similar to how Action Text's CSS was included in our application.css, the bolded *require* lines include Action Text's JavaScript in our main application.js pack. We can use *require* in our JavaScript files to include other JavaScript files from our own application (e.g., app/javascript/shiny.js) or to include JavaScript files from our app's *dependencies* found in our *node_modules* directory. (The latter is where our *trix* and *@rails/actiontext* JavaScript dependencies are found.)

Action Text Database Storage

The last task our *action_text:install* command performed was to generate a migration to store our Action Text data. After running the migration, we see the following table added to our db/schema.rb, as shown in Listing 11-4.

Listing 11-4. Action Text Table Added to db/schema.rb

https://gist.github.com/nicedawg/b4d79afe726e026afae59821a3b70385

```
...
  create_table "action_text_rich_texts", force: :cascade do |t|
    t.string "name", null: false
    t.text "body"
    t.string "record_type", null: false
    t.integer "record_id", null: false
    t.datetime "created_at", precision: 6, null: false
    t.datetime "updated_at", precision: 6, null: false
    t.index ["record_type", "record_id", "name"], name: "index_action_text_
    rich_texts_uniqueness", unique: true
  end
...
```

Similar to the *active_storage_attachments* table from the previous chapter's work, the *action_text_rich_texts* table is a *polymorphic* table, meaning it can belong to many different types of Active Record models by using the *record_type* column to store the class name of the model a particular *action_text_rich_texts* row belongs to, along with the *record_id* column to identify which particular record (of type *record_type*) it belongs to.

For illustration, consider the sample data which might appear in the *action_text_ rich_texts* database table in Table 11-1.

Table 11-1. *Sample Data in the action_text_rich_texts Database Table*

id	name	body	record_type	record_id
1	body	<p>Hey!</p>	Article	1
2	body	<p>Yo</p>	FAQ	1
3	excerpt	<p>Hi</p>	Article	1
4	body	<p>:-)</p>	Article	2

In this sample data, we see that

- Article 1 has a body of "<p>Hey!</p>" and an excerpt of "<p>Hi</p>".

- FAQ 1 has a body of "<p>Yo</p>".

- Article 2 has a body of "<p>:-)</p>", but no excerpt.

As you can see, this structure is very flexible. It can hold the content for any attribute of any model. This usually is much more convenient than needing to define separate database storage each model's rich text needs.

Using Action Text in Our Blog

Now that we've investigated how Action Text adds its CSS, JavaScript, and database storage needs to our app, we can enhance our blog with greater understanding of what's happening behind the scenes. In the following steps, we will allow our users to create articles with HTML bodies.

Updating the Article Model

First, we need to make our Article model aware that we want to use Action Text for its *body* attribute.

In Listing 11-5, we declare in our Article model that we want to use Action Text to handle its *body* attribute.

Listing 11-5. Adding Action Text to Article#body

https://gist.github.com/nicedawg/98424877354b24411de2dbe5d2a1fa79

```
class Article < ApplicationRecord
  validates :title, :body, presence: true

  belongs_to :user
  has_and_belongs_to_many :categories
  has_many :comments

  has_one_attached :cover_image
  attr_accessor :remove_cover_image
  after_save { cover_image.purge if remove_cover_image == '1' }

  has_rich_text :body

  scope :published, -> { where.not(published_at: nil) }
  scope :draft, -> { where(published_at: nil) }
  scope :recent, -> { where('articles.published_at > ?', 1.week.ago.to_
  date) }
  scope :where_title, -> (term) { where("articles.title LIKE ?",
  "%#{term}%") }

  def long_title
    "#{title} - #{published_at}"
  end

  def published?
    published_at.present?
  end

  def owned_by?(owner)
    return false unless owner.is_a?(User)
    user == owner
  end
end
```

By adding *has_rich_text :body*, a few things happened behind the scenes. Now, *Article#body* is a *has_one* relation which returns the relevant *ActionText::RichText* object from the *action_text_rich_texts* table, rather than returning the value of the *body* column from the *articles* table. Also, assigning to the body (e.g., article.body = "<p>Hey!</p>") now assigns the given value to the body attribute of the *ActionText::RichText* related object, rather than the article's old *body* attribute. Lastly, adding *has_rich_text :body* added a couple of scopes to our class to make it easier to include the related ActionText::RichText objects, helping us avoid N+1 queries. We'll demonstrate this later in the chapter.

Migrating Our Data

You may have noticed in the previous section that one side effect of using *has_rich_content :body* is that the value is retrieved from (and stored in) a different table. If we were starting from scratch, no problem. However, we have some data in our *articles* table's *body* column which is now being ignored! To preserve our data (and for illustration), we'll migrate our *body* data from the *articles* table to the *action_text_rich_texts* table. Then we'll add a migration to remove the *body* column from the *articles* table; since we no longer need it, we should remove it to prevent possible confusion down the road.

First, let's generate a migration to copy our *body* data from the *articles* table to the *action_text_rich_texts* table. Run the following command to generate the migration file:

```
> rails g migration MigrateArticleBodyToActionText
```

Next, modify the generated migration file to look like Listing 11-6. (Note: In my case, that's db/migrate/20200305025834_migrate_article_body_to_action_text.rb, but your timestamp will differ.)

Listing 11-6. Migrating Article Body Data to ActionText::RichText
https://gist.github.com/nicedawg/5654a9de5ac781d71462912af754d659

```
class MigrateArticleBodyToActionText < ActiveRecord::Migration[6.0]
  def up
    execute <<-SQL
      INSERT INTO action_text_rich_texts (
        name,
        body,
        record_type,
        record_id,
        created_at,
```

323

```
        updated_at
      ) SELECT
        'body' AS name,
        body,
        "Article",
        id,
        created_at,
        updated_at
      FROM articles
    SQL
  end

  def down
    execute <<-SQL
      DELETE FROM action_text_rich_texts
    SQL
  end
end
```

Let's talk about this migration. First, notice we defined separate *up* and *down* methods in this migration; we need to execute some custom SQL, so we need to declare what should happen in each direction.

When migrating *up*, we added some SQL to create *action_text_rich_texts* records using our *articles* data. We used the *INSERT INTO .. SELECT...* syntax which most SQL databases understand. It may look complicated, but it's essentially saying "for each record in the *articles* table, create a record in the *action_text_rich_texts* by mapping these values to those."

Let's run the migration and then query the database directly to see how our data looks:

```
> rails db:migrate
> rails dbconsole
sqlite> .headers on
sqlite> .mode column
sqlite> SELECT * FROM articles;
sqlite> SELECT * FROM action_text_rich_texts;
sqlite> .exit
```

Let's explain those sqlite commands. "*.headers on*" adds headers to the display of output in the SQLite console. "*.mode column*" formats the output to be in a column layout. We took the time to configure these options to make the next two steps easier to read. Then, we get the contents of the *articles* and *action_text_rich_texts* tables. You should see the same number of records in each, and you should see the *action_text_rich_texts* table populated with data that matches the *article* record to which it corresponds.

Now that we are confident the *data* looks okay, we can try it out in *rails console*:

```
> rails console
irb(main):001:0> Article.first.body
  (0.4ms)  SELECT sqlite_version(*)
  Article Load (0.2ms)  SELECT "articles".* FROM "articles" ORDER BY
  "articles"."id" ASC LIMIT ?   [["LIMIT", 1]]
  ActionText::RichText Load (0.2ms)  SELECT "action_text_rich_texts".* FROM
  "action_text_rich_texts" WHERE "action_text_rich_texts"."record_id" = ?
  AND "action_text_rich_texts"."record_type" = ? AND "action_text_rich_
  texts"."name" = ? LIMIT ?   [["record_id", 1], ["record_type", "Article"],
  ["name", "body"], ["LIMIT", 1]]
  Rendered /Users/brady.somerville/.rbenv/versions/2.6.5/lib/ruby/
  gems/2.6.0/gems/actiontext-6.0.2.1/app/views/action_text/content/_layout.
  html.erb (Duration: 1.8ms | Allocations: 478)
=> #<ActionText::RichText id: 9, name: "body", body: #<ActionText::Content
"<div class=\"trix-conte...">, record_type: "Article", record_id: 1,
created_at: "2020-02-25 02:23:56", updated_at: "2020-02-29 15:41:47">
```

As the console output shows, *Article.first.body* did a few things. First, it loaded the Article object. Then, it loaded its corresponding *ActionText::RichText* object for the *body* attribute. Then it loaded an action_text template! Lastly, it returned the body as an instance of the *ActionText::RichText* class. Notice the body value of the *ActionText::RichText* object—it's actually an instance of the *ActionText::Content* class. We won't dig even further at this point, but just know this means our simple *Article#body* attribute now has a lot of new behavior attached to it.

Now that we know our *Article* model is fetching its *body* content from Action Text's database tables, let's add a database migration to remove the *body* column from the *articles* table. This isn't necessary, but since we aren't using it (and we're **sure** we don't need its data anymore), we'll remove it to keep things tidy.

Run the following Rails command to generate another migration:

```
> rails g migration RemoveBodyFromArticles body:text
```

By following the naming convention and adding the name and data type of the column we wish to remove, Rails generates exactly the migration we need, as seen in Listing 11-7.

Listing 11-7. Migration to Remove the Body Column from the Articles Table
https://gist.github.com/nicedawg/176b87f36550f8269fa4afcf73f4502e

```
class RemoveBodyFromArticles < ActiveRecord::Migration[6.0]
  def change

    remove_column :articles, :body, :text
  end
end
```

This migration will remove the *body* column from the *articles* table when migrating upward and will add the column back when calling *rails db:rollback*. However, when rolling back, it won't restore the data. We're okay with that, because we know we don't need it, but be aware that extra steps would be necessary if that were not the case.

Run `rails db:migrate` to actually remove the unneeded column from *articles*:

```
> rails db:migrate
```

At this point, we feel confident that our *Article* model is correctly integrated with Action Text, so let's continue enhancing our blog application.

Updating the Article View

After having updated our *Article* model to use Action Text for its *body*, if you were try to load the root path (or /articles path) of our application, you would see an error: "NoMethodError in Articles#index: undefined method `strip' for #<ActionText::RichTex t:0x00007ff6f6b51478>". We shouldn't be too surprised; we changed what type of object *article.body* returns, so we have to deal with it a little differently.

We were using *simple_format* in the article partial template to safely allow links (and other basic HTML) in the display of our article bodies. Modify your app/views/articles/_article.html.erb file to match Listing 11-8.

Listing 11-8. Displaying Action Text Content in _article.html.erb

`https://gist.github.com/nicedawg/2c3d1d2f14899ffb944099879935857c`

```erb
<div class="article">
  <h3>
    <%= link_to article.title, article %>
    <% if article.owned_by? current_user %>
      <span class="actions">
        <%= link_to 'Edit', edit_article_path(article) %>
        <%= link_to 'Delete', article, confirm: 'Are you sure?', method:
        :delete %>
      </span>
    <% end %>
  </h3>
  <hr>
  <% if article.cover_image.attached? %>
    <%= image_tag article.cover_image.variant(resize_to_limit: local_
    assigns.fetch(:cover_image_options, [200, 200])) %>
    <hr>
  <% end %>
  <%= article.body %>
</div>
```

After updating app/views/articles/_article.html.erb, we can now load the various pages that display an article body without error. Nothing really looks different than before, but that's good! Our article bodies don't have any HTML in them. *Yet.*

Updating the Article Form

Now, almost everything's in place. The support system for articles having HTML in their *body* fields is there; we just need to update the form to use a WYSIWYG editor.

Again, Action Text makes this easy. Edit your app/views/articles/_form.html.erb to match Listing 11-9.

Listing 11-9. Updating the Article Form to Use the Trix Editor for Its Body Input

https://gist.github.com/nicedawg/d76b2b3ad4e4b1dd5eefd2af2f1a5a3f

```erb
<%= form_with(model: article, local: true) do |form| %>
  <% if article.errors.any? %>
    <div id="error_explanation">
      <h2><%= pluralize(article.errors.count, "error") %> prohibited this
      article from being saved:</h2>

      <ul>
        <% article.errors.full_messages.each do |message| %>
          <li><%= message %></li>
        <% end %>
      </ul>
    </div>
  <% end %>

  <div class="field">
    <%= form.label :title %>
    <%= form.text_field :title %>
  </div>

  <div class="field">
    <%= form.label :cover_image %>
    <%= form.file_field :cover_image %>

    <% if article.cover_image.attached? %>
      <p>
        <%= image_tag article.cover_image.variant(resize_to_limit:
        [50, 50]) %>
        <br>
        <%= form.label :remove_cover_image do %>
          <%= form.check_box :remove_cover_image %> Remove this image
        <% end %>
      </p>
    <% end %>
  </div>
```

```erb
  <div class="field">
    <%= form.label :location %>
    <%= form.text_field :location %>
  </div>

  <div class="field">
    <%= form.collection_check_boxes(:category_ids, Category.all, :id,
    :name) do |b| %>
      <% b.label { b.check_box + b.text } %>
    <% end %>
  </div>

  <div class="field">
    <%= form.label :excerpt %>
    <%= form.text_field :excerpt %>
  </div>

  <div class="field">
    <%= form.label :body %>
    <%= form.rich_text_area :body %>
  </div>

  <div class="field">
    <%= form.label :published_at %>
    <%= form.datetime_select :published_at %>
  </div>

  <div class="actions">
    <%= submit_or_cancel(form) %>
  </div>
<% end %>
```

As you can see, all we had to do was replace the *text_area* form helper we were using for the *body* attribute with the *rich_text_area* form helper which Action Text provides. Edit an article, and see our WYSIWYG editor for the body tag in action! Your article form should look something like Figure 11-1.

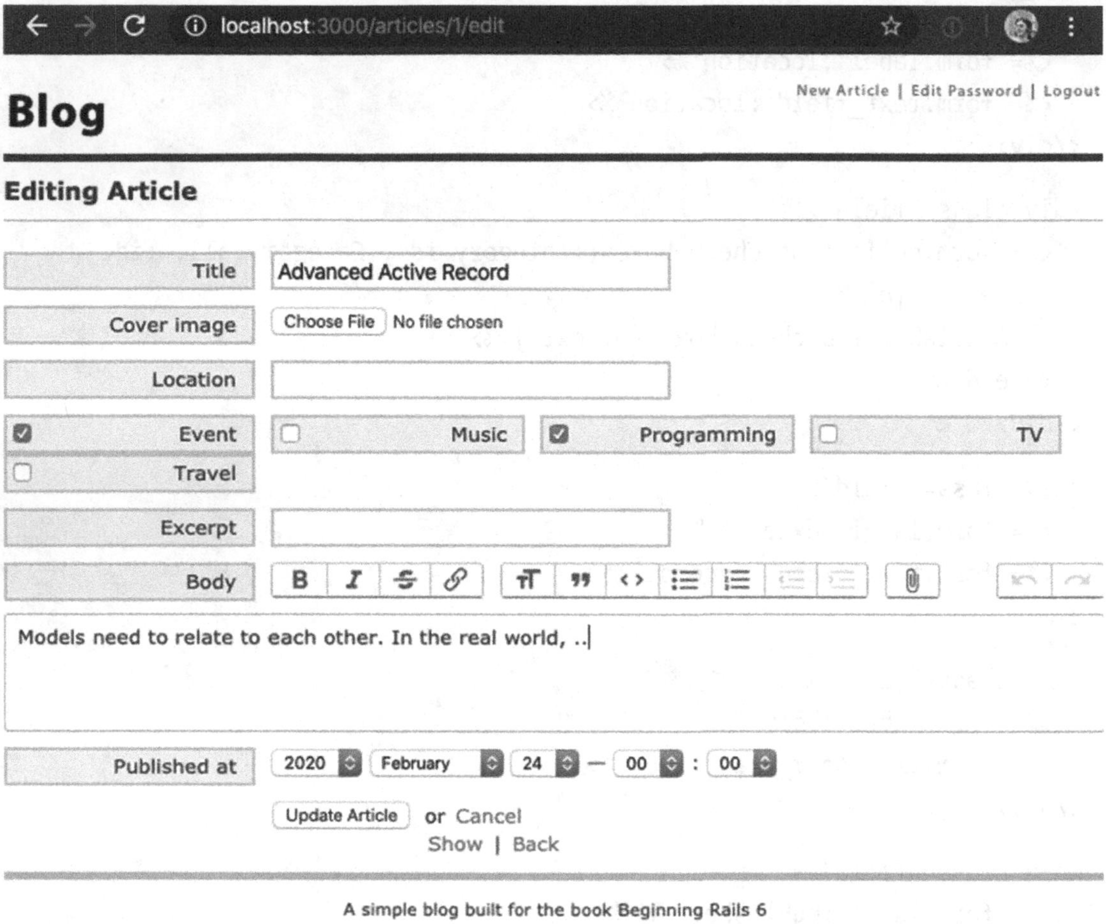

Figure 11-1. *Article form using Trix as WYSIWYG editor for the body field*

Try it out! Restart your Rails server to be sure all of our new code is loaded, and use the article form to add content to your body, using Trix's toolbar to make some of your content bold and add links, lists, and other formatting. Then view the article, and see your fancy formatting in the body tag.

Cleaning Up N+1 Queries

In an earlier section in this chapter, we described what happened when we added *has_rich_text :body* to our *Article* model. One of the benefits we described was the inclusion of scopes to help us deal with N+1 queries.

Why is this necessary? While viewing your *rails server* output, load the root path (which renders each article in your database), and notice how many SQL queries are executed. See Listing 11-10 for an example.

Listing 11-10. Too Many SQL Queries for Loading Articles
https://gist.github.com/nicedawg/70ba78c747b96fa0ec4d7a924b760586

```
Started GET "/" for ::1 at 2020-03-04 23:04:50 -0600
Processing by ArticlesController#index as HTML
  Rendering articles/index.html.erb within layouts/application
  Article Load (0.2ms)  SELECT "articles".* FROM "articles"
  ↳ app/views/articles/index.html.erb:4
  User Load (0.2ms)  SELECT "users".* FROM "users" WHERE "users"."id" = ?
  LIMIT ?  [["id", 2], ["LIMIT", 1]]
  ↳ app/controllers/application_controller.rb:6:in `current_user'
  CACHE User Load (0.0ms)  SELECT "users".* FROM "users" WHERE "users"."id"
  = ? LIMIT ?  [["id", 2], ["LIMIT", 1]]
  ↳ app/models/article.rb:29:in `owned_by?'
  ActiveStorage::Attachment Load (0.2ms)  SELECT "active_storage_
  attachments".* FROM "active_storage_attachments"...
  ↳ app/views/articles/_article.html.erb:12
  ActionText::RichText Load (0.2ms)  SELECT "action_text_rich_texts".* FROM
  "action_text_rich_texts"...
  ↳ app/views/articles/_article.html.erb:16
  User Load (0.3ms)  SELECT "users".* FROM "users" WHERE "users"."id" = ?
  LIMIT ?  [["id", 1], ["LIMIT", 1]]
  ↳ app/models/article.rb:29:in `owned_by?'
  ActiveStorage::Attachment Load (0.3ms)  SELECT "active_storage_
  attachments".* FROM "active_storage_attachments"...
  ↳ app/views/articles/_article.html.erb:12
  ActionText::RichText Load (0.3ms)  SELECT "action_text_rich_texts".* FROM
  "action_text_rich_texts"...
  ↳ app/views/articles/_article.html.erb:16
  CACHE User Load (0.0ms)  SELECT "users".* FROM "users" WHERE "users"."id"
  = ? LIMIT ?  [["id", 1], ["LIMIT", 1]]
```

```
↳ app/models/article.rb:29:in `owned_by?'
ActiveStorage::Attachment Load (0.2ms)  SELECT "active_storage_
attachments".* FROM "active_storage_attachments"...
↳ app/views/articles/_article.html.erb:12
ActionText::RichText Load (0.2ms)  SELECT "action_text_rich_texts".* FROM
"action_text_rich_texts"...
↳ app/views/articles/_article.html.erb:16
ActiveStorage::Attachment Load (0.2ms)  SELECT "active_storage_
attachments".* FROM "active_storage_attachments"...
↳ app/views/articles/_article.html.erb:12
ActionText::RichText Load (0.2ms)  SELECT "action_text_rich_texts".* FROM
"action_text_rich_texts"...
↳ app/views/articles/_article.html.erb:16
Rendered collection of articles/_article.html.erb [4 times] (Duration:
48.2ms | Allocations: 13120)
Rendered articles/index.html.erb within layouts/application (Duration:
49.9ms | Allocations: 13897)
[Webpacker] Everything's up-to-date. Nothing to do
Completed 200 OK in 68ms (Views: 64.7ms | ActiveRecord: 2.6ms |
Allocations: 19139)
```

To help make the output easier to read, we truncated and omitted extremely long lines. But scanning the output, we see a pattern; over and over again, we query the same three tables: users, active_storage_attachments, and action_text_rich_texts.

At this point, we only have a few articles, so the performance hit of making at least three queries may not be noticeable. But each article in our database would result in at least three queries being executed, so imagine if we had 50 articles or 100. This doesn't scale, so we need to deal with these N+1 queries we've accumulated along the way.

To combat these N+1 queries in our articles index, we just need to make a simple change to our ArticlesController. Modify your app/controllers/articles_controller.rb so it resembles Listing 11-11.

Listing 11-11. Fixing N+1 Queries in ArticlesController

https://gist.github.com/nicedawg/e47509b6a42e7732475c0db89bf40b65

```
class ArticlesController < ApplicationController
  before_action :authenticate, except: [:index, :show]
  before_action :set_article, only: [:show, :edit, :update, :destroy]

  # GET /articles
  # GET /articles.json
  def index
    @articles = Article.includes(:user).with_rich_text_body.with_attached_
    cover_image.all
  end

  # rest of code omitted for brevity
end
```

Instead of simply calling *Article.all*, we add a few things to eliminate our N+1 queries. First, we use *.includes(:user)* to hint to Active Record that we want to know the user which each article belongs to. (*:user* is the name of the relevant association, so that's what we provide to *includes*. Next, we chain the *with_rich_text_body* scope. This scope was added automatically to our Article class when we added *has_rich_content :body* and similarly hints to Rails we want to efficiently load the relevant *action_text_rich_texts* records for each article. Lastly, we chain the *with_attached_cover_image* scope, which Active Storage automatically added to our class when we added *has_one_attached :cover_image* in the previous chapter.

Now that we've addressed these N+1 queries, watch the *rails server* output again while you load the root path. It should resemble Listing 11-12.

Listing 11-12. No More N+1 Queries When Loading Articles

https://gist.github.com/nicedawg/cfe9422f14763cbf831a224d7c74b8c5

```
Started GET "/" for ::1 at 2020-03-04 23:27:15 -0600
Processing by ArticlesController#index as HTML
  Rendering articles/index.html.erb within layouts/application
  Article Load (0.2ms)  SELECT "articles".* FROM "articles"
  ↳ app/views/articles/index.html.erb:4
```

```
User Load (0.4ms)  SELECT "users".* FROM "users" WHERE "users"."id" IN
(?, ?)  [["id", 2], ["id", 1]]
↳ app/views/articles/index.html.erb:4
ActionText::RichText Load (0.4ms)  SELECT "action_text_rich_texts".* FROM
"action_text_rich_texts"...
↳ app/views/articles/index.html.erb:4
ActiveStorage::Attachment Load (0.3ms)  SELECT "active_storage_
attachments".* FROM "active_storage_attachments"...
↳ app/views/articles/index.html.erb:4
User Load (0.1ms)  SELECT "users".* FROM "users" WHERE "users"."id" = ?
LIMIT ?  [["id", 2], ["LIMIT", 1]]
↳ app/controllers/application_controller.rb:6:in `current_user'
Rendered collection of articles/_article.html.erb [4 times] (Duration:
12.5ms | Allocations: 3421)
Rendered articles/index.html.erb within layouts/application (Duration:
24.7ms | Allocations: 7684)
[Webpacker] Everything's up-to-date. Nothing to do
Completed 200 OK in 36ms (Views: 32.9ms | ActiveRecord: 1.5ms |
Allocations: 13062)
```

Again, note that we truncated and omitted some extremely long lines for clarity. But look again for the SELECT statements. Instead of dozens of SELECT statements, there are only a few! This is a good sign that our optimizations were effective.

Summary

In this chapter, we ran the *action_text:install* command and investigated what changes it made to our app in order to support using *Trix* as a WYSIWYG editor. Then, we enhanced our blog application by allowing users to create HTML in their articles' bodies without needing to learn HTML.

While we ended up covering most of what you need to know to work with Action Text, `https://edgeguides.rubyonrails.org/action_text_overview.html` is a great resource for future reference.

CHAPTER 12

Sending and Receiving Email

It's a rare web application that doesn't need to send email from time to time. For example, you may want to send messages to welcome users who sign up on your website, send "reset password" links, or confirm orders placed with an online store. Rails ships with a library called Action Mailer, which provides developers with an easy-to-use yet powerful tool to handle email.

This chapter explains how Action Mailer works and how to use it in your applications. You first learn how to configure it, and then you'll see a few examples of how to send email in various formats.

In addition to sending email, your Rails app can also *receive* email with the help of Action Mailbox—a new feature in Rails 6. With Action Mailbox, we can receive email destined for different email addresses, parse the email however we want, and then decide what action to take (if any) in response to that email. For example, we could allow authors to send an email to our app, which would then parse the email and create an unpublished article—great for allowing authors to save ideas for an article when it's not convenient for them to use the browser. Toward the end of the chapter, we'll add the ability for our blog to do just that.

Note If you need to get the code at the exact point where you finished Chapter 11, download the source code zip file from the book's page on `www.apress.com` and extract it on your computer.

335

© Brady Somerville, Adam Gamble, Cloves Carneiro Jr and Rida Al Barazi 2020
B. Somerville et al., *Beginning Rails 6*, https://doi.org/10.1007/978-1-4842-5716-6_12

Setting Up Action Mailer

Like Active Record and Action Pack, Action Mailer is one of the components that make up the Rails framework. It works much like the other components of Rails: mailers are implemented to behave like controllers, and mailer templates are implemented as views. Because it's integrated into the framework, it's easy to set up and use, and it requires very little configuration to get going.

When you send email using an email client such as Outlook or a web-based email application like Gmail or Yahoo Mail, your messages are sent via a mail server. Unlike a web server, Rails doesn't provide a built-in mail server. You need to tell Action Mailer where your email server is located and how to connect to it. This sounds a bit complicated, but it's really quite easy. Depending on the kind of computer you're using, you may have a mail server built in (this is true of most UNIX systems). If not, you can use the same server that you use to process your regular email. If this is the case, you can find your server information in your email client settings, as provided by your Internet service provider (ISP), or in the settings section of your web-based email application, like Gmail.

Configuring Mail Server Settings

Before you can send email from your Rails application, you need to tell Action Mailer how to communicate with your mail server. Action Mailer can be configured to send email using either `sendmail` or a Simple Mail Transfer Protocol (SMTP) server. SMTP is the core Internet protocol for relaying email messages between servers. If you're on Linux, OS X, or any other UNIX-based system, you're in luck: you can use `sendmail`, and as long as it's in the standard location (`/usr/bin/sendmail`), you don't need to configure anything. If you're on Windows or if you want to use SMTP, you have some work to do.

Action Mailer options are set at the class level on `ActionMailer::Base`. The best place to set these options is in your environment files, located in the `config` directory of your application. You can also add your configuration in an initializer file in `config/initializers`; doing so ensures that your settings apply for all environments. In most cases, though, you have different settings for the development and production environments; so it may be wiser to add settings in any of the environment-specific configuration files (`config/environments/*.rb`), because this takes precedence over the global configuration.

This section describes how to set up Action Mailer to use SMTP, because it works on all systems and is the default delivery method. To do this, you supply the SMTP settings via the `smtp_settings` option. The `smtp_settings` method expects a hash of options, most of which are shown in Table 12-1.

Table 12-1. *Server Connection Settings*

Setting	Description
address	The address of your mail server. The default is `localhost`.
port	The port number of your mail server. The default is port 25.
domain	If your email server responds to different domain names, you may need to specify your domain name here.
authentication	If your mail server requires authentication, you need to specify the authentication type here. This can be one of `:plain`, `:login`, or `:cram_md5`.
user_name	The username you use to authenticate when you connect to the mail server, if your server requires authentication.
password	The password you use to authenticate when you connect to the mail server, if your server requires authentication.

Storing Sensitive Secrets

Since we know we're going to need to set some sensitive information in our configuration—our user_name and password for our SMTP server—we need to know where to put them. We *could* just put them directly in our config file. While that would be the simplest choice, it's not the safest choice. Our config files may be version controlled, deployed to servers, or copied to developers' laptops—and our sensitive information will be sitting there in plain text, vulnerable to misuse. How can we prevent this?

Naturally, there are various ways to prevent this. A common approach is to put sensitive configuration values in environment variables which are *not* version controlled and must be manually added and updated to servers and workstations as they're needed. The Rails application would then fetch these values from the special *ENV* hash. This approach works well, but can be tedious to maintain. For example, when a code change requires a new environment variable, care must be taken to ensure the servers are updated with the new environment variables in conjunction with deploying the code. This can be an error-prone manual task.

Rails now offers an integrated approach, called *credentials*. With Rails' approach to handling sensitive information, we generate a secret key in config/master.key which is *not* to be version controlled. (But it can and should be shared with other developers and servers.) This secret key can then be used to encrypt and decrypt a YAML file which stores our sensitive data–in config/credentials.yml.enc. This strikes a good balance between security and convenience; we only share the master key once, and then future updates to the contents of config/credentials.yml.enc are shared via version control, and we avoid the risks of storing sensitive data in plain text.

To safely store our SMTP username and password, we will use Rails' credentials system. (Note: If you downloaded the source code for this book, you received an encoded credentials file—config/credentials.yml.enc—for which you don't have the key. Simply remove that file before beginning.) First, let's run the Rails command to edit our encrypted credentials file:

```
> rails credentials:edit
```

Running this command will open an editor with the unencrypted contents of config/credentials.yml.enc. Now we can edit our sensitive credentials, and when we save and close our editor, the contents will be encrypted again and saved.

Easy enough, but there's one complication—*which* editor will it use? Like many CLI (command-line interface) programs, *rails credentials* delegates that decision to the *$EDITOR* environment variable on your system. Depending on your system, this may be a console-based editor like *nano* or *vim*, or on Windows it could be *Notepad*. If the default editor isn't to your liking, use your favorite search engine to find how to set your preferred default editor for command-line programs like *rails credentials:edit*.

After running *rails credentials:edit* to open your unencrypted credentials in your editor, edit your credentials file to match Listing 12-1, but with *your* SMTP username and password, of course. (Note: Your secret_key_base value will likely be different. That's okay!)

Listing 12-1. Adding SMTP Credentials via rails credentials:edit
https://gist.github.com/nicedawg/d1691274c9b99de6cf81a80a89d3ae3f

```
# Used as the base secret for all MessageVerifiers in Rails, including the
one protecting cookies.
```

```
secret_key_base: 42cd449ceeb465562463941be28c64e7786cfe482fcf8b5e4f51f5605c
6b1a155b3cb2ef1baa221e27c5dc41b778a0dc91b26f956aa6a3f295ae098a67a3f891

smtp:
  user_name: "beginningrails@gmail.com"
  password: "changeme"
```

Save and close your editor, and your config/credentials.yml.enc file will be created or updated to include your encrypted information. Now that we have our sensitive data securely stored, we can configure our SMTP settings in our config files and reference our encrypted credentials rather than store them in plain text.

Let's configure our SMTP settings now. Listing 12-2 shows a typical configuration for a server that requires authentication, in this case, Gmail. You can use this sample configuration as a starting point to configure your connection. Change each of the settings to connect to your own SMTP server. You may need to search for correct SMTP settings for your particular email service. If you're using sendmail as the delivery method, add *config.action_mailer.delivery_method = :sendmail*; then, everything should "just work."

In addition to configuring our SMTP settings, we also go ahead and set *default_url_ options* to include our *host* URL in the development environment so that links in our emails can point back to our app.

Listing 12-2. Sample Action Mailer Configuration Using SMTP, in config/ environments/*.rb https://gist.github.com/nicedawg/0424d7892cbb3ef3e0fa 87f2a777f40c

```
Rails.application.configure do
  # Settings specified here will take precedence over those in config/
  application.rb.

  # In the development environment your application's code is reloaded on
  # every request. This slows down response time but is perfect for
  development
  # since you don't have to restart the web server when you make code
  changes.
  config.cache_classes = false
```

```
# Do not eager load code on boot.
config.eager_load = false

# Show full error reports.
config.consider_all_requests_local = true

# Enable/disable caching. By default caching is disabled.
# Run rails dev:cache to toggle caching.
if Rails.root.join('tmp', 'caching-dev.txt').exist?
  config.action_controller.perform_caching = true
  config.action_controller.enable_fragment_cache_logging = true

  config.cache_store = :memory_store
  config.public_file_server.headers = {
    'Cache-Control' => "public, max-age=#{2.days.to_i}"
  }
else
  config.action_controller.perform_caching = false

  config.cache_store = :null_store
end

# Store uploaded files on the local file system (see config/storage.yml
for options).
config.active_storage.service = :local

# Don't care if the mailer can't send.
config.action_mailer.raise_delivery_errors = false

config.action_mailer.default_url_options = { host: 'http://
localhost:3000' }

# Gmail SMTP server setup
config.action_mailer.smtp_settings = {
  address: "smtp.gmail.com",
  enable_starttls_auto: true,
  port: 587,
  authentication: :plain,
  user_name: Rails.application.credentials.smtp[:user_name],
```

```
   password: Rails.application.credentials.smtp[:password],
}

config.action_mailer.perform_caching = false

# Print deprecation notices to the Rails logger.
config.active_support.deprecation = :log

# Raise an error on page load if there are pending migrations.
config.active_record.migration_error = :page_load

# Highlight code that triggered database queries in logs.
config.active_record.verbose_query_logs = true

# Debug mode disables concatenation and preprocessing of assets.
# This option may cause significant delays in view rendering with a large
# number of complex assets.
config.assets.debug = true

# Suppress logger output for asset requests.
config.assets.quiet = true

# Raises error for missing translations.
# config.action_view.raise_on_missing_translations = true

# Use an evented file watcher to asynchronously detect changes in source
code,
# routes, locales, etc. This feature depends on the listen gem.
   config.file_watcher = ActiveSupport::EventedFileUpdateChecker
end
```

Make sure to modify the options to match your own connection details for your email provider. Restart your server if it's running, and your application is ready to send email. If your server fails to restart, check the error messages and look closely at your config/environments/development.rb file and your encrypted credentials via *rails credentials:edit* to make sure your changes match the listings.

> **Note**   If you need to use any advanced Action Mailer settings, the Rails API has
> a good chunk of information at `https://api.rubyonrails.org/classes/`
> `ActionMailer/Base.html`.

Configuring Application Settings

In addition to the mail server settings, Action Mailer has a set of configuration
parameters you can tweak to make the library behave in specific ways according to
the application or the environment. For reference, Table 12-2 lists the most common
configuration options. Just like the server settings, these can be specified in an initializer
file or in the environment-specific configuration files (`config/environments/*.rb`).

Table 12-2. *Common Action Mailer Application Settings*

Option	Description
`raise_delivery_errors`	Determines if exceptions should be raised when an error occurs during email delivery.
`delivery_method`	Determines which subsystem to use to deliver emails. Valid options are *:smtp*, *:sendmail*, *:file*, and *:test*. Additional options for the chosen subsystem may be required.
`perform_deliveries`	Indicates whether emails should actually be delivered.
`deliveries`	Keeps an array of all delivered emails when the delivery method is set to `:test`. This is useful when writing tests as we can inspect the delivered messages without sending them anywhere.
`default_options`	Allows you to specify default arguments for the *mail* method used inside mailers (e.g., setting default *from* or *reply_to* addresses).
`default_url_options`	Allows you to specify default arguments for URL helpers used inside your mailers (e.g., setting *host* so generated URLs have the correct domain name).
`asset_host`	Allows you to specify the base URL used when including assets like images in your emails.

Note   When you create a new Rails application, the configuration files automatically use sensible defaults for each of the development, test, and production environments. Take a quick look in `config/environments` to see how Action Mailer behaves in development, production, and test mode to make sure you understand your application's behavior.

Sending Email

Now that you have Action Mailer configured, it's time to see it in action. This section explores all the possibilities in the Action Mailer world, starting with basic text-only email and then adding extra email options such as attachments.

To demonstrate Action Mailer, let's enhance the blog application by allowing users to send email to their friends, so they can share information about a specific article. This is a common feature in today's web applications, affectionately referred to as "send to friend."

By now, you know that Rails provides helpful generators to get started writing your own code. You saw generators in action when you created models and controllers in previous chapters. The mailer generator works just like the other generators.

Enter the following command to generate the `NotifierMailer` class with one method named `email_friend`:

```
$ rails g mailer Notifier email_friend
```

```
      create    app/mailers/notifier_mailer.rb
      invoke    erb
      create      app/views/notifier_mailer
      create      app/views/notifier_mailer/email_friend.text.erb
      create      app/views/notifier_mailer/email_friend.html.erb
      invoke    test_unit
      create      test/mailers/notifier_mailer_test.rb
      create      test/mailers/previews/notifier_mailer_preview.rb
```

As we can see, the generator created several files, which we'll briefly describe before diving into more detail.

First, it created the NotifierMailer class in app/mailers/notifier_mailer.rb. By convention, any other mailers we create will be located in app/mailers as well. Inspecting NotifyMailer, we notice two things: First, the NotifyMailer class contains the email_friend method we requested on the command line. Second, we see that it is a subclass of ApplicationMailer class (found in app/mailers/application_mailer.rb), which is in turn a subclass of the `ActionMailer::Base` class. This gives us a chance to make app-wide changes to our mailers (by setting default options or changing layouts) while still inheriting all the features ActionMailer::Base provides.

Next, we see that it also created two template files in the `views` directory (`email_friend.text.erb` and `email_friend.html.erb`) which correspond to the `email_friend` method (action) found in our mailer class. These template files will control the HTML and text content of our emails. (Though most prefer to view the HTML version of an email, it's still considered a best practice to include a plain-text alternative. As you can see, Action Mailer encourages this best practice.)

Doesn't this look familiar? Just like controllers, Action Mailer classes contain methods that, when triggered, execute some code and render a related view of the same name, unless otherwise specified.

Lastly, the generator created a test file for our mailer, which we won't use yet. It also created a preview file, which we will cover later in this chapter.

Before we dive into our NotifierMailer implementation, let's take a quick look at our ApplicationMailer class, as seen in Listing 12-3.

Listing 12-3. ApplicationMailer Class in `app/mailers/application_mailer.rb`
`https://gist.github.com/nicedawg/d77cbbcf9705fbe917cf3caeddaaa5cb`

```
class ApplicationMailer < ActionMailer::Base
  default from: 'from@example.com'
  layout 'mailer'
end
```

We see a couple of things happening here. First, the *default* method is called on the hash *from: 'from@example.com'*. This sets the given email address as the default, making it unnecessary to specify the same *From* address for each mailer action we might add. It would be a good idea to go ahead and change this *From* address to be the same as the account you configured in your SMTP settings in config/environments/development.rb, to stave off any possible delivery problems.

We also see that the *layout* is set to mailer. Similar to how view templates rendered by controller actions are usually wrapped in a *layout* template, mailer templates are by default as well. This default "mailer" layout is defined in app/views/layouts/mailer.html.erb and app/views/layouts/mailer.text.erb. If you want to make changes that affect all (or most) of your mailer templates, these mailer layout template files are the perfect place to do so.

Now, we're ready to look at the NotifierMailer class we generated. In Listing 12-4, we see that the *email_friend* method already has some code, which will be the starting point for most of the methods you write using Action Mailer.

Listing 12-4. NotifierMailer Class in app/mailers/notifier.rb
https://gist.github.com/nicedawg/7db1799fd4eaa504d1a81ddc41930333

```
class NotifierMailer < ApplicationMailer

  # Subject can be set in your I18n file at config/locales/en.yml
  # with the following lookup:
  #
  #   en.notifier_mailer.email_friend.subject
  #
  def email_friend
    @greeting = "Hi"

    mail to: "to@example.org"
  end
end
```

We see a comment about setting up our subject line for the email which our *email_friend* mailer action will send in our I18n (internationalization) file. We won't do that now, but we will cover internationalization in a later chapter in this book.

Next, in the email_friend method body, the first line defines an instance variable named @greeting; just like in controllers, instance variables are also available in your views.

Also in the email_friend method body, we see that the *mail* method is called with a parameter of *to: "to@example.org"*, specifying the email address that will receive this message. The *mail* method accepts an options hash that specifies the various headers of the message. Table 12-3 lists the available options we can use to configure an individual message.

Table 12-3. *Mail Method Options*

Option	Description	Example
subject	The subject of the email message to be sent.	subject: "Action Mailer is powerful"
to	A string or array of email addresses to which the message will be sent.	to: "friend@example.com"
from	A string specifying the sender of the email message.	from: "sender@example.com"
reply_to	A string specifying the reply-to email address.	reply: "sender@example.com"
date	The date header. The default is the current date.	date: Time.now
cc	A string or array of email addresses to carbon copy with the message.	cc: "admin@example.com"
bcc	A string or array of email addresses to blind carbon copy with the message.	bcc: ["support@example.com", "sales@example.com"]

Handling Basic Email

Let's start enhancing the blog application by adding "Notify a Friend" functionality to the article page. The first iteration is a very basic example that sends an email (with both HTML and plain-text formats) containing a brief message.

The first piece of the puzzle is to make a change to the routes file, to include a route for the action that will be called after the user submits the form. Let's add a member route to articles using the member method to give a notify_friend_article route. Make sure your config/routes.rb file looks like the code in Listing 12-5.

Listing 12-5. Added a notify_friend Action to config/routes.rb: https://gist.github.com/nicedawg/1b848339e03a9ce2204836e744d9c272

```
Rails.application.routes.draw do
  root to: "articles#index"
  resources :articles do
    member do
```

```
    post :notify_friend
  end
  resources :comments
end
resources :users
resource :session
get "/login", to: "sessions#new", as: "login"
get "/logout", to: "sessions#destroy", as: "logout"
end
```

Note   Using the `member` method inside your `resources` block helps define a route that requires the `id` of the resource. Custom member routes are similar to the default member routes, such as `edit_article_path` and `article_path`. Following the same convention, you can define collection routes using the `collection` method. Custom collection routes are similar to the default collection routes, such as `articles_path`, which don't require an `id`.

Now that we have the route in place, let's show users a link which, when clicked, shows a form where they can enter the email address of the friend to whom they want to send a message. (Please note, a feature like this *could* be abused. In a production environment, it may be necessary to add security measures to restrict usage of a form like this to prevent malicious users using your form to send unsolicited emails. That's beyond the scope of this book, but be aware.)

Let's update the article's show view to include the new link and form partial directly after rendering the article's partial. Add the code shown in Listing 12-6 in app/views/articles/show.html.erb.

Listing 12-6. "Email a Friend" Link and Partial Added to app/views/articles/show.html.erb:

https://gist.github.com/nicedawg/5fac226dd94990290eb2deb18d67951d

```
<%= render partial: @article, locals: { cover_image_options: [500, 500] } %>

<%= link_to 'Email a friend', '#', onclick: "document.
querySelector('#notify_friend').style.display = 'block';return false;" %>
```

```
<div id="notify_friend" style="display:none;">
  <%= render 'notify_friend', article: @article %>
</div>

<h3>Comments</h3>

<div id="comments">
  <%= render @article.comments %>
</div>

<%= link_to "new comment", new_article_comment_path(@article), remote:
true, id: 'new_comment_link' %>
```

We added a link which may look a little strange. We set its URL to '#', which is one way to make a link clickable without it navigating anywhere. We're only using the link to trigger some JavaScript when clicked—namely, to display the "Notify a Friend" form. (We also added *return false* to the *onclick* handler to prevent the browser from navigating.)

We also added a partial—*notify_friend*—and passed the article as a local variable. This partial doesn't exist yet, but we'll create it next. We wrapped the partial in a container which will be hidden by default. We gave the container an *id* so that the preceding link can reference it and display the form. Generally, it's best to keep your JavaScript behavior separate from your HTML—perhaps in app/javascript/—but this works for now and keeps us focused on our goal. And that's okay!

Next, we need to add the partial for the "Notify a Friend" form we referenced in the preceding listing. Let's create this partial in app/views/articles/_notify_friend. html.erb so it looks like the code in Listing 12-7.

Listing 12-7. "Notify a Friend" Partial in app/views/articles/_notify_friend.html. erb: https://gist.github.com/nicedawg/c39b08e008df3daab297ba9998b0f178

```
<%= form_with(url: notify_friend_article_path(article)) do |form| %>
  <div class="field">
    <%= form.label :name, 'Your name' %>
    <%= form.text_field :name %>
  </div>
```

```
<div class="field">
  <%= form.label :email, "Your friend's email" %>
  <%= form.text_field :email %>
</div>
<div class="actions">
  <%= form.submit 'Send' %> or
  <%= link_to 'Cancel', '#', onclick: "document.querySelector('#notify_
  friend').style.display='none';return false;" %>
</div>
<% end %>
```

This form is pretty standard. We configured it to send the name and email values to the new route we added. And remember that, by default, *form_with* will send its data via Ajax. The only other thing to note is the Cancel link; it's similar to the "Email a Friend" link from the previous listing, except that it *hides* the form.

Now, when you go to any article page, you'll see a link to email a friend. Because you don't want to show the form all the time, you made the form hidden. If users are interested in recommending the article by sending an email to a friend, they can click the link, and the form will be revealed through the help of some simple JavaScript. The end result is shown in Figures 12-1 and 12-2.

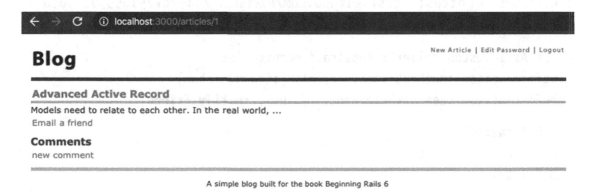

Figure 12-1. *Article page without "Notify a Friend" form*

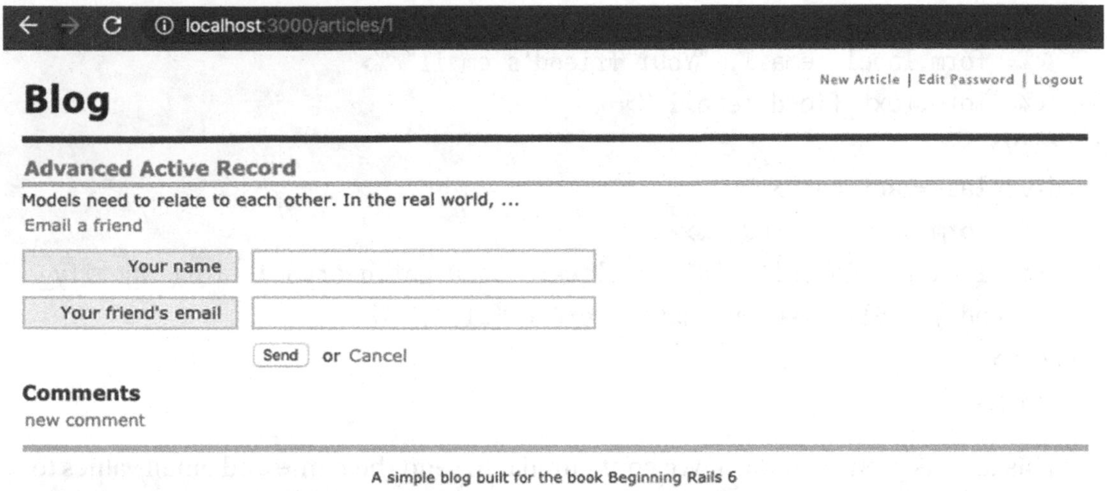

Figure 12-2. *Article page with visible "Notify a Friend" form*

The new form is ready to go, but the articles controller doesn't know how to handle its submitted data yet. The form is configured to submit to an action called notify_ friend, but that action doesn't exist. Let's update the articles controller and add the notify_friend method (and to find the article for it) as shown in Listing 12-8.

Listing 12-8. The notify_friend Action Added to app/controllers/articles_ controller.rb: https://gist.github.com/nicedawg/9447cf251055501a1d3a41 05af4fa208

```
class ArticlesController < ApplicationController
  before_action :authenticate, except: [:index, :show]
  before_action :set_article, only: [:show, :notify_friend]

  # GET /articles
  # GET /articles.json
  def index
    @articles = Article.includes(:user).with_rich_text_body.with_attached_
    cover_image.all
  end

   # .... code omitted for brevity ...

  # DELETE /articles/1
  # DELETE /articles/1.json
```

```
def destroy
  @article = current_user.articles.find(params[:id])
  @article.destroy
  respond_to do |format|
    format.html { redirect_to articles_url, notice: 'Article was
    successfully destroyed.' }
    format.json { head :no_content }
  end
end

def notify_friend
  NotifierMailer.email_friend(@article, params[:name], params[:email]).
  deliver
  redirect_to @article, notice: 'Successfully sent a message to your
  friend'
end

private
  # Use callbacks to share common setup or constraints between actions.
  def set_article
    @article = Article.find(params[:id])
  end

  # Never trust parameters from the scary internet, only allow the white
  list through.
  def article_params
    params.require(:article).permit(:title, :cover_image, :remove_cover_
    image, :location, :excerpt, :body, :published_at, category_ids: [])
  end
end
```

First, we modified the *before_action* so that it would also set *@article* for our new action. Then, we added the *notify_friend* action to deliver our message. The *notify_friend* action is short and readable, but let's dig a little deeper. Let's use the rails console to see what's going on:

```
> rails console
irb(main):001:0> NotifierMailer.email_friend
```

```
 Rendering notifier_mailer/email_friend.html.erb within layouts/mailer
Rendered notifier_mailer/email_friend.html.erb within layouts/mailer
(Duration: 1.1ms | Allocations: 226)
 Rendering notifier_mailer/email_friend.text.erb within layouts/mailer
Rendered notifier_mailer/email_friend.text.erb within layouts/mailer
(Duration: 0.4ms | Allocations: 101)
NotifierMailer#email_friend: processed outbound mail in 13.1ms
=> #<Mail::Message:70146235556720, Multipart: true, Headers: <From: from
@example.com>, <To: to@example.org>, <Subject: Email friend>, <Mime-
Version: 1.0>, <Content-Type: multipart/alternative; boundary="--==_mimepar
t_5e6ada2fab7e7_110243fcc3142bfd48643f"; charset=UTF-8>>
```

A lot happened there. We see that our mailer action rendered our mailer templates, and it constructed a message which it returned—apparently an instance of a class named Mail::Message. Let's inspect that instance to find out more about it:

```
irb(main):002:0> email = _
=> #<Mail::Message:70146235556720, Multipart: true, Headers: <From: from@
example.com>, <To: to@example.org>, <Subject: Email friend>, <Mime-Version:
1.0>, <Content-Type: multipart/alternative; boundary="--==_mimepart_5e6ada2
fab7e7_110243fcc3142bfd48643f"; charset=UTF-8>>
irb(main):003:0> email.class.name
=> "ActionMailer::MessageDelivery"
```

We used a handy shortcut—the underscore—as an alias for the last object returned by rails console and assigned its value to a variable we defined called *email*, for more convenient investigation.

Then, we asked for the name of its class and were surprised to find out that it's ActionMailer::MessageDelivery, not Mail::Message as we thought. Why did that happen? ActionMailer::MessageDelivery is a thin wrapper around Mail::Message—it relies on Mail::Message for its expertise in manipulating emails and adds some methods to facilitate the delivery of these emails. It's *such* a thin wrapper that it delegates almost every method call to the Mail::Message object it contains—even the *inspect* method inherited from the base Object class, which rails console uses to print the value of the last returned object. That's really interesting!

Now, let's see what we can do with this object:

```
irb(main):004:0> email.methods    # note: output shortened for brevity
=> [:subject, :subject=, :errors, :to_yaml, :decoded, :add_file, :filename,
:from, :content_type, :to, :charset, :action, :<=>, :content_type=, :==,
:[], :[]=, :sender, :boundary, :references, :attachment, :delivery_method,
:inspect, :method_missing, :multipart?, :parts, :from_address, :recipients_
addresses, :to_addresses, :cc_addresses, :x_original_to_addresses,
:bcc_addresses, :to_s, :deliver, :deliver!, ..., :reply_to=, :resent_
bcc, :body=, ... :message, :deliver_now!, :deliver_later, :deliver_now,
:processed?, :deliver_later!, :__setobj__, :marshal_dump, :marshal_load]
irb(main):005:0> email.deliver
Delivered mail 5e6adb06191e8_110243fcc3142bfd48652b@bardy.local.mail
(984.5ms)
Date: Thu, 12 Mar 2020 19:59:50 -0500
From: from@example.com
To: to@example.org
Message-ID: <5e6adb06191e8_110243fcc3142bfd48652b@bardy.local.mail>
Subject: Email friend

... omitted for brevity ...

=> #<Mail::Message:70146235556720, Multipart: true, Headers: <Date: Thu, 12
Mar 2020 19:59:50 -0500>, <From: from@example.com>, <To: to@example.org>,
<Message-ID: <5e6adb06191e8_110243fcc3142bfd48652b@bardy.local.mail>>,
<Subject: Email friend>, <Mime-Version: 1.0>, <Content-Type: multipart/
alternative; boundary="--==_mimepart_5e6ada2fab7e7_110243fcc3142bfd48643f";
charset=UTF-8>, <Content-Transfer-Encoding: 7bit>>
```

We see that our email object has a long list of messages we can send it; many are for inspecting the details of the email message itself. Others are for managing the delivery of it. There were too many methods to include in the listing, but we included some of the more interesting ones. We see several methods with "deliver" in their name. We used *:deliver* in our controller already, but we also see *:deliver_later* and *:deliver_now*; the next chapter will explain those in more depth, though we can easily imagine what they might do.

Lastly, we ran *email.deliver*, and the rails console output indicated the delivery was performed—or at least *attempted*.

We don't need to remember all these details every time we send an email; we just need to remember that we call the mailer action as a class method on the mailer class and then call *deliver* (e.g., *NotifierMailer.email_friend.deliver*).

We're not quite ready to send our new email. In the previous code change, we added some code to send the article, the name of the sender, and the email address of the recipient to our mailer action—but the mailer action isn't ready to receive it yet. Let's update our mailer action to receive this data and to make use of it when constructing the message. Listing 12-9 shows these changes.

Listing 12-9. Updated NotifierMailer in app/mailers/notifier_mailer.rb: https://gist.github.com/nicedawg/a9d4779d99d442d9beddf76d169e92b6

```
class NotifierMailer < ApplicationMailer
  def email_friend(article, sender_name, receiver_email)
    @article = article
    @sender_name = sender_name

    mail to: receiver_email, subject: 'Interesting Article'
  end
end
```

We added three arguments which correspond to the arguments we added to the controller action in Listing 12-8: article, sender_name, and receiver_email. We assigned two of those values—article and sender_name—to instance variables so they will be available for use in our mailer templates. Then, we modified the *mail* method call to send the email to the *receiver_email* address with the subject "Interesting Article."

We can now test to see if our email will actually be sent. It won't have the *content* we want yet, but we'll change that soon. Go ahead and try! Fill out the form in your browser, and send the message to your own email address. If all goes according to plan, you should receive an email that looks something like Figure 12-3.

Figure 12-3. *Message delivered to a user's inbox*

If you didn't get the message, don't worry. Sending email can be tricky, but there are a few things we can try.

First, look at your server output. Do you see any errors? If so, it may be a syntax error in your code which you can fix. Address any errors by making sure your code matches the preceding listings, and try again.

Does it look like everything was successful, but you still didn't receive the message? Checking your Spam or Junk folder or simply waiting another minute could clear this up. However, there could be an SMTP error that's being hidden. Edit your config/ environments/development.rb file, and change the following option so it says *config. action_mailer.raise_delivery_errors = true*. (It was set to *false*, meaning SMTP delivery errors would be suppressed.) Then restart your Rails server and try to send the message again. Perhaps this will reveal the problem.

Email providers must continuously evolve to fight security risks and spam. It's quite likely that a security feature or spam-blocking feature from your email provider is blocking your delivery attempts. For instance, if using a Gmail account with two-factor authentication enabled, you may need to go to your Google Account settings page, visit the Security section, and add an "app password" for your Rails app and then replace the password in your SMTP settings (via *rails credentials:edit*) with the new app password in order to send email from your Rails app.

Unfortunately, we cannot provide solutions for every type of SMTP delivery problem that might exist with every provider—and even if we did, the solutions would soon be obsolete! But knowing how to reveal the problem (via *raise_delivery_errors)* and using your favorite search engine, you're bound to solve the problem. But if not, don't worry. We can still *preview* the emails, even if they can't be delivered right now.

Previewing Email

Hopefully, you were able to successfully send the email from your app. But if not, don't worry. We can still preview what the email *would* look like with the help of another feature of Action Mailer—*previews.*

With Action Mailer's previews, we can configure a mailer action to be previewed with some predefined data for its templates and then view the HTML and plain-text variations of that mailer action in our web browser—without having to send the email.

Certainly this is helpful when you're having trouble sending emails from your development environment, but even if you don't have any delivery problems, using Action Mailer previews helps shorten the feedback loop for making incremental changes to your mailers. Instead of filling out a form and waiting for the message to be sent to your email account, simply refresh your browser! We'll walk through the steps necessary to make our *email_friend* mailer action previewable.

First, we need to define a subclass of ActionMailer::Preview specifically for previewing mailer actions in our NotifierMailer class. Thankfully, when we generated the mailer in an earlier section, it already created one for us, located in test/mailers/previews/notifier_mailer_preview.rb. It already has almost everything we need; however, we need to pass to the *email_friend* method the arguments which it expects. Modify your NotifierMailerPreview class so it matches Listing 12-10.

Listing 12-10. NotifierMailerPreview in `test/mailers/previews/notifier_mailer_preview.rb`

`https://gist.github.com/nicedawg/c5522dc35fcb2f4cdca3b3b29edab451`

```
# Preview all emails at http://localhost:3000/rails/mailers/notifier_mailer
class NotifierMailerPreview < ActionMailer::Preview

  # Preview this email at http://localhost:3000/rails/mailers/notifier_
  mailer/email_friend
  def email_friend
    NotifierMailer.email_friend(Article.first, 'Sender T. Sendington',
    'ree.seever@example.com')
  end
end
```

Instead of passing arguments to *email_friend* based on user input, we're predefining the values which will be sent to the mailer action for the purpose of previewing.

Now, visit http://localhost:3000/rails/mailers in your browser. If all is well, you should see "Notifier Mailer" listed, with a link to "email_friend" nested underneath it. Click "email_friend," and you should see the preview, similar to Figure 12-4.

Figure 12-4. *Action Mailer preview of NotifierMailer#email_friend*

Notice that we see essentially every important part of the message—the From address, the Subject, the content, and more. Also, notice the Format menu; we see we're currently viewing the HTML version of our email, but can easily switch to viewing the plain-text version as well.

Please be aware that email clients may not display the email exactly as it appears here. Email clients tend to support a subset of HTML and CSS, and each email client has its particular quirks. A good rule of thumb is to keep your layout and styles simple and to test your messages with a variety of popular email clients.

Now that we can preview our "Email a Friend" message, let's add the content we want to send. We should include the sender's name and a brief description of why we're sending this email so the recipient understands why they're receiving this email. We should also include the article's title and a link back to the article. So let's update our *email_friend* mailer action text and HTML templates to match Listings 12-11 and 12-12, respectively.

Listing 12-11. NotifierMailer Template in app/views/notifier_mailer/email_
friend.text.erb:

https://gist.github.com/nicedawg/a68c65b8b15b21be7a6346e8e3375969

```
Your friend, <%= @sender_name %>, thinks you may like the following
article:
<%= @article.title %>: <%= article_url(@article) %>
```

Listing 12-12. HTML email_friend Template in app/views/notifier_mailer/
email_friend.html.erb:

https://gist.github.com/nicedawg/1cc96d3de7b9bdf3bb0980bd87a2803e

```
<p>
  Your friend, <em><%= @sender_name %></em>, thinks you may like the
  following article:
</p>

<p>
  <%= link_to @article.title, article_url(@article) %>
</p>
```

Now that we've updated our text and HTML versions of our mailer action, try
previewing the email again in your browser by visiting http://localhost:3000/rails/
mailers/notifier_mailer/email_friend. Much better!

If you were able to successfully send email from your Rails app via SMTP, try using
the "Email a Friend" form to send yourself this email. It looks pretty good, as shown in
Figure 12-5. If your users don't have a rich email client and can't read HTML mail, they
are shown the plain-text version.

Figure 12-5. *HTML message delivered to a user's inbox*

Note   If you think maintaining both text and HTML versions of an email message is a lot of work, it may be safer to stick with the HTML message. While it is best practice to send both, most email users prefer the HTML version.

Adding Attachments

In some cases, you may want to add attachments to an email message. Action Mailer makes this a straightforward task by providing an *attachments* helper. You tell *attachments* which file you want to attach to the email, and it does its magic.

Let's walk through an example of attaching a file to an email message. We could send the article's cover image (if available) when a user sends an email about that article to a friend. To attach this image file to the email you created in the previous section, add a call to the attachments method in the email_friend method in the NotifierMailer class, as shown in Listing 12-13.

Listing 12-13. Adding an Attachment to the Mailer in app/mailers/notifier_mailer.rb:

https://gist.github.com/nicedawg/bdf43103d0cb0f896047d9c458600afc

```
class NotifierMailer < ApplicationMailer
  def email_friend(article, sender_name, receiver_email)
    @article = article
    @sender_name = sender_name
```

```
if @article.cover_image.present?
  attachments[@article.cover_image.filename.to_s] = @article.cover_
  image.download
end

  mail to: receiver_email, subject: 'Interesting Article'
  end
end
```

First, since articles don't require a cover image, we only attempt to add the attachment if a cover image is present. Then, we set the name of the attachment to the file name of the cover image. We could have named it anything we wanted, as long as it had the right extension so that the recipient can view it properly. To set the contents of the attachment, we used the *download* method—provided by Active Storage to give you the raw data of the attached file. The resulting message preview looks like Figure 12-6. Notice the link to the attachment.

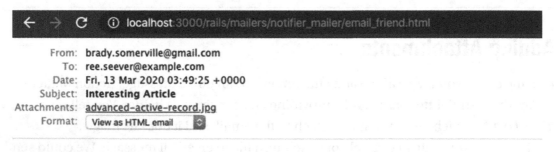

Figure 12-6. *Message with an attachment delivered to a user's inbox*

Tip   In addition to sending dynamic attachments like the preceding example, you can also add a static attachment that exists on disk by using the *File.read* method. For instance, if you wanted to send an image found in app/assets/images/blog.png, you'd use *File.read(Rails.root.join('app', 'assets', 'images', 'blog.png'))* when adding an attachment.

Letting Authors Know About Comments

Just to make sure you've grasped how to send email from your Rails applications, this section quickly goes over the complete flow to add another mailer action.

In Chapter 6, we added an *after_create* callback to the Comment model to email the author of an article after a comment was created—but we never implemented the email. Let's do that now! We will change five files. First, we'll add a new action to the Notifier Mailer class; next, we will add new HTML and text mailer templates with the contents of the email to send; then, we will add a previewer for our new mailer action so we can easily test it; finally, we add code to the *after_create* callback in the Comment model to invoke the mailer when a new comment is created. Listings 12-14 to 12-18, respectively, show the code for these modifications.

Listing 12-14. Adding the comment_added Method to app/mailers/notifier_mailer.rb:

https://gist.github.com/nicedawg/b6572b22e3627a93072b5a1eb2dead50

```ruby
class NotifierMailer < ApplicationMailer
  def email_friend(article, sender_name, receiver_email)
    @article = article
    @sender_name = sender_name

    if @article.cover_image.present?
      attachments[@article.cover_image.filename.to_s] = @article.cover_
      image.download
    end

    mail to: receiver_email, subject: 'Interesting Article'
  end

  def comment_added(comment)
    @article = comment.article
    mail to: @article.user.email, subject: "New Comment for '#{@article.
    title}'"
  end
end
```

Listing 12-15. The comment_added HTML Mailer Template in app/views/
notifier_mailer/comment_added.html.erb:
https://gist.github.com/nicedawg/f60a353d255661cdb181ad8306cecf62

```
<p>
  Someone added a comment to one of your articles <i><%= @article.title
  %></i>.
</p>
<p>
  Go read the comment:
  <%= link_to @article.title, article_url(@article) %>
</p>
```

Listing 12-16. The comment_added Text Mailer Template in app/views/notifier_
mailer/comment_added.text.erb:
https://gist.github.com/nicedawg/4d0690011557da8bf7526a76760995e3

```
Someone added a comment to one of your articles: "<%= @article.title"

Go read the comment:
  <%= article_url(@article) %>
```

Listing 12-17. Adding a Previewer for NotifierMailer#comment_added in
test/mailers/previews/notifier_mailer_preview.rb:
https://gist.github.com/nicedawg/8f6ebddb661a4939f7732dc9de000695

```
# Preview all emails at http://localhost:3000/rails/mailers/notifier_mailer
class NotifierMailerPreview < ActionMailer::Preview

  # Preview this email at http://localhost:3000/rails/mailers/notifier_
  mailer/email_friend
  def email_friend
    NotifierMailer.email_friend(Article.first, 'Sender T. Sendington',
    'ree.seever@example.com')
  end

  def comment_added
    comment = Article.first.comments.build(
```

```
      name: 'Anonymous Reader',
      email: 'guesswho@example.com',
      body: 'This article changed my life.',
    )
    NotifierMailer.comment_added(comment)
  end
end
```

Listing 12-18. Updates to app/model/comment.rb:
https://gist.github.com/nicedawg/a523e8af12c2559d539351aeb8d9f66d

```
class Comment < ApplicationRecord
  belongs_to :article

  validates :name, :email, :body, presence: true
  validate :article_should_be_published

  after_create :email_article_author

  def article_should_be_published
    errors.add(:article_id, 'is not published yet') if article && !article.
    published?
  end

  def email_article_author
    NotifierMailer.comment_added(self).deliver
  end
end
```

Most of the code changes we made probably look familiar to you. However, we did something in the preview class we should mention: we *built* a comment belonging to the first article to use in our mailer. Why did we do this? When the preview action runs, it is connected to your development database. If we had chosen to create a comment instead of building one, then every time you previewed the email, it would add another comment to your database. While that's not necessarily a problem, you may not want that to happen. By building instead of creating, the comment is never saved to the database. Alternatively, we could have manually created a comment for the first article so we could preview this email—but if we deleted that comment during the course of development, this preview would suddenly be broken.

Another thing we should point out is the *email_article_author* method in the Comment model; we passed *self* as the argument to *NotifierMailer.comment_added*. That's because the mailer action expects a comment, and in this context, the comment is the current object, which can be referred to as *self*.

Now that those changes have been made, create an article with your user account and add some comments. You should receive one email message per comment. If you want to, you could add the comment text to the email; that way, you wouldn't need to go to the article page to read the comment. You could easily implement that by changing the mailer view.

Receiving Email via Action Mailbox

So far, you've seen that Action Mailer has extensive support for sending all types of email messages. But what if your application needs to receive email? Action Mailbox is a new feature in Rails 6 which makes it as easy as possible to receive emails into your app and process them.

Though Action Mailbox makes it as easy as it can to receive and parse emails, it can still be tricky to set up. Being able to actually receive email may involve domain name registration, deploying your application to a publicly available web host, signing up for third-party email services, or configuring mail servers to call a Rails command when receiving certain messages.

Walking you through the process of configuring your app to receive actual email would be too difficult, as the variety of systems and services to integrate with is too great and may require payment. However, Action Mailbox offers a tool in development mode to let you submit emails to your app via a form. So we'll use that tool to help us as we modify our blog to let our authors submit draft articles via email. If at some point you decide to send actual email to your app, be sure to check out the Action Mailbox guide at `https://edgeguides.rubyonrails.org/action_mailbox_basics.html`.

Installation

To add Action Mailbox capabilities to our blog, we must begin by running Action Mailbox's installation command:

```
> rails action_mailbox:install
Copying application_mailbox.rb to app/mailboxes
      create  app/mailboxes/application_mailbox.rb
Copied migration 20200314210550_create_action_mailbox_tables.action_
mailbox.rb from action_mailbox
```

As we see from the command's output, it did a couple of things. First, it created an ApplicationMailbox class. Then, it created a migration file; Action Mailbox keeps track of which messages it has received and processed in a database table. So let's run the migrations to add this new database table to our database:

```
> rails db:migrate
== 20200314210550 CreateActionMailboxTables: migrating ==================
-- create_table(:action_mailbox_inbound_emails)
   -> 0.0069s
== 20200314210550 CreateActionMailboxTables: migrated (0.0071s) ===========
That's it! Next, let's take a look at configuring Action Mailbox.
```

Configuration

Action Mailbox has a few configuration options, as shown in Table 12-4. We won't deviate from the defaults in our blog, but it's still helpful to take a look and see what's possible. Per usual, these values can be changed by putting *config.action_mailbox.[setting] = [value]* in the appropriate config/environments/ files or in config/application.rb to set the value for all environments.

Table 12-4. *Action Mailbox Configuration Options*

Option	Description
ingress	Specifies which adapter to use to receive emails. Valid options include *:relay*, *:mailgun*, *:mandrill*, *:postmark*, and *:sendgrid*. Depending on the adapter chosen, additional credentials may be required.
logger	Specifies which logger Action Mailbox should use for its logging output. By default, it will use the standard Rails logger.
incinerate	Action Mailbox stores the emails it receives for a certain amount of time and then deletes them. If you wish to keep them forever, set this value to *false*.
incinerate_ after	By default, when *incinerate* is true, Action Mailbox will destroy emails after storing them for 30 days. You can alter the storage policy by changing this value. (e.g., config.action_mailbox.incinerate_after = 60.days).
queues	Action Mailbox uses queues to schedule routing and incineration jobs. We haven't talked about queues yet, but we will in the next chapter when we discuss Active Job. For now, just know this option gives you a chance to rename the queues which Action Mailbox uses by default.

Now that we've installed Action Mailbox and perused its options (though we didn't need to change any yet), let's get started on enhancing our blog by allowing authors to create draft articles via email.

Creating Draft Articles via Email

Before we jump in to adding this feature, let's think about the various things we need to do in order to accomplish this.

First, we need to give each author a special email address, so that when we receive an email, we know *what* it's for (creating a draft article) and we know *whom* it's for. Ideally, we'll make this a hard-to-guess email address to help prevent the public from being able to create draft articles for the author.

Then, we'll need to process the email. Based on the email's *To:* address, subject, and body, we'll create a draft article associated with the right user, the right subject, and the draft body.

Finally, we'll send an acknowledgement email to the author, so they know our app successfully processed their content. It will also have a convenient link to allow them to edit their draft article.

Assigning Authors a Special Email Address

First, let's give each author a unique email address which they can use to create draft articles via email. To do this, we will add a secret token to each user record for this purpose and display it on their "Edit Password" page.

Let's generate and run the necessary migration:

```
> rails g migration add_draft_article_token_to_users draft_article_
token:token
      invoke  active_record
      create      db/migrate/20200314215947_add_draft_article_token_to_users.rb
> rails db:migrate
== 20200314215947 AddDraftArticleTokenToUsers: migrating ================
-- add_column(:users, :draft_article_token, :string)
   -> 0.0034s
-- add_index(:users, :draft_article_token, {:unique=>true})
   -> 0.0016s
== 20200314215947 AddDraftArticleTokenToUsers: migrated (0.0053s) =========
```

Notice we gave a hint to the migration generator that our new field—draft_article_ token—is a *token*. Rails handles that specially. We can see in the output that it created our field as a string in the database, but also added a unique index to the column, ensuring that each user has a *different* token. (If two users had the same draft_articles_ token, we might end up creating a draft article associated with the wrong user!)

Next, we'll modify our User class so that it will treat the *draft_article_token* like a token, as shown in Listing 12-19. By doing so, it will automatically set a random, unique token when a user is being created. It also gives the User class a method called *regenerate_draft_article_token* we could use if we needed to.

We'll also add a method to return the full special email address for convenience, so we don't end up repeating it throughout the blog's code base.

Listing 12-19. Adding draft_article_token to User Model
https://gist.github.com/nicedawg/6848c1a2348a1afa28406f93ced19e97

```ruby
require 'digest'

class User < ApplicationRecord
  attr_accessor :password

  validates :email, uniqueness: true
  validates :email, length: { in: 5..50 }
  validates :email, format: { with:  /\A[^@][\w.-]+@[\w.-]+[.][a-z]
{2,4}\z/i }
  validates :password, confirmation: true, if: :password_required?
  validates :password, length: { in: 4..20 }, if: :password_required?
  validates :password, presence: true, if: :password_required?

  has_one :profile
  has_many :articles, -> { order 'published_at DESC, title ASC' },
           dependent: :nullify
  has_many :replies, through: :articles, source: :comments

  has_secure_token :draft_article_token

  before_save :encrypt_new_password

  def self.authenticate(email, password)
    user = find_by email: email
    return user if user && user.authenticated?(password)
  end

  def authenticated?(password)
    self.hashed_password == encrypt(password)
  end

  def draft_article_email
    "#{draft_article_token}@drafts.example.com"
  end

  protected
```

```
  def encrypt_new_password
    return if password.blank?
    self.hashed_password = encrypt(password)
  end

  def password_required?
    hashed_password.blank? || password.present?
  end

  def encrypt(string)
    Digest::SHA1.hexdigest(string)
  end
end
```

After this code change, new users will automatically receive a unique token. And we can easily generate the user's special draft article email address. But what about our existing users? We can use this code in the rails console to generate draft_article_token values for them and then verify it worked:

```
> rails c
irb(main):001:0> User.find_each { |u| u.regenerate_draft_article_token }
    .... SQL output ...
irb(main):002:0> User.first.draft_article_token
  User Load (0.3ms)  SELECT "users".* FROM "users" ORDER BY "users"."id"
  ASC LIMIT ?  [["LIMIT", 1]]
=> "qzi2k2g9ULwZhVqFQTKUet5M"
```

Now that we have secure draft article tokens for each user (and will automatically create tokens for new users), let's show our authors their unique, secure email address they can use to send draft articles via email.

Perhaps near the top of the "new article" form would be a good place to show them this email address. We could also explain how the process works. Let's add this to our app/views/articles/new.html.erb, as Listing 12-20 shows.

Listing 12-20. Showing the Draft Article Email at the Top of app/views/articles/
new.html.erb

https://gist.github.com/nicedawg/6a6dbb6049f28c9873ed0d963488e477

```
<h1>New Article</h1>

<p>
  <em>Did you know that you can submit draft articles via email?</em>
  Send an e-mail to <%= mail_to current_user.draft_article_email %> with
  the title in your subject, and your draft content in the body.
</p>

<%= render 'form', article: @article %>

<%= link_to 'Back', articles_path %>
```

After making these changes, go to the New Article page in your browser. It should resemble Figure 12-7.

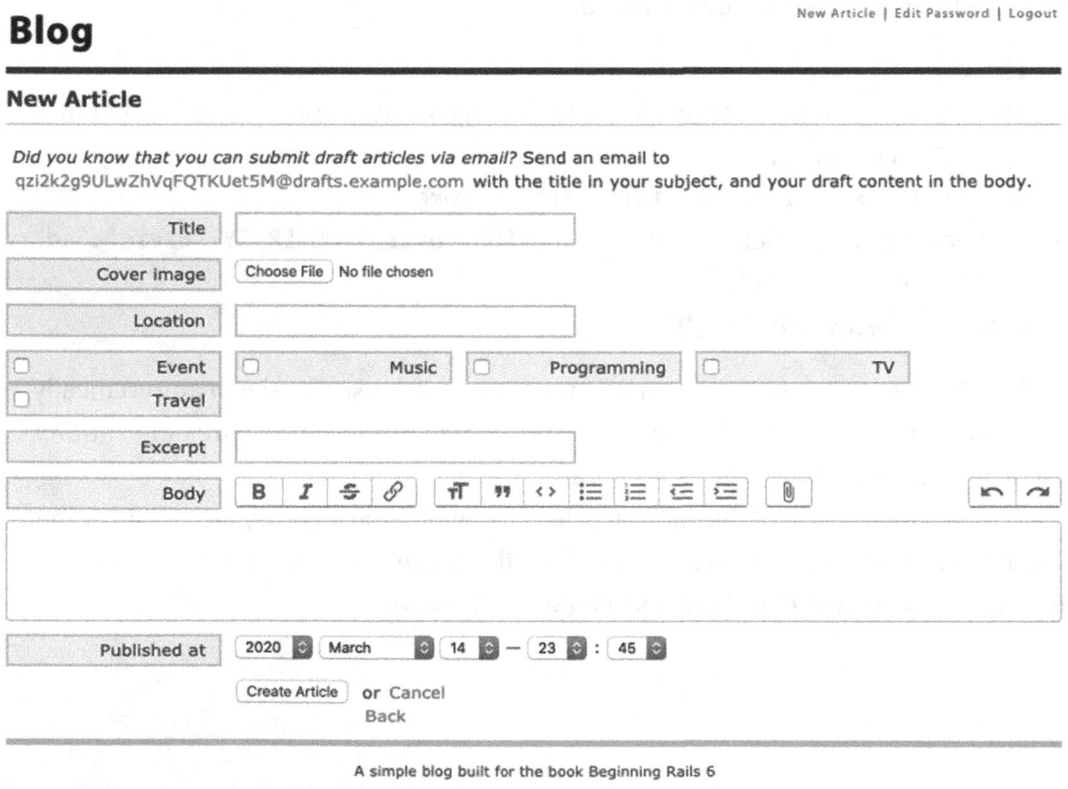

Figure 12-7. *New article form with special draft article email address*

With these changes, authors are aware of their special draft article email address and can start sending email to our blog to create draft articles. But what will our application do with those emails when it receives them? We clearly have more work to do. Next, we'll add code to process these emails and create draft articles from them.

Processing the Email

We need a place to put code that can handle incoming emails which are meant to create draft articles. It needs to be able to find the right author record and then create an article with the right title and body. If we wanted to take this action in response to an incoming HTTP request, we'd do that in a *controller*. But when receiving email input, we'll do that in a *mailbox*.

In an Action Mailbox context, a mailbox receives emails and decides what to do with them. We can have many mailboxes, each one for a particular purpose, similar to controllers. Since we're going to be creating draft articles from emails, we should name our new mailbox accordingly.

To create our new mailbox, run the following Rails command:

```
> rails g mailbox draft_articles
      create  app/mailboxes/draft_articles_mailbox.rb
      invoke  test_unit
      create    test/mailboxes/draft_articles_mailbox_test.rb
```

As we can see, the generator created our DraftArticlesMailbox class in the app/ mailboxes directory and also added a placeholder test file for us (which we won't use yet.)

If you view the DraftArticlesMailbox class, you'll see it's a blank state. It has an empty *process* method, and that's it. We'll need to update the DraftArticlesMailbox class in app/ mailboxes/draft_articles_mailbox.rb to match Listing 12-21.

Listing 12-21. Processing Emails in app/mailboxes/draft_articles_mailbox.rb
https://gist.github.com/nicedawg/fdb5245cb9a8235d6f0894f0d4dc31f5

```
class DraftArticlesMailbox < ApplicationMailbox
  before_processing :require_author

  def process
    author.articles.create(
      title: mail.subject,
```

371

```
    body: mail.body,
  )
end

private

def require_author
  bounce_with DraftArticlesMailer.no_author(mail.from) unless author
end

def author
  @author ||= User.find_by(draft_article_token: token)
end

def token
  mail.to.first.split('@').first
end
end
```

This isn't a *ton* of code, but there's a bit to unpack here. First, we see that our DraftArticlesMailbox class inherits from ApplicationMailbox. Any mailboxes we create to work with Action Mailbox should inherit from this class.

Next, we see *before_processing :require_author*. Similar to how Action Controller allows you to define filters to run before, after, or around your controller action, Action Mailbox allows you to define filters to run before, after, or around your *process* method. Here, we reference a method we added called *require_author* which we'll explain in a minute. We could have put the code for *require_author* at the top of our *process* method, but extracting it to a separate method keeps our *process* method tidy and encourages reuse. So now we understand the general idea—before we process the email, we make sure we could locate the right user object.

Before we dig into the methods we added, let's talk about some magic that Action Mailbox added to our class. First, notice how we referenced something called *mail* a few times in our class. Where did that come from? Action Mailbox provides that to our class—and it returns the object representing the email we're processing. So we can use it to access the email's To, Subject, and Body fields and more.

We also used a method called *bounce_with*; this method marks the inbound email record as "bounced" (so the system knows it was processed but failed), and the method takes an ActionMailer::MessageDelivery instance as an argument. Action Mailbox will then deliver this message in response to the failure. This is an elegant way to let you do both things—mark as bounced and deliver an error message—with very little code.

Now we can understand the code we added more clearly. In *require_author*, we bounce a message back to the sender unless we can find a valid author.

In *author*, we search for the user record with the right token. You may not have seen the ||= operator yet, often referred to as the "or equals" operator. Using this in conjunction with an instance variable, as we did in the *author* method, is a common pattern called *memoization*—which attempts to prevent redundant, expensive queries. We refer to *author* multiple times in this class, but don't need to actually execute an SQL query more than once. So the *author* method returns the value of @author if it has a value. Otherwise, it executes the User.find_by query, assigns the value to @author, and *then* returns the value.

In *token*, we access the object representing the email and get its *to* value…which rightly returns an array of email addresses (since an email's To field may have multiple recipients). For our purposes, we assume the first address is the one we want, and then we split the address based on the @ symbol and take the first piece of the resulting array to return the token portion of our email address.

Finally, to the meat of the class. The *process* method creates an article associated with the author found via the token in the email address and sets its title and body based on the email's subject and body, respectively.

You might notice the explanation of this class is longer than the code itself, a tribute to the concise readability of well-written Ruby code. The code is rather self-documenting. Even if you don't know what's happening behind the scenes, a developer could read the code and have a good sense of the class's intentions.

There's one more matter to take care of. We referenced a mailer and mailer action which don't yet exist. Let's take care of that now:

```
> rails g mailer draft_articles no_author
      create  app/mailers/draft_articles_mailer.rb
      invoke  erb
      create    app/views/draft_articles_mailer
      create    app/views/draft_articles_mailer/no_author.text.erb
      create    app/views/draft_articles_mailer/no_author.html.erb
      invoke  test_unit
      create    test/mailers/draft_articles_mailer_test.rb
      create    test/mailers/previews/draft_articles_mailer_preview.rb
```

We need to implement the *no_author* mailer action to send a message back to the sender, informing them we couldn't process their email. Edit your `DraftArticlesMailer` to match Listing 12-22.

Listing 12-22. Sending Notifications That the Draft Article Couldn't Be Created
https://gist.github.com/nicedawg/653f0fefb94f8afda2e1021a0b6287e4

```
class DraftArticlesMailer < ApplicationMailer
  def no_author(to)
    mail to: to, subject: 'Your email could not be processed' do |format|
      content = 'Please check your draft articles email address and try
      again.'
      format.html { render plain: content }
      format.text { render plain: content }
    end
  end
end
```

Notice how in addition to specifying the "To:" address and subject of the message, this time we passed a block which takes *format* as an argument. This lets us provide the content inline for our HTML and text formats. Since we just want to send a plain, simple message for now, we'll do this instead of creating separate mailer view template files.

Before we finish with our DraftArticlesMailer, we should update its preview. Let's edit test/mailers/previews/draft_articles_mailer_preview.rb so DraftArticlesMailerPreview matches Listing 12-23.

Listing 12-23. Update DraftArticlesMailerPreview
https://gist.github.com/nicedawg/d24dcc1464e41ef468589ee4ad2e8755

```
class DraftArticlesMailerPreview < ActionMailer::Preview
  def no_author
    DraftArticlesMailer.no_author('test@example.com')
  end
end
```

Now we can preview our new mailer via http://localhost:3000/rails/mailers if we want to.

Finally, our mailbox is prepared to turn emails into draft articles when it can and send an email back to the sender when it can't find the right user. That sounds good, but how will our app know to send emails to our new DraftArticlesMailbox? We have a little more work to do.

Next, we need to update our ApplicationMailbox to send the right emails to our DraftArticlesMailbox. We know we only need to handle emails addressed to sometoken@drafts.example.com, so let's edit ApplicationMailbox to look like Listing 12-24.

Listing 12-24. Routing Emails to Our DraftArticlesMailbox in ApplicationMailbox
`https://gist.github.com/nicedawg/1ac117138347346a67bf7a82f9117023`

```
class ApplicationMailbox < ActionMailbox::Base
  routing /@drafts\./i => :draft_articles
end
```

We added a *routing* line which says "if the *To:* address of the email has '@drafts.' in it, then send it to the DraftArticlesMailbox." If you have multiple mailboxes in your app, you will likely need multiple *routing* calls to send emails to the right mailboxes. Note that the routes will be processed in top-down order, executing the first match (similar to Action Pack's router). Action Mailbox's router also allows the symbol *:all* instead of a regular expression to say "send all emails to this mailbox."

Now that we've added the mailbox and routed the right types of email to it, let's see if it works! As mentioned in the beginning of the chapter, Action Mailbox provides a helpful tool in development to "send" emails to your app. Visit http://localhost:3000/rails/conductor/action_mailbox/inbound_emails/ in your browser, and you should see a page that says "All Inbound Emails" and has an empty table. This page lists all of your ActionMailbox::InboundEmail records in your database.

Click the "Deliver new inbound email" link, and you should see a form with fields for creating an ActionMailbox::InboundEmail record. Populate the "From" field with your email address and the "To" field with the draft article email address shown on your New Article page, provide a title and body, and click "Deliver inbound email." Before submitting, your screen will look something like Figure 12-8.

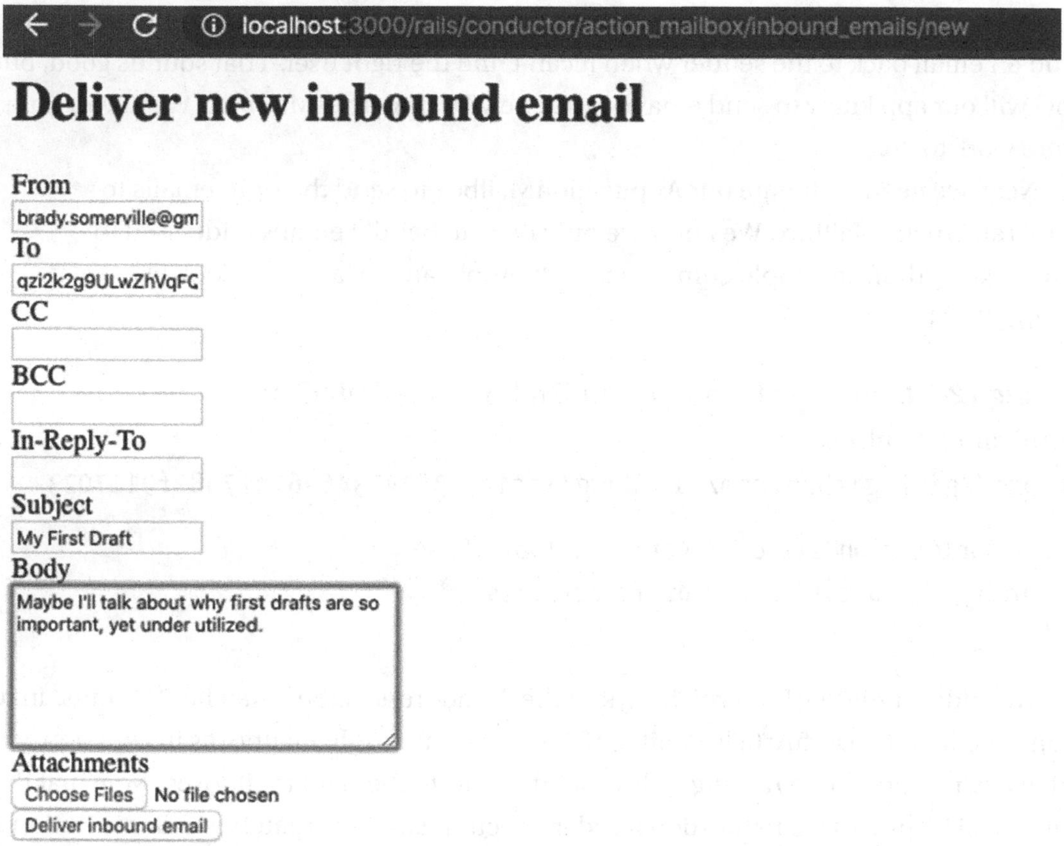
localhost:3000/rails/conductor/action_mailbox/inbound_emails/new
Deliver new inbound email
From
brady.somerville@gm
To
qzi2k2g9ULwZhVqFC
CC
BCC
In-Reply-To
Subject
My First Draft
Body
Maybe I'll talk about why first drafts are so important, yet under utilized.
Attachments
Choose Files
No file chosen
Deliver inbound email

Figure 12-8. *Testing our new mailbox with a new inbound email*

Once you submit the email, your app should receive the email, route it to the DraftArticlesMailbox, find your user record based on the token from the *To:* address, and create an article with the subject of your email as its title and the body of your email as its body.

Did it work? Go back to your blog's root URL, http://localhost:3000. If the email was able to be processed, you will see the unpublished article there. (Hmm, we ought to change that! We won't take time to do it now, but a live blog wouldn't want to serve unpublished articles to the public.)

If it didn't work, make sure you addressed your email correctly. The dev tool we used to send an email redirected to a details page for the email we sent. It shows the full source of the email we generated and gives us a chance to send it again.

If the email was addressed correctly, then check over our recent code changes closely. You may also look in your server's output for clues, though sending/processing an email generates quite a bit of logging.

Now that we can create draft articles by processing an email, we've almost finished adding our feature. However, there's one last thing that will make it more polished—letting the author know their email has been processed.

Responding to the Author

As our feature currently stands, the author is left wondering if the email they sent to create a draft article *actually* created a draft article. Rather than leaving them worried or in doubt, we can send them an email to acknowledge their submission and even to give them a helpful link to edit the draft article.

First, let's add a mailer action to the DraftArticleMailer called *created*, as shown in Listing 12-25.

Listing 12-25. Adding DraftArticleMailer#created Action
https://gist.github.com/nicedawg/760e8a533498503ab8f7133318830fe6

```
class DraftArticlesMailer < ApplicationMailer
  def created(to, article)
    @article = article
    mail to: to, subject: 'Your Draft Article has been created.'
  end

  def no_author(to)
    mail to: to, subject: 'Your email could not be processed' do |format|
      content = 'Please check your draft articles email address and try
      again.'
      format.html { render plain: content }
      format.text { render plain: content }
    end
  end
end
```

And let's add the HTML and text mailer view templates for this new mailer action as shown in Listings 12-26 and 12-27, respectively.

Listing 12-26. app/views/draft_articles_mailer/created.html.erb
https://gist.github.com/nicedawg/9ba9ca657cd66e34a6b0cbaf82f0edf9

```
<p>
  Your draft article has been successfully created.
</p>

<p>
  You may edit your article here:
  <%= link_to @article.title, edit_article_url(@article) %>
</p>
```

Listing 12-27. app/views/draft_articles_mailer/created.text.erb
https://gist.github.com/nicedawg/b5ed9f8d972b90cdf0baeac23ca5f668

```
Your draft article has been successfully created.

You may edit your article here:
  <%= edit_article_url(@article) %>
```

Next, let's update our DraftArticlesMailerPreview class in test/mailers/previews/ draft_articles_mailer_preview.rb, as shown in Listing 12-28, so we can preview our new *created* mailer action.

Listing 12-28. test/mailers/previews/draft_articles_mailer_preview.rb
https://gist.github.com/nicedawg/adeaf5ae0325a1c6c1a5b460861f2099

```
class DraftArticlesMailerPreview < ActionMailer::Preview
  def created
    DraftArticlesMailer.created('test@example.com', Article.first)
  end

  def no_author
    DraftArticlesMailer.no_author('test@example.com')
  end
end
```

Now that we're all set up to preview and send the *DraftArticlesMailer.created* message, the last thing we need to do is to have our DraftArticlesMailbox send this message when it's appropriate. Let's update our DraftArticlesMailbox so it looks like Listing 12-29.

Listing 12-29. Updating DraftArticlesMailbox to Send "Created" Email
https://gist.github.com/nicedawg/b6bdb5d3289079cd7f91c6e6657658d2

```
class DraftArticlesMailbox < ApplicationMailbox
  before_processing :require_author

  def process
    article = author.articles.create!(
      title: mail.subject,
      body: mail.body,
    )

    DraftArticlesMailer.created(mail.from, article).deliver
  end

  private

  def require_author
    bounce_with DraftArticlesMailer.no_author(mail.from) unless author
  end

  def author
    @author ||= User.find_by(draft_article_token: token)
  end

  def token
    mail.to.first.split('@').first
  end
end
```

In this last code change, we changed *author.articles.create* to say *author.articles.
create!* instead. This will ensure that if the article can't be created, an exception will be
raised and the *process* method will stop before sending the *created* message. If *create!*
succeeds, then we'll construct our *created* message using the "From" address of the
sender, and the resulting draft article, and then deliver it.

Try it out! Visit http://localhost:3000/rails/conductor/action_mailbox/inbound_
emails/ to resend an email or to send a new email. If your Action Mailer delivery works
correctly and you use your email address as the "From" message, then in response to

your email to create a draft article, you will receive an acknowledgement email with a link to the newly created draft article. It did take a bit of work to make it happen, but in retrospect, that was a really cool feature to add with not *that* much work.

Summary

In this chapter, we learned how to send email from our web application using Action Mailer. We configured Action Mailer to talk to our mail server and learned the most common configuration parameters we can use to fine-tune how Action Mailer works with our application.

We learned that Action Mailer allows us to send email messages based on view templates and how to use implicit parts for text and HTML messages, as well as how to use the `attachments` helper to add attachments to our messages. We also learned how to preview messages so we don't even have to deliver them while developing.

We also learned how to receive and process email using Action Mailbox. This chapter only scratched the surface, but serves as a good starting point. Should your application ever need to perform this task, you know where to look when you need more information.

Now that our app is sending (and even receiving) emails, it's time to talk about another component of Rails—Active Job. In the next chapter, we'll discuss how it can be used to improve performance of your application when performing tasks that have the potential to bog it down.

CHAPTER 13

Active Job

Web applications often need to perform long-running tasks in response to a request. For example, in the previous chapter, we modified our blog to send emails. While it's true that sending an email usually only takes a second or so, web developers are often concerned with *milliseconds*. So what's the big deal with some requests taking a second or two?

For illustration, imagine going to your local Post Office to drop off a package for delivery. There are a few employees at the counter accepting packages for delivery and a long line of customers waiting to be helped. When it's finally your turn to be helped at the counter, you hand the package to the employee, and they say, "Thank you! Please wait here at the counter with me until we have delivered your package." No wonder why the line was so long! The employees can't help other customers while waiting for your package to be delivered, and you can't do anything else while you're waiting either. How absurd, right?! We don't need to stand there and wait for the delivery to be *completed*. We just need to know that the delivery was *scheduled*, and we'll trust the system to work as it should.

The illustration is absurd, but this is exactly what happens in our web applications when we perform lengthy tasks in the middle of a request, before returning a response to the user. Perhaps a typical request can be serviced in 200 ms—but if we actually try to deliver an email in the middle of the request, that request may take 1 or 2 seconds to complete. For small web applications, this may be acceptable. But at a larger scale, this could mean you need additional expensive servers to handle the load.

This is exactly the type of problem which Active Job strives to solve. With Active Job, we can *schedule* a job (like email delivery) to be performed later, so that it doesn't block the server from handling other requests and doesn't block the client from going about *their* business too. Whenever we have a lengthy operation to perform in response to a request and the client doesn't need to know immediately if the operation succeeded or not—just that it was *scheduled* to be performed—then using a job runner like Active Job is a great way to service these requests efficiently.

© Brady Somerville, Adam Gamble, Cloves Carneiro Jr and Rida Al Barazi 2020
B. Somerville et al., *Beginning Rails 6*, https://doi.org/10.1007/978-1-4842-5716-6_13

Active Job isn't the first or only solution to this problem for Rails developers. For years, developers have solved this problem with *cron* jobs, custom software, or third-party job queuing frameworks, like *Resque*, *Delayed::Job*, and *Sidekiq*. Active Job doesn't even necessarily replace these frameworks; it provides a simple default implementation of a job queueing framework and acts as an *adapter* so that a developer can switch between job queueing frameworks without needing to overhaul their code.

In this chapter, first we will learn about Active Job configuration. Then, we will explore the anatomy of an Active Job class to learn about its capabilities. Finally, we will improve the performance of our blog application by sending our emails through Active Job.

Configuring Active Job

You may be surprised to find out that not only is Active Job already installed in our blog application but we've already used it (indirectly). In the previous chapter, when we used the built-in tool to send an email to our blog application, some Action Mailbox and Active Storage jobs were scheduled and performed in order to analyze the submitted email and to route it to the appropriate Mailbox class. (If you'd like to see for yourself, revisit that section of the previous chapter and watch the server output when you submit the email. Look for lines that begin with *[ActiveJob]*.)

As you can see, Rails makes using a job queueing system as easy as possible—no configuration necessary! However, it's important to note that the default implementation which Active Job includes is not appropriate for production use, mainly because it stores the information about the scheduled jobs in memory—meaning that if your Rails server is stopped, it loses track of the jobs it might still need to perform.

But as mentioned before, Active Job also acts as an *adapter* to work with more robust job frameworks which *are* suitable for production environments; tools like *Sidekiq*, *Delayed::Job*, and *Resque* can keep track of jobs which need to be performed, offer administrative tools, and other advanced features. So this means we can use Active Job in development with no fuss and, when the need arises in production, can do a little extra work to integrate with a production-ready job runner—without needing to change how our jobs were written.

The only Active Job configuration option we're likely to set is *config.active_job. queue_adapter*, which tells Active Job which job queueing system we want to use. Table 13-1 shows the most common values we might use for this option. As usual, we can configure these options in config/application.rb when we want the setting to apply across all environments or in each specific config/environments/*.rb file.

Table 13-1. *Common Values for config.active_job.queue_adapter*

Option	Description
:async	This is the default implementation provided by Active Job. It performs the jobs *asynchronously*—outside of the client/server request cycle. This adapter is only appropriate for development and testing, as it will lose track of scheduled jobs when the server process is restarted.
:inline	This is another implementation provided by Active Job. Unlike the *async* implementation, the *inline* implementation performs the jobs *during* the request cycle. This option loses the performance gains which the *:async* adapter provides, but may be necessary for custom Rake tasks which schedule jobs to work properly.
:test	This is another implementation provided by Active Job, meant to be used in your testing environment. This adapter lets your tests decide whether the jobs should actually be performed or not and makes it easy for your tests to assert whether or not certain jobs were queued or performed.
:backburner, *:delayed_job,* *:que, :que_* *classic,* *:resque, :sidekiq,* *:sneakers,* *:sucker_punch*	These adapters are provided by Active Job, but require configuration and installation of a third-party job framework to actually queue and perform jobs. For production use, it's highly recommended to choose one of these alternatives.

We will stick with Active Job's default *:async* adapter for now, so no configuration changes needed. But when you're ready to use Active Job in production, see `https://api.rubyonrails.org/v6.0.2.1/classes/ActiveJob/QueueAdapters.html` for a list of supported adapters.

Creating an Active Job

We have described the problem that Active Job seeks to solve and explored its configuration a little bit—but how does one *create* a job?

Purely for illustration (and for fun), let's create a silly job called *GuessANumberBetweenOneAndTenJob*. While this job won't be useful for us in a practical sense, it will demonstrate various aspects of Active Job classes which *will* serve you practically in the future.

We'll start out simple and then enhance this job as we go along. First, let's use the Rails generator to create our Job class:

```
> rails g job guess_a_number_between_one_and_ten
    invoke  test_unit
    create  test/jobs/guess_a_number_between_one_and_ten_job_test.rb
    create  app/jobs/guess_a_number_between_one_and_ten_job.rb
```

Now, let's edit app/jobs/guess_a_number_between_one_and_ten_job.rb so that it matches Listing 13-1.

Listing 13-1. app/jobs/guess_a_number_between_one_and_ten_job.rb
https://gist.github.com/nicedawg/3189d0b82a40401a7d17ba1333cf1c2d

```ruby
class GuessANumberBetweenOneAndTenJob < ApplicationJob
  queue_as :default
  def perform(my_number)
    guessed_number = rand(1..10)

    if guessed_number == my_number
      Rails.logger.info "I guessed it! It was #{my_number}"
    else
      Rails.logger.error "Is it #{guessed_number}? No? Hmm."
    end
  end
end
```

First, we see that our Job class inherits from ApplicationJob, which is defined in our application in app/jobs/application_job.rb. If you inspect ApplicationJob, you'll see it inherits from ActiveJob::Base. This is similar to how our Active Record models, controllers, and mailers work. ApplicationJob provides a place to add functionality to *all* of our application's jobs while also endowing each of our Job classes with all of Active Job's functionality.

Next, we see *queue_as :default*. Active Job allows you to define separate queues for categorizing your jobs and treating them differently. For example, some jobs may be higher priority than others; you could put them in a queue named "critical," for example, and configure your server to prioritize them.

Next, we see we defined a *perform* method. Our Job classes must always have a *perform* method; this is the method which will be executed when the job is performed. As you can see, you can provide arguments to your *perform* method.

Our *perform* method implements a simple game; we provide our number (which should be between 1 and 10), and the job will pick a random number between 1 and 10. If the random number matches the number we passed in, it declares victory in the logged output. If the random number doesn't match our number (and most of the time it won't), then it admits defeat in the logged output.

Performing a Job

Let's try it out! Open your rails console (or *reload!* it), and let's perform the job:

```
> rails c
irb(main):001:0> GuessANumberBetweenOneAndTenJob.new.perform(3)
Is it 5? No? Hmm.
=> true
```

Of course, since the job guesses randomly, your output is likely different. You may have even gotten lucky, and the job guessed your number on the first try! Go ahead and rerun the job until it finally guesses your number if you'd like. (On most systems, you can just press the "up" arrow on your keyboard to pull up the previous commands and then press Enter again.)

Performing a Job *Later*

Well, that was a little fun, maybe. But we didn't make use of Active Job's asynchronous execution of our job. Let's go back to our rails console and run our job a little differently:

```
irb(main):002:0> GuessANumberBetweenOneAndTenJob.perform_later(3)
Enqueued GuessANumberBetweenOneAndTenJob (Job ID: fc5eb7b6-b1ab-4011-ba4c-
cac73e999f3c) to Async(default) with arguments: 3
```

```
=> #<GuessANumberBetweenOneAndTenJob:0x00007fda1c172ae8 @arguments=[3],
@job_id="fc5eb7b6-b1ab-4011-ba4c-cac73e999f3c", @queue_name="default",
@priority=nil, @executions=0, @exception_executions={}, @provider_job_
id="c1fe1985-449a-4100-812c-9bab5923694b">
irb(main):003:0> Performing GuessANumberBetweenOneAndTenJob (Job ID:
fc5eb7b6-b1ab-4011-ba4c-cac73e999f3c) from Async(default) enqueued at
2020-03-28T18:48:45Z with arguments: 3
I guessed it! It was 3
Performed GuessANumberBetweenOneAndTenJob (Job ID: fc5eb7b6-b1ab-4011-ba4c-
cac73e999f3c) from Async(default) in 4.99ms
```

As you can see, I got lucky this time, but you likely won't. We ran our job a little differently—instead of *.new.perform(3)*, we used *perform_later(3)*. Our code in the *perform* method was still executed, but all the extra output from the rails console command shows us that this small change resulted in our job being "enqueued" and then "performed" later. Sure, it was only milliseconds later, but you get the idea.

Admittedly, that was maybe even *less* fun. It's interesting to see the job being queued up and then performed asynchronously, but it didn't add anything to our game. (But it did teach us how to execute our job asynchronously!) Let's enhance our silly game, though.

Retrying a Failed Job

Next, let's change our job so that it *retries* the job if it fails to guess the correct number. Modify your job so it looks like Listing 13-2.

Listing 13-2. Retrying Our Job When It Fails to Guess the Right Number
https://gist.github.com/nicedawg/784bfce14529a6e5432dd5eb542b8c8c

```
class GuessANumberBetweenOneAndTenJob < ApplicationJob
  queue_as :default

  class GuessedWrongNumber < StandardError; end

  retry_on GuessedWrongNumber, attempts: 8, wait: 1

  def perform(my_number)
```

```
    guessed_number = rand(1..10)

    if guessed_number == my_number
      Rails.logger.info "I guessed it! It was #{my_number}"
    else
      raise GuessedWrongNumber, "Is it #{guessed_number}? No? Hmm."
    end
  end
end
```

Our changes were fairly minimal. First, we defined a custom exception called *GuessedWrongNumber*, which inherits from *StandardError*, as is common practice for custom exceptions. This syntax may look strange; we haven't yet defined a class inside of another class, and the semicolon looks out of place. It's okay, though; defining a class within another class is perfectly valid, and when all you need is inheritance, defining a class within a single line is valid too.

Next, we configured our job to retry when the *GuessedWrongNumber* exception is raised during execution of the job. The default for *retry_on* is five attempts, but we decided to be generous and give our job eight attempts to guess the right number. We could have also accepted the default of waiting 3 seconds between retries, but we chose to only wait 1 second.

Finally, instead of simply logging the error, we *raise* our custom exception with a custom error message, so that the *retry_on* behavior will kick in. This has the overall effect of retrying our job up to eight times, 1 second apart, when the job fails to guess the correct number.

Let's go ahead and try this out in our rails console:

```
irb(main):003:0> reload!
irb(main):004:0> GuessANumberBetweenOneAndTenJob.perform_later(3)
Enqueued GuessANumberBetweenOneAndTenJob ....
Performing GuessANumberBetweenOneAndTenJob .....
Error performing GuessANumberBetweenOneAndTenJob... GuessANumberBetweenOneA
ndTenJob::GuessedWrongNumber (Is it 9? No? Hmm.): ...
 ... backtrace omitted ...
Retrying GuessANumberBetweenOneAndTenJob in 1 seconds, due to a GuessANumbe
rBetweenOneAndTenJob::GuessedWrongNumber.
Performing GuessANumberBetweenOneAndTenJob ...
```

```
Error performing GuessANumberBetweenOneAndTenJob…
… backtrace omitted ...
Retrying GuessANumberBetweenOneAndTenJob in 1 seconds…
… many retries and their backtraces omitted …
Stopped retrying GuessANumberBetweenOneAndTenJob due to a GuessANumberBetwe
enOneAndTenJob::GuessedWrongNumber, which reoccurred on 8 attempts.
```

You may have noticed that we omitted a *lot* of output. The majority of the output we omitted (which you might be scrolling through) is from *backtraces*—a long list of file names, line numbers, and method names which show you the method calls that led to your exception. Those aren't helpful to us right now—we know exactly where our GuessedWrongNumber exception came from. But in real-world debugging, it's often helpful to look closely at these backtraces to establish a context for the conditions in which an error occurred.

Skipping over the backtraces, you'll see a series of messages from Active Job which inform you that it has enqueued your job, that it's performing it, that an error occurred, that it's going to retry the job, and then perhaps that it finally gave up because it reached the maximum retry attempts allowed.

While this is a silly example, being able to retry your jobs when certain exceptions occur is very useful. For example, maybe your job consumes a third-party API; if that third-party API has a brief outage and your job is written to handle the exception that such an outage might raise, your job can be smart enough to try again later, when it very well may succeed. By expecting and handling such exceptions, we can develop more robust applications.

Discarding a Failed Job

Sometimes, when a certain exception is raised, we may want to *discard* our job. In certain situations, the job may no longer be applicable. For instance, perhaps a job is run to update a particular article—but by the time the job is performed, that article has been destroyed and can no longer be found.

Similar to *retry_on*, Active Job gives us the ability to call *discard_on* for certain exceptions. To illustrate this, we'll discard our job in the event that the number we provide isn't an integer between 1 and 10. Let's modify our job so it matches Listing 13-3.

Listing 13-3. Discarding Our Job When Provided an Invalid Number
https://gist.github.com/nicedawg/80779e72918f83c86a81bd5115b92271

```
class GuessANumberBetweenOneAndTenJob < ApplicationJob

  class ThatsNotFair < StandardError; end
  class GuessedWrongNumber < StandardError; end

  discard_on ThatsNotFair
  retry_on GuessedWrongNumber, attempts: 8, wait: 1

  def perform(my_number)
    unless my_number.is_a?(Integer) && my_number.between?(1, 10)
      raise ThatsNotFair, "#{my_number} isn't an integer between 1 and 10!"
    end

    guessed_number = rand(1..10)

    if guessed_number == my_number
      Rails.logger.info "I guessed it! It was #{my_number}"
    else
      raise GuessedWrongNumber, "Is it #{guessed_number}? No? Hmm."
    end
  end
end
```

Similar to how we added the ability to retry, we added the ability to discard the job by first defining a custom exception called *ThatsNotFair*. Then, we configured the job to be discarded when the *ThatsNotFair* exception is raised during job execution. Finally, we added some logic to the *perform* method to raise our custom exception (with a custom error message) if we tried to cheat the system by providing a number which isn't an integer between 1 and 10.

Let's try it out in the rails console:

```
irb(main):043:0> GuessANumberBetweenOneAndTenJob.perform_later(11)
Enqueued GuessANumberBetweenOneAndTenJob ....
Performing GuessANumberBetweenOneAndTenJob ...
```

```
Error performing GuessANumberBetweenOneAndTenJob .... GuessANumberBetweenOn
eAndTenJob::ThatsNotFair (11 isn't an integer between 1 and 10!):
... backtrace omitted ...
Discarded GuessANumberBetweenOneAndTenJob due to a GuessANumberBetweenOneAn
dTenJob::ThatsNotFair
```

Again, this is a silly example, but it shows us how we can choose how to handle certain exceptions in our jobs—sometimes by retrying, sometimes by discarding.

Improving Our Blog with Active Job

How can we use what we've learned about Active Job to improve our blog application? What long-running tasks do we have which we can defer to a background process to speed up our response time, so that both the client and server can move on to submitting and responding to more requests?

Converting our email delivery to use Active Job for asynchronous delivery is the lowest-hanging fruit. Thankfully, this is such a common need that we won't have to write custom Job classes to manage asynchronous email delivery; Action Mailer anticipated our need and provided us with a *deliver_later* method we can use (instead of simply using *deliver*) to convert our email delivery from happening in the *middle* of our request cycle to happening *outside* of the request cycle.

In the previous chapter, we could have opted to use *deliver_later*; it would have worked just fine, with no installation or configuration necessary. However, we decided to introduce it in *this* chapter so you could appreciate its usefulness (and understand better what's happening behind the scenes).

Before we begin converting our emails to be delivered asynchronously with *deliver_later*, let's do a little casual benchmarking of the current performance of our requests which send email synchronously.

For example, let's use the "Email a Friend" form on an article's show page. (Hopefully in the previous example, you were able to successfully deliver email from your application. But even if not, you should still be able to see the performance improvements of handing your deliveries off to Active Job.)

Go ahead and send yourself an email using the "Email a Friend" form, and then look at the server output for something that looks like the following:

Started POST "/articles/1/notify_friend" for ::1 at 2020-03-28 15:21:42
-0500
Processing by ArticlesController#notify_friend as JS
... output omitted ...
NotifierMailer#email_friend: processed outbound mail in 18.0ms
Delivered mail 5e7fb1d6e22ea_9abe3feeb76d503412331@Bradys-MacBook-Pro-2.
local.mail **(2685.5ms)**
... email contents omitted ...
Redirected to http://localhost:3000/articles/1
Completed 200 OK in **2758ms** (ActiveRecord: 0.6ms | Allocations: 20009)

We omitted some of the output for clarity. Look for the line that signifies that the request for "POST /articles/:id/notify_friend" began, and then look for the numbers that correspond with that request. In my example, it took 2685 ms (2.6 s) to deliver the email. The request as a whole (including the email delivery) took about 2.7 seconds to process.

Try it a few more times, taking note of these numbers, and establish an idea of the average response time. You're likely to see a bit of a range, but perhaps an average response time of around 2 seconds, depending on your development machine, as well as the performance of the email provider you're using to send your email.

Now, let's convert this mailer to deliver asynchronously using Active Job. Simply edit your app/controllers/article_controller.rb to match Listing 13-4.

Listing 13-4. Sending "Email a Friend" Using Active Job https://gist.github.
com/nicedawg/52a9cdf57e671d41de0e6044c4d5b555

```
class ArticlesController < ApplicationController
  before_action :authenticate, except: [:index, :show]
  before_action :set_article, only: [:show, :notify_friend]

  .. code omitted ...

  def notify_friend
    NotifierMailer.email_friend(@article, params[:name],
    params[:email]).deliver_later
    redirect_to @article, notice: 'Successfully sent a message to your friend'
  end

  ... code omitted ...
end
```

With that small change, now try sending that same email to yourself by filling out the "Email a Friend" form again. Let's try a few times to see what the new average response time is:

```
Started POST "/articles/1/notify_friend" ...
Processing by ArticlesController#notify_friend as JS
… output omitted ...
[ActiveJob] Enqueued ActionMailer::MailDeliveryJob (Job ID: cdcfdc12-7275-
4faf-bd9a-d546acb54688) to Async(mailers) with arguments: "NotifierMailer",
"email_friend", "deliver_now", ….
Redirected to http://localhost:3000/articles/1
Completed 200 OK in 42ms (ActiveRecord: 0.7ms | Allocations: 19614)

… output omitted ...
Started GET "/articles/1" …
[ActiveJob] [ActionMailer::MailDeliveryJob] Performing...
[ActiveJob] [ActionMailer::MailDeliveryJob] [cdcfdc12-7275-4faf-bd9a-
d546acb54688] Delivered mail … (2292.7ms)
[ActiveJob] [ActionMailer::MailDeliveryJob] [cdcfdc12-7275-4faf-bd9a-
d546acb54688] Performed ... in 2337.68ms
```

Reading logs can be a bit tricky, so we omitted some output to focus on the important parts. We see that the response to the "notify_friend" request was drastically reduced from somewhere in the realm of 2 seconds to 40 milliseconds. We can now process about 50 of these requests in the time it used to take to handle one!

One might be tempted to say, "Big deal, 2 seconds isn't long at all." However, in a production environment, a performance increase like this is very valuable. Not only will your users appreciate a snappier response time but forcing browsers to wait for the email to be delivered (like the illustration of the Post Office at the beginning of this chapter) will lead to long lines of customers waiting for someone to be able to handle *their* request. They'll eventually get tired of waiting and give up or receive an error. However, with a job framework like Active Job, we can easily defer certain time-consuming tasks to be performed later for an easy win.

While we're at it, let's go ahead and convert our other mailer deliveries to use Active Job too. Listings 13-5 and 13-6 show where to change our remaining usages of *deliver* to *deliver_later* in order to speed up our response times.

Listing 13-5. Sending "Comment added" Mailer Asynchronously https://gist.github.com/nicedawg/c28d5a14e7182d606ef5bf01b68779ee

```ruby
class Comment < ApplicationRecord
  belongs_to :article

  validates :name, :email, :body, presence: true
  validate :article_should_be_published

  after_create :email_article_author

  def article_should_be_published
    errors.add(:article_id, 'is not published yet') if article && !article.
    published?
  end

  def email_article_author
    NotifierMailer.comment_added(self).deliver_later
  end
end
```

Listing 13-6. Sending "Draft article created" Mailer Asynchronously https://gist.github.com/nicedawg/64cda2012f5dcf9662561480f0c3ba31

```ruby
class DraftArticlesMailbox < ApplicationMailbox
  before_processing :require_author

  def process
    article = author.articles.create!(
      title: mail.subject,
      body: mail.body,
    )

    DraftArticlesMailer.created(mail.from, article).deliver_later
  end

  private

  def require_author
```

```
    bounce_with DraftArticlesMailer.no_author(mail.from) unless author
  end

  def author
    @author ||= User.find_by(draft_article_token: token)
  end

  def token
    mail.to.first.split('@').first
  end
end
```

Summary

In this chapter, we learned about Active Job and the types of problems it solves. To illustrate some of Active Job's capabilities, we created a silly game using Active Job and learned how to invoke a job synchronously and asynchronously via the rails console. We then learned how to retry and discard jobs in reaction to certain types of errors.

Finally, we learned how easy it is to convert our mail deliveries to use Active Job and saw how it greatly improved response times when a request attempted to deliver an email.

While we stuck with Rails' default *:async* adapter for convenience, we learned that we should choose a more robust job backend for production usage—but that our Job classes wouldn't necessarily need to change when switching backends.

What's next? While testing out our improvements to our email delivery, you may have realized that our "Email a Friend" form isn't very robust. If you submit it with blank or invalid information, our blog acts like that's perfectly fine and even says, "Successfully sent a message to your friend." If submitting this form led to the creation of an Active Record model, we could simply add validations to that model to fix this problem, but it doesn't create an instance of an Active Record model. In the next chapter, we'll explore Active Model and learn how we can use it to add validations and other helpful things to classes which aren't stored in the database.

CHAPTER 14

Active Model

We learned in previous chapters that Active Record gives us the tools we need to perform a variety of activities on our models. For example, we added validations to our User model to make sure email addresses are unique and valid. We also added a callback to our Comment model to email the article's author anytime a comment is created. We were able to pass instances of these models to the *form_with* helper in their respective form partials to get default values and error messages with minimal effort. Powerful stuff!

But at the end of the previous chapter, we realized that our "Email a Friend" form is lacking these features. Currently, if one were to fill out that form without populating any values or by supplying an invalid email address, our blog application would happily accept those invalid values and even claim to have successfully sent the email!

We *could* create a new Active Record model to represent these "Email a Friend" submissions to give us validations, callbacks, and other Active Record goodies, but that would require us to create a database table to store these submissions. That's not necessarily *wrong*, but sometimes we want these benefits of Active Record without needing the database-related functionality. (In our example, we don't have a desire to store these "Email a Friend" submissions—just to validate them.)

We *could* also reinvent the wheel and make our own validation functions, our own callback mechanisms, and other features we need. But that's time-consuming and error-prone.

What if we could have the parts of Active Record we need, without the parts we don't need? This is precisely where Active Model comes in; in fact, you might be surprised to learn that Active Record validations, callbacks, and many other features are actually supplied by Active Model!

In this chapter, we'll learn how to mix in some of the most commonly used Active Model modules into POROs (Plain Old Ruby Objects) to gain some of the best features of Active Record in models which don't need database storage.

© Brady Somerville, Adam Gamble, Cloves Carneiro Jr and Rida Al Barazi 2020
B. Somerville et al., *Beginning Rails 6*, https://doi.org/10.1007/978-1-4842-5716-6_14

After a brief tour of some of the most commonly used Active Model modules, we'll improve our blog application by using Active Model to improve how we handle "Email a Friend" submissions.

A Tour of Active Model

Like many well-designed libraries, Active Model is composed of several modules, each focused on a specific set of behaviors. This type of organization allows the developer to choose which parts of Active Model they need, rather than being forced to include the whole set of behaviors.

In this section, we'll explore some of the most commonly used modules in Active Model and learn how they can enhance our POROs. For illustration, let's build a Car class, which will have nothing to do with our blog application. After we've toured some of the most commonly used modules of Active Model, we'll leave this Car class behind and go to work improving our blog application.

Let's add a simple Car class to app/models/car.rb, as shown in Listing 14-1.

Listing 14-1. Basic Car Class to Help Illustrate Active Model Modules
https://gist.github.com/nicedawg/a1ba973abc0a29df829ef46ab78b20de

```
class Car
  attr_accessor :make, :model, :year, :color

  def paint(new_color)
    self.color = new_color
  end
end
```

Notice that our Car class does not inherit from any parent classes. That's perfectly fine! We defined a few attributes and added a *paint* method which will change our car's color, but that's it. Let's open our rails console (or *reload!* an existing one) and see what this simple class can do:

```
> rails c
irb(main):001:0> c = Car.new(make: 'Mazda', model: 'B3000', year: 1998,
color: 'green')
```

```
Traceback (most recent call last):
        3: from (irb):9
        2: from (irb):9:in `new'
        1: from (irb):9:in `initialize'
ArgumentError (wrong number of arguments (given 1, expected 0))
irb(main):002:0> c = Car.new
=> #<Car:0x00007fe42bab6528>
irb(main):003:0> c.make = 'Mazda'
=> "Mazda"
irb(main):004:0> c.model = 'B3000'
=> "B3000"
irb(main):005:0> c.year = 1998
=> 1998
irb(main):006:0> c.color = 'green'
=> "green"
irb(main):007:0> c
=> #<Car:0x00007fe42a9f9118 @make="Mazda", @model="B3000", @year=1998,
@color="green">
```

We tried to instantiate a new car by supplying its attributes in the constructor—
the *new* method. That works with Active Record models, but not this Car class. So we
instantiated a new car with no arguments and assigned each attribute a value one by
one. That worked as expected, but not being able to supply a hash of attributes and their
values to the constructor will be inconvenient. Hopefully, we can fix that.

ActiveModel::Attributes

Good news—we can fix that! As it turns out, ActiveModel::AttributeAssignment supplies
the very thing we need. First, let's include the module in our Car class and override the
initialize method so that it matches Listing 14-2.

Listing 14-2. Including ActiveModel::AttributeAssignment in the Car Class
https://gist.github.com/nicedawg/96ffbaed32abc8ef78acc90149345343

```ruby
class Car
  include ActiveModel::AttributeAssignment

  attr_accessor :make, :model, :year, :color

  def initialize(attributes = {})
    assign_attributes(attributes) if attributes

    super()
  end

  def paint(new_color)
    self.color = new_color
  end
end
```

In the preceding listing, we included the ActiveModel::AttributeAssignment module in our Car class. Generally, that means that our Car class gains new methods from the module we included. One such method we gained is *assign_attributes*—a method that takes a hash of key-value pairs and uses the corresponding setter for each key to assign the value from the hash.

Another thing that warrants explanation is our *initialize* method. Every Ruby object has an *initialize* method, usually supplied by a parent class. Whenever the *new* message is sent to a class, Ruby creates a new object from the class and then calls the *initialize* method on that new object. We wanted to be able to assign a hash of attributes when we call *Car.new*, so this is the right place to do it! Our *initialize* method takes an argument (with the default being an empty hash) and then calls the *assign_attributes* method on our car object with that hash, if it exists.

Finally, we call *super()*, to make sure that any *initialize* methods on our parent classes are called as well. The parentheses after the call to *super* might strike you as strange—it's not typical Ruby code style to affix empty parentheses to method calls. However, *super* is a little special; with no parentheses, its default behavior is to send the arguments of the method it's in to its parents also. That's often helpful, but in our case, it would cause an error, as our parent class does not expect any arguments.

That was a little tedious. For a feature we might like to use frequently—the ability to assign attributes via our model's constructor—this feels a little like the tedious boilerplate code which we've come to expect that Ruby on Rails can help us avoid. Don't worry; later in this chapter, we'll learn how to avoid needing to take these steps.

Now that we've made these changes, let's reload our console and see what happens:

```
irb(main):008:0> reload!
irb(main):009:0> c = Car.new(make: 'Mazda', model: 'B3000', year: 1998,
color: 'green')
=> #<Car:0x00007fc56fedc5d8 @make="Mazda", @model="B3000", @year=1998,
@color="green">
irb(main):010:0> c.assign_attributes(color: 'blue')
=> {"color"=>"blue"}
irb(main):011:0> c
=> #<Car:0x00007fc56faba608 @make="Mazda", @model="B3000", @year=1998,
@color="blue">
```

We're making progress! Slowly, but surely, our Car model is becoming a little easier to work with—thanks to ActiveModel::AttributeMethods.

ActiveModel::Callbacks

Next, let's use our *paint* method to change our car's color to black:

```
irb(main):012:0>c.paint('black')
=> "black"
irb(main):013:0> c
=> #<Car:0x00007fe42a9f9118 @make="Mazda", @model="B3000", @year=1998,
@color="black">
```

That worked just fine, as we expected it would. However, we remembered that if you change your car's color, you're supposed to notify your local Department of Motor Vehicles. Also, we'd like to remind people to keep their new paint jobs waxed for protection. We could certainly do these things in our *paint* method, but if this was an Active Record object, we'd be able to do these in *callbacks* to keep our *paint* method focused. With the ActiveModel::Callbacks module, we can do just that! Let's update our Car model to match Listing 14-3 to add support for callbacks to our class.

Listing 14-3. Extending Our Car Class with ActiveModel::Callbacks

https://gist.github.com/nicedawg/0bcaa23b2450a9d81859ed28d7089719

```ruby
class Car
  include ActiveModel::AttributeAssignment
  extend ActiveModel::Callbacks

  attr_accessor :make, :model, :year, :color

  define_model_callbacks :paint

  before_paint :keep_it_waxed
  after_paint :notify_dmv

  def initialize(attributes = {})
    assign_attributes(attributes) if attributes

    super()
  end

  def paint(new_color)
    run_callbacks :paint do
      Rails.logger.info "Painting the car #{new_color}"
      self.color = new_color
    end
  end

  private

  def keep_it_waxed
    Rails.logger.warn "Be sure to keep your new paint job waxed!"
  end

  def notify_dmv
    Rails.logger.warn "Be sure to notify the DMV about this color change!"
  end
end
```

First, we *extended* our class with the ActiveModel::Callbacks module. Why *extend* rather than *include*? The main reason is that ActiveModel::Callbacks adds *class methods* to our class, while ActiveModel::AttributeAssignment added *instance methods*. If in doubt, consult the source code of the module you wish to use in your class, or use your favorite search engine to find example usage.

Next, we used the class method *define_model_callbacks* to register a new lifecycle event—namely, *:paint*—for which we might want to run code before, after, or around that event.

Then, we configured our class to run *keep_it_waxed* before the car is painted and to run *notify_dmv* after the car is painted. (We added those methods as private methods, which simply log some output.)

Finally, we modified our *paint* method to call *run_callbacks :paint*. (The fact that we named our callback event *:paint* and the fact it happens in a method called *paint* are just a coincidence. The callback name does not need to match any method names.) By wrapping our assignment of *color* in the *run_callbacks* block, this provides enough information for our code to know when to run any applicable callback methods. We also added a logging statement inside the callback to indicate when the color is actually being changed.

Let's reload our rails console and try it out:

```
irb(main):014:0> reload!
irb(main):015:0> c = Car.new(make: 'Mazda', model: 'B3000', year: 1998,
color: 'green')
irb(main):016:0> c.paint('gray')
Be sure to keep your new paint job waxed!
Painting the car gray
Be sure to notify the DMV about this color change!
=> "gray"
```

Alright! We see that our registered callback methods were performed in the right order. Once again, Active Model has added some powerful behavior to our Car class with not *too* much effort. However, we just realized we have a slight flaw in our logic surrounding notifying the DMV about color changes. Often, someone might paint their car the same color to repair paint damage, but to keep the same look. In that case, there's no need to notify the DMV. We only need to notify them if the color actually changed.

ActiveModel::Dirty

We need to modify our Car class to only notify the DMV if the paint color actually changed—not when the car was repainted the same color.

If we were notifying the DMV in our *paint* method, we could simply compare the requested color to the current color. But we chose to notify the DMV in a *before_paint* callback and no longer have access to the requested color.

The ActiveModel::Dirty can help us here. Active Record uses this module to keep track of which attributes have changed. By including ActiveModel::Dirty in our Car class, we can achieve the same functionality, albeit with a little more work.

You might wonder, why is this module called *Dirty*? Often, in programming, an entity is called "dirty" if it has been modified, but the new values have not been saved or finalized. Since this module helps us keep track of which attributes have been changed (but not finalized), Dirty is an appropriate name.

Let's update our Car model to match Listing 14-4 to include ActiveModel::Dirty and make the associated changes so that we only notify the DMV if the color actually changed.

Listing 14-4. Including ActiveModel::Dirty in Our Car Class
https://gist.github.com/nicedawg/97a87d1f4bd19f7577bd500fbe51632a

```
class Car
  include ActiveModel::AttributeAssignment
  extend ActiveModel::Callbacks
  include ActiveModel::Dirty

  attr_accessor :make, :model, :year, :color

  define_attribute_methods :color
  define_model_callbacks :paint

  before_paint :keep_it_waxed
  after_paint :notify_dmv, if: :color_changed?

  def initialize(attributes = {})
    assign_attributes(attributes) if attributes

    super()
  end
```

```
  def paint(new_color)
    run_callbacks :paint do
      Rails.logger.info "Painting the car #{new_color}"
      color_will_change! if color != new_color
      self.color = new_color
    end
  end

  private

  def keep_it_waxed
    Rails.logger.warn "Be sure to keep your new paint job waxed!"
  end

  def notify_dmv
    Rails.logger.warn "Be sure to notify the DMV about this color change!"
    changes_applied
  end
end
```

First, we included the ActiveModel::Dirty module to add methods to our class which can help keep track of which attributes' values have changed. But unlike with Active Record, we don't get this behavior on our attributes automatically—we must define which attributes will be tracked and must manually set when an attribute's value is changing and when we should consider the change to be complete.

To declare that we want to track the "dirty" status of the *color* attribute, we add the *define_attribute_methods :color* line to our class. If we had more attributes we wanted to track, we could add them to this same line.

Next, we added a condition to our *notify_dmv* callback, so that we only perform *notify_dmv* if the color actually changed.

However, since this model is not an Active Record model, it's up to us to keep track of when the color attribute has changed and when we should consider the changes to be applied. So we call the *color_will_change!* method in our *paint* method only if the new color does not match the current color. By calling *color_will_change!*, the *color* attribute is now considered "dirty," and *color_changed?* will return true.

Finally, in our *notify_dmv* method, after having warned the user, we call *changes_applied* to clear the "dirty" status from our attributes. If we had not done this, any subsequent calls to *color_changed?* would return true—even if we're repainting the car with the same color!

Let's try out our new code changes in the rails console:

```
irb(main):017:0> reload!
irb(main):018:0> c = Car.new(make: 'Mazda', model: 'B3000', year: 1998,
color: 'green')
=> #<Car:0x00007fc57171dd40 @make="Mazda", @model="B3000", @year=1998,
@color="green">
irb(main):019:0> c.paint('black')
Be sure to keep your new paint job waxed!
Painting the car black
Be sure to notify the DMV about this color change!
=> "black"
irb(main):020:0> c.paint('black')
Be sure to keep your new paint job waxed!
Painting the car black
=> "black"
irb(main):021:0> c.paint('red')
Be sure to keep your new paint job waxed!
Painting the car red
Be sure to notify the DMV about this color change!
=> "red"
```

After reloading the console and re-instantiating our Car object with the color green, we painted it black and saw the warning to notify the DMV, as we expected. Next, we repainted the car black. As we hoped, we did *not* see the DMV warning. Finally, to be certain, we painted the car red and saw the DMV warning again.

Our Car class is certainly becoming more featureful. Another wishlist item of ours is validation. Will we be able to add Active Record–style validations to our Car class?

ActiveModel::Validations

As we've seen in previous chapters, being able to validate our models is essential. Active Record makes it easy and elegant to validate models—but our Car class is not an Active Record model. Are we doomed to reinvent the wheel?

No! In fact, you may have guessed by now that Active Record actually gets its validation functionality from Active Model. So let's update our Car class to match Listing 14-5 so that we can benefit from Active Model's Validations module.

Listing 14-5. Including ActiveModel::Validations in Our Car Class

https://gist.github.com/nicedawg/a68604460656afe78f6a0739477d7918

```
class Car
  include ActiveModel::AttributeAssignment
  include ActiveModel::Dirty
  include ActiveModel::Validations

  attr_accessor :make, :model, :year, :color

  validates :make, :model, :year, :color, presence: true
  validates :year, numericality: { only_integer: true, greater_than: 1885,
  less_than: Time.zone.now.year.to_i + 1 }

  define_attribute_methods :color
  define_model_callbacks :paint

  before_paint :keep_it_waxed
  after_paint :notify_dmv, if: :color_changed?

  def initialize(attributes = {})
    assign_attributes(attributes) if attributes

    super()
  end

  def paint(new_color)
    run_callbacks :paint do
      Rails.logger.info "Painting the car #{new_color}"
      color_will_change! if color != new_color
      self.color = new_color
    end
  end

  private

  def keep_it_waxed
    Rails.logger.warn "Be sure to keep your new paint job waxed!"
  end
```

```
def notify_dmv
  Rails.logger.warn "Be sure to notify the DMV about this color change!"
  changes_applied
end
end
```

First, we included ActiveModel::Validations into our class. If you look closely, we also removed ActiveModel::Callbacks. Why? It turns out that ActiveModel::Validations already includes ActiveModel::Callbacks, so we don't need to include it separately.

Next, we added validations to ensure that all of our attributes are present and also to ensure that the year is reasonable.

Now, let's use our rails console to check our validations:

```
irb(main):022:0> reload!
irb(main):023:0> c = Car.new(make: 'Mazda', model: 'B3000', year: 1998,
color: 'green')
=> #<Car:0x00007fc56fbcda68 @make="Mazda", @model="B3000", @year=1998,
@color="green">
irb(main):024:0> c.valid?
=> true
irb(main):025:0> c = Car.new(make: 'Tesla', model: 'Cybertruck', year:
2022, color: 'shiny metal')
=> #<Car:0x00007fc56fbf73b8 @make="Tesla", @model="Cybertruck", @year=2022,
@color="shiny metal">
irb(main):026:0> c.valid?
=> false
irb(main):027:0> c.errors.full_messages.to_sentence
=> "Year must be less than 2021"
```

There we have it! Simply by including ActiveModel::Validations, we gained the ability to define validation rules, to check an object's validity, and to see the validation errors—just like we've done in previous chapters with Active Record.

There are more Active Model modules we could explore, but we've covered some of the most commonly used modules. However, we're not quite ready to apply our knowledge to our blog application; there's one more Active Model module to cover.

ActiveModel::Model

So far, we've added attribute assignment, callbacks, dirty tracking, and validation to our Car class by adding various Active Model modules to our class and making relevant code changes.

Though we've made significant enhancements to our Car class with not *that* much code, it is beginning to feel a little heavy. We miss the elegance of Active Record classes which give us so much functionality for free.

There's a bit of bad news too: our Car class is not ready to be used in our Rails app the same way we can use Active Record objects throughout the app. Rails favors convention over configuration, and Active Record objects follow suit. We can pass an instance of an Active Record object to a path helper, to a *form_with* helper, to a *render* call... and Rails does the right thing. Unfortunately, as our Car class currently stands, using instances of the Car class in Action Pack and Action View will require more configuration than convention.

Yes, there are some more Active Model modules we could include to change our Car class to play more nicely with Action Pack and Action View, but we're already starting to feel that our Car class is getting a little too complicated.

Thankfully, we have ActiveModel::Model to rescue us. The *Model* module from Active Model is a bit of a super-module. ActiveModel::Model itself includes the AttributeAssignment and Validations modules, as well as a few more (Conversion, Naming, Translation) which will help our Car model play nicely with Action Pack and Action View. It also implements the behavior which we added manually in our *initialize* method.

In other words, simply by including this module and then removing some code, we'll have more functionality than when we started!

Let's improve our Car model by changing it to match Listing 14-6.

Listing 14-6. Including ActiveModel::Model in Our Car Class
https://gist.github.com/nicedawg/f38da1df450cc5860eebb420cc47220a

```
class Car
  include ActiveModel::Dirty
  include ActiveModel::Model

  attr_accessor :make, :model, :year, :color
```

```ruby
  validates :make, :model, :year, :color, presence: true
  validates :year, numericality: { only_integer: true, greater_than: 1885,
  less_than: Time.zone.now.year.to_i + 1 }

  define_attribute_methods :color
  define_model_callbacks :paint

  before_paint :keep_it_waxed
  after_paint :notify_dmv, if: :color_changed?

  def paint(new_color)
    run_callbacks :paint do
      Rails.logger.info "Painting the car #{new_color}"

      color_will_change! if color != new_color
      self.color = new_color
    end
  end

  private

  def keep_it_waxed
    Rails.logger.warn "Be sure to keep your new paint job waxed!"
  end

  def notify_dmv
    Rails.logger.warn "Be sure to notify the DMV about this color change!"
    changes_applied
  end
end
```

As you can see, we included ActiveModel::Model and removed the modules
we no longer need to manually include. We also removed our *initialize* method as
ActiveModel::Model gives us the ability to assign attributes in our class's constructor.

If you'd like to, reload your rails console and try out the features again—assigning
attributes in the constructor, the callbacks, tracking change status, and validations. It all
still works, with a little less code!

But the additional modules which ActiveModel::Model has included have given us some new functionality, so that instances of our Car class will work smoothly with Action Pack and Action View.

For instance, ActiveModel::Model includes ActiveModel::Naming, which adds a method called *model_name* to our class. Various Action Pack and Action View components will use the values of the ActiveModel::Name object it returns in order to generate routes, parameter keys, translation keys, and more. See the following example:

```
irb(main):028:0> reload!
Reloading...
=> true
irb(main):029:0> c = Car.new(make: 'Mazda', model: 'B3000', year: 1998,
color: 'green')
=> #<Car:0x00007fc5715e4c80 @make="Mazda", @model="B3000", @year=1998,
@color="green">
irb(main):030:0> c.model_name
=> #<ActiveModel::Name:0x00007fc571607c08 @name="Car", @klass=Car,
@singular="car", @plural="cars", @element="car", @human="Car",
@collection="cars", @param_key="car", @i18n_key=:car, @route_key="cars",
@singular_route_key="car">
```

Now that we've explored various Active Model modules and learned how to enhance our simple Car class to behave more like an Active Record module, we're ready to apply what we've learned to our blog.

Enhancing Our Blog with Active Model

You might remember that the issue which spawned this chapter (besides the fact that it's valuable to know about Active Model) is that our "Email a Friend" form is not up to our standards; it doesn't validate the input and claims to have "successfully sent the message" even if the user left all the fields blank or entered a syntactically invalid email address in the form!

We weren't sure how to handle this, because we didn't really want to create an Active Record model for "Email a Friend" submissions. At the moment, we have no need to store or retrieve these submissions. And we didn't want to reinvent the wheel or bloat our controller by adding validation code and error messaging in an unconventional way.

But now that we know how to create a model that mostly behaves like the Active Record models we're used to working with, we're ready to fix this.

Create an EmailAFriend Model

Using what we've learned from Active Model, let's create an EmailAFriend model in app/models/email_a_friend.rb. Make sure it matches the code in Listing 14-7.

Listing 14-7. EmailAFriend Model in app/models/email_a_friend.rb
https://gist.github.com/nicedawg/45fd55a2f9527675b18c8505352e8463

```
class EmailAFriend
  include ActiveModel::Model

  attr_accessor :name, :email

  validates :name, :email, presence: true
  validates :email, format: { with: URI::MailTo::EMAIL_REGEXP }
end
```

This model is simple enough. We included ActiveModel::Model to gain validations and other methods which will let the EmailAFriend model work well with Action Pack and Action View. The validator which checks the format of the email address uses a regular expression which is provided by the URI module—a part of any standard Ruby installation. (Note: This validator only checks that the email address is *syntactically* valid—that is to say, that it adheres to the rules for the format of an email address. It does not ensure that the domain is valid or that it accepts email or that a mailbox exists for that user.)

If we try out our model in the rails console, it looks good so far:

```
irb(main):031:0> reload!
irb(main):032:0> email_a_friend = EmailAFriend.new(name: 'Brady', email:
'brady.somerville@gmail.com')
=> #<EmailAFriend:0x00007fc575826800 @name="Brady", @email="brady.
somerville@gmail.com">
irb(main):033:0> email_a_friend.valid?
=> true
irb(main):034:0> email_a_friend = EmailAFriend.new(name: 'Brady', email:
'brady.somerville')
```

```
=> #<EmailAFriend:0x00007fc57281bae8 @name="Brady", @email="brady.
somerville">
irb(main):035:0> email_a_friend.valid?
=> false
irb(main):036:0> email_a_friend.errors.full_messages.to_sentence
=> "Email is invalid"
```

Now that our model can validate that a name and properly formatted email address were supplied, we can rework our controller and views to make use of our new model.

Update Controller/Views to Use Our New Model

Now that our EmailAFriend model is in place, let's update our blog application to use it. First, we will modify the *show* action in our ArticlesController to provide a new *EmailAFriend* object. Update your ArticlesController to match Listing 14-8.

Listing 14-8. Provide a New EmailAFriend Object to ArticlesController#show
https://gist.github.com/nicedawg/69a3789f84e91a63e68345ab7d4be814

```
class ArticlesController < ApplicationController
  ... code omitted ...

  # GET /articles/1
  # GET /articles/1.json
  def show
    @email_a_friend = EmailAFriend.new
  end

  ... code omitted ...
end
```

Next, we need to update our view layer to use this new instance variable to build the form. Let's modify app/views/articles/_notify_friend.html.erb to match Listing 14-9 to do just that.

Listing 14-9. Use @email_a_friend in app/views/articles/_notify_friend.html.erb
https://gist.github.com/nicedawg/b985133d8c917cb3367953ba4dc6ee0c

```
<%= form_with(model: @email_a_friend, url: notify_friend_article_
path(article), id: 'email_a_friend') do |form| %>
  <% if @email_a_friend.errors.any? %>
    <div id="error_explanation">
      <h2><%= pluralize(@email_a_friend.errors.count, "error") %>
      prohibited this from being submitted:</h2>

      <ul>
        <% @email_a_friend.errors.full_messages.each do |message| %>
          <li><%= message %></li>
        <% end %>
      </ul>
    </div>
  <% end %>

  <div class="field">
    <%= form.label :name, 'Your name' %>
    <%= form.text_field :name %>
  </div>
  <div class="field">
    <%= form.label :email, "Your friend's email" %>
    <%= form.text_field :email %>
  </div>
  <div class="actions">
    <%= form.submit 'Send' %> or
    <%= link_to 'Cancel', '#', onclick: "document.querySelector('#notify_
    friend').style.display='none';return false;" %>
  </div>
<% end %>
```

Nothing surprising there. As we've done before, we simply added *model:*
@email_a_friend to tell the *form_with* helper that we wanted our form to be based
on the object we passed. We also told the *form_with* helper we wanted the resulting

form to have the id "email_a_friend," which will be handy in a minute. Finally, we also added a snippet of code similar to what we've used elsewhere in order to display any error messages in the form.

If you were to try out the Email a Friend form now, you would see that nothing has really changed yet. That's to be expected, as we haven't yet added the code to make sure the Email a Friend submission was valid.

To do that, let's go back to the ArticlesController and change its *notify_friend* action to match Listing 14-10.

Listing 14-10. Validating Email a Friend in ArticlesController#notify_friend
`https://gist.github.com/nicedawg/5dc3292f1944af645df85afd9c627753`

```
class ArticlesController < ApplicationController
  ... code omitted ...

  def notify_friend
    @email_a_friend = EmailAFriend.new(email_a_friend_params)

    if @email_a_friend.valid?
      NotifierMailer.email_friend(@article, @email_a_friend.name, @email_a_
      friend.email).deliver_later
      redirect_to @article, notice: 'Successfully sent a message to your
      friend'
    else
      render :notify_friend, status: :unprocessable_entity
    end
  end

  private
    # Use callbacks to share common setup or constraints between actions.
    def set_article
      @article = Article.find(params[:id])
    end

    # Never trust parameters from the scary internet, only allow the white
    list through.
    def article_params
```

```
    params.require(:article).permit(:title, :cover_image, :remove_cover_
    image, :location, :excerpt, :body, :published_at, category_ids: [])
  end

  def email_a_friend_params
    params.require(:email_a_friend).permit(:name, :email)
  end
end
```

First, note the new private method we added at the bottom—*email_a_friend_ params*. It's always good practice to make sure that we whitelist the params we expect to receive. This has the effect of saying "the only params we'll accept for an EmailAFriend model are name and email."

Now take a close look at the changes we made to the *notify_friend* action. We instantiate a new EmailAFriend object using the params submitted from our form. If the object is valid, we do what we've always done—we schedule the email to be delivered, and we redirect with a success notice. However, instead of just grabbing the name and email straight from the *params* hash, we now get them from our instance of the EmailAFriend class.

Finally, we added an *else* clause. If the submission was *not* valid, we need to show the form again with the relevant error message. We also return a status of *:unprocessable_ entity*, which translates to HTTP status code 422.

We have one last thing to do. When an "Email a Friend" submission is invalid, we render a *:notify_friend* template—but that doesn't exist yet! We know that the submission is sent via Ajax, so we will need to create a new JavaScript template in app/views/ articles/notify_friend.js.erb. Let's add that now, as shown in Listing 14-11.

Listing 14-11. Adding app/views/articles/notify_friend.js.erb
https://gist.github.com/nicedawg/b4bd7f04722ca6ad14e518bb0829b539

```
document.querySelector('#email_a_friend').innerHTML = "<%= escape_javascript
render partial: 'notify_friend', locals: { article: @article } %>";
```

When this JS template is rendered, it instructs the browser to find the element with the id "email_a_friend"—which is our "Email a Friend" form—and replaces its content with the output of the *notify_friend* partial which we're already using. When this template is rendered as the result of the submission being invalid, it will include the error messages that explain why the form couldn't be submitted.

Try It Out

Now everything's in place. Try it out! Try submitting a blank "Email a Friend" form; you should see error messages about Name and Email being blank and Email being invalid. Try adding a Name but not an Email; you should see the error messages about Email, but not Name. Try adding an invalid Email; you should see an error message stating that the email address is invalid. Finally, submit valid information, and you should be redirected with a success message just like before!

Summary

In this chapter, we covered the use of several Active Model modules and saw how we can use them to enhance our POROs (Plain Old Ruby Objects) with Active Record–type behaviors. We then learned that ActiveModel::Model includes a few of the most commonly used modules and most importantly gives our model what it needs to play nice with Action Pack and Action View conventions.

There are some Active Model modules we did not cover, and we didn't exhaustively cover each module, but that's okay. Knowing that Active Model exists and understanding the types of things it can do is good enough for now. When you're ready for more information about Active Model, a good place to start is the official Rails guide, found at `https://guides.rubyonrails.org/active_model_basics.html`. Also, don't be afraid to find the source code and look through it. It's true that sometimes the source code may include things you don't fully understand, but often you can get the basic idea. A lot of Rails code—Active Model included—is well designed and documented and is much more accessible than you might think. You might even learn some new tricks!

What's next? We'll take a brief look at Action Cable—an exciting component of Rails which uses WebSockets to add some "real-time" capabilities to our applications.

CHAPTER 15

Action Cable

Introduction

The backbone of web development has been—and still is—the traditional request cycle; the client makes an HTTP request, and the server handles the request by performing some action and returning an HTTP response. In the context of a browser-based application, a human being is usually the initiator of this cycle, by clicking a link or submitting a form, for example.

Over time, though, web applications *themselves* have sought to be the initiator. For example, web-based email clients have an arguably richer UI when new mail shows up automatically, not just when the user refreshes the page. Imagine how frustrating it would be to use a web-based instant messaging service where you only see new messages when you reload the page.

Web developers have often met the demands of these richer UI needs through *polling*—periodically making Ajax requests to check if any new data might warrant action. For example, that web-based email client might have some JavaScript that calls an API endpoint to check for new mail. This strategy has helped build multimillion-dollar software projects and has worked amazingly well, but it does have some problems of its own; for example, the overhead of repeatedly checking for new information (when quite likely there is none) can become a critical performance issue for the server and even sometimes the client.

WebSockets solved that problem with the wide adoption of the WebSocket API by most commonly used browsers. Instead of browsers needing to constantly poll the server for new data, browsers can establish—and keep open—a connection through which *either* side can send messages. For example, that web-based email client doesn't have to keep checking for new mail; the page can just sit there, and the server will tell it when it has new mail! This strategy can be much more efficient, making your users happier and hopefully reducing server costs too.

© Brady Somerville, Adam Gamble, Cloves Carneiro Jr and Rida Al Barazi 2020
B. Somerville et al., *Beginning Rails 6*, https://doi.org/10.1007/978-1-4842-5716-6_15

Rails developers have already been using WebSockets in their applications by using gems such as *faye-websocket, websocket-rails,* and others. However, Rails 5 introduced an integrated approach with Action Cable.

In this chapter, we'll first try to get our mental model straight; Action Cable introduces a few new concepts that can be tricky to keep straight, so we'll do our best to firm up our understanding before moving on. Then, we'll briefly discuss the configuration of Action Cable and then get to work applying Action Cable to our blog application; we'll add an impressive but simple feature—in-page notifications when a new article is posted.

Concepts

Action Cable introduces a lot of new terminology into Rails—connections, channels, streams, broadcasting, subscriptions, and more. It's worth our time to get familiar with these terms before moving on; otherwise, it will be easy to get confused when diving into the code.

To aid our understanding of these concepts, we'll use Cable TV as an analogy. Analogies are by nature somewhat flawed, and this author doesn't *actually* know how Cable TV really works, but this analogy may help nonetheless.

The base of the Action Cable stack is the *connection*, represented by ActionCable::Connection. This *connection* represents an actual WebSocket connection. A user of your application will usually have, at most, one connection per browser window (or tab). The connection typically doesn't care what type of data it might send or receive; it's simply an established method of communication. In our Cable TV analogy, we can think of the physical connection of the cable to our TVs. Each TV must be connected to the cable provider in order to watch Cable TV.

The next layer of the Action Cable stack is the *channel*, represented by ActionCable::Channel. A channel is a logical (as opposed to physical) division within a connection. Channels are often organized according to interests, or purposes. (For instance, our blog app might have an ArticlesChannel, a CommentsChannel, and a UsersChannel.) Communications sent through these channels all take place within the same connection, but they're separated by naming conventions. Back to our analogy, we can watch many channels over a single connection. (Thankfully, we don't need a separate connection for each channel!)

Another important Action Cable term is *streams*. Streams are yet another logical division within channels. For example, an ArticlesChannel may have a stream named "articles:42", which handles sending and receiving data specifically regarding the article with id 42. Our Cable TV analogy begins to break down a bit, but perhaps this is similar to the way that some TV channels have specific "sub-channels" for viewers in different time zones.

Another important Action Cable concept is *subscriptions*. Users can only send and receive data over channels to which they have *subscribed*. With Action Cable, this is done by some JavaScript being run by the user's browser. With Cable TV, this is done by sending your Cable TV provider some money every month. But the idea is the same; you may only stream data from channels to which you've subscribed.

One last Action Cable concept we'll mention is *broadcasting*. With Action Cable, a *broadcast* is when the server sends data to a channel's stream so that any listening subscribers can receive it. Thinking about Cable TV, this makes a lot of sense. Cable TV channels don't keep a list of TVs to which they need to send their streaming content; they simply *broadcast* it, and only subscribers who are tuned in at that moment will be able to receive that data. (Of course, on-demand video and DVRs complicate the analogy.)

Hopefully, taking the time to describe these concepts and making a naive analogy to Cable TV was helpful. One wonders if the Rails developers had Cable TV in mind when developing Action Cable; the naming of its various components seems to beg the analogy. Whether they did or not, it does demonstrate the power of analogies and thoughtful class names when developing; whenever we can, we should strive for our classes and concepts to have names that paint vivid pictures of what they do in a broad sense and how they relate to other components of the system in which they live.

So how does Action Cable fit in with what we've known so far? Does Action Cable replace our traditional request cycle of submitting HTTP requests and receiving HTTP responses?

Rarely in web development would Action Cable replace our HTTP request and response cycle; rather, it works within it. Here's how:

First, a web page would be requested by a user entering an address in their browser or clicking a link, for example. They make an HTTP request and receive an HTTP response, typically with HTML, JavaScript, and CSS in the response.

Then, while the web page is loaded, perhaps an Action Cable connection would be established, and the browser may subscribe to one or more Action Cable channels. This connection would stay open, with both the client and server waiting for any messages sent through these channels.

Perhaps some data would be broadcasted through streams in those channels from the server to the browser; the browser may then execute some JavaScript in response to the data received and update the UI or even request a new web page.

Or perhaps the user will initiate some action that causes data to be streamed from the client to the server through a channel, and the server may decide to execute some Ruby code in response to the data received.

While this introduction was rather dense, hopefully taking the time to build a mental model of Action Cable was worth the effort. Now that we understand the purpose Action Cable serves, let's take a quick look at how to configure it before we dive into using it in our application.

Configuration

Thankfully, like other Rails components we've looked at, Action Cable works great out of the box in development mode. However, like other Rails components we've looked at, additional configuration is necessary to ensure a robust production environment. We won't need to change our configuration in this chapter. Table 15-1 shows a brief overview of the most common configuration options, what they're used for, and why one might want to use them.

Table 15-1. *Common Action Cable Configuration Options*

Option	Description
adapter	Specifies which type of message queue service to use, which handles the data sent between server and client. Acceptable values are *:async,* *:redis,* and *:postgres. :async* is suitable for development but not production. *:postgres* and *:redis* are more robust options for production, but require additional configuration and running services. These values are conventionally set in config/cable.yml and allow environment-specific settings, similar to config/database.yml
allowed_request_origins	Specifies which origins are allowed to make requests of your Action Cable server. In development, this is set by default to allow requests from localhost. In a production environment, you most likely want this set to the domain of your web application. You may choose to disable this whitelist of allowed origins by setting `action_cable.disable_request_forgery_protection = true`, but this could be a security risk and should be chosen carefully.
worker_pool_size	For performance, to avoid running Action Cable logic in the main server thread, Action Cable creates a number of threads dedicated for its own use. With this setting, you can configure how many threads to use. More isn't always better; finding the right size can require careful analysis.
mount_path	By default, Action Cable request URLs are constructed with a base of "/cable". This setting allows a custom base path for Action Cable URLs.

Application

Time to put our knowledge to use! For the sake of illustration (and for having a super-fancy blog), we'll add a cool new feature—"new article notifications"—so that visitors who are currently viewing the site will see an alert pop-up on the page they're currently viewing to inform them of a new article that was posted while they were reading.

To add this new feature, we'll need to add some functionality to both the server side of our application and the client side.

On the server side, we'll create an ArticlesChannel, meant to be used for various Action Cable communications relating to articles. We'll then modify our Article model to *broadcast* a message over a stream in that channel when a new article has been published.

On the client side, we'll add some JavaScript to automatically subscribe visitors to that channel and to react to data received over that stream, so that when the server sends the "New Article" message, their browser can do the work to display the notification in "real time."

Server-Side Changes

ApplicationCable::Connection

At the bottom of the Action Cable stack, we find ApplicationCable::Connection. Though we won't need to change it in our blog, we'll talk about it briefly. Take a look at app/channels/application_cable/connection.rb, as shown in Listing 15-1.

Listing 15-1. ApplicationCable::Connection in app/channels/
application_cable/connection.rb
https://gist.github.com/nicedawg/f986c253814b6eda79989f8c83c9b27f

```
module ApplicationCable
  class Connection < ActionCable::Connection::Base
  end
end
```

Similar to other Rails components we've seen, Action Cable provides a base class in our app, which inherits from the library's base class. This gives us a convenient place to override any functionality at this layer of the stack. A frequent use case would be to add an *identifier* here, as shown in https://guides.rubyonrails.org/action_cable_overview.html#connection-setup. For instance, we may want to only allow Action Cable connections to be established by logged-in users or users with certain privileges. This isn't the case in our blog—most of our users will not be logged in, but just know that this is possible.

ApplicationCable::Channel

The next layer in the Action Cable stack is ApplicationCable::Channel. Again, we won't need to change it for the features we've planned for our blog, but it's still worth mentioning. Take a look at app/channels/application_cable/channel.rb as shown in Listing 15-2.

Listing 15-2. ApplicationCable::Channel in app/channels/application_cable/channel.rb

https://gist.github.com/nicedawg/4a0ceb9894c3f84026a0d01c2554c8a2

```
module ApplicationCable
  class Channel < ActionCable::Channel::Base
  end
end
```

Similar to ApplicationCable::Connection, ApplicationCable::Channel starts out as a class which simply inherits from ActionCable::Channel::Base, but provides a place for us to add functionality which could apply to any Channel classes we add to our app.

ArticlesChannel

Now that we've got the lay of the land, let's get to work! You may remember from the "Concepts" section that Action Cable channels are similar to Action Pack controllers in some regards. Channels should be organized into logical units; since we're adding the ability to push notifications from the server to the client when a new article is published, it makes sense to create an ArticlesChannel.

Let's create ArticlesChannel in app/channels/articles_channel.rb, as shown in Listing 15-3.

Listing 15-3. ArticlesChannel in app/channels/articles_channel.rb

https://gist.github.com/nicedawg/35ad4063d663aaa3c871f5f2da38ddda

```
class ArticlesChannel < ApplicationCable::Channel
  def subscribed
    stream_from "articles:new"
  end
end
```

First, notice that our ArticlesChannel class inherits from ApplicationCable::Channel. This endows our ArticlesChannel class with the functionality it needs so it can behave like an Action Cable channel.

Next, we implemented the *subscribed* method. This method is called whenever a client subscribes to the ArticlesChannel. When a client subscribes to our ArticlesChannel, we connect them with a stream within this channel called "articles:new". The name of this stream isn't significant; we didn't have to use a semicolon, nor is there any magical convention. However, we should name our streams in a way that clearly indicates the stream's purpose for our own sanity.

Finally, on the server side, we need to broadcast data to this channel's stream we just created when appropriate. For this feature, we want to broadcast to this stream whenever an article has been *published*. Sounds simple enough, but we must remember that an article can be created and published at the same time or an article could be created as a draft article but not yet published or a published article could also be updated. Since we want to be careful not to send notifications for unpublished articles or notifications for articles which were already published, we have to think carefully about how we'll do this. We want to broadcast a notification whenever an article is saved (whether created or updated), but only if it went from not being published to being published.

Let's modify our Article model to broadcast a notification to our new "articles:new" stream in this scenario, as shown in Listing 15-4.

Listing 15-4. Broadcasting "New Article" Message When an Article Is Published
https://gist.github.com/nicedawg/f46dfa59f351a012d26d47f71c42d86a

```
class Article < ApplicationRecord
  validates :title, :body, presence: true

  belongs_to :user
  has_and_belongs_to_many :categories
  has_many :comments

  has_one_attached :cover_image
  attr_accessor :remove_cover_image
  after_save { cover_image.purge if remove_cover_image == '1' }
  after_save :broadcast_new_article

  has_rich_text :body
```

```
scope :published, -> { where.not(published_at: nil) }
scope :draft, -> { where(published_at: nil) }
scope :recent, -> { where('articles.published_at > ?', 1.week.ago.to_date) }
scope :where_title, -> (term) { where("articles.title LIKE ?",
"%#{term}%") }

def long_title
  "#{title} - #{published_at}"
end

def published?
  published_at.present?
end

def owned_by?(owner)
  return false unless owner.is_a?(User)
  user == owner
end

private

def broadcast_new_article
  if published? && saved_change_to_published_at?
    ActionCable.server.broadcast(
      "articles:new",
      new_article: ArticlesController.render(
        partial: 'articles/new_article_notification',
        locals: { article: self }
      )
    )
  end
end
end
```

First, we added an *after_save* callback. Then, in our new *broadcast_new_article* method, we broadcast the data about the recently saved article only if it is currently published and if the recent save changed the value of published_at.

The *saved_change_to_published_at?* method warrants discussion. In the previous chapter, we discussed various methods which the *ActiveModel::Dirty* module adds to our Active Model (and therefore Active Record)–based classes. Sometimes we want to know if an attribute's value *will* change. However, in this context, we want to know if it *did* change after a successful save. ActiveModel::Dirty doesn't know anything about persisting data to the database, so it can't help us there. But Active Record adds a method to each of our persisted attributes in the form of *saved_change_to_{attr}?*. So we made use of that helpful method to only send the broadcast when we want to.

Then we used ActionCable.server.broadcast to send some data through the "articles:new" stream. The first argument is the name of the stream we wish to broadcast on. (This matches the name we used in the ArticlesChannel.) The remaining arguments are the data we wish to broadcast, which could be anything we want! We decided to pass an argument called "new_article," which will contain the HTML we want to send to the client to display. In order to construct that HTML, we called ArticlesController.render with a partial which we haven't yet defined and passed a local variable "article" with the value of "self," which is the Article object which was just saved.

Note that we didn't *have* to broadcast HTML to the stream; we could have sent the individual attributes of the article which we need for the notification as a hash, and the client side would receive that hash in JSON form and could have constructed the HTML to show the notification. Either approach is fine, but for our purposes, sending HTML is easier.

So, to wrap up our server-side changes for this feature, let's create this *new_article_ notification* partial we referenced earlier. Create a new partial in app/views/articles/_ new_article_notification.html.erb to match Listing 15-5.

Listing 15-5. Partial View Template for New Article Notifications
https://gist.github.com/nicedawg/170ebe6de3d4b14fcfdffa7129008713

```
<div id="new-article-notification">
  <h3>New Article Published!</h3>

  <%= link_to article.title, article %>
</div>
```

Simple enough! We don't need to show a lot of content in our notification. We decided, however, to give the outer container of this markup an id so we can reference it in the client-side code.

We've finished building the server-side portions of our feature; now, when an article is published, an HTML representation of a notification is broadcasted with Action Cable. However, at this point, we're only *sending* the data. Let's move on to the client-side changes so that browsers can *receive* the data and display the notification.

Client-Side Changes

First, we'll add some JavaScript to subscribe to the channel we created, so that we can receive and display notifications when an article is published.

Let's add this JavaScript to app/javascript/channels/articles_channel.js, as shown in Listing 15-6.

Listing 15-6. Subscribing to the "New Article" Stream
https://gist.github.com/nicedawg/1bed41f4adc3bc30099180e4e00db653

```
import consumer from "./consumer"

consumer.subscriptions.create("ArticlesChannel", {
  received(data) {
    if (data.new_article) {
      this.displayNewArticleNotification(data.new_article);
    }
  },

  displayNewArticleNotification(newArticle) {
    const body = document.querySelector('body');
    body.insertAdjacentHTML('beforeend', newArticle);

    const newArticleNotification = document.querySelector('#new-article-
    notification');
    setTimeout(() => {
      body.removeChild(newArticleNotification);
    }, 3000);
  }
})
```

First, we import *consumer* into our JavaScript. We didn't create this file; rather, Rails supplied it for us. This import gives us a *consumer* object we can use to create *subscriptions* to the *channels* which Action Cable serves. Using our Cable TV analogy

427

from earlier, a *consumer* can be thought of as a Cable TV subscriber. They only need one connection, but can choose to subscribe to zero or more channels.

Next, we used *consumer.subscriptions.create* to subscribe to the ArticlesChannel we created earlier. The second argument to the create function call is a Javascript object with a couple of functions we defined.

The first function, *received*, is a function which we must implement if we wish to act on broadcasted data received from the channel we subscribed to. The broadcasted data is passed to our *received* function. In our implementation, we check to see if the broadcasted data includes a *new_article* property. If it does, then we call another function which we created to handle new article notifications.

The second function, *displayNewArticleNotification*, is a function we wrote. We could have put all the logic for displaying a new article notification in the *received* function, but it's good practice to keep functions small for maintainability when possible. In this function, we insert the HTML for the new article notification (which the server constructed and sent) into the body of the page and then set a timer to automatically remove the notification in 3 seconds.

By this point, everything should be working! However, the notifications won't be very noticeable because we're stuffing them down at the bottom of the page. And they won't look very good. Our visitors may not even notice them. Let's add some CSS to place these notifications in the top-right corner of the page. Let's add some styles to app/assets/stylesheets/articles.scss so that it matches Listing 15-7.

Listing 15-7. Styling New Article Notifications in articles.scss
https://gist.github.com/nicedawg/8dc15f36e36ffc495464b551222d6f27

```
#new-article-notification {
  background-color: lightgray;
  max-width: 50%;
  position: fixed;
  top: 10px;
  right: 10px;
  padding: 10px;
  border-radius: 10px;
  z-index: 10;
  box-shadow: 3px 5px #888;
}
```

This isn't a book about CSS or visual design; there are undoubtedly better ways of styling these notifications. But these styles are good enough for now! We give the notification a background color so it stands out. We restrict the width to 50% so it doesn't cover the whole screen. We make the notification's position "fixed" so that it's positioned relative to the viewport (the portion of the web page the user is viewing). This ensures the notification is always visible, no matter where the user has scrolled. We use *top* and *right* to position the notification 10 pixels from the top and right of the viewport, so it's near (but not butting up against) the top-right corner. We add a little padding to the notification and give it slightly rounded corners for aesthetics. We bump up the z-index a little so that it will display "on top of" any elements it may intersect with and give the notification a little drop shadow to give the appearance of floating above the page.

Try It Out

That's it! It's time to try out our "finished" product. We'll want to use two browser windows to see the full effect. Let's use one browser window to create a published article and a second browser window to observe our notification.

So in your first browser window, go ahead and pull up the "New Article" form, but don't submit it yet.

Then, in your second window, go to the home page, or view an article show page; it doesn't really matter which page of our blog your second window is viewing.

Finally, with both browsers visible if possible, create a new article in your first browser window, and watch the notification appear nearly instantly in your second browser window—with no refreshing (or polling) necessary. (Remember that we set up our notifications to disappear after 3 seconds, so look quickly!) If everything went according to plan, your notification should look something like Figure 15-1.

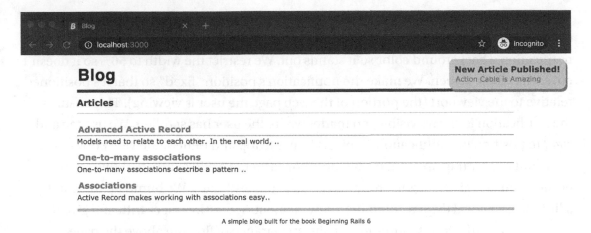

Figure 15-1. *New article notification via Action Cable*

Pretty neat! To get here, we did have to talk about a lot of new concepts, but looking back I hope you'll agree that Action Cable makes it *relatively* easy to add real-time functionality to your application with WebSockets.

If this didn't work for you, don't worry! Take a look at your Rails server output for indications of server-side errors, and look at your browser's console for indications of client-side errors. Often, there's an error message that points you straight to the culprit. Sometimes it's not so easy, so review the previous code listings and make sure your code matches.

Summary

In this chapter, we covered a lot of new ground. We invested the time to understand how WebSockets satisfy a need for efficient bidirectional server communication and how they can lead to richer user experiences. We then learned how Action Cable supplies a framework for working with WebSockets in Rails and how to configure it for production use. Then, we dove in and added a cool new feature to our blog with the power of Action Cable.

We only scratched the surface of Action Cable; for more information, a good place to start is the Rails guide, at `https://guides.rubyonrails.org/action_cable_overview.html`.

What's next? As our blog application has grown in complexity through the chapters, it has become more *fragile*; making a change in one area of our app may have unintended consequences in other areas of our app. One way to guard against this is to have a robust automated test suite, so that your code will tell you there's a problem before your users do. In the next chapter, we will dip our toes into the deep topic of testing your Rails application.

CHAPTER 16

Testing Your Application

When an application is in its infancy, its developers may be able to keep a complete mental model of the whole system. Changes to the system are relatively easy to reason about, easy to implement, and easy to verify they're working as intended.

However, most applications change over time. And as they grow, developers lose the ability to keep a complete mental model of the whole system. When that happens, bugs are introduced more frequently, as a seemingly innocuous change in one part of the application can have surprising and unintended consequences in another area of the code. Developers start to feel this burden; changes take longer to reason about, are harder to implement, and are more time-consuming to verify. Increasingly, it feels like every release introduces new bugs, and even bug fixes introduce new bugs.

When we start breaking our application more frequently, we get nervous about introducing changes. Perhaps we know how we *want* to add a new feature, but we deem it too risky and settle for compromises in code quality. For example, maybe instead of changing a critical code path to support a new feature, we'll add an *if* statement to take another nearly identical but slightly different code path for our new feature, so that if we break something, at least it will only be the *new* feature we're breaking.

These compromises in code quality—sometimes referred to as *technical debt*—are easier for *now*, but harder to deal with *later*; a future requirement may necessitate changing *both* of these critical code paths; perhaps at that point in the future, we'll feel brave enough to do what we wanted in the first place. But if we were reluctant to change *one* critical piece of code, we probably won't want to change *two* critical pieces of code. So maybe we'll just tack on another and another and so on. Left unchecked, this technical debt grows until the application is nearly unmaintainable.

How can we, as developers, avoid this? Automated testing is one of the most important things we can do to improve the quality of our code, reduce the cost of change, and keep our software (relatively) bug-free. Rails (and the Ruby community at large) takes testing seriously. Not surprisingly, Rails goes out of its way to make testing hassle-free.

© Brady Somerville, Adam Gamble, Cloves Carneiro Jr and Rida Al Barazi 2020
B. Somerville et al., *Beginning Rails 6*, https://doi.org/10.1007/978-1-4842-5716-6_16

The basic idea of automated testing is simple: you write code that exercises your program and tests your assumptions. Instead of just opening a browser and adding a new user manually to check whether the process works, you write a test that automates the process—something repeatable. With a test in place, every time you modify the code that adds a new user, you can run the test to see if your change worked—and, more important, whether your seemingly innocuous change broke something else.

If you stop and think about it, you're already testing your software. The problem is that you're doing it manually, often in an ad hoc fashion. You may make a change to the way users log in, and then you try it in your browser. You make a change to the sign-up procedure, and then you take it for a spin. As your application grows in size, it becomes more and more difficult to manually test like this, and eventually you miss something important. Even if you're not testing, you can be sure that your users are. After all, they're the ones using the application in the wild, and they'll find bugs you never knew existed. The best solution is to replace this sort of visual, ad hoc inspection with automatic checking.

Testing becomes increasingly important when you're refactoring existing code. *Refactoring* is the process of improving the design of code without changing its behavior. The best way to refactor is with a test in place acting as a safety net. Because refactoring shouldn't result in an observable change in behavior, it shouldn't break your tests either. It's easy, therefore, to see why many programmers won't refactor without tests.

Given the importance placed on testing, it may seem odd that this book leaves a discussion of this until Chapter 16. Ideally, you should be writing tests as you go, never getting too far ahead without testing what you've written. But we decided that explaining how to test would be overwhelming while you were still learning the basics of Ruby and the Rails framework. Now that you have a good deal of knowledge under your belt, it's time to tackle testing.

Note   If you need to get the code at the exact point where you finished Chapter 15, download the zip file from `www.apress.com` and extract it onto your computer.

How Rails Handles Testing

Because Rails is an integrated environment, it can make assumptions about the best ways to structure and organize your tests. Rails provides

1. Test directories for controller, model, mailer, helper, system, and integration tests (and more)

2. Fixtures for easily working with database data

3. An environment explicitly created for testing

The default Rails skeleton generated by the `rails` command creates a directory just for testing. If you open it, you'll see subdirectories for each of the aforementioned test types:

```
test
 |-- channels          <-- Action Cable tests
 |-- controllers        <-- controller tests
 |-- fixtures            <-- test data
 |-- helpers            <-- helper tests
 |-- integration        <-- integration tests
 |-- jobs                <-- Active Job tests
 |-- mailboxes        <-- Action Mailbox tests
 |-- mailers             <-- Action Mailer tests
 |-- models            <-- model tests
 |-- system            <-- system tests
```

Several of these directories should look familiar. You can probably imagine what types of things will be tested in the channels, controllers, helpers, jobs, mailboxes, mailers, and models directories. But a few directories probably won't look familiar. Fixtures? Integration? System? What are these for? We'll cover integration and system tests later in the chapter, but let's take a quick look at fixtures now.

Fixtures are textual representations of table data written in YAML—a data serialization format. Fixtures are loaded into the database before your tests run; you use them to populate your database with data to test against. Look at the users fixtures file in `test/fixtures/users.yml`, as shown in Listing 16-1.

Listing 16-1. Users Fixtures in `test/fixtures/users.yml`

```
# Read about fixtures at https://api.rubyonrails.org/classes/ActiveRecord/
FixtureSet.html

one:
  email: MyString
  password: MyString

two:
  email: MyString
  password: MyString
```

Rails generated the users fixtures file for us when we generated the User model. As you can see, the file has two fixtures, named *one* and *two*. Each fixture has both attributes `email` and `password` set to `MyString`; but, as you recall, you renamed the `password` column `hashed_password` back in Chapter 6. Let's update the users fixtures file to reflect the new column name and use meaningful data. Listing 11-2 shows the updated fixture.

Listing 16-2. Updated Users Fixtures in `test/fixtures/users.yml`: https://gist.github.com/nicedawg/393f21dc9e39a70be49b18970a8967ad

```
# Read about fixtures at https://api.rubyonrails.org/classes/ActiveRecord/
FixtureSet.html

eugene:
  email: eugene@example.com
  hashed_password: e5e9fa1ba31ecd1ae84f75caaa474f3a663f05f4 # => secret

lauren:
  email: lauren@example.com
  hashed_password: e5e9fa1ba31ecd1ae84f75caaa474f3a663f05f4 # => secret
```

Remember that every time we generated a model or a controller while building the blog application, Rails automatically generated test files for us. This is another example of its opinionated nature—Rails thinks we should test, so it goes out of its way to remind us.

You may also recall that Rails created three SQLite databases for the blog application: one for development (which is all you've been using thus far), one for production, and one for testing. Not surprisingly, Rails uses the testing database just for testing.

Rails drops and re-creates this test database on every run of the test suite. Make sure you don't list your development or production database in its place, or all your data will be gone.

Unit Testing Your Rails Application

You know that Rails generated some tests automatically. Let's open one of them now and take a look. Let's start with the `Article` test, located in `test/models/article_test.rb`, as shown in Listing 16-3.

Listing 16-3. Generated `Article` Unit Test in `test/models/article_test.rb`

```
require 'test_helper'

class ArticleTest < ActiveSupport::TestCase
  # test "the truth" do
  #   assert true
  # end
end
```

Although there's not much to it (all it does is show you how to test that `true` is, in fact, true), this test gives you a template from which to build your real tests. It has the following elements:

1. The test class is a subclass of ActiveSupport::TestCase, which is Rails' enhanced version of the Minitest::Test class, which comes from the Ruby testing framework, `minitest`.

2. Tests are implemented as blocks using the `test` method, with the first parameter as the description of that test—`"the truth"` in this case.

3. Within a test case, *assertions* are used to test expectations. The "Testing with Assertions" section later in this chapter explains how these work.

If you peek inside the `test/models` directory, you'll see a similar test case for every model we've generated so far: `Article`, `Comment`, `Category`, `User`, and `Profile`. Each looks almost exactly the same as the `Article` test. Let's run the unit tests now using the *rails test:models* command from your command prompt and see what happens:

```
$ rails test:models
```

```
Run options: --seed 50142

# Running:

Finished in 0.140507s, 0.0000 runs/s, 0.0000 assertions/s.
0 runs, 0 assertions, 0 failures, 0 errors, 0 skips
```

In this case, there are no tests yet (the ones generated are commented out). If there were tests and the test passed, you would see a . (dot) character. When the test case produces an error, you would see an E. If any assertion fails to return true, you would see an F. Finally, when the test suite is finished, it prints a summary.

Also, you may have noticed that your *seed* was different. By default, your tests are run with a random *seed* value so that your tests are run in a different order each time. That helps us avoid writing order-dependent tests by making sure each test can pass independently of which tests have run before.

Also, we ran *rails test:models* because we only want to run the tests within our *test/ models* directory right now. We could run *rails test* to run *most* of our tests (more on that later) or *rails test test/models/article_test.rb* to run the tests in a specific file or even *rails test test/models/article_test.rb:26* to run a specific test case within a file based on the provided line number. See *rails test -h* for more information.

Testing the Article Model

Let's test the Article model. If you recall from Chapter 5, one of the first things you did with your Article model was basic CRUD operations. Well, testing that you can create, read, update, and delete articles is a great place to start. Here's a quick summary of the specific things you test in this chapter:

1. Creating a new article

2. Finding an article

3. Updating an article

4. Destroying an article

Before you begin, you'll need to create a few fixtures (remember that a fixture is a textual representation of test data).

Creating Fixtures

Let's create a fixture for an article so we can test it. Open the `test/fixtures/articles.yml` file and replace its content with the code as shown in Listing 16-4.

Listing 16-4. Articles Fixtures in `test/fixtures/articles.yml`: `https://gist.github.com/nicedawg/27d1df26c994bbd0c7579498cd8d91e7`

```
welcome_to_rails:
  user: eugene
  title: "Welcome to Rails"
  published_at: <%= 3.days.ago %>
```

We named this fixture *welcome_to_rails* so our tests can refer to it clearly. We declared *eugene* (a users fixture we added in the previous step) as the owner of the article, gave it a title, and used a little ERb to set the *published_at* datetime to 3 days ago. Our article still needs a body, but we can't declare it here; you may remember that when we added Action Text in Chapter 11, the *body* attribute was moved to Action Text's storage, so we'll need to modify our ActionText::RichText fixtures file, found in test/fixtures/action_text/rich_texts.yml so that it matches Listing 16-5.

Listing 16-5. Action Text Fixtures in `test/fixtures/action_text/rich_texts.yml`: `https://gist.github.com/nicedawg/210608fc3d5730b49032c73ce1d500fe`

```
welcome_to_rails_body:
  record: welcome_to_rails (Article)
  name: body
  body:  <p>Rails is such a nice web framework written in ruby</p>
```

Here, we named this fixture *welcome_to_rails_body*, because that accurately defines this fixture. Its *record* value is a special syntax that identifies the type (Article) and id (welcome_to_rails) of the record to which this rich text belongs. The *name* indicates which attribute of the parent record it belongs to, and the *body* value declares the contents of this Action Text record. This fixture is a little more complicated than the previous ones, because it's a polymorphic record, as you might remember from Chapter 11, but even then, fixtures still make it easy to work with.

The data in our fixtures files will be inserted automatically into our test database before our tests run. With our fixtures in place, we're ready to start creating test cases!

> **Tip**   Fixtures are parsed by ERb before they're loaded, so you can use ERb in them just as you can in view templates. This is useful for creating dynamic dates, as we did in `published_at: <%= 3.days.ago %>`.

The following sections present the test cases one at a time, beginning with *create*.

Adding a Create Test

Open the `test/models/article_test.rb` file and create the first test case by deleting the `test "the truth"` method and replacing it with a test called `test "should create article."` Your file should look like Listing 16-6.

Listing 16-6. The Create Article Test in `test/models/article_test.rb`: https://gist.github.com/nicedawg/e0d35b3317dbd1040ad93688f8db605d

```ruby
require 'test_helper'

class ArticleTest < ActiveSupport::TestCase
  test 'should create article' do
    article = Article.new

    article.user = users(:eugene)
    article.title = 'Test Article'
    article.body = 'Test body'

    assert article.save
  end
end
```

The `"should create article"` test case is standard article creation fare. We created a new article in the same way we would create one from the console. The only real difference is on the last line of the test case—*assert article.save*. We know that *article.save* will return true if the save was successful and that it will return false if the save failed. *assert* is a method available to us in our tests which will mark the test as successful if given a true value and mark the test as failed if given a false value. Therefore, if the article saves successfully, the test passes; otherwise, it fails.

> **Note**   Fixtures can be accessed in your test cases by name. Use
> `fixture(:name)`, where `fixture` is the plural name of the model and `:name`
> is the symbolized name of the fixture you're after. This returns an Active Record
> object on which you can call methods. Here, you get at the eugene users fixture
> using `users(:eugene)`.

Let's run our new test to see if it passes:

```
$ rails test:models
```

```
Run options: --seed 13876

# Running:

.

Finished in 0.285145s, 3.5070 runs/s, 3.5070 assertions/s.
1 runs, 1 assertions, 0 failures, 0 errors, 0 skips
```

Just as the output from the test says, you ran one test (`test "should create
article"`), which included one assertion (`assert article.save`), and everything
passed. Life is good!

A best practice is to test your tests. That may sound silly, but it's easy to write a test
that gives you a false positive. (This is why some developers prefer to write failing tests
before writing the code that makes them pass.) A quick check for the test we just wrote
would be to comment out the line in our test where we set the article's title; since the
article requires a title, the test should fail. Give it a try!

The *assert* method is one of many assertion methods available to us. Before we
go any further, let's take a closer look at assertions as they pertain to `minitest` and
`ActiveSupport::TestCase`.

Testing with Assertions

Assertions are statements of expected outcome. If the assertion turns out to be correct,
the assertion passes. If the assertion turns out to be false, the assertion fails, and
`minitest` reports a failure.

While one *could* get by with only the *assert* method, many more assertion methods are available to us for convenience; minitest ships with a bevy of built-in assertions, and Rails adds some of its own. First, let's look at some of the most commonly used minitest assertions as shown in Table 16-1.

***Table 16-1.** Standard minitest Assertion Methods*

Assertion Method	Description
assert(test, msg = nil)	Fails unless *test* is truthy.
assert_empty(object, msg = nil)	Fails unless *object* is empty.
assert_equal(expected, actual, msg = nil)	Fails unless *exp* == *act*.
assert_in_delta(expected_float, actual_float, delta = 0.001, msg = nil)	Fails unless *expected_float* is within *delta* of *actual_float*.
assert_includes(collection, object, msg = nil)	Fails unless *collection* includes *object*.
assert_instance_of(klass, object, msg = nil)	Fails unless *object* is an instance of the *klass* class.
assert_kind_of(klass, object, msg = nil)	Fails unless *object* is a kind of *klass*. (Note: Unlike *assert_instance_of*, which checks the object's class directly, *assert_kind_of* considers the object's ancestors.)
assert_match(matcher, object, msg = nil)	Fails unless *matcher* =~ *object*.
assert_nil(object, msg = nil)	Fails unless *object* is nil.
assert_raises(exception_class, msg) do ... end	Fails unless block raises an exception of type *exception_class*.
assert_respond_to(*object, method, msg = nil)*	Fails unless *object* responds to a method named *method*.

As you might have noticed, most of these assertion methods support an optional parameter to supply a custom failure message if desired. Including a custom failure message in most cases is not necessary, but it may occasionally be helpful.

Also, note that some methods show a *klass* argument. Why the misspelling? In Ruby, *class* is a keyword; when using a variable to store a reference to a class, we can't use *class* as the variable name; it's common practice to use the name *klass*.

Minitest also provides *refute* variations of these methods, which simply inverse the logic of the corresponding assertion. For example, *refute_empty* will pass when the provided object *isn't* empty. However, for backward compatibility with *test-unit*, Rails' previous built-in testing framework (and arguably for readability), Rails provides aliases for these *refute* variations such as these: assert_not_empty, assert_not_equal, assert_no_match, and so on.

While we showed some of the most common assertion methods, there are more. When you find that an assertion is overly complicated and hard to read, it may be a good idea to check https://guides.rubyonrails.org/testing.html#rails-meets-minitest to see if perhaps a different assertion method would make your test more readable.

Adding a Find Test

Now that we know more about assertion methods, we're ready to add more tests. Next on the list is testing that we can successfully *find* an article. We'll use the data in the fixture we created to help us. Add the method shown in Listing 16-7 after the "should create article" test.

Listing 16-7. Test Case for Finding an Article in test/models/article_test.rb: https://gist.github.com/nicedawg/71fbefeec56ce2ada47e956d3115b243

```
require 'test_helper'

class ArticleTest < ActiveSupport::TestCase
  test 'should create article' do
    article = Article.new

    article.user = users(:eugene)
    article.title = 'Test Article'
    article.body = 'Test body'

    assert article.save
  end

  test 'should find article' do
    article_id = articles(:welcome_to_rails).id
    assert_nothing_raised { Article.find(article_id) }
  end
end
```

Our new test verifies that we can find an article of the given id. First, we grab the *id* attribute from the fixture, and then we test that we can use *Article.find* to retrieve it. We use the assertion *assert_nothing_raised* because we know that *find* raises an exception if the record can't be found. If no exception is raised, we know that finding works. Again, run the test and see what happens:

```
$ rails test test/models
```

```
Run options: --seed 22750

# Running:

..

Finished in 0.249469s, 8.0170 runs/s, 4.0085 assertions/s.
2 runs, 1 assertions, 0 failures, 0 errors, 0 skips
```

Sure enough, finding works! So far, so good.

Adding an Update Test

Next, let's test updating an article. Add the test "should update article" case, as shown in Listing 16-8.

Listing 16-8. Test Case for Updating an Article in test/models/article_test.rb: https://gist.github.com/nicedawg/24dc226151646294245b7c1f2380dd0b

```ruby
require 'test_helper'

class ArticleTest < ActiveSupport::TestCase
  test 'should create article' do
    article = Article.new

    article.user = users(:eugene)
    article.title = 'Test Article'
    article.body = 'Test body'

    assert article.save
  end
```

```
test 'should find article' do
  article_id = articles(:welcome_to_rails).id
  assert_nothing_raised { Article.find(article_id) }
end

test 'should update article' do
  article = articles(:welcome_to_rails)
  article.update(title: 'New title')
  assert_equal 'New title', article.reload.title
end
end
```

First, we find the "Welcome to Rails" article from our fixtures file, and then we update the article with a new title and assert that when the article is reloaded, it has the new title. Once again, run the test and see what happens:

```
$ rails test:models
```

```
Run options: --seed 25358

# Running:

...

Finished in 0.270023s, 11.1102 runs/s, 7.4068 assertions/s.
3 runs, 2 assertions, 0 failures, 0 errors, 0 skips
```

Adding a Destroy Test

Only one more test to go: destroy. We'll find an article, destroy it, and assert that Active Record raises an exception when you try to find it again. Listing 16-9 shows the test.

Listing 16-9. Test Case for Destroying an Article in test/models/article_test.rb: https://gist.github.com/nicedawg/813a3e5f9bf5d3fdbfe888a2dc4e3360

```
require 'test_helper'

class ArticleTest < ActiveSupport::TestCase
  test 'should create article' do
    article = Article.new
```

```ruby
    article.user = users(:eugene)
    article.title = 'Test Article'
    article.body = 'Test body'

    assert article.save
  end

  test 'should find article' do
    article_id = articles(:welcome_to_rails).id
    assert_nothing_raised { Article.find(article_id) }
  end

  test 'should update article' do
    article = articles(:welcome_to_rails)
    article.update(title: 'New title')
    assert_equal 'New title', article.reload.title
  end

  test 'should destroy article' do
    article = articles(:welcome_to_rails)
    article.destroy
    assert_raise(ActiveRecord::RecordNotFound) { Article.find(article.id) }
  end
end
```

The `assert_raise` assertion takes as an argument the class of the exception you expect to be raised for whatever you do inside the given block. Because you've deleted the article, you expect Active Record to respond with a `RecordNotFound` exception when you try to find the article you just deleted by `id`. Run the test and see what happens:

```
$ rails test test/models
```

```
Run options: --seed 26110

# Running:

....

Finished in 0.275000s, 14.5455 runs/s, 10.9091 assertions/s.
4 runs, 3 assertions, 0 failures, 0 errors, 0 skips
```

We've done it! We've successfully tested the *happy path* for each CRUD operation for our Article model.

Testing Validations

We have a few validations on our `Article` model, specifically for the presence of a title and body. Because we want to make sure these are working as expected, we should test them too. Let's add the method shown in Listing 16-10 to our test to prove that we can't create invalid articles.

Listing 16-10. Test Case for Validations in test/models/article_test.rb: https://gist.github.com/nicedawg/603e64d1846086488873757624745245

```ruby
require 'test_helper'

class ArticleTest < ActiveSupport::TestCase
  test 'should create article' do
    article = Article.new

    article.user = users(:eugene)
    article.title = 'Test Article'
    article.body = 'Test body'

    assert article.save
  end

  test 'should find article' do
    article_id = articles(:welcome_to_rails).id
    assert_nothing_raised { Article.find(article_id) }
  end

  test 'should update article' do
    article = articles(:welcome_to_rails)
    article.update(title: 'New title')
    assert_equal 'New title', article.reload.title
  end

  test 'should destroy article' do
    article = articles(:welcome_to_rails)
```

```
    article.destroy
    assert_raise(ActiveRecord::RecordNotFound) { Article.find(article.id) }
  end

  test 'should not create an article without title nor body' do
    article = Article.new
    assert !article.save

    assert_not_empty article.errors[:title]
    assert_not_empty article.errors[:body]
    assert_equal ["can't be blank"], article.errors[:title]
    assert_equal ["can't be blank"], article.errors[:body]
  end
end
```

This is pretty straightforward, although you may have to read it a few times before it clicks. First, we instantiate a new Article object in the local variable article. Without having given it any attributes, we expect it to be invalid, so we assert that *article.save* returns false. (Notice the *!*, which negates truth). Next, we access the errors hash to explicitly check for the attributes we expect to be invalid:

```
assert_not_empty article.errors[:title]
assert_not_empty article.errors[:body]
```

We also want to check that the validation responses are what we expect. To do this, we use the assert_equal assertion. Here's its basic syntax:

```
assert_equal(expected, actual)
```

To check the error messages, we again access the errors hash, but this time we ask for the specific messages associated with the given attribute:

```
    assert_equal ["can't be blank"], article.errors[:title]
    assert_equal ["can't be blank"], article.errors[:body]
```

Finally, we assert that article.save returns false using *!article.save*. Run the test one more time:

```
$ rails test:models
```

```
Run options: --seed 28498

# Running:

.....

Finished in 0.335649s, 14.8965 runs/s, 32.7723 assertions/s.
5 runs, 11 assertions, 0 failures, 0 errors, 0 skips
```

Feels good, doesn't it? Our tests pass now, but any application being used is likely to change as requirements change. What if one day we decide to make a change to the Article model and remove the validation requirements for the *title* attribute? If that were to happen, our test would fail. If you want to try it, open the Article model in app/models/article.rb and remove *:title* from the *validates* line which checks for presence, and then run the tests again.

When our requirements change, we often need to update our tests. We recommend updating the tests *first* (which should make them fail) and *then* updating the code (which makes them pass). This is also known as test-driven development (TDD).

Though we added several tests for our Article model, we certainly didn't test everything that the Article model can do—nor did we write unit tests for our other models—but hopefully we've gained a good understanding of how to write unit tests for our models. Next, we'll learn how to test another critical component of our application—our controllers.

Functional Testing Your Controllers

Tests to specifically check your controllers are called *functional* tests. When we tested our models, we didn't test them in the context of the web application—there were no web requests and responses, nor were there any URLs to contend with. This focused approach lets you hone in on the specific functionality of the model and test it in isolation. Alas, Rails is great for building web applications; and although unit testing models is important, it's equally important to test the full request/response cycle.

Testing the Articles Controller

Functional tests aren't that much different from unit tests. The main difference is that Rails sets up request and response objects for us; these objects act just like the live requests and responses we get when running the application via a web server. If we open the `articles` controller test in `test/controllers/articles_controller_test.rb` (which Rails generated for us when we scaffolded the articles controller in an earlier chapter) and examine the first few lines, as shown in Listing 16-11, we can see how this is done.

Listing 16-11. Setup of a Controller Test in `test/controllers/articles_ controller_test.rb`

```
require 'test_helper'

class ArticlesControllerTest < ActionDispatch::IntegrationTest
  # ...
end
```

Just as in the unit test we worked with earlier, the first thing we do is require *test_ helper*. The `test_helper.rb` file sets up some common environment variables and generally endows `minitest` with specific methods that make testing Rails applications easier.

Note   You can think of `test_helper` as being akin to `application_helper`. Any methods you define here are available to all your tests.

Notice that `ArticlesControllerTest` is a subclass of `ActionDispatch::Integratio nTest`, which performs some magic for us behind the scenes. It gives our tests the ability to send HTTP requests to our controller, make assertions against the response from the controller, and make assertions on the *cookies*, *flash*, and *session* hashes which our controller action may have modified. It also prepares three instance variables for us to use in our tests: the first is `@controller` as an instance variable of `ArticlesController`, after which it instantiates both `@request` and `@response` variables, which are instances of `ActionDispatch::Request` and `ActionDispatch::TestResponse`, respectively.

Most of the time, we don't need to worry about all this. Still, it's important to know what's going on. Because the test we're looking at was created by the scaffold generator, it has quite a bit more code than we would get from the standard controller generator. There's a problem with this code, though: these test cases will not pass—at least not without some modification. Warts and all, this gives us a good start and serves well as a template.

As you look over the `articles` controller test file, notice that each test case tests a specific request for an action on the controller. There's a test for every action: `index`, `show`, `new`, `create`, `edit`, `update`, and `destroy`. Let's walk through each test case, making adjustments as we go.

Creating a Test Helper Method

Before we start testing our ArticlesController actions, we realize that in order to create an article, our application expects a logged-in user. In fact, it's conceivable that many of our tests may expect a logged-in user. This is a perfect job for a test helper, because it can be shared across many tests. We'll create a helper method called *login_as* that accepts a user's name and makes the necessary request to log them in. We can use this method for any test case that requires a login.

While we're editing our test_helper file, we'll go ahead and include the Turbolinks::Assertions module into the ActionDispatch::IntegrationTest; doing so will make sure that when we make assertions about being redirected in response to a Turbolinks request, our tests will still work seamlessly.

To begin, open test/test_helper.rb in your editor and make the highlighted changes, as shown in Listing 16-12.

Listing 16-12. The login_as Test Helper in test/test_helper.rb:
https://gist.github.com/nicedawg/304592e83622cafa9297747d40dcab1f

```
ENV['RAILS_ENV'] ||= 'test'
require_relative '../config/environment'
require 'rails/test_help'

class ActiveSupport::TestCase
  # Run tests in parallel with specified workers
  parallelize(workers: :number_of_processors)
```

```
# Setup all fixtures in test/fixtures/*.yml for all tests in alphabetical order.
fixtures :all

# Add more helper methods to be used by all tests here...
ActionDispatch::IntegrationTest.include Turbolinks::Assertions

def login_as(user)
  post session_url(email: users(user).email, password: 'secret')
end
end
```

The login_as method is pretty simple. It simply takes the provided fixture id for a user and sends a POST request to session_url—just like a real user of our app would—with their email address and password.

Now that we've created a handy shortcut to log in a user during our tests and included the Turbolinks::Assertions module, we're ready to proceed with our tests, beginning with the index action.

Getting ArticlesControllerTest to Pass

Since we changed the id of our articles fixture in a previous step, we need to update the *setup* method in our test. (If we tried to run the test without making this change, every single test case in this file would fail with an error like "No fixture named 'one' found for fixture set 'articles.'") Modify your test/controllers/articles_controller_test.rb so that it matches Listing 16-13.

Listing 16-13. Updated Setup for test/controllers/articles_controller_test.rb: https://gist.github.com/nicedawg/b3c1492071238170aca06160f4a5061c

```
require 'test_helper'

class ArticlesControllerTest < ActionDispatch::IntegrationTest
  setup do
    @article = articles(:welcome_to_rails)
  end

  test "should get index" do
    get articles_url
```

```
  assert_response :success
end

test "should get new" do
  get new_article_url
  assert_response :success
end

test "should create article" do
  assert_difference('Article.count') do
    post articles_url, params: { article: { body: @article.body, excerpt:
    @article.excerpt, location: @article.location, published_at:
    @article.published_at, title: @article.title } }
  end

  assert_redirected_to article_url(Article.last)
end

test "should show article" do
  get article_url(@article)
  assert_response :success
end

test "should get edit" do
  get edit_article_url(@article)
  assert_response :success
end

test "should update article" do
  patch article_url(@article), params: { article: { body: @article.body,
  excerpt: @article.excerpt, location: @article.location, published_at:
  @article.published_at, title: @article.title } }
  assert_redirected_to article_url(@article)
end

test "should destroy article" do
  assert_difference('Article.count', -1) do
    delete article_url(@article)
  end
```

```
    assert_redirected_to articles_url
  end
end
```

The setup method is executed before every test case. In this case, the setup method assigns the *:welcome_to_rail*s article record from the fixtures to an instance variable @article; the @article variable is available to all test cases in the ArticlesControllerTest class.

Our controller tests define methods that correspond to HTTP verbs (get, post, patch, and delete) and provide our route helpers, which we can use to make requests. The first line of the "should get index" test makes a GET request for the index action using *get articles_url*. Here's the full syntax you use for these requests:

```
http_method(path, parameters, headers, env, xhr, as)
```

In the case of the "should get index" test, we have no parameters to submit along with the request, so our call is simple. It makes a GET request to the index action just as if you had done so with a browser. Try looking at your log/test.log file as you run a controller test; you should see output that looks just like your server output when using your application with a browser in development mode.

After the request has been made, we use *assert_response :success* to prove that the request had a successful HTTP response code.

The *assert_response* assertion is a custom assertion defined by Rails (i.e., it's not part of the standard minitest library), and it does exactly what its name implies: it asserts that the actual response status matches the expected status.

Every time you make an HTTP request, the server responds with a status code. When the response is successful, the server returns a status code of 200. When an error occurs, it returns 500. And when the browser can't find the resource being requested, it returns 404. In our assertion, we used the shortcut *:success*, which is the same as 200. We could have used *assert_response(200)*, but it's easier to remember words like *success* or *error* than HTTP status codes, which is why we avoid using the numeric codes whenever possible. Table 16-2 lists the shortcuts available when using assert_response.

Table 16-2. *Status Code Shortcuts Known to* `assert_response`

Symbol	Meaning
`:success`	Status code was 200.
`:redirect`	Status code was in the 300–399 range.
`:missing`	Status code was 404.
`:error`	Status code was in the 500–599 range.

Tip You can pass an explicit status code number to `assert_response`, such as `assert_response(501)` or its symbolic equivalent `assert_response(:not_implemented)`. See `https://www.iana.org/assignments/http-status-codes/http-status-codes.xhtml` for the full list of codes and default messages you can use.

Let's run the test for the index action. (Note: This command assumes your code matches the preceding listing. If not, you may need to adjust the line number used in the command to ensure you're running the right test.)

```
$ rails test test/controllers/articles_controller_test.rb:8
```

```
Run options: --seed 30227

# Running:

.

Finished in 0.559850s, 1.7862 runs/s, 1.7862 assertions/s.
1 runs, 1 assertions, 0 failures, 0 errors, 0 skips
```

Good! Our index action test case passes. It's true that all we tested was the status code of the response; we didn't test that the correct content was included in the response or the right view templates were rendered, for example. This used to be possible with Rails out of the box, but Rails 5 removed this from controller tests, because they felt that controller tests should be focused on the *effects* of executing a particular controller action, not the details of *how* it does it.

So why would we write a controller test if we're going to write another kind of test that also runs our controller actions, but with richer tools for assertions? Well, often we might not. But as you gain experience writing more tests, you'll see there are always trade-offs involved; for example, tests which use an actual browser to more accurately simulate a user's experience may be a more accurate test of your system as a whole, but those tests are magnitudes slower than a controller test.

A common strategy is to use faster tests to cover the full range of all possible scenarios in your application while using slower (but more thorough) tests to cover your application's critical paths.

It is possible, by adding the *rails-controller-testing* to our project, to add the ability to assert instance variable assignments and which templates were rendered back into our controller tests, but we'll follow the recommendations of the Rails team; besides, we'll learn later in this chapter how to write other types of tests which will give us richer tools for verifying the content of a response.

Okay, back to our tests. Let's run the entire ArticlesControllerTest and see where we stand:

```
$ rails test test/controllers/articles_controller_test.rb
```

```
Run options: --seed 8758

# Running:

F

Failure:
ArticlesControllerTest#test_should_get_new [/Users/brady/Sites/beginning-
rails-6-blog/test/controllers/articles_controller_test.rb:15]:
Expected response to be a <2XX: success>, but was a <302: Found> redirect
to <http://www.example.com/login>
Response body: <html><body>You are being <a href="http://www.example.com/
login">redirected</a>.</body></html>

rails test test/controllers/articles_controller_test.rb:13

... more failures omitted ...

Finished in 0.483794s, 14.4690 runs/s, 16.5360 assertions/s.
7 runs, 8 assertions, 5 failures, 0 errors, 0 skips
```

Oh my. Out of our seven test cases, five failed. Don't worry; often, there's a single root cause which, when fixed, can clear up multiple test cases.

Looking at the preceding failure output, we see that the "should get new" test case failed because we expected it to be successful, but instead it redirected to the login page. Of course! We only allow logged-in users to access the new article form, to create an article, to edit an article, to update an article, and to destroy an article!

So let's use the *login_as* test helper method we created where it's needed and see if our tests will now pass. Modify test/controllers/articles_controller.rb to match Listing 16-14.

Listing 16-14. Adding login_as to Test Cases in ArticlesControllerTest: https://gist.github.com/nicedawg/ec58c6d0b771078a308580fbc2c1743c

```ruby
require 'test_helper'

class ArticlesControllerTest < ActionDispatch::IntegrationTest
  setup do
    @article = articles(:welcome_to_rails)
  end

  test "should get index" do
    get articles_url
    assert_response :success
  end

  test "should get new" do
    login_as :eugene
    get new_article_url
    assert_response :success
  end

  test "should create article" do
    login_as :eugene
    assert_difference('Article.count') do
      post articles_url, params: { article: { body: @article.body, excerpt:
      @article.excerpt, location: @article.location, published_at:
      @article.published_at, title: @article.title } }
    end
```

```ruby
    assert_redirected_to article_url(Article.last)
  end

  test "should show article" do
    get article_url(@article)
    assert_response :success
  end

  test "should get edit" do
    login_as :eugene
    get edit_article_url(@article)
    assert_response :success
  end

  test "should update article" do
    login_as :eugene
    patch article_url(@article), params: { article: { body: @article.body,
    excerpt: @article.excerpt, location: @article.location, published_at:
    @article.published_at, title: @article.title } }
    assert_redirected_to article_url(@article)
  end

  test "should destroy article" do
    login_as :eugene
    assert_difference('Article.count', -1) do
      delete article_url(@article)
    end

    assert_redirected_to articles_url
  end
end
```

Let's run our test again and see if we made a dent in our test failures:

```
$ rails test test/controllers/articles_controller_test.rb
```

```
Run options: --seed 42474

# Running:

.......

Finished in 0.675501s, 10.3627 runs/s, 13.3234 assertions/s.
7 runs, 9 assertions, 0 failures, 0 errors, 0 skips
```

Hurrah! Our tests pass now! We *could* declare victory and end on a high note, but we realize that these tests were supplied by our scaffolding; while they're very useful to have, they only cover the *happy path*—that is to say, they only make assertions on what we think of as typical interactions.

Handling Edge Cases

However, we often want our tests to cover edge cases. For instance, we only allow the *owner* of an article to edit the article. We don't allow just *any* logged-in user to edit *any* article. To be sure we don't accidentally remove this security restriction, we should write tests that cover the scenario of user A trying to edit user B's article.

Let's add tests to prove that logged-in users who are *not* the owner are *not* allowed to edit, update, or destroy another's article. Let's modify ArticlesControllerTest in test/controllers/articles_controller_test.rb to match Listing 16-15.

Listing 16-15. Handling Security in ArticlesControllerTest
https://gist.github.com/nicedawg/36039c7dd6feed0883c526a924e712d7

```
require 'test_helper'

class ArticlesControllerTest < ActionDispatch::IntegrationTest
  setup do
    @article = articles(:welcome_to_rails)
  end
```

```ruby
  test "should get index" do
    get articles_url
    assert_response :success
  end

  test "should get new" do
    login_as :eugene
    get new_article_url
    assert_response :success
  end

  test "should create article" do
    login_as :eugene
    assert_difference('Article.count') do
      post articles_url, params: { article: { body: @article.body, excerpt:
      @article.excerpt, location: @article.location, published_at:
      @article.published_at, title: @article.title } }
    end

    assert_redirected_to article_url(Article.last)
  end

  test "should show article" do
    get article_url(@article)
    assert_response :success
  end

  test "should get edit" do
    login_as :eugene
    get edit_article_url(@article)
    assert_response :success
  end

  test "should raise RecordNotFound when non-owner tries to get edit" do
    login_as :lauren
    assert_raises(ActiveRecord::RecordNotFound) do
      get edit_article_url(@article)
    end
  end
```

```ruby
test "should update article" do
  login_as :eugene
  patch article_url(@article), params: { article: { body: @article.body,
  excerpt: @article.excerpt, location: @article.location, published_at:
  @article.published_at, title: @article.title } }
  assert_redirected_to article_url(@article)
end

test "should raise RecordNotFound when non-owner tries to update article" do
  login_as :lauren
  assert_raises(ActiveRecord::RecordNotFound) do
    patch article_url(@article), params: { article: { body: @article.
    body, excerpt: @article.excerpt, location: @article.location,
    published_at: @article.published_at, title: @article.title } }
  end
end

test "should destroy article" do
  login_as :eugene
  assert_difference('Article.count', -1) do
    delete article_url(@article)
  end

  assert_redirected_to articles_url
end

test "should raise RecordNotFound when non-owner tries to destroy
article" do
  login_as :lauren
  assert_raises(ActiveRecord::RecordNotFound) do
    delete article_url(@article)
  end
end
end
```

As you can see, we added additional tests next to our existing edit, update, and destroy tests which assert that an exception is raised when a user attempts to modify an article which they *don't* own. In each case, we logged in as Lauren (because we know our articles fixture is owned by Eugene) and attempted the edit/update/delete operation which Eugene was able to successfully complete, but verified that Lauren was unable to do so. Very powerful!

Looking at our articles controller, it seems our controller test has covered most of its functionality; however, we realize we haven't yet covered the *notify_friend* action. Let's modify our ArticlesControllerTest in tests/controllers/articles_controller_test.rb to add a couple of tests to cover the scenarios when a reader submits the "Email a Friend" form with both valid and invalid information, as shown in Listing 16-16.

Listing 16-16. Covering notify_friend in ArticlesControllerTest
https://gist.github.com/nicedawg/b1da893b01ff4e3e3eff5778ef8b912f

```ruby
require 'test_helper'

class ArticlesControllerTest < ActionDispatch::IntegrationTest
  setup do
    @article = articles(:welcome_to_rails)
  end

  # ... code omitted for brevity ...

  test "should raise RecordNotFound when non-owner tries to destroy
  article" do
    login_as :lauren
    assert_raises(ActiveRecord::RecordNotFound) do
      delete article_url(@article)
    end
  end

  test "should redirect to article url when submitting valid email a friend
  form" do
    post notify_friend_article_url(@article), params: {
      email_a_friend: { name: 'Joe', email: 'joe@example.com' }
    }, xhr: true
    assert_redirected_to article_url(@article)
  end
```

```
test "should respond with unprocessable_entity when submitting invalid
email a friend form" do
  post notify_friend_article_url(@article), params: {
    email_a_friend: { name: 'Joe', email: 'notAnEmail' }
  }, xhr: true
  assert_response :unprocessable_entity
end
end
```

The first test proves that when a valid "Email a Friend" form submission is sent to the ArticlesController, the response is a redirect to the article show page. And the next test proves that when *invalid* data is sent, an HTTP status code for "unprocessable entity" is returned. Note that we supplied an additional option to our *post* calls which we haven't used yet—*xhr: true*. We know that these requests to submit the "Email a Friend" form use Ajax, so we set *xhr: true* so that the request will indicate it expects a JavaScript response.

Now that we've added these test cases, let's run the entire controller test again and see what happens:

```
$ rails test test/controllers/articles_controller_test.rb
```

```
Run options: --seed 9405

# Running:
F

Failure:
ArticlesControllerTest#test_should_redirect_to_article_url_when_submitting_
valid_email_a_friend_form [/Users/brady/Sites/beginning-rails-6-blog/test/
controllers/articles_controller_test.rb:77]:
Expected response to be a Turbolinks visit to <http://www.example.com/
articles/517600287> but was a visit to <http://www.example.com/login>.
Expected "http://www.example.com/articles/517600287" to be === "http://www.
example.com/login".
rails test test/controllers/articles_controller_test.rb:73

F
```

```
Failure:
ArticlesControllerTest#test_should_respond_with_unprocessable_entity_when_
submitting_invalid_email_a_friend_form [/Users/brady/Sites/beginning-rails-
6-blog/test/controllers/articles_controller_test.rb:84]:
Expected response to be a <422: unprocessable_entity>, but was a <200: OK>
Response body: Turbolinks.clearCache()
Turbolinks.visit("http://www.example.com/login", {"action":"replace"}).
Expected: 422
  Actual: 200
rails test test/controllers/articles_controller_test.rb:80

.........

Finished in 0.763068s, 15.7260 runs/s, 20.9680 assertions/s.
12 runs, 16 assertions, 2 failures, 0 errors, 0 skips
```

Hmm. Our new tests failed. Looking closely at the failure output, we see both responses redirected to the login path. What? We don't require a visitor to be logged in to send an email to a friend, do we?

In fact, we do! This was clearly an oversight on our part (perhaps you realized this earlier). Looking at the top of ArticlesController, we require authentication for all actions except for *index* and *show*. When we added the *notify_friend* action in a previous chapter, we should have also excluded *notify_friend* from requiring authentication. Not only can tests help prevent future bugs, they can help us find *current* bugs! Let's fix this bug in our application by modifying ArticlesController in app/controllers/articles_controller.rb to match Listing 16-17.

Listing 16-17. Fix Bug in ArticlesController Which Required Authentication to Send Email to a Friend

https://gist.github.com/nicedawg/68d8c626d3f3dd9cf37d6bdb56c93f87

```ruby
class ArticlesController < ApplicationController
  before_action :authenticate, except: [:index, :show, :notify_friend]
  before_action :set_article, only: [:show, :notify_friend]

  # ... code omitted for brevity ...
end
```

Run the test again, and we should see that our `ArticlesController` now passes all of its tests.

In case you're still on the fence about whether writing automated tests is worth the effort, try running this entire test file again and observe how long it takes to run; quite likely, it takes less than one second. Consider how long it would take to verify these scenarios manually—a few minutes at best. (And if you're like me, you might forget to manually verify one or two of them.) Also consider the fact that writing tests helped us find an embarrassing bug!

We've covered some of the most common scenarios when writing controller tests, but testing is a deep topic. When you're ready for more information, the Rails guide at `https://guides.rubyonrails.org/testing.html#functional-tests-for-your-controllers` is a great resource.

Next, we'll take a look at other types of tests we can write.

Running the "Full" Test Suite

Up until this point, we've been using the *rails test* command with arguments, in order to run certain tests. But we mentioned that if we run the *rails test* command with no arguments, it runs *most* of the tests. (It will exclude any *system* tests, which we'll describe later.)

So let's try running the *rails test* command and see if we have any more broken tests:

```
$ rails test
```

```
Run options: --seed 40931

# Running:

.........E

Error:
NotifierMailerTest#test_email_friend:
ArgumentError: wrong number of arguments (given 0, expected 3)
    app/mailers/notifier_mailer.rb:2:in `email_friend'
    test/mailers/notifier_mailer_test.rb:6:in `block in
<class:NotifierMailerTest>'
rails test test/mailers/notifier_mailer_test.rb:4
.....E
```

```
Error:
DraftArticlesMailerTest#test_no_author:
ArgumentError: wrong number of arguments (given 0, expected 1)
    app/mailers/draft_articles_mailer.rb:8:in `no_author'
    test/mailers/draft_articles_mailer_test.rb:6:in `block in <class:DraftA
rticlesMailerTest>'
rails test test/mailers/draft_articles_mailer_test.rb:4

...

Finished in 0.704911s, 26.9538 runs/s, 38.3027 assertions/s.
19 runs, 27 assertions, 0 failures, 2 errors, 0 skips
```

Looking closely at the failures, we see we have a couple of mailer tests which need attention. That makes sense; we used the Rails generator to create these mailer classes, but never updated their tests to reflect the changes we made. Let's fix these mailer tests.

Mailer Tests

Mailers can be just an integral part of your application as controllers and models and deserve to be tested as well. Again, Rails gives us tools to make doing so as easy as possible.

We saw in the previous section that we have some failing mailer tests, since we didn't update the generated tests when we updated our mailers, so let's fix that.

First, let's focus on the failure from our NotifierMailerTest. Looking at the test (in test/mailers/notifier_mailer_test.rb) and the mailer (in app/mailers/notifier_mailer.rb) side by side, we see that the problem is that in the test, we're not passing any parameters to the *email_friend* method. We also see that our test's assertions are no longer valid. Let's edit our NotifierMailerTest to fix the test, as shown in Listing 16-18.

Listing 16-18. Fixing NotifierMailerTest
https://gist.github.com/nicedawg/c467c97ddfce1dbfd99bf6641ed2e06f

```
require 'test_helper'

class NotifierMailerTest < ActionMailer::TestCase
  def setup
```

```
    @article = articles(:welcome_to_rails)
    @sender_name = 'Reed'
    @receiver_email = 'to@example.com'
  end

  test "email_friend" do
    mail = NotifierMailer.email_friend(@article, @sender_name, @receiver_email)

    assert_emails 1 do
      mail.deliver_now
    end

    assert_equal "Interesting Article", mail.subject
    assert_equal ["to@example.com"], mail.to
    assert_equal ["from@example.com"], mail.from
    assert_match "Your friend, <em>#{@sender_name}</em>", mail.body.encoded
    assert_match @article.title, mail.body.encoded
  end
end
```

First, we added a *setup* method to run before the test, to fetch the article and set the sender and receiver information. We could have done this in the test itself, but this helps keep the test clearer and encourages reuse for future tests.

Then, we passed the parameters that *NotifierMailer.email_friend* expects. This fixes the immediate problem our previous test run showed us, but we made some more changes.

After that, we used a special assertion method—*assert_emails*—which Action Mailer provides to prove that if we call *deliver_now* on the mailer object, one email is "delivered."

Then, we updated the existing assertions to match what we expect the email to look like. We could have chosen to ensure that *every character* in the body of the email is exactly what we expect, but we decided to just check for the critical pieces. (As mentioned before, writing tests involves trade-offs; writing extremely thorough tests may give you more confidence, but it takes longer to write the tests, and the tests become too brittle—too easily broken by insignificant changes.)

After updating this mailer test, let's run the test again:

```
$ rails test test/mailers/notifier_mailer_test.rb
```

```
Run options: --seed 46405

# Running:

E

Error:
NotifierMailerTest#test_email_friend:
ActionView::Template::Error: Missing host to link to! Please provide the
:host parameter, set default_url_options[:host], or set :only_path to true
    app/views/notifier_mailer/email_friend.html.erb:6
    app/mailers/notifier_mailer.rb:10:in `email_friend'
    test/mailers/notifier_mailer_test.rb:14:in `block (2 levels) in
    <class:NotifierMailerTest>'
    test/mailers/notifier_mailer_test.rb:13:in `block in
    <class:NotifierMailerTest>'
rails test test/mailers/notifier_mailer_test.rb:10
Finished in 0.279585s, 3.5767 runs/s, 0.0000 assertions/s.
1 runs, 0 assertions, 0 failures, 1 errors, 0 skips
```

Now we have a new error, which is a form of progress! This error may look familiar; back in Chapter 12, we had to configure this *default_url_options* setting to send emails in development. We need to also configure this setting for our test environment. Modify your config/environments/test.rb file to match Listing 16-19.

Listing 16-19. Configuring Action Mailer Default URL Host in Test Environment
https://gist.github.com/nicedawg/b99964ceadc6f2bd4efef52e14caabbc

```
# The test environment is used exclusively to run your application's
# test suite. You never need to work with it otherwise. Remember that
# your test database is "scratch space" for the test suite and is wiped
# and recreated between test runs. Don't rely on the data there!

Rails.application.configure do
```

```
# Settings specified here will take precedence over those in config/
application.rb.

# ... settings omitted for brevity ...

config.action_mailer.perform_caching = false

# Tell Action Mailer not to deliver emails to the real world.
# The :test delivery method accumulates sent emails in the
# ActionMailer::Base.deliveries array.
config.action_mailer.delivery_method = :test
config.action_mailer.default_url_options = { host: 'http://example.com' }

# Print deprecation notices to the stderr.
config.active_support.deprecation = :stderr

# Raises error for missing translations.
# config.action_view.raise_on_missing_translations = true
end
```

Now, running the NotifierMailer test again should show success! We still have a failing DraftArticlesMailer test, though. Let's quickly fix that. Let's modify our code in test/mailers/draft_articles_mailer_test.rb to match Listing 16-20.

Listing 16-20. Fixing DraftArticlesMailerTest
https://gist.github.com/nicedawg/f03b344103e4a4f66370fe668b8be576

```
require 'test_helper'

class DraftArticlesMailerTest < ActionMailer::TestCase
  test "no_author" do
    mail = DraftArticlesMailer.no_author('to@example.org')
    assert_equal "Your email could not be processed", mail.subject
    assert_equal ["to@example.org"], mail.to
    assert_equal ["from@example.com"], mail.from
    assert_match "Please check your draft articles email address and try
    again.", mail.body.encoded
  end
end
```

These fixes were fairly minor; we provided the parameter which *no_author* expected and updated a couple of assertions to match reality. Now, try running the *rails test* command again. Success!

We only scratched the surface of Action Mailer tests, and we haven't even talked about Action Cable tests, Active Job tests, or Action Mailbox tests. Entire books are devoted to testing the Rails framework; we won't cover all types of testing here, but hopefully you feel more comfortable with testing Rails applications than you did before.

We're not quite done with testing yet, though. Up to this point, we've covered unit test models and mailers, as well as writing functional controller tests which gave us the ability to quickly make *some* assertions about our controller's behavior, but we realized those controller tests had some limitations. We'd like to have some tests—even if they're slower—that approach testing the actual user experience.

System Testing

Rails defines one more type of test, and it's the highest level of the bunch. System tests go much further than the controller tests we wrote earlier. Unlike controller tests, which basically just look for response codes, system tests can span multiple controllers and actions with full session support. System tests either are run by a Rack::Test driver, which is like a barebones simulated web browser, or can even be run by an actual browser installed on your workstation! They're the closest you can get to simulating actual interaction with a web application. They test that the individual pieces of your application integrate well together.

It should be noted that Rails also supports another, similar type of test, called *integration* tests, though many developers feel there's too much overlap between controller tests, integration tests, and system tests and opt for leaving integration tests out of their test suite. We won't cover integration tests in this chapter, but check out `https://guides.rubyonrails.org/testing.html#integration-testing` if you'd like to learn more.

System Testing the Blog Application

Let's get started by writing some system tests. In fact, we already have one; in an earlier chapter, when we used the generator to scaffold our articles controller, Rails created the test/system/articles_test.rb file for us. Let's go ahead and try to run it:

```
$ rails test:system
```

```
Run options: --seed 27728

# Running:

Capybara starting Puma...
* Version 4.3.1 , codename: Mysterious Traveller
* Min threads: 0, max threads: 4
* Listening on tcp://127.0.0.1:55167

... output omitted ...

[Screenshot]: /Users/brady/Sites/beginning-rails-6-blog/tmp/screenshots/
failures_test_updating_a_Article.png
E

Error:
ArticlesTest#test_updating_a_Article:
StandardError: No fixture named 'one' found for fixture set 'articles'
    test/system/articles_test.rb:5:in `block in <class:ArticlesTest>'

... output omitted ...

Finished in 5.770051s, 0.6932 runs/s, 0.0000 assertions/s.
4 runs, 0 assertions, 0 failures, 4 errors, 0 skips
```

First of all, you may have been surprised to see that when running this system test, suddenly some Chrome browser windows opened and closed; don't worry—your workstation hasn't gone crazy! System tests in Rails are configured to use Chrome by default; those windows were actually launched by running the system test.

Looking at the test output, we see our tests failed, but for a familiar reason; we need to update the fixture name. We'll fix that in a moment, but let's keep looking at this test output.

First, we see "Capybara starting Puma..."; Capybara is a gem which Rails now includes and configures by default which gives your system tests the ability to control a real browser and to help make assertions. Puma is a Ruby server that can handle web requests and pass them to your Rails app. System tests start their own server so that the test environment is kept isolated from your development environment. It's possible to change Capybara and Puma configuration in your test environment, but it's nice to know it works out of the box.

Also, notice how when a test fails, a screenshot is generated; this can be very useful! Those browser windows flew by so fast, we wouldn't have had a chance to see what was wrong; but the screenshot taken at the point of failure can sometimes help us debug our system tests.

Before we fix our fixture reference in our test, let's make a quick change so that when we run our system tests, Chrome windows don't take over our screen. Our system tests can continue to use Chrome in "headless" mode, which simply means in a way that isn't visible on your workstation. Let's switch to headless Chrome by modifying test/application_system_test_case.rb to match Listing 16-21.

Listing 16-21. Switching System Tests to Use Headless Chrome by Default
https://gist.github.com/nicedawg/17d775d3bea48b5274e15f5bed9b41b5

```
require "test_helper"

class ApplicationSystemTestCase < ActionDispatch::SystemTestCase
  driven_by :selenium, using: :headless_chrome, screen_size: [1400, 1400]
end
```

As you can see, this ApplicationSystemTestCase class is a convenient place to change defaults for our system tests. It was using *selenium*—a library which knows how to control web browsers—to control Chrome, with a given screen size. By changing this to *headless_chrome*, our system tests will still run with the Chrome browser, but invisibly. It's also possible to use other browsers, like Firefox and others; see https://github.com/teamcapybara/capybara#selenium for more information.

Run the system tests again with *rails test:system*; we should see the same failures as before, but without browser windows popping up during the test run. But now you know how easy it is to switch back to using visible Chrome windows if you want.

Okay, let's get back to fixing our system test. First, let's fix our immediate problem—the reference to our articles fixture. Modify the reference in the *setup* method of your test/system/articles_test.rb so it matches Listing 16-22.

Listing 16-22. Fixing Articles Fixture Reference in test/system/articles_test.rb

https://gist.github.com/nicedawg/a16e2ae42319be3641ca9d4bb57f0827

```
require "application_system_test_case"

class ArticlesTest < ApplicationSystemTestCase
  setup do
    @article = articles(:welcome_to_rails)
  end

  test "visiting the index" do
    visit articles_url
    assert_selector "h1", text: "Articles"
  end

  test "creating a Article" do
    visit articles_url
    click_on "New Article"

    fill_in "Body", with: @article.body
    fill_in "Excerpt", with: @article.excerpt
    fill_in "Location", with: @article.location
    fill_in "Published at", with: @article.published_at
    fill_in "Title", with: @article.title
    click_on "Create Article"

    assert_text "Article was successfully created"
    click_on "Back"
  end

  test "updating a Article" do
    visit articles_url
    click_on "Edit", match: :first

    fill_in "Body", with: @article.body
    fill_in "Excerpt", with: @article.excerpt
    fill_in "Location", with: @article.location
```

```
    fill_in "Published at", with: @article.published_at
    fill_in "Title", with: @article.title
    click_on "Update Article"

    assert_text "Article was successfully updated"
    click_on "Back"
  end

  test "destroying a Article" do
    visit articles_url
    page.accept_confirm do
      click_on "Destroy", match: :first
    end

    assert_text "Article was successfully destroyed"
  end
end
```

We fixed the reference to our articles fixture, but before running our system test again, let's take a closer look at how this test works.

First, the overall structure looks familiar; just like the other tests we've written, there's an optional *setup* method, and each test case is declared just like we've done before.

However, we see some new methods in our test cases; *visit* is a Capybara method which tells our browser to navigate to a particular URL. *assert_selector* is another Capybara method which lets us make assertions like "there is an H1 tag with the text 'Articles.'" *click_on* is another Capybara method which finds a button or link with the provided text (or even CSS selector) and tells the browser to click it. *fill_in* is yet another Capybara method that fills in an input field with provided data.

Capybara provides a vast array of methods (with options) to give you the ability to perform almost any browser function in your system tests; by default, Capybara only interacts with *visible* elements and will typically wait up to a couple of seconds for a given element to appear on the screen. There are too many methods and options to list here; visit https://github.com/teamcapybara/capybara#the-dsl for more information when you're ready.

Running the system test again, we see new errors. (Remember, that's progress!)

```
$ rails test:system
```

```
Run options: --seed 6356

# Running:

... output omitted ...

E

Error:
ArticlesTest#test_creating_a_Article:
Capybara::ElementNotFound: Unable to find link or button "New Article"
    test/system/articles_test.rb:15:in `block in <class:ArticlesTest>'
rails test test/system/articles_test.rb:13

Finished in 5.833557s, 0.6857 runs/s, 0.1714 assertions/s.
4 runs, 1 assertions, 0 failures, 3 errors, 0 skips
```

We see that our tests for creating, updating, and destroying an article failed, due to being unable to find links or buttons with the given tests. Similar to our controller test earlier in this chapter, we realize that only logged-in users are allowed to perform these actions, so we'll need to add code to sign in a user for these tests.

Also, we remember that we only show the Edit and Destroy links when the logged-in author is hovering over the title, so we'll need to add a hover command to those tests in order for those tests to pass. Also, this generated test wasn't updated to reflect that we changed the article body to be handled by Action Text nor to reflect that the *Published At* field is a series of select boxes instead of a text input.

Let's edit our test in test/system/articles_test.rb to match Listing 16-23 to address these problems. We'll explain further after the listing.

Listing 16-23. Fixing Articles System Test in test/system/articles_test.rb
https://gist.github.com/nicedawg/9e37f7000fd9761762c312bfcd92d24b

```
require "application_system_test_case"

class ArticlesTest < ApplicationSystemTestCase
  setup do
```

```ruby
  @article = articles(:welcome_to_rails)
  @user = users(:eugene)
end

def sign_in(user)
  visit login_url

  fill_in "email", with: user.email
  fill_in "password", with: 'secret'

  click_button "Login"
end

def fill_in_rich_text(locator, content)
  find(locator).base.send_keys(content)
end

def set_datetime_select(locator, datetime)
  select datetime.strftime("%Y"),  from: "#{locator}_1i" # Year
  select datetime.strftime("%B"),  from: "#{locator}_2i" # Month
  select datetime.strftime("%-d"), from: "#{locator}_3i" # Day
  select datetime.strftime("%H"),  from: "#{locator}_4i" # Hour
  select datetime.strftime("%M"),  from: "#{locator}_5i" # Minutes
end

test "visiting the index" do
  visit articles_url
  assert_selector "h1", text: "Articles"
end

test "creating a Article" do
  sign_in(@user)

  visit articles_url
  click_on "New Article"

  fill_in_rich_text("#article_body", @article.body)
  fill_in "Excerpt", with: @article.excerpt
  fill_in "Location", with: @article.location
  set_datetime_select("article_published_at", @article.published_at)
```

```
    fill_in "Title", with: @article.title
    click_on "Create Article"

    assert_text "Article was successfully created"
  end

  test "updating a Article" do
    sign_in(@user)

    visit articles_url

    find(".article a", match: :first).hover
    find(".article .actions a", text: "Edit").click

    fill_in_rich_text("#article_body", @article.body)
    fill_in "Excerpt", with: @article.excerpt
    fill_in "Location", with: @article.location
    set_datetime_select("article_published_at", @article.published_at)
    fill_in "Title", with: @article.title
    click_on "Update Article"

    assert_text "Article was successfully updated"
  end

  test "destroying a Article" do
    sign_in(@user)

    visit articles_url

    find(".article a", match: :first).hover

    find(".article .actions a", text: "Delete").click

    assert_text "Article was successfully destroyed"
  end
end
```

Whew! It took several changes, and some of them were complicated; we'll explain the changes, but don't worry if these changes don't seem self-evident. It took this author several tries, Internet searches, and debugging using test output and screenshots to figure it out. System tests are often more tedious to implement and more fragile (since minor changes *anywhere* in the application can cause them to break), but the effort is worth it.

First, we loaded the *eugene* user in our *setup* method so we can log him in when necessary.

Next, we created a *sign_in* method which takes a user and performs the necessary Capybara operations to log them in. This method would be a great candidate for moving to our ApplicationSystemTestCase class so it can be shared between multiple system tests, but this is fine for now.

Next, we realized we couldn't simply *fill_in "Body"*, as test failures indicate that element didn't exist (or wasn't visible). Of course, we replaced the simple text area for an article's body with the Action Text control in an earlier chapter. Unfortunately, there doesn't seem to be an elegant way to populate the content for an Action Text rich text field, so we resort to some lower-level Capybara methods. We use *find* to grab a reference to a particular DOM element and then use *base.send_keys* to simulate typing into a specific element. Since this was a little tricky to figure out, we decided to make it a method called *fill_in_rich_text*; again, this would be a great candidate for sharing and should probably be moved elsewhere, but it's fine for now.

Next, we realized that *fill_in "Published at"* wouldn't work, as our Published At field isn't a simple text box, but rather a series of select boxes. Again, since this was tricky to figure out, we made it a separate method called *set_datetime_select*. Like our other custom methods, this is a great candidate for sharing between other system tests, but it's fine here for now.

For our *creating an Article* test, we added a call to sign in the user, replaced the commands to populate the *body* and *published_at* fields with our custom commands, and removed the final *click_on "Back"* command because we had made changes to our app that rendered that final command invalid.

Our changes to the *updating an Article* test were similar, though we couldn't just *click_on "Edit"*; we had to use some commands to find the first article link and hover over it and then click the Edit link within the article's *.actions* DOM element.

Finally, our changes to the *destroying an Article* test were similar, except we had to remove the *page.accept_confirm* method, since our "Delete" link doesn't trigger a confirmation dialog when clicked.

Running our system tests now, we should see sweet success:

```
$ rails test:system
```

```
Run options: --seed 29652

# Running:

Capybara starting Puma...
* Version 4.3.1 , codename: Mysterious Traveller
* Min threads: 0, max threads: 4
* Listening on tcp://127.0.0.1:50734
... output omitted ...

....

Finished in 6.055268s, 0.6606 runs/s, 0.6606 assertions/s.
4 runs, 4 assertions, 0 failures, 0 errors, 0 skips
```

Notice the runtime of our system tests; we only had four tests, but they took 6 seconds to run. Compared to our other tests—19 tests that took less than 1 second—system tests are quite a bit slower. It's true that 6 seconds is not long at all, but imagine your application having hundreds of system tests; soon, the entire test suite may take 15, 20, 30, or even 60 minutes to run! As mentioned earlier, a challenge of writing automated tests for your application is deciding which types of tests to write for certain features of your application.

For fun, try running the tests again with visible Chrome by changing the reference to *:headless_chrome* in your test/application_system_test_case.rb file back to *:chrome*. If you watch closely, you'll see the browser windows open and start navigating, filling out forms, and submitting forms by themselves!

Summary

This chapter served as an introduction to the Rails philosophy behind testing and stressed its importance as part of the development cycle. We toured some of the most common types of tests—unit tests for our models, controller tests, mailer tests, and system tests, but we only scratched the surface.

While it's not feasible to cover everything there is to know about testing your Rails application in this chapter, hopefully you gained a good foundation and know where to look for more information.

Hopefully you've also understood how testing is an important part of the development cycle. Despite the fact that we left it until near the end of this book, it's not something we should treat as an afterthought. Now that you know how to write a Rails application and how to test it, you can combine the steps: write some code, and then test it. As you get into the code/test rhythm (or better yet, test/code), you'll find that you can write better, more reliable software. And you may sleep a little better at night too, knowing that your code changes have a safety net.

We should also mention that Rails' default testing framework, minitest, is only a default choice. There are several other test frameworks available for the Ruby community. In fact, test frameworks become almost like a religion to developers. RSpec (`https://rspec.info/`) is a very popular choice, as is test-unit (`https://test-unit.github.io/`), which was actually the default Rails test framework before minitest. There is also Cucumber (`https://cucumber.io/`), which uses a language called Gherkin that lets you write tests in a more human-friendly manner.

No matter which framework you decide to use, make sure you test early and often. Not only does it ensure your application does what you expect but it is also frequently used as a source of documentation by developers moving into your project for the first time.

The next chapter will look at preparing your applications for a global audience through the use of Rails' built-in internationalization and localization support.

CHAPTER 17

Internationalization

Internationalization in Rails used to be a complex task until Rails version 2.2 came out with internationalization and localization support built in. Since then, launching an application in another language or even multiple languages has become a relatively simple task.

What is internationalization, and why do we care? According to Wikipedia:

> Internationalization is the process of designing a software application so that it can be adapted to various languages and regions without engineering changes. Localization is the process of adapting internationalized software for a specific region or language by translating text and adding locale-specific components.

—https://en.wikipedia.org/wiki/Internationalization_and_
  localization)

This chapter explains internationalization and localization support in Rails. First, we'll set up internationalization in our blog application with English as the main language; then we'll localize it to another language; and, finally, we'll support both languages and allow users to pick the language they want.

Internationalization and *localization* are long words, so developers use short names for them. The short name for internationalization is i18n, which is the first and the last letters of the word with the count of how many characters are in between. Following the same logic, localization's short name is l10n.

Note If you need to get the code at the exact point where you finished Chapter 16, download the source code zip file from the book's page on `www.apress.com` and extract it on your computer.

479

© Brady Somerville, Adam Gamble, Cloves Carneiro Jr and Rida Al Barazi 2020
B. Somerville et al., *Beginning Rails 6*, https://doi.org/10.1007/978-1-4842-5716-6_17

Internationalization Logic in Rails

The i18n and l10n support in Rails is based on a single module that takes care of all the translation and locale changes for you; this module is called *I18n* and is added to your Rails application automatically by the *i18n* gem, which is a dependency of the *activesupport* gem, which is in turn a dependency of Rails.

I18n's main method is *translate*, which simply looks up locale-specific content by looking for a translation text in a locale file, normally located in config/locales.

Locales are like languages but are more specific to regions. For example, *en* represents English in general, whereas *en-us* represents US English and *en-uk* represents UK English. In Rails, those differences are reflected in the translation files, mainly for localization options like time, date formats, and currency.

If you look in the config/locales directory, you'll see a file called en.yml; it's a YAML file that defines the English translations for your application. Open the file, and you'll see something similar to the code in Listing 17-1.

Listing 17-1. The Default English Locale File in config/locales/en.yml

```
# Files in the config/locales directory are used for internationalization
# and are automatically loaded by Rails. If you want to use locales other
# than English, add the necessary files in this directory.
#
# To use the locales, use `I18n.t`:
#
#     I18n.t 'hello'
#
# In views, this is aliased to just `t`:
#
#     <%= t('hello') %>
#
# To use a different locale, set it with `I18n.locale`:
#
#     I18n.locale = :es
#
# This would use the information in config/locales/es.yml.
#
```

```
# The following keys must be escaped otherwise they will not be retrieved by
# the default I18n backend:
#
# true, false, on, off, yes, no
#
# Instead, surround them with single quotes.
#
# en:
#   'true': 'foo'
#
# To learn more, please read the Rails Internationalization guide
# available at https://guides.rubyonrails.org/i18n.html.

en:
  hello: "Hello world"
```

These locale files are written in the YAML format. It starts with the locale symbol, which is also the translation file name; in this case, it's *en*. Then, the file lists the translations in a key-value pair style: the en.yml example defines the translation of *hello* as "Hello world."

Now, let's see the translation in action by trying the I18n module in the console. Launch it with `rails console`:

```
>> I18n.translate "hello"
=> "Hello world"
>> I18n.t "hello"
=> "Hello world"
```

We pass the *key* to the `translate` method, and it returns the corresponding *value* from the current locale, which in our case is English. The I18n module has the *t* method as an alias for the *translate* method, which you used in the previous example.

In Rails, there is the concept of a "current locale." At any time, we can determine the current locale by calling the *I18n.locale* method. When you don't set the locale yourself, it's set to a default locale, normally *en*. You can access the default locale by calling *I18n.default_locale*. Let's check the current locale and the default locale in our rails console:

```
>> I18n.locale
=> :en
>> I18n.default_locale
=> :en
```

To change the locale or the default locale, we can use the *I18n.locale=* and *I18n.default_locale=* methods. Let's try to change the locale to Brazilian Portuguese, for which the locale symbol is pt-br:

```
>> I18n.locale = 'pt-br'
I18n::InvalidLocale ("pt-br" is not a valid locale)
>> I18n.available_locales
=> [:en]
```

Trying to change our locale to Brazilian Portuguese failed with an error saying it's not valid. Of course, 'pt-br' *is* a valid locale code, but we ran *I18n.available_locales* to see which locales our application allows and found our application does not allow *pt-br*. Only *en* is available by default. To change that, let's edit our config/application.rb to match Listing 17-2.

Listing 17-2. Allowing Brazilian Portuguese Locale in config/application.rb
https://gist.github.com/nicedawg/c945ddb11ff1a79d3f3e46f0a430c85e

```
require_relative 'boot'

require 'rails/all'

# Require the gems listed in Gemfile, including any gems
# you've limited to :test, :development, or :production.
Bundler.require(*Rails.groups)

module Blog
  class Application < Rails::Application
    # Initialize configuration defaults for originally generated Rails
      version.
    config.load_defaults 6.0

    # Settings in config/environments/* take precedence over those
      specified here.
```

```
# Application configuration can go into files in config/initializers
# -- all .rb files in that directory are automatically loaded after
    loading
# the framework and any gems in your application.

I18n.available_locales = [:en, :'pt-br']
  end
end
```

Now, let's exit our rails console and restart it to pick up our configuration change and try again:

```
>> I18n.available_locales
=> [:en, :"pt-br"]
>> I18n.locale = 'pt-br'
=> "pt-br"
>> I18n.translate('hello')
=> "translation missing: pt-br.hello"
```

First, we checked *I18n.available_locales* after making our configuration change and see that *pt-br* is now available for our application to use. Next, we set the current locale to *pt-br*, and then we tried to look up the translation for "hello," but received a string saying the translation is missing.

To define the translation for *hello* in Brazilian Portuguese, let's create a new translation file named after the locale symbol pt-br.yml in config/locales, as shown in Listing 17-3.

Listing 17-3. The Brazilian Portuguese Locale File in config/locales/pt-br.yml: https://gist.github.com/nicedawg/e7d2a090aebc9994c147e6ae1ada408d

```
pt-br:
  hello: "Ola mundo"
```

Rails doesn't reload locale files automatically, unlike other files. So let's exit the console, restart it to make sure Rails loads the new translation file, and try again:

```
>> I18n.locale
=> :en
>> I18n.locale = 'pt-br'
```

```
=> "pt-br"
>> I18n.t "hello"
=> "Ola mundo"
```

That's how simple it is! All we need are the translation files, each with several translations in key-value pairs. We access those translations by passing the corresponding key to the *I18n.translate* method or its alias *I18n.t*.

Rails manages all of its internals using the I18n module. For example, all the Active Record validation messages we saw in Chapters 5 and 6 are called by using the *translate* method and referring to a translation key. If you change the locale, Rails has no translation for those error messages. Check it out:

```
>> I18n.locale = 'pt-br'
=> "pt-br"
>> article = Article.new
=> #<Article id: nil, title: nil, published_at: nil, created_at: nil,
    updated_at: nil, excerpt: nil, location: nil, user_id: nil>
>> article.save
=> false
>> article.errors.full_messages
=> ["Title translation missing: pt-br.activerecord.errors.models.article.
attributes.title.blank", "Body translation missing: pt-br.activerecord.
errors.models.article.attributes.body.blank", "User translation missing:
pt-br.activerecord.errors.models.article.attributes.user.required"]
```

Active Record tried to get the translations for the error messages, but it couldn't find them in the Brazilian Portuguese translation file. Thankfully, these helpful messages include the missing i18n keys. So let's add them by updating pt-br.yml so it looks like the code in Listing 17-4.

Listing 17-4. Updated Brazilian Portuguese Locale File in config/locales/pt-br. yml: https://gist.github.com/nicedawg/e3bc0ab4810e66f99570baa7685e39bd

```
pt-br:
  hello: "Ola mundo"

  activerecord:
    errors:
```

```
models:
  article:
    attributes:
      title:
        blank: não pode ficar em branco
      body:
        blank: não pode ficar em branco
      user:
        required: deve existir
```

Notice how we nested the keys. The "translation missing" message we saw earlier in the console included a list of names: pt-br, activerecord, errors, models, article, attributes, body, and blank. Those names represent the path inside the pt-br translation file. I18n calls the blank key, for example, by using dots to connect it and its parents; the translate call which Rails tried to use behind the scenes was *I18n.translate('activerecord.errors.models.article.attributes.title.blank')*.

Now that we have added the translations, let's try it from the console again. (Don't forget to restart your console!)

```
>> I18n.locale = 'pt-br'
=> "pt-br"
>> article = Article.new
=> #<Article id: nil, title: nil, published_at: nil, created_at: nil,
   updated_at: nil, excerpt: nil, location: nil, user_id: nil>
>> article.save
=> false
>> I18n.translate('activerecord.errors.models.article.attributes.title.
   blank')
=> "não pode ficar em branco"
>> article.errors.full_messages
=> ["Title não pode ficar em branco", "Body não pode ficar em branco",
   "User deve existir"]
```

Congratulations! You just translated the error messages for the validations on our Article model's title, body, and user attributes to Brazilian Portuguese. Now that we understand how I18n works, let's set it up in our blog application.

Setting Up i18n in the Blog Application

Rails at its core uses i18n, but so far our application's code *hasn't* been using it. We'll need to make sure that all hardcoded text and strings in our code are replaced with a call to the *I18n.translate* method.

This may sound like a lot of work, but it's fairly simple in this case because our application is still small. We encourage you to use the *I18n.translate* method in your project as early as possible; it's only a little bit of work up front, but you'll avoid having to do a *lot* of work later; it gets more difficult as your project grows.

Let's begin with our models. The only one that has a hardcoded string is the Comment model, which includes a custom validation with an error message. Let's replace this error message with an *I18n.t* call to a key and add that key to our en.yml translation file. Listing 17-5 shows how the Comment model should look after our changes.

Listing 17-5. Updated Comment Model in app/models/comment.rb:
https://gist.github.com/nicedawg/ed1cfec6013e4b8319ad334f7e0aa646

```
class Comment < ApplicationRecord
  belongs_to :article

  validates :name, :email, :body, presence: true
  validate :article_should_be_published

  after_create :email_article_author

  def article_should_be_published
    errors.add(:article_id, I18n.t('comments.errors.not_published_yet')) if
    article && !article.published?
  end

  def email_article_author
    NotifierMailer.comment_added(self).deliver_later
  end
end
```

Notice how we used the dot notation in the *comments.errors.not_published_yet* key. It's good practice to keep the locale file organized; doing so helps us find the translation more easily when our file gets bigger. Because the error message is added to the comment object, we add it under comments; and because it's an error message, we drill a step deeper and place it under errors.

Don't forget to add the translation to your en.yml translation file. It should look like Listing 17-6 after we clean it up and update it with the new translation. (Notice that we removed the "Hello world" translation since we don't need it.)

Listing 17-6. Updated English Locale File in config/locales/en.yml: https://gist.github.com/nicedawg/d248b48ab77675319f185c148d7afe0b

```
en:
  comments:
    errors:
      not_published_yet: is not published yet
```

Now, let's move on to localizing our controllers. If you check all the controllers, you'll see that each of our controllers has hardcoded strings in their flash messages. First, let's fix ArticlesController. Listing 17-7 shows how it should look after our changes.

Listing 17-7. Updated ArticlesController in app/controllers/articles_controller. rb: https://gist.github.com/nicedawg/8b8fe899b5a3079ceb1932f81fd0b3c8

```
class ArticlesController < ApplicationController
  before_action :authenticate, except: [:index, :show, :notify_friend]
  before_action :set_article, only: [:show, :notify_friend]

  # ... code omitted for brevity ...

  # POST /articles
  # POST /articles.json
  def create
    @article = current_user.articles.new(article_params)

    respond_to do |format|
      if @article.save
```

```ruby
        format.html { redirect_to @article, notice: t('articles.create_
        success') }
        format.json { render :show, status: :created, location: @article }
      else
        format.html { render :new }
        format.json { render json: @article.errors, status: :unprocessable_
        entity }
      end
    end
  end

  # PATCH/PUT /articles/1
  # PATCH/PUT /articles/1.json
  def update
    @article = current_user.articles.find(params[:id])
    respond_to do |format|
      if @article.update(article_params)
        format.html { redirect_to @article, notice: t('articles.update_
        success') }
        format.json { render :show, status: :ok, location: @article }
      else
        format.html { render :edit }
        format.json { render json: @article.errors, status: :unprocessable_
        entity }
      end
    end
  end

  # DELETE /articles/1
  # DELETE /articles/1.json
  def destroy
    @article = current_user.articles.find(params[:id])
    @article.destroy
    respond_to do |format|
      format.html { redirect_to articles_url, notice: t('articles.destroy_
      success') }
```

```
    format.json { head :no_content }
  end
end

def notify_friend
  @email_a_friend = EmailAFriend.new(email_a_friend_params)

  if @email_a_friend.valid?
    NotifierMailer.email_friend(@article, @email_a_friend.name, @email_a_
    friend.email).deliver_later
    redirect_to @article, notice: t('articles.notify_friend_success')
  else
    render :notify_friend, status: :unprocessable_entity
  end
end

# … code omitted for brevity ...
end
```

There are two things to notice here. First, we simply used the *t* method without the I18n module, unlike what we did in the console and the model; that's because the I18n module is integrated with Action Pack to keep things cleaner in the controllers, helpers, and views. Second, we also nested the messages under `articles`—again, to keep things cleaner.

Let's do the same with the other controllers, also nesting them under their corresponding name: users controller translations will go under *users*, the comments controller will go under *comments*, the application controller will go under *application*, and the sessions controller will go under *session*.

Updating the rest of the controllers is fairly simple, albeit a little tedious. Rather than fill this chapter with lengthy code listings for each controller, you can either replace the remaining hardcoded strings from the remaining controllers yourself, using Listing 17-9 as a guide for which I18n keys to use, or you can download the updated files from `www.apress.com`.

Next, let's look at our view templates. They're very similar, so let's just look at a single view template here. Listing 17-8 shows the `article` partial after using translations, with changes in bold.

Listing 17-8. Updated article Partial in app/views/articles/_article.html.erb: https://gist.github.com/nicedawg/8af9eb4565c3667b02015446863609dd

```erb
<div class="article">
  <h3>
    <%= link_to article.title, article %>
    <% if article.owned_by? current_user %>
      <span class="actions">
        <%= link_to t('general.edit'), edit_article_path(article) %>
        <%= link_to t('general.delete'), article, confirm: t('general.are_
        you_sure'), method: :delete %>
      </span>
    <% end %>
  </h3>
  <hr>
  <% if article.cover_image.attached? %>
    <%= image_tag article.cover_image.variant(resize_to_limit: local_
    assigns.fetch(:cover_image_options, [200, 200])) %>
    <hr>
  <% end %>
  <%= article.body %>
</div>
```

As with our controllers, so many of our view templates have hardcoded strings to replace, that it's not feasible to list all the code changes in this chapter. Instead, using Listing 17-9 as a guide, let's go through each of our view templates, replacing hardcoded strings with the corresponding I18n keys. Alternatively, you can download the updated files from www.apress.com.

After updating your code, we're one step away from completing the i18n setup. We still need to add the translations to the default locale file, config/locales/en.yml. Listing 17-9 shows the updated translation file.

Listing 17-9. English Locale File After Implementing i18n Support in config/locales/en.yml: https://gist.github.com/nicedawg/0836f3cc393bbc530834673c4878e7d9

```
en:
```

```
general:
  are_you_sure: Are you sure?
  back: Back
  cancel: Cancel
  create: Create
  delete: Delete
  edit: Edit
  editing: Editing
  footer: A simple blog built for the book Beginning Rails 6
  email_a_friend: Email a friend
  search: Search
  send_email: Send email
  show: Show
  title: Blog
  update: Update
  your_name: Your name
  your_friend_email: Your friend's email
  or: or
application:
  access_denied: Please log in to continue
articles:
  editing_article: Editing Article
  listing_articles: Listing Articles
  new_article: New Article
  article: article
  create_success: Article was successfully created.
  update_success: Article was successfully updated.
  destroy_success: Article was successfully destroyed.
  articles: Articles
  notify_friend_success: Successfully sent a message to your friend
  remove_this_image: Remove this image
  new_article_published: New Article Published!
users:
  new_user: New user
  edit_password: Edit Password
```

```
  editing_user: Editing user
  create_success: User successfully added.
  update_success: Updated user information successfully.
sessions:
  email: Email
  password: Password
  login: Login
  logout: Logout
  successful_login: Logged in successfully
  invalid_login: Invalid login/password combination
  logout_success: You successfully logged out
comments:
  name: Name
  email: Email
  body: Body
  comments: Comments
  new_comment: New comment
  create_success: Thanks for your comment
  create_failure: Unable to add comment
  destroy_success: Comment deleted
  add: Add
  errors:
    not_published_yet: is not published yet
```

While we may have missed some strings here and there and though it was a little tedious, it wasn't too difficult to add i18n support to our blog.

Let's restart our Rails server to be sure the most recent locale configuration is loaded and then browse through the site; we shouldn't see any differences yet, as we just moved the hardcoded strings from our controllers and view templates into our locale file. Although i18n support is in place, we're still using English as our locale. To *really* see i18n in action, let's change the locale and try Brazilian Portuguese.

Localizing the Blog Application to Brazilian Portuguese

Localizing an i18n-ready Rails application is amazingly simple. All we have to do is add a new translation file and configure our Rails application to use that locale as the default locale, and we're good to go.

In this section, we will localize our blog application for Brazilian Portuguese. As mentioned earlier, since the locale symbol for Brazilian Portuguese is `pt-br`, we must change the `config/locales/pt-br.yml` file. We will use the same keys as our English translation file, but with Brazilian Portuguese text instead of English.

This separation between the translation files and our application code is very helpful; it gives us the ability to send the translation file to a translator, for example. When we get it back, we just plug it into our application, and we're all set. Listing 17-10 shows the newly created Brazilian Portuguese translation file.

Listing 17-10. Brazilian Portuguese Locale File in config/locales/pt-br.yml: https://gist.github.com/nicedawg/fc77bc122698a71c960883954f66a231

```
pt-br:
  general:
    are_you_sure: Tem certeza?
    back: Volta
    cancel: Cancelar
    create: Criar
    delete: Apagar
    edit: Editar
    editing: Editando
    footer: Um blog simples desenvolvido para o livro
    email_a_friend: Avisar um amigo
    search: Pesquisar
    send_email: Mandar email
    show: Mostrar
    title: Blog
    update: Atualizar
    your_name: Seu nome
    your_friend_email: O email do seu amigo
```

```
    or: ou
  application:
    access_denied: "Por favor, efetue o login para continuar"
  articles:
    editing_article: Editando Artigo
    listing_articles: Listando Artigos
    new_article: Novo Artigo
    article: artigo
    create_success: Artigo foi criado com sucesso.
    update_success: Artigo foi atualizado com sucesso.
    articles: artigos
    notify_friend_success: Seu amigo foi avisado a respeito desse artigo
    remove_this_image: Remova esta imagem
  users:
    new_user: Novo Usuario
    edit_password: Editar senha
    editing_user: Editando usuario
    create_success: Usuario editado com sucesso.
    update_success: Usuario atualizado com sucesso.
  sessions:
    email: Email
    password: Senha
    login: Logar
    logout: Desconectar
    successful_login: Logado com sucesso
    invalid_login: Senha ou Email invalidos
    logout_success: Voce desconectou do sistem com sucesso
  comments:
    name: Nome
    email: Email
    body: Conteudo
    comments: Comentarios
    new_comment: Novo Comentario
    create_success: Obrigado pelo comentario
    create_failure: Nao foi possivel adicionar o comentario
```

```
      destroy_success: Comentario deletado
      add: Adicionar
      errors:
        not_published_yet: ainda nao foi publicado

activerecord:
  errors:
    models:
      article:
        attributes:
          title:
            blank: "não pode ficar em branco"
          body:
            blank: "não pode ficar em branco"
          user:
            required: deve existir

date:
  formats:
    default: "%d/%m/%Y"
    short: "%d de %B"
    long: "%d de %B de %Y"

  day_names:
    - Domingo
    - Segunda
    - Terça
    - Quarta
    - Quinta
    - Sexta
    - Sábado
  abbr_day_names:
    - Dom
    - Seg
    - Ter
    - Qua
    - Qui
```

```
        - Sex
        - Sáb
    month_names:
        - Janeiro
        - Fevereiro
        - Março
        - Abril
        - Maio
        - Junho
        - Julho
        - Agosto
        - Setembro
        - Outubro
        - Novembro
        - Dezembro
    abbr_month_names:
        - Jan
        - Fev
        - Mar
        - Abr
        - Mai
        - Jun
        - Jul
        - Ago
        - Set
        - Out
        - Nov
        - Dez
    order:
        - :day
        - :month
        - :year
```

Now we've added these translations for Brazilian Portuguese—but our blog application won't use them yet. One way we can see them in action is to change the default locale of our app from *en* to *pt-br*. Let's do that by adding a configuration to your config/application.rb file. Listing 17-11 shows the updated config/application.rb file with the added lines in bold.

Listing 17-11. Setting the Default Locale to Brazilian Portuguese in config/application.rb: https://gist.github.com/nicedawg/2243de835fb57064e993311 f479687dc

```
require_relative 'boot'

require 'rails/all'

# Require the gems listed in Gemfile, including any gems
# you've limited to :test, :development, or :production.
Bundler.require(*Rails.groups)

module Blog
  class Application < Rails::Application
    # Initialize configuration defaults for originally generated Rails
      version.
    config.load_defaults 6.0

    # Settings in config/environments/* take precedence over those
      specified here.
    # Application configuration can go into files in config/initializers
    # -- all .rb files in that directory are automatically loaded after
        loading
    # the framework and any gems in your application.

    I18n.available_locales = [:en, :'pt-br']
    I18n.default_locale = 'pt-br'
  end
end
```

Restart your Rails server, and check out your new Brazilian Portuguese blog application! We localized the application in two simple steps: adding the translation files and setting up the locale. Figure 17-1 shows the blog application with its Brazilian Portuguese face.

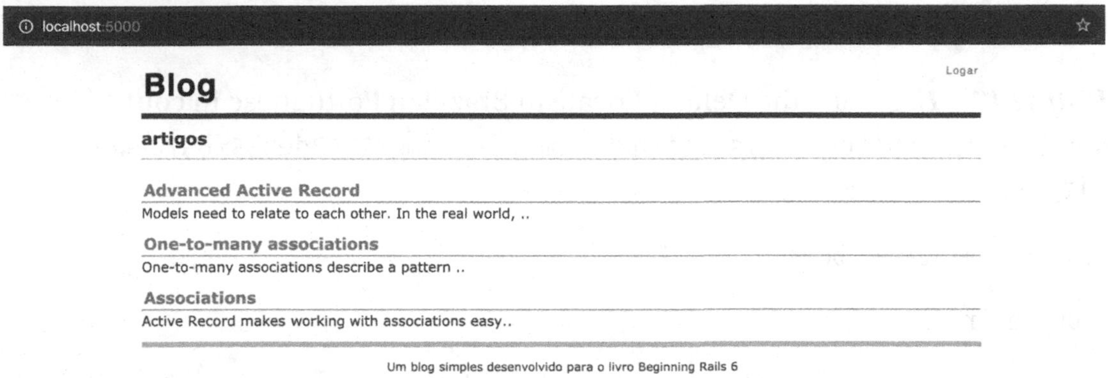

Figure 17-1. *Brazilian Portuguese localized interface*

We may have missed some strings to translate here and there, but you get the idea!

Also, it's worth noting that our internationalization and localization work so far has only dealt with our user interface—*not* with our data. For example, the link to login and logout is localized—but our article titles and bodies are not. This isn't an oversight, but a real distinction; as developers, we know what our UI will consist of, so we can include translations of our UI text with our code changes. However, data is by nature dynamic; how reasonable would it be, for example, to deploy new changes to our config/locale files every time an author publishes a new article?

In order to localize our data—in our case, article titles and bodies, for example— other solutions such as *mobility* (https://github.com/shioyama/mobility) and *globalize* (https://github.com/globalize/globalize) are helpful. Typically, solutions like these add additional storage to fields you wish to translate (like article titles and bodies), allowing editors to supply content for each locale and for your Rails app to display the correct translated content based on the locale. We won't cover using a gem like these in this chapter, but just know that these types of solutions exist.

Bilingual Blog

We learned earlier that all it takes to change the locale is to set the I18n.locale configuration to the locale of choice. How about giving users the power to do that themselves? To do so, we'll implement a controller filter that sets the locale depending on user input and provides the user with a language selector from which to choose the locale.

Let's create a helper in the application helper called *language_selector* that shows the available locales for the user to choose from. Listing 17-12 shows *application_helper* with the new helper method in bold.

Listing 17-12. language_selector Helper Method in app/helpers/application_helper.rb: https://gist.github.com/nicedawg/7a144e3c0e695bfddb23fe593f2daa85

```
module ApplicationHelper
  def language_selector
    if I18n.locale == :en
      link_to "Pt", url_for(locale: 'pt-br')
    else
      link_to "En", url_for(locale: 'en')
    end
  end

  def submit_or_cancel(form, name = t("general.cancel"))
    form.submit + " #{t("general.or")} " + link_to(name,
'javascript:history.go(-1);', class: 'cancel')
  end
end
```

In the *language_selector* method, we show a link to the language that isn't currently selected. We do that by linking to the URL the user is currently on, with an extra *:locale* parameter using the *url_for* helper.

The user should always be able to change the language; so we'll add this function to our application layout. Listing 17-13 shows the updated application layout with the new helper call in bold.

Listing 17-13. Calling language_selector in app/views/layouts/application.html.erb: https://gist.github.com/nicedawg/1f22173e59a45a6fcf6ec9821452e251

```
<!DOCTYPE html>
<html>
  <head>
    <title><%= t("general.title") %></title>
    <%= csrf_meta_tags %>
```

```erb
    <%= csp_meta_tag %>

    <%= stylesheet_link_tag 'application', media: 'all', 'data-turbolinks-
    track': 'reload' %>
    <%= javascript_pack_tag 'application', 'data-turbolinks-track':
    'reload' %>
  </head>

  <body>
    <div id="header">
      <h1><%= link_to t("general.title"), root_path %></h1>
      <%= language_selector %>

      <div id="user_bar">
        <% if logged_in? %>
          <%= link_to t("articles.new_article"), new_article_path %> |
          <%= link_to t("users.edit_password"), edit_user_path(current_
          user) %> |
          <%= link_to t("sessions.logout"), logout_path %>
        <% else %>
          <%= link_to t("sessions.login"), login_path %>
        <% end %>
      </div>
    </div>
    <div id="main">
      <%= content_tag :p, notice, class: 'notice' if notice.present? %>
      <%= content_tag :p, alert, class: 'alert' if alert.present? %>
      <%= yield %>
    </div>
    <div id="footer">
      <%= t("general.footer") %>
    </div>
  </body>
</html>
```

Finally, let's use *around_action* in our ApplicationController that sets the locale to the requested locale; adding it here allows us to switch locales from *any* page. See `https://edgeguides.rubyonrails.org/i18n.html#managing-the-locale-across-requests` for more information; there's an important warning about using *I18n. with_locale* instead of *I18n.locale=* in your Rails application. With the latter, it's possible that some requests may be served with the wrong locale! To avoid this problem, be sure to use *I18n.with_locale* when possible. Listing 17-14 shows the updated application controller with the new additions in bold.

Listing 17-14. Using around_action to Set the Locale in app/controllers/ application_controller.rb: `https://gist.github.com/nicedawg/ bb57d52a99a2a3874929da5d8ce19f9a`

```
class ApplicationController < ActionController::Base
  helper_method :current_user, :logged_in?

  around_action :set_locale

  def set_locale(&action)
    session[:locale] = params[:locale] if params[:locale]
    I18n.with_locale(session[:locale] || I18n.default_locale, &action)
  end

  def current_user
    return unless session[:user_id]
    @current_user ||= User.find_by(id: session[:user_id])
  end

  def authenticate
    logged_in? || access_denied
  end

  def logged_in?
    current_user.present?
  end

  def access_denied
    redirect_to(login_path, notice: t('application.access_denied')) and
return false
  end
end
```

In our *around* action, we look for a requested locale in the params hash. If one was present, we store the requested locale in the session. Then, we call *I18n.with_locale*, passing it the requested locale (or our default locale as a fallback) and the requested controller action to execute. This has the effect of setting the desired locale in the application for the rest of the request, but then cleaning up after itself and reverting back to the default locale when the request has been completed.

Let's change the application locale configuration back to English—so users can select their language of choice—by removing the config.i18n.default_locale line from config/application.rb (Listing 17-15).

Listing 17-15. Change Our Default Locale Back to "en" in config/application.rb: https://gist.github.com/nicedawg/90243d4c911513d601e7026dbf298edc

```
require_relative 'boot'

require 'rails/all'

# Require the gems listed in Gemfile, including any gems
# you've limited to :test, :development, or :production.
Bundler.require(*Rails.groups)

module Blog
  class Application < Rails::Application
    # Initialize configuration defaults for originally generated Rails
      version.
    config.load_defaults 6.0

    # Settings in config/environments/* take precedence over those
      specified here.
    # Application configuration can go into files in config/initializers
    # -- all .rb files in that directory are automatically loaded after
        loading
    # the framework and any gems in your application.

    I18n.available_locales = [:en, :'pt-br']
  end
end
```

Restart your server and try the application, as shown in Figure 17-2.

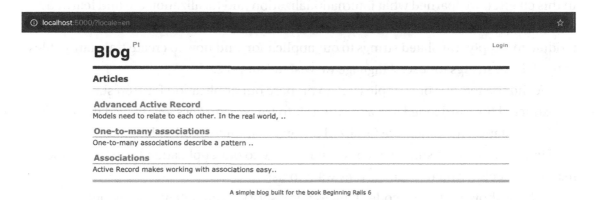

Figure 17-2. *Language selector in the English interface*

The application loads in English because it's the default locale. Click the Pt link, and see how everything switches to Brazilian Portuguese, as shown in Figure 17-3.

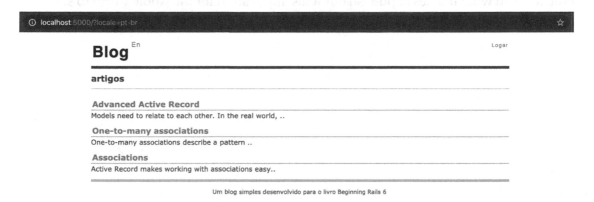

Figure 17-3. *Brazilian Portuguese interface with the language selector link*

Congratulations! Not only do you have a bilingual blog application but you also know how easy it is to add more languages.

Summary

In this chapter, we learned what internationalization and localization are and learned what it takes to build a multilingual Rails application. We learned how to use the I18n module to supply translated strings to our application and how to create translation files to hold these strings for each language we wish to support.

We did the tedious but simple work to prepare our application for i18n support; we extracted the hardcoded text and strings into translation keys and placed them in a locale translation file. Then, we localized the application to another language.

Finally, we made a simple but powerful change to our application to allow our blog readers to decide which language they want to use.

To have shown *all* of the code changes necessary to completely localize our application would have been too much. Be sure to check out this book's companion source code for a more complete implementation.

The next, and final, chapter in the book will cover how to deploy your Rails apps; up until this time, our application has only been running on our personal workstations. It's time to learn what it takes to publish our Rails application for the whole world to see!

CHAPTER 18

Deploying Your Rails Applications

At some point, you may decide it's time to share your Rails application with the world. Though Rails offers a first-class local development environment, it's not feasible to host your public-facing web application from your development environment; besides potentially violating your residential Internet service's terms of service, you'd have to deal with dynamic IP addresses, opening your firewall (and a host of potential security issues), and many more issues. Instead, when you're ready to launch your application for public use, you'll need to deploy your Rails application to a suitable hosting environment.

Options for hosting web applications have changed a lot over the years. Years ago, there were two main options—shared hosting or dedicated hosting. With shared hosting, you would be given limited access to a server used by other customers' web applications as well. You would be able to upload files and perhaps configure some settings, but have limited (or no) access to the command line for advanced usage. Shared hosting was cheaper, but limited; it worked well for static HTML sites, or even web applications built in languages such as PHP which often just worked—as long as your application would work on the versions of the language (and other supporting services) that the shared hosting environment offered.

Dedicated hosting, on the other hand, gave application developers full control over their hosting environment; by leasing a physical server in a rack in some data center somewhere, you would then have (nearly) full control over the server. You could perform command-line actions as the *root* user, installing whatever software your hosting environment needed. While having full control sounds nice, it comes at a cost—in addition to the higher *financial* costs of dedicated hosting, the developers had to pay the higher *maintenance* costs of correctly configuring their system, keeping up-to-date with

© Brady Somerville, Adam Gamble, Cloves Carneiro Jr and Rida Al Barazi 2020
B. Somerville et al., *Beginning Rails 6*, https://doi.org/10.1007/978-1-4842-5716-6_18

security patches, and more. These higher costs, though, were sometimes necessary to support web applications written in languages such as Java or which required supporting services not offered by shared hosting environments.

However, as virtualization technology improved, hosting providers began offering *virtual private servers*—a kind of hybrid of shared and dedicated hosting—which gave developers full control over a shared slice of a server. This brought the *financial* costs of dedicated hosting down, but didn't address the higher *maintenance* costs of dedicated hosting.

Then, hosting providers began offering what became known as PAAS—Platform as a Service. Services like Heroku and AWS Elastic Beanstalk gave developers a way to deploy more sophisticated web applications without having to concern themselves with server configuration and maintenance, thus attempting to reduce both the financial and maintenance costs of using dedicated servers.

Why the long history lesson? It's important to understand the variety of hosting services available and their strengths and weaknesses and to know which are appropriate for hosting your Rails application.

Rails applications are not suited for cheap, shared hosting plans as first described in this section. Why? For example, gems often need the ability to compile code during installation. Copying your compiled gems from your development environment to the hosting environment would most likely fail terribly. Also, with Rails applications, the web server (like Apache or Nginx) needs to be configured to communicate with the Rails server via a TCP port or socket—it can't simply load the requested file from the directory, like PHP or Classic ASP. Most shared hosting plans simply don't support this.

Rails applications would work great on "dedicated" hosting platforms—whether you're leasing a physical server or paying for a virtualized server (like from the AWS EC2 service.) However, as mentioned before, you're signing up for lots of server administration. While there is a vast amount of information available on the Internet to help you configure your hosting environment, not everyone has the interest or time to learn.

So that brings us to the PAAS option. For many developers, this is a great approach. While the financial cost of hosting on a PAAS may be slightly higher than hosting on a virtual server, the maintenance costs are much lower, allowing the application developer to focus on application development, rather than system administration.

In this chapter, we'll illustrate deploying a Rails application to Heroku. There are many fine options, but Heroku is well known and respected for their ease of use and is a great way for us to get our blog application up for the whole world to see, with minimal effort.

Set Up an Account with Heroku

The first step in this process is to set up an account with Heroku. Don't worry, Heroku offers a free account which doesn't need a credit card. Point your browser to `www.heroku.com`, and you should see something like Figure 18-1.

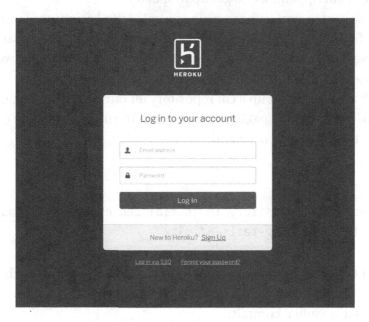

Figure 18-1. *Setting up a Heroku account*

Click the Sign Up link and enter an email address. Heroku will then send you an email with a confirmation link. Once you click that link, you'll be asked for a password and password confirmation. You're now the proud owner of a shiny new Heroku account. This will let you deploy Rails (and other) apps to your heart's content.

Heroku has a piece of software that facilitates interacting with your Heroku apps on your computer. It's called the Heroku Toolbelt (`https://toolbelt.heroku.com/`). Go to that URL and follow the instructions for installing the Heroku Toolbelt in your development environment. Once it's been installed, you should be able to run the *heroku* command in your CLI and see usage information.

Preparing Your Git Repository

Now that we've set up a Heroku account and installed the command-line tools, we'll need to make a couple of small changes to our app so we can deploy it. Heroku's method of deployment is Git, a tool most developers are already using. If you are unfamiliar with Git, you can check out Appendix C to get up to speed.

Usually, we'd want to start using version control at the *beginning* of our project, for maximum benefit. Having a readily accessible history of all your code changes *while you're developing* is incredibly useful. To keep this book's focus on Rails, we waited until now (when we *needed* it) to introduce the idea.

Unless you have already set up a Git repository for our application, you'll need to do so now. Go to the terminal, making sure you're in the directory where our project is stored, and type the following command:

```
$ git init
```

```
Initialized empty Git repository in Initialized empty Git repository in /
Users/brady/Sites/beginning-rails-6/.git/
```

This told Git that we want this directory to be a repository, meaning that Git will now keep track of the files you want it to. Let's tell it to keep track of all the files in this directory and make an initial commit:

```
$ git add .
$ git commit -m 'Initial Commit'
```

```
master (root-commit) ea1c9dd] Initial Commit
 186 files changed, 11061 insertions(+)
 create mode 100644 .browserslistrc
 create mode 100644 .gitignore
...
```

Your output might be slightly different, but it should add all files to your Git repository. This means that Git is now keeping track of the files and will notice when you make changes. You can then either decide to commit those changes or get rid of them. Once you have committed changes, Git has built-in support for pushing those changes to a remote server. Likewise, it can pull the changes from a remote server to your local repository. This is why so many developers use a source control system like Git; it makes it so easy to collaborate. It also happens to be the way you deploy your application to Heroku.

Creating Your Heroku App

So let's tell Heroku we are ready to create an app. The first step is to create the app on Heroku. You can do this on their web control panel, or you can do it from the command line. We prefer to use the command-line interface. You need to authenticate the Heroku Toolbelt you previously installed, but that's a simple task. Once that is done, you can move straight into creating your application on Heroku:

```
$ heroku login
```

```
heroku: Press any key to open up the browser to login or q to exit:
Opening browser to https://cli-auth.heroku.com/auth/cli/browser/7921344c-
4ce8-4fee-96c5-0938c1eb6f83
heroku: Waiting for login...
```

As prompted, press a key to open your browser to Heroku's authentication page, and then click the "Log In" button. When successful, the web page will say you can close it, and the *heroku login* command will complete, showing "Logged in as" with your email address.

Now, we're ready to create the Heroku instance for our application. We simply need to run the *heroku create* command from our terminal, while in our project's directory:

```
$ heroku create
```

```
Creating app... done, ⬡ evening-ocean-78121
https://evening-ocean-78121.herokuapp.com/ | https://git.heroku.com/
evening-ocean-78121.git
```

Notice that it called the app *evening-ocean-78121*. If you don't specify a name, Heroku will choose a random name for you. If you would like to specify a name, type it after the Heroku create line, like so:

```
$ heroku create beginning-rails-6-brady
```

```
Creating ⬡ beginning-rails-6-brady... done
https://beginning-rails-6-brady.herokuapp.com/ | https://git.heroku.com/
beginning-rails-6-brady.git
```

Since Heroku names must be unique, you obviously won't be able to use *beginning-rails-6-brady*, but you can be creative and choose your own, like maybe chunky-bacon.

Installing PostgreSQL

To support deploying to Heroku, we'll need to make one more change. We've been using *SQLite* as our database, but it's not supported in Heroku. Why? SQLite stores its data in a file—and filesystems in Heroku are ephemeral, meaning they can suddenly be reset to their initial state. This may seem like an unfair limitation, but relying on the local filesystem in production blocks the ability to scale to running your application with more servers. Also, SQLite just isn't suited for production usage; it's fine for a few users at a time, but is not built to handle much more than that.

Instead, Heroku offers support for PostgreSQL—a much more robust database server suitable for production environments. While Rails makes it possible to use SQLite locally but PostgreSQL in production, Heroku strongly recommends switching to PostgreSQL locally. One reason is that even though Active Record does a great job at abstracting the differences and keeping the actual database being used easily swappable, it is *possible* to write database-specific code, leading to problems only found in the production environment.

Also, deployments to Heroku will fail if they detect the sqlite3 gem in our Gemfile.lock file. It's *possible* to regenerate our Gemfile.lock file just before each deploy to omit the sqlite3 gem, but it would be a constant hassle and not worth it in the long run. So let's bite the bullet and install PostgreSQL.

Visit `www.postgresql.org/download/` and follow the instructions for your development platform to install PostgreSQL on your system. Some platforms have downloadable installers, while others have instructions for installing PostgreSQL via your system's package manager.

Once successfully installed, you should be able to open a new command prompt and run *psql*—PostgreSQL's command-line tool. You should see something like the following, though your output may vary:

```
$ psql -U postgres
```

```
psql (12.2)
Type "help" for help.

postgres=# select VERSION();
                                version
-------------------------------------------------------------------------
 PostgreSQL 12.2 on x86_64-apple-darwin19.4.0, compiled by Apple clang
version 11.0.3 (clang-1103.0.32.59), 64-bit
(1 row)

postgres=# exit
```

At this point, PostgreSQL is installed and working on your system. Now it's time to configure our Rails application to use PostgreSQL instead of SQLite.

Switching to PostgreSQL

You may remember that in your application's folder, there is a file named Gemfile. This file stores a list of all the "gems" your project uses. Gems are little pieces of code that are easy to pull into your project to add features. Rails itself is a gem, and when we started this project, a whole host of gems were pulled in. Along the way, we've added a gem or two ourselves.

To facilitate the easiest out-of-the-box environment for developers, Rails includes and uses the *sqlite* gem and configures the databases (in config/database.yml) to use SQLite by default.

So let's change our application to use PostgreSQL instead. Let's edit our Gemfile to match Listing 18-1.

Listing 18-1. Changing Gemfile to Use PostgreSQL Instead of SQLite `https://gist.github.com/nicedawg/7d2567221075d2ff12a5aa87f3eb57f0`

```
source 'https://rubygems.org'
git_source(:github) { |repo| "https://github.com/#{repo}.git" }

ruby '2.6.5'


# Bundle edge Rails instead: gem 'rails', github: 'rails/rails'
```

```
gem 'rails', '~> 6.0.2', '>= 6.0.2.1'
# Use PostgreSQL as the database for Active Record
gem 'pg'
# Use Puma as the app server
gem 'puma', '~> 4.1'

# ... rest of contents omitted ...
```

Be sure to remove the line that starts with "*gem 'sqlite3'*," and save the Gemfile. Next, we'll run *bundle install* to install the new gem on our machine and to generate a new Gemfile.lock (so that other environments will install the same version of our gems):

```
$ bundle install
```

When all goes well, you'll see the list of installed gems scroll by, including our newly added *pg* gem. If there's an error installing the *pg* gem, it may be that you're missing a library needed for its installation. (For example, on Ubuntu, you may need to install the *libpq-dev* package.)

After successfully installing the *pg* gem, we need to let Git know that we want to commit the changes to the Gemfile and Gemfile.lock files:

```
$ git add Gemfile Gemfile.lock
$ git commit -m "Replace sqlite gem with pg"
```

```
[ch-18 2dcb4f5] Replace sqlite gem with pg
 2 files changed, 4 insertions(+), 4 deletions(-)
```

We've replaced the *sqlite3* gem with the *pg* gem, but our switch to using PostgreSQL is not yet complete; we need to configure our application to use the right database adapter. Edit your config/database.yml so that it matches Listing 18-2.

Listing 18-2. Switching to PostgreSQL in config/database.yml https://gist.github.com/nicedawg/889466f0eb905eb867beae7156c2705d

```
default: &default
  adapter: postgresql
  pool: <%= ENV.fetch("RAILS_MAX_THREADS") { 5 } %>
  timeout: 5000
```

```
development:
  <<: *default
  database: beginning_rails_6_development
```

```
# Warning: The database defined as "test" will be erased and
# re-generated from your development database when you run "rake".
# Do not set this db to the same as development or production.
test:
  <<: *default
  database: beginning_rails_6_test
```

```
production:
  <<: *default
  database: beginning_rails_6_production
```

We're almost done! If you were to restart your Rails app now and try to load it in your browser, you'd see an error saying "database beginning_rails_6_development does not exist." So let's run the *rails db:setup* to recreate our databases in PostgreSQL and to use db/seeds.rb to add some records:

```
$ rails db:setup
```

```
Created database 'beginning_rails_6_development'
Created database 'beginning_rails_6_test'
```

Restart your Rails server, and click around in your app. Everything should still work the same as it did before. If you run into trouble that seems like it could be database related, running *rails db:reset* is an option, since we don't have any data we care about. Installing PostgreSQL may be a little tricky, but switching your Rails app to use it is easy!

Deploying to Heroku

Now we're ready to deploy our app! It's as easy as one command, though be patient; it will take a few minutes:

```
$ git push heroku master
```

Enumerating objects: 1019, done.

Counting objects: 100% (1019/1019), done.

Delta compression using up to 8 threads

Compressing objects: 100% (609/609), done.

Writing objects: 100% (1019/1019), 254.30 KiB | 16.95 MiB/s, done.

Total 1019 (delta 573), reused 691 (delta 378), pack-reused 0

remote: Compressing source files... done.

remote: Building source:

remote:

remote: !   Warning: Multiple default buildpacks reported the ability to handle this app. The first buildpack in the list below will be used.

remote: Detected buildpacks: Ruby,Node.js

remote: See https://devcenter.heroku.com/articles/ buildpacks#buildpack-detect-order

remote: -----> Ruby app detected

remote: -----> Installing bundler 1.17.3

remote: -----> Removing BUNDLED WITH version in the Gemfile.lock

remote: -----> Compiling Ruby/Rails

remote: -----> Using Ruby version: ruby-2.6.5

remote: -----> Installing dependencies using bundler 1.17.3

remote: Running: bundle install --without development:test --path vendor/bundle --binstubs vendor/bundle/bin -j4 --deployment

remote: The dependency tzinfo-data (>= 0) will be unused by any of the platforms Bundler is installing for. Bundler is installing for ruby but the dependency is only for x86-mingw32, x86-mswin32, x64-mingw32, java. To add those platforms to the bundle, run `bundle lock --add-platform x86-mingw32 x86-mswin32 x64-mingw32 java`.

remote: Fetching gem metadata from https://rubygems.org/............

remote: Fetching rake 13.0.1

remote: Installing rake 13.0.1

 ...

remote: -----> Launching...

remote: Released v6

remote: **https://evening-ocean-78121.herokuapp.com/ deployed to Heroku**

```
remote:
remote: Verifying deploy... done.
To https://git.heroku.com/evening-ocean-78121.git
 * [new branch]      HEAD -> master
```

There is a lot of output from the command, and your output may differ, but at the end you will see something like

https://evening-ocean-78121.herokuapp.com/ deployed to Heroku

This means that the deployment worked! Go ahead and visit the URL to view your app in production (or run *heroku open*), but don't get too excited, because it's certainly an error page. "We're sorry, but something went wrong." How can we tell *what* went wrong? We can run the convenient *heroku logs* command:

```
$ heroku logs
```

Look carefully at the output. You'll see an error that says something like "PG::UndefinedTable: ERROR: relation "articles" does not exist." We need to create our database tables! Unfortunately, we can't simply run the *db:setup* or *db:migrate* command for two reasons: First, trying to create the database fails due to some limitations from Heroku, as *they* take care of creating the database their custom way. Second, one of our migrations (from Chapter 11) has some SQL in it which is specific to SQLite 3. Rather than modifying the migration file, which has risks not unlike traveling into the past and changing history, we can run this command to allow us to recreate the database from our db/schema.rb file, rather than building it back up from scratch using our migrations:

```
$ heroku run rails db:schema:load DISABLE_DATABASE_ENVIRONMENT_CHECK=1
```

Setting the "DISABLE_DATABASE_ENVIRONMENT_CHECK" environment variable was necessary because Rails thankfully tries to protect us from doing destructive things to our production database.

After successfully creating the database tables, we can view the blog running on Heroku. It looks good, except it's rather empty. Let's populate some records using the *db:seed* command:

```
$ heroku run rails db:seed
```

Looking at the output, things *started* out well; the command created a user and created some categories, but as soon as it tried to create an article, it failed. Reading the output closely, we see the following error:

```
Gem::LoadError: Error loading the 'redis' Action Cable pubsub adapter.
Missing a gem it depends on? redis is not part of the bundle. Add it to
your Gemfile.
```

Ah! By default, Rails configures Action Cable to use a *redis* adapter in the production environment. While Heroku does offer a free *redis* add-on for light usage, they require a valid credit card on file; though a completely reasonable request, we don't want to require that of our readers, so we'll change our app to use the *async* adapter for the production environment instead. (As mentioned in Chapter 15 earlier, this is not recommended for production environments, but is fine for this illustration.) Change your config/cable.yml so it matches Listing 18-3.

Listing 18-3. Using Action Cable's async Adapter in Production—config/cable. yml https://gist.github.com/nicedawg/9be89c0d6a29a0dbc1cb3786f8b3346e

```
development:
  adapter: async

test:
  adapter: test

production:
  adapter: async
```

After saving the change, then let's commit our changes to Git and redeploy:

```
$ git add config/cable.yml
$ git commit -m "Use async Action Cable adapter in production"
$ git push heroku master
```

Now that we've hopefully fixed our *redis* issue, let's try to seed our database again. If we simply ran the same *db:seed* command as before, it would fail because our db/seeds. rb file is not *idempotent*; if it were *idempotent*, we could run it multiple times, and the overall effect would be as if it had run once. Rather than changing our db/seeds.rb file (which is a good idea—as db/seeds.rb is best when idempotent) or manually removing records, we'll use a command we haven't used yet:

```
$ heroku run rails db:seed:replant DISABLE_DATABASE_ENVIRONMENT_CHECK=1
```

Again, we had to add the *DISABLE_DATABASE_ENVIRONMENT_CHECK* environment variable to our command, because it's destructive; it clears *all* the database records before it runs *db:seed*. You wouldn't want to do this if your database had records you cared about, but we're still getting started, so it's fine.

Now that we have some seed data in our Heroku app, click around. Things should look mostly normal!

Perhaps you'd like to add another user. Our blog application doesn't have a section to allow the creation of new users; we'd previously done that through the *rails console* command. Thankfully, Heroku made it easy to access your production rails console. Let's add another user:

```
$ heroku run console
> Running console on □ evening-ocean-78121... up, run.4864 (Free)
Loading production environment (Rails 6.0.2.1)
irb(main):001:0> User.create(email: 'brady.somerville@gmail.com', password:
'hunter2', password_confirmation: 'hunter2')
=> #<User id: 4, email: "brady.somerville@gmail.com", hashed_password:
[FILTERED], created_at: "2020-04-25 23:29:45", updated_at: "2020-04-25
23:29:45", draft_article_token: "JQVnjHF5cXVW2VfJb5h5j4YW">
```

That's It!

Feel free to take your newly deployed Rails application for a spin; if you find any problems, remember to use the *heroku logs* command to help troubleshoot. (For example, sending the "Email a Friend" form fails to send the email. If up for a challenge, use *heroku logs* to find the error, and use knowledge gained from this book to fix the problem. You can do it!)

There is one caveat; remember how earlier in this chapter, when talking about needing to replace SQLite, we mentioned that one reason was because the filesystem is ephemeral? Our application has another dependency on the local filesystem: Active Storage. For convenience, it's configured to store uploaded files on the local filesystem. However, in Heroku, this means that your uploaded files may suddenly disappear. For real production usage, we'd want to configure our app to store uploaded files in a service such as AWS S3. Trying to cover that in this book would've been a bit of a detour; if interested, visit the following URL for more information: https://devcenter.heroku.com/articles/active-storage-on-heroku.

That's all there is to deploying your app with Heroku! Anyone with a web browser now has access to your application. This deployment is suitable for most small apps and even larger applications if you decide. Heroku allows you to purchase extra "dynos" or servers to scale your application to support heavier loads. You can do this by visiting Heroku's web console.

Sure, we hit a few bumps along the way, but it wasn't *that* bad and gave us a chance to exercise our troubleshooting skills along the way.

Deploying to Heroku is only one of the many different ways you can deploy your Rails applications. One of the more popular, but more complex, solutions is called Capistrano (`https://github.com/capistrano/capistrano`). Capistrano gives you more control over your app's deployment steps and is a good option for apps running in more complex environments than a PAAS. Capistrano deployment is out of the scope of this book, but knowing that other deployment solutions exist is important.

Whole books could be written on the topics of server configuration and application deployment, but hopefully this chapter provided you with a quick way to let the masses use your Rails applications with as little pain as possible.

Summary

In this chapter, we talked about various types of web hosting, understood a bit about the hosting needs for a Rails application, and discussed the benefits (and limitations) of using PAAS options (like Heroku).

Then, we created a Heroku account, created a Heroku app, and configured our project to be deployed to Heroku via Git. However, we ran into a few bumps—needing to switch our database to PostgreSQL, reconfiguring Action Cable to use the *async* adapter in production (which isn't recommended, but easiest for now), and then re-seeding our database. But this gave us a chance to learn a bit more, and now you know how to view logs from Heroku and open the Rails console in Heroku.

What's next? While this is the end of our tour of Rails 6, it's only the beginning of your journey. While it's true that there's always more to learn, we hope we've provided you with the foundational knowledge you need to build the web applications of your dreams.

APPENDIX A

Databases 101

Let's begin with some simple definitions. A *database* is a piece of software that governs the storage, retrieval, deletion, and integrity of data. Databases are organized into *tables*. Tables have *columns* (or, if you prefer, *fields*), and data are stored in *rows*. If you're familiar with spreadsheets, then the idea is fairly similar. Of course, databases blow spreadsheets out of the water in terms of power and performance.

Some databases are *relational*—meaning they model their data in a way that makes use of relationships between tables. In this book, we use SQLite and Postgres, both of which are relational databases, and you may have seen already how we use these relationships to associate users with articles, for example. Other databases may model their data with other, non-relational approaches, such as simple key-value pairs.

Structured Query Language (SQL) is the standard way of communicating with *relational* databases. Using SQL, you can view column information, fetch a particular row or a set of rows, and search for rows containing certain criteria. You also use SQL to create, drop, and modify tables, as well as insert, update, and destroy the information stored in those tables. SQL is a fairly large topic, so a complete treatment is beyond the scope of this book. That said, you need to know the basics, so consider this a crash course.

Note The output in this appendix assumes you've followed the code in the book up to Chapter 5. If you read this appendix at a different point and implement the code, you may get different output.

519

© Brady Somerville, Adam Gamble, Cloves Carneiro Jr and Rida Al Barazi 2020
B. Somerville et al., *Beginning Rails 6*, https://doi.org/10.1007/978-1-4842-5716-6

Examining a Database Table

The examples in this chapter will use SQLite, as they do throughout this book. If you're following along using a different piece of database software or depending on the state of your database according to your progress throughout this book, some commands may not work, or the responses you see may be slightly different. While SQLite commands differ from those offered by other databases, the same general concepts apply.

To start the SQLite utility tool, run the `rails dbconsole` command from the book's project folder on your computer:

```
$ rails dbconsole
```

```
SQLite version 3.28.0 2019-04-15 14:49:49
Enter ".help" for usage hints.
sqlite>
```

As you can see, you can enter the *.help* command at the SQLite prompt to see a helpful list of commands. Knowing how to exit any command-line interface is helpful too; simply type *.exit* and press Enter. If that doesn't work, perhaps your prompt is in a strange state from an unbalanced quote or something; Ctrl+D will generally allow you to exit your prompt as well.

To list the tables present in your database, you can use the SQLite *.tables* command:

```
sqlite> .tables
```

```
articles           schema_migrations
```

As you can see, the database has two tables: *articles* and *schema_migrations*. You don't get a lot of information about the tables from the .tables command, but that can be achieved by using the SQLite *.schema* command:

```
sqlite> .schema articles
```

```
CREATE TABLE IF NOT EXISTS "articles" ("id" integer NOT NULL PRIMARY KEY,
"title" varchar DEFAULT NULL, "body" text, "published_at" datetime DEFAULT
NULL, "created_at" datetime(6) NOT NULL, "updated_at" datetime(6) NOT
NULL, "excerpt" varchar DEFAULT NULL, "location" varchar DEFAULT NULL);
```

The result of this command is an SQL statement that describes all the fields in the articles table. Each field has a *type*, which defines the kind of data it can store. The id field has a type of *integer*, title has a type of varchar, and body is a text field. Although it may sound strange, a type of varchar means the field has a variable number of characters up to a defined maximum.

The id column is the one to pay attention to here. It's the *primary key*—a unique identifier for a particular row. Because this key is essential, it absolutely needs to be not null, and it must be unique; instead of managing these requirements in our application code, we let the database manage its value by automatically incrementing its number each time a new row is created. Many databases also choose to *index* records by their primary key, which makes retrieving the record much quicker. Notice how this is specified in the articles table column description: NOT NULL PRIMARY KEY. These are special commands that tell SQLite how to handle this particular field.

Let's look at some data from the articles table:

```
sqlite> SELECT * FROM articles;
```

```
1|Advanced Active Record|2020-04-19 00:00:00|2020-04-19...
2|One-to-many associations|2020-04-19 00:00:00|2020-04-19...
3|Associations|2020-04-19 00:00:00|2020-04-19 23:10:10.283152...
```

Here, instead of using an SQLite command (which starts with a ". "), we're using the SQL SELECT statement to view this table's data. SQL statements are largely compatible between different database engines. As you can see in this example, this table has three records. You probably have different records in your database; the main point here is understanding the commands to see the data, not the data itself.

Working with Tables

The most common use of databases (not only in the context of Rails) is to implement CRUD functionality: create, read, update, and delete. Corresponding to the CRUD components are the most commonly used SQL commands: INSERT, SELECT, UPDATE, and DELETE, as shown in Table A-1.

Table A-1. *Common SQL Commands*

Operation	SQL Command
Create	INSERT
Read	SELECT
Update	UPDATE
Delete	DELETE

The following sections use the articles table presented in the previous section to show some examples of how these commands work. Remember that it's not necessary to have a complete understanding of SQL to work with Rails. The whole point of Active Record is to alleviate the tedium of needing to construct complex SQL statements to view and otherwise manipulate your data.

Selecting Data

The SELECT statement is a powerful and useful SQL command. Using SELECT, you can query (or request information from) the database and mine it for information. You can give SELECT any number of fields, a set of conditions to be applied to the data to be returned, a limit on the number of rows it returns, and instructions on how to order its results.

Earlier, you used the SELECT statement to see the data in the articles table:

```
SELECT * FROM articles;
```

The asterisk (*) character is a wildcard that means *every column*. This statement says, "Show me the values in every column for every row in the articles table." This is the easiest way to look at the contents of a table. But you don't often need to see every single row; and for tables with a lot of data, you could end up with a really large list. So, sometimes it isn't very efficient to select everything. Fortunately, you can also select specific columns by name. For example, to select only the title column, do this:

```
sqlite> SELECT title FROM articles;
```

Advanced Active Record
One-to-many associations
Associations

Instead of returning all fields, this command returns only the one requested: `title`. To return both the `title` and the `published_at` fields, add `published_at` to the list of columns to select:

```
sqlite> SELECT title, published_at FROM articles;
```

```
Advanced Active Record|2020-04-19 00:00:00
One-to-many associations|2020-04-19 00:00:00
Associations|2020-04-19 00:00:00
```

In both cases, the command returns all rows. If there were 100 rows in the table, they would all be returned. But what if you need to find a particular row? This is where *conditions* come into play. To supply conditions to a SELECT statement, you use the WHERE clause:

```
SELECT fields FROM table WHERE some_field = some_value;
```

Let's apply this to the `articles` table by finding a row by its primary key:

```
sqlite> SELECT * FROM articles WHERE id = 1;
```

```
1|Advanced Active Record|2020-04-19 00:00:00|2020-04-19 23:10:10.223714...
```

This query returns only the row whose primary key, `id`, matches the condition. You can use this technique on any field—`id`, `title`, or `published_at`—or all of them combined. Conditions can be chained together using AND and further modified using OR. For example, the following query returns only records whose titles match the word "associations" *and* whose published_at date is after a certain value:

```
SELECT * FROM articles WHERE title LIKE "%active%" AND published_at >
"2020-04-01"
```

Inserting Data

To insert a row into a table, you use the INSERT command. INSERT requires a table name, a list of fields, and a list of values to insert into those fields. Here's a basic INSERT statement for the `articles` table:

```
sqlite> INSERT INTO articles(title, created_at, updated_at) VALUES('Intro
to SQL', datetime("now"), datetime("now"));
```

This INSERT command creates a new record in the articles table with the title "Intro to SQL" and the created_at and updated_at columns set to the current timestamp, since we used the SQLite function *datetime("now")* for those values.

SQLite doesn't give any indication that any happened, which means your command was accepted and didn't generate any errors. To see what was inserted, you again use the SELECT command:

```
sqlite> SELECT * FROM articles;
```

```
1|Advanced Active Record|2020-04-19 00:00:00|2020-04-19 23:10:10.223714...
2|One-to-many associations|2020-04-19 00:00:00|2020-04-19
   23:10:10.270343...
3|Associations|2020-04-19 00:00:00|2020-04-19 23:10:10.283152|2020-04-19...
4|Intro to SQL||2020-04-26 20:57:35|2020-04-26 20:57:35|||
```

We now have four rows in our table. Notice that in the INSERT statement, we didn't specify the id field. That's because, as you recall, it's handled automatically by the database. If we were to specify a value for the id, we wouldn't have a reliable way to guarantee its uniqueness and could cause an error if we attempted to insert a duplicate value. The database automatically inserts an id value into the field that's greater than the largest existing id.

Updating Data

If you want to change the values in a row, you use the UPDATE statement. UPDATE is similar to INSERT, except that like SELECT, it can be modified (or constrained) by *conditions*. If you want to change the title for the "Intro to SQL" article, you can do so like this:

```
sqlite>  UPDATE articles SET title = 'Introduction to SQL' WHERE id = 4;
```

Again, SQLite is silent, which means the command has been accepted. The fact that you use the primary key to find and update the row is significant. Although you can match any value in any column, the only surefire way to ensure you're updating the row you want is to use the primary key. You can confirm that the value was updated with another query:

```
sqlite> SELECT title FROM articles WHERE id = 4;
```

Introduction to SQL

Sure enough, the `title` field has been updated.

Deleting Data

Of course, not all information in a database will stay there forever. Sometimes you need to delete records, such as when a product goes out of stock or a user cancels their account. That's the purpose of the `DELETE` statement. It works a lot like the `UPDATE` statement, in that it accepts conditions and deletes the rows for any records that match the conditions. If you want to delete the article with the `id` of 4, the `DELETE` statement is as follows:

```
sqlite> DELETE FROM articles WHERE id = 4;
```

SQLite receives the command and deletes the record identified by the `id` you specified. And, of course, if you subsequently search for the record, you find that it no longer exists:

```
sqlite> SELECT * FROM articles WHERE id = 4;
sqlite>
```

> **Caution**   When you use either the `UPDATE` or `DELETE` command, you're making changes to existing data; so be careful to use a `WHERE` clause to limit the records you're updating or deleting. A good practice is to always run a `SELECT` command first to make sure your query returns the records you're expecting; then, later run the `UPDATE` or `DELETE` command with the same conditions.

Understanding Relationships

It's good practice to avoid duplication in your database by creating distinct tables to store certain kinds of information. Then, you can relate records from these two tables to each other using an *association*. This makes more sense when you see it in action, so let's use the `articles` table for our example again.

First, let's add a new column to the articles table named *author*. First, we'll use it to store the author name, so we'll make it a varchar data type:

```
sqlite> ALTER TABLE articles ADD COLUMN author varchar;
sqlite> SELECT id, title, author FROM articles;
1|Advanced Active Record|
2|One-to-many associations|
3|Associations|
```

We don't have any data for our authors, so let's change that:

```
sqlite> UPDATE articles SET author = "Brady Summerville";
sqlite> SELECT id, title, author FROM articles;
1|Advanced Active Record|Brady Summerville
2|One-to-many associations|Brady Summerville
3|Associations|Brady Summerville
```

There's quite a bit of duplication in the author field. This can potentially create problems. Although you could search for all articles by a particular author using a standard SELECT query, what would happen if someone's name were misspelled? Any articles by the misspelled author wouldn't show up in the query. And if there were such a typo, you'd need to update a lot of records in order to fix it. Moreover, searching on a text field like "author" is rather slow when compared with searching using an integer type.

We can improve this design significantly by putting authors in their own table and referencing each author's unique id (primary key) in the articles table instead of the name. Let's do that now. Let's create a new table called authors and add the author_id field to the articles table so it can store an integer instead of text.:

```
sqlite> CREATE TABLE "authors" ("id" integer NOT NULL PRIMARY KEY, "name" varchar);
sqlite> ALTER TABLE articles ADD COLUMN author_id integer;
```

At this point, our articles table has both an author field (for the author's name) and an author_id field (to point to a record in the authors table), and we have an empty authors table. First, let's populate the authors table from the data in the articles table:

```
sqlite> INSERT INTO authors SELECT NULL, author FROM articles GROUP BY author;
```

This command is a little more complex; instead of specifying values for the INSERT statement to use, we supplied a SELECT statement to dynamically get those values. The authors table expects an id and a name, so we SELECT NULL (a keyword for *nothing*) for the id, so that the primary key will be generated automatically, and we select the *author* field from articles. To make sure we don't create duplicate records in the *authors* table, we used "GROUP BY author" in our SELECT statement to ensure each author's name is only used once. Now, we can verify our authors table has the data we expect:

```
 sqlite> select * from authors;
1|Brady Summerville
```

Next, we would want to get rid of the *author* field from the *articles* table, but we shouldn't do that yet since we haven't yet populated our *author_id* column to store the associations. So let's do that next:

```
sqlite> UPDATE articles SET author_id = (SELECT id FROM authors WHERE name
= author);
sqlite> SELECT id, title, author, author_id FROM articles;
1|Advanced Active Record|Brady Summerville|1
2|One-to-many associations|Brady Summerville|1
3|Associations|Brady Summerville|1
```

First, we set the *author_id* column for each record in the *articles* table using the UPDATE command combined with a *subquery*. Instead of needing to hardcode which id to use for the *author_id* column, we selected the id from the *authors* table where its *name* value matched the article's *author* value.

Then, to verify our work, we selected the fields we're interested in and saw that our articles table now has the correct *author_id* values for each *articles* record.

Now that our *articles* table has the *author_id* field, it no longer needs to store the name of the author, since the *authors* table now stores that. So let's remove the *author* column from the *articles* table:

```
sqlite> CREATE TABLE "articles_temp" ("id" integer NOT NULL PRIMARY KEY,
"title" varchar DEFAULT NULL, "published_at" datetime DEFAULT NULL,
"created_at" datetime(6) NOT NULL, "updated_at" datetime(6) NOT NULL,
"excerpt" varchar DEFAULT NULL, "location" varchar DEFAULT NULL, author_id
integer);
```

```
sqlite> INSERT INTO articles_temp (id, title, published_at, created_at,
updated_at, excerpt, location, author_id) SELECT id, title, published_at,
created_at, updated_at, excerpt, location, author_id FROM articles;

sqlite> ALTER TABLE articles RENAME TO articles_old;
sqlite> ALTER TABLE articles_temp RENAME TO articles;
```

That was a lot, so let's explain; many database engines support a simple command to drop a column, but SQLite does not—so our only option is to create a new table *without* the column we want.

So first, we created a new table called "articles_temp" with all the columns except for the *author* column we wanted to remove. Then, we used an INSERT .... SELECT statement to copy the data from *articles* to *articles_temp*. Next, we renamed *articles* to *articles_old*. (We could have used *DROP TABLE articles*, but maybe it's a good idea to keep the original *articles* table until we make sure things went according to plan.) And finally, we renamed *articles_temp* to *articles*:

```
sqlite> SELECT * FROM articles;
1|Advanced Active Record|2020-04-19 00:00:00|2020-04-19
23:10:10.223714|2020-04-19 23:10:10.233432|||1
2|One-to-many associations|2020-04-19 00:00:00|2020-04-19
23:10:10.270343|2020-04-19 23:10:10.273669|||1
3|Associations|2020-04-19 00:00:00|2020-04-19 23:10:10.283152|2020-04-19
23:10:10.286340|||1
```

We can see now that our new *articles* table still has the data we expected—and our unwanted *author* field has been replaced with *author_id*. But how can we use the *author_id* to get the author's name for each article?

The *author_id* column is considered to be a *foreign key*, because it references the primary key of the table it relates to: in this case, the author who wrote the article. If you now look at the data from both tables, you'll see that we've eliminated the duplication:

```
sqlite> SELECT id, author_id, title FROM articles;
```

```
sqlite> SELECT id, author_id, title FROM articles;
1|1|Advanced Active Record
2|1|One-to-many associations
3|1|Associations
sqlite> SELECT * FROM authors;
1|Brady Summerville
```

We can now use this relationship in our SELECT queries by joining the two tables together using their association. In this association, the author_id in the articles table is equal to the id column in the authors table. Adding the JOIN directive requires only a slight change to the SQL:

```
sqlite> SELECT articles.id, title, name FROM articles
JOIN authors ON articles.author_id = authors.id;
```

```
1|Advanced Active Record|Brady Summerville
2|One-to-many associations|Brady Summerville
3|Associations|Brady Summerville
```

By using JOIN, we're able to combine the two tables and get the author names returned with the articles' information. This is the crux of relational databases. Updating an author's name is now easy because there is only one instance of a given author.

It turns out that our author name *does* have a typo; before we moved the author names to the *authors* table, we would've had to update every instance of the misspelled name in the *articles* table. But now, we can simply update the appropriate author record to correct the mistake:

```
sqlite>  UPDATE authors SET name = 'Brady Somerville' WHERE id = 1;
```

This changes the name of the author with the id of 1 to "Brady Somerville." When we run the JOIN query again, we'll see that all instances of the author's name have been updated:

```
sqlite> SELECT articles.id, title, name FROM articles
JOIN authors ON articles.author_id = authors.id;
```

```
1|Advanced Active Record|Brady Somerville
2|One-to-many associations|Brady Somerville
3|Associations|Brady Somerville
```

SQL and Active Record

This brings this database crash course to a close. This was by no means a complete reference, nor was it intended to be. Its purpose was to illustrate the basics of how databases work and to introduce you to their native language: SQL. Now that you have a taste, you can safely enter the world of Active Record, where most of this tedious work is handled for us.

Why did we bother showing you this if Active Record takes care of most of it for you? Because it's important to know what Active Record is doing behind the scenes. Although you can effectively use Active Record like a black box, you'll eventually need to debug your programs and figure out why something isn't working the way you expect. Having a basic understanding of SQL helps. Moreover, every bit of SQL that Active Record generates is logged by Rails. You can find the logs in the log/ directory of your application. Now, when you see these SQL commands in the logs, you'll have a good idea what they mean.

The Rails Community

Rails development is driven by a vibrant and passionate community of open source developers. The Rails community encourages its members to participate actively in Rails development. You can start by asking questions and discussing new features. As your knowledge increases, you can help others by writing about your own experiences in a personal blog, answering questions on the mailing list, contributing to the Wiki, and fixing bugs and writing patches to make Rails even better. Whatever your intention, rest assured that participating in the community will help you get the most out of Rails.

Beginning Rails 6 Mailing List

As a companion to this book, we're establishing a mailing list for those interested in exchanging ideas or asking questions to the authors or other Rails developers. You can discuss changes in the Rails framework; or, if you find a bug in the framework, you can discuss proposed solutions. You can subscribe to this list at `https://groups.google.com/group/beginning-rails`.

Rails Discussion Forums

You can browse and join several Rails-related discussion forums:

- *Ruby on Rails Discussions:* A forum with categories for general discussion about using Rails, as well as discussion about technical aspects of Rails core. For more information, visit `https://discuss.rubyonrails.org/` and become an active member of the community.

- *Ruby on Rails Security:* A Google Group for those who want to keep abreast of Rails security concerns. You can subscribe to this group at `https://groups.google.com/group/rubyonrails-security`.

© Brady Somerville, Adam Gamble, Cloves Carneiro Jr and Rida Al Barazi 2020
B. Somerville et al., *Beginning Rails 6*, https://doi.org/10.1007/978-1-4842-5716-6

- *Ruby on Rails @ StackOverflow:* View questions and answers tagged with *ruby-on-rails* on one of the most widely used forums by developers from around the world at `https://stackoverflow.com/questions/tagged/ruby-on-rails`.

- *Ruby Weekly:* Sign up at `https://rubyweekly.com/` and receive a weekly email with Ruby-related news, articles, job postings, and more.

- *reddit for rubyists:* Visit `www.reddit.com/r/ruby/` for an infinitely scrollable feed of all things pertaining to Ruby development.

- *Medium:* While `https://medium.com/` hosts articles on a wide range of topics, many useful guides and interesting articles about Ruby and Rails development are hosted there.

Rails Chat

If you prefer real-time discussions about Rails, you may want to check out

- *Ruby on Rails Link:* A Slack channel which joins Rails developers from around the world, with dozens of channels for topic-specific conversations. For more information, visit `www.rubyonrails.link`.

- *#rubyonrails Internet Relay Chat (IRC) channel:* Hosted on the Freenode IRC network, the #rubyonrails channel hosts discussion centered around the Rails framework.

Whether in forums, chat, StackOverflow posts, or wherever, remember to be kind when asking for help, or when helping others.

If asking for help, be sure to provide as much information as you can, and be patient while waiting for a response. Remember that help usually comes from volunteers who aren't getting paid to help you, so show them the same courtesy you'd expect.

And if giving help, it's equally important to be kind! We were all once beginners and sometimes didn't even know *how* to ask the right question! Don't discourage beginners by being harsh; gently correct them and encourage them.

Note   Internet Relay Chat (IRC) is a type of real-time Internet chat, where users talk about their interests in topic-specific areas called *channels*. All you need to connect to IRC is IRC client software. The most commonly used IRC clients are the shareware mIRC (`www.mirc.com/`) for Windows and the open source Colloquy (`https://colloquy.app/`) for Mac.

Rails Blogs and Podcasts

The number of blogs dedicated to Rails information is rapidly growing, and most of the new Rails features are covered in blogs or podcasts even before they're released to the public. You can subscribe to the blogs of your choice to keep up with news in the Rails world.

The following are some of the more rewarding Rails-related blogs you can visit, including the official Rails podcast:

- *https://weblog.rubyonrails.org*: The official Rails blog. You'll find information about upcoming releases, new functionality in Rails, and news that's considered important (such as documentation updates and Rails adoption worldwide).

- *www.rubyflow.com*: A Ruby community site where people post interesting and new things about Ruby or Rails.

- *https://5by5.tv/rubyonrails*: A weekly podcast covering topics related to Ruby on Rails, open source programming, and development in general.

Rails Guides

The Rails community has an excellent set of documentation called Rails guides, which you can find at `https://guides.rubyonrails.org`. We've referred to it several times throughout this book. It's a great effort to document various parts of the frameworks, from basic beginner-oriented documentation to more advanced material.

Rails APIs

It's close to impossible to remember the names, methods, and possible parameters of all the functions and classes in Ruby and Rails. To help you with your coding tasks, we recommend that you keep the Ruby and Rails application programming interface (API) documentation open or at least that you put them in your favorites. The API documentation contains all the information about specific functions you're trying to use, including the function source code.

You can find the Rails API documentation at `https://api.rubyonrails.org`. The Ruby API is at `https://ruby-doc.org/core`. For more user-friendly and searchable API documentation, go to `https://apidock.com/rails`.

Rails Source and Issue Tracking

The Rails source code can be found at `https://github.com/rails/rails`. It's powered by the GitHub, a hosting service for projects using the Git revision control system. GitHub allows you to download the Rails source code using a web interface. You can subscribe to the Git change log using RSS to be notified about changes to the Rails source code.

You can also participate in the development of Rails by submitting bug reports and patches to the GitHub account at `www.github.com/rails/rails` or by looking at existing issues and trying to fix them. It might seem overwhelming, but don't let that deter you; the more time you spend reading code you don't understand, the more you begin to understand it. Soon, you could be a contributing member of the Rails project and not just a user of it!

APPENDIX C

Git

Developers normally work in teams. You write plenty of code; sometimes you test some and decide to delete it, and other times you decide to stick to it. Managing this can be a painful process, which is why you can use Source Control Management (SCM) software to help you focus on what you do best—writing beautiful code. Git is rapidly becoming the preferred SCM of developers everywhere.

What Is Source Control Management?

SCM software helps you keep track of code changes and gives you the ability to easily collaborate on that code with your teammates. The two main features of many SCMs are

- *Versioning:* When you're using SCM for your project, files and directories in the project are tracked. Every time you make changes to your files, you can save those changes as a new version. Your project then has several versions—one for every change set—giving you the ability to browse those changes and revert to any one at any time.

- *File merging:* Let's say you worked on a file and your colleague, John, worked on that same file and you both committed (submitted) your files to the SCM system. Both files are merged by SCM of your involvement; if SCM can't handle the merge for any reason, it lets you know and gives you some useful information about how to manually merge conflicting changes yourself.

535

© Brady Somerville, Adam Gamble, Cloves Carneiro Jr and Rida Al Barazi 2020
B. Somerville et al., *Beginning Rails 6*, https://doi.org/10.1007/978-1-4842-5716-6

How Does It Work?

Generally, when you add your code base to an SCM system, a *repository* is created, which is the store of all the versions of your code base. Then, you can take a copy of that repository and work on it; this is normally called your *working copy*. You can add files, change or delete some, and then *commit* those changes and send them back to the repository as a new revision. If your colleague John is working with you on the same code base, he can check out or pull those changes from the repository to update his working copy, letting the SCM take care of any necessary file merging (Figure C-1).

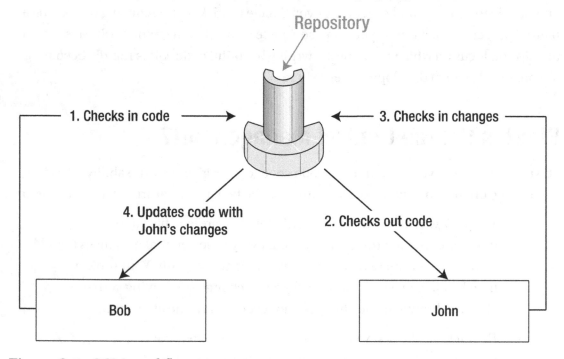

Figure C-1. *SCM workflow*

Git

The Git SCM was developed by Linus Torvalds for managing the Linux kernel source code. It's also been used for several million open source projects, including Rails.

Git is different from other SCMs because it's a *distributed* source control system. This means that instead of having a single repository on your server that all your teammates use to check out working copies (*client-server* or *centralized* SCM), each team member has their own repository along with a working copy, and you all *push* a copy of that repository to a remote repository.

This approach has some great benefits, such as the ability to work and commit your code, even if you're offline, and being able to operate on your repository more quickly.

Now that you have a good understanding of what an SCM is and how it works, let's install Git and try it.

Installing Git

Installing Git is relatively easy. Thanks to open source contributions, several Git installation packages are available to facilitate a quick installation for most platforms.

Installing on Windows

If you're on Windows, one option for installing Git is from the official source: `https://git-scm.com/download/win`. Simply download the installer, accept the default options, and you'll end up with Git Bash for command-line usage, as well as Git GUI for a graphical interface. Use the Git Bash tool for executing commands mentioned in this appendix.

Installing on macOS

To install Git on macOS, there are a few easy options.

If you've already installed the Xcode Command-Line Tools, you may already have it. Try running *git --version* from your terminal. It should either report the version of Git that's already installed or offer to install it for you.

It's also possible to install Git using the Homebrew package manager, via *brew install git*. If you don't yet have Homebrew installed, visit `https://brew.sh/` for installation instructions, or consult Chapter 2.

Installing on Linux

Most Linux distributions ship with a package manager. The most common one is the Debian package manager `apt`, and Git is part of its library.

To install Git using `apt`, run the following `apt-get` command from the terminal:

```
sudo apt-get install git
```

Accept if the package manager asks your permission to use additional disk space for this installation. When the installation is complete, Git is ready to use.

Setting Global Parameters

Every commit you make in your repository has flags for the user who executed the commit; those flags are the user's name and email address. Now that you have Git installed on your system, it's important to set a global username and email address for Git to use for any new repository you work on.

To set global parameters, you use the `git config` command with the `--global` option, followed by the parameters you want to set. Listing C-1 shows the command to set up both the `user.name` and `user.email` parameters.

Listing C-1. Setting the Global Git Username and Email

```
git config --global user.name "dude"
git config --global user.email my.email@example.com
```

These parameters can be set on a repository level as well; you can do that by using the same commands but without the `--global` option in your repository's working directory.

Initializing a Repository

Often, we need to initialize a new repository for our application. Let's begin by creating a test application, making sure to be outside of any directories which are already under version control:

```
$ rails new testapp
```

```
      create
      create  README.md
      create  Rakefile
      create  .ruby-version
      create  config.ru
      create  .gitignore
      create  Gemfile
         run  git init from "."
Initialized empty Git repository in /Users/brady/Sites/testapp/.git/
      create  package.json
      ...
```

Notice that *rails new* took care of initializing a new Git repository for us! If it hadn't or if we wanted to initialize a new Git repository for a project which didn't already have one, we could have done the following:

```
$ cd testapp
$ git init
```

```
Initialized empty Git repository in /Users/brady/Sites/testapp/.git/
```

The git init command initializes an empty local repository for the application, but it doesn't add any files to the repository. To determine which files we can add to the repository, we can use the *git status* command:

```
$ git status
```

```
On branch master

No commits yet

Untracked files:
  (use "git add <file>..." to include in what will be committed)
    .browserslistrc
    .gitignore
    .ruby-version
    Gemfile
    Gemfile.lock
    README.md
    Rakefile
    app/
    babel.config.js
    bin/
    config.ru
    config/
    db/
    lib/
    log/
    package.json
```

```
    postcss.config.js
    public/
    storage/
    test/
    tmp/
    vendor/
    yarn.lock

nothing added to commit but untracked files present (use "git add" to track)
```

As you can see, all the folders and files of the Rails application are in the *untracked files* list, which means that they're not under Git's control. To start tracking those files, we need to *add* them to the track list; as this indicates, we can do this by using the `git add` command. (While sometimes *git* may seem a bit perplexing to use, you'll find it often includes helpful hints in its output—so read closely!)

Ignoring Files

Before we add those files, let's think a little: Do we want *all* of our files to be tracked? Are there *any* files we don't want to track? Normally, those would be configuration files that contain passwords, such as `database.yml`, the `tmp` folder, log files, and SQLite databases. If we add those files, our teammates will have this information, and it may even conflict with their files. A worst-case scenario involves our Git repository becoming public and sensitive secrets falling into the hands of malicious users.

To skip those files in any `git add` and `git status` commands and to tell Git to never bother you about them again, we must configure Git to ignore them. We can do that by declaring those files in a hidden configuration file called `.gitignore`, which is normally stored at the root of your working copy (in this case, at the root of the `testapp` directory). The `.gitignore` file is a regular text file; it is generated by Rails in all new projects. View it using the text editor of your choice, and you'll see that it looks like the code in Listing C-2.

Listing C-2. The .gitignore File Content in testapp/.gitignore: https://gist.github.com/nicedawg/085165a26189b3913ee1fdca860ae1e9

```
# Ignore bundler config.
/.bundle

# Ignore the default SQLite database.
/db/*.sqlite3
/db/*.sqlite3-journal
/db/*.sqlite3-*

# Ignore all logfiles and tempfiles.
/log/*
/tmp/*
!/log/.keep
!/tmp/.keep

# Ignore uploaded files in development.
/storage/*
!/storage/.keep

/public/assets
.byebug_history

# Ignore master key for decrypting credentials and more.
/config/master.key

/public/packs
/public/packs-test
/node_modules
/yarn-error.log
yarn-debug.log*
.yarn-integrity
```

As you can see, the files and folders listed in the .gitignore file weren't listed in the git status command you issued earlier. To help make sure we don't commit any unwanted or sensitive information to our Git repository, Rails initializes new projects with a preconfigured .gitignore, especially made for Rails projects.

There may be times when we need to modify which files should or shouldn't be tracked by Git; simply add a pattern to exclude the file(s) you wish to exclude, and that's it!

Adding and Committing

We can add all of the untracked files to our repository by using the *git add* command and passing a dot to it, which refers to the current directory and all its content. Be cautious when using *"git add ."* to make sure you aren't adding files that don't belong in the repository:

```
$ git add .
```

Try the git status command again:

```
$ git status
```

```
On branch master

No commits yet

Changes to be committed:
  (use "git rm --cached <file>..." to unstage)
    new file:   .browserslistrc
    new file:   .gitignore
    new file:   .ruby-version
    new file:   Gemfile
    new file:   Gemfile.lock
    new file:   README.md
    new file:   Rakefile
  ...
```

The git status command still shows all the files, because the git add command just added those files to be committed, but they aren't committed yet. Notice how instead of being shown in the "untracked files" list, they're now included in the "changes to be committed." Another way of phrasing this using Git terminology is that these changes have been "staged." (Notice the helpful command to *unstage* a file. Running this command won't delete the file from your filesystem; it will simply remove the file from the list of changes to be committed.)

In order to commit the changes you added to the commit list, we use the *git commit* command. Use the –m argument to include a message describing the purpose of and the changes in this commit:

```
$ git commit -m "Empty Rails application"
```

```
master (root-commit) 15c012e] Empty Rails application
 91 files changed, 9213 insertions(+)
 create mode 100644 .browserslistrc
 create mode 100644 .gitignore
 create mode 100644 .ruby-version
 create mode 100644 Gemfile
 create mode 100644 Gemfile.lock
 create mode 100644 README.md
 create mode 100644 Rakefile
 ....
```

Congratulations! You've completed your first commit to your local repository! If we check the git status command now, we'll see that there are no changes to be added or committed:

```
$ git status
```

```
On branch master
nothing to commit, working tree clean
```

Now, let's change a file. For example, let's edit app/views/layouts/application.html. erb to include *<p>Hey!</p>* in the body of the page. Save the file, and now let's check our status again:

```
$ git status
```

```
On branch master
Changes not staged for commit:
  (use "git add <file>..." to update what will be committed)
  (use "git restore <file>..." to discard changes in working directory)
    modified:   app/views/layouts/application.html.erb

no changes added to commit (use "git add" and/or "git commit -a")
```

Git knows that we changed the file since the last time we committed changes, so shows the file as *modified*, but not yet staged for commit.

Instead of using *"git add ."*, like we did before, we can add this specific file:

```
$ git add app/views/layouts/application.html.erb
$ git status
```

```
On branch master
Changes to be committed:
  (use "git restore --staged <file>..." to unstage)
    modified:   app/views/layouts/application.html.erb
```

Now, the file is still modified, but labeled as *to be committed*. You could then run the *git command -m "Updated layout"* command to commit the change. When reasonable, it's best to carefully add specific files; using *"git add ."* without looking at your *git status* closely will inevitably lead to unwanted files being added to your repository.

Branching and Merging

Let's say you decide to test out a major refactor on your project and you're not sure if it will work out and don't want to break the code for everyone else. Meanwhile, you need to be able to keep working on the main project without changes from your experiment breaking your application. To have a safe place to experiment with your project's code, you need to create a *branch*. A branch is a duplicate of your project's code that you can work on in parallel with the master copy of the same project.

When you called the `git init` command earlier, Git initialized a new repository for your application with a default branch called `master`. To create a new branch in the repository, use the `git checkout -b` command followed by the name of the new branch you want to create:

```
$ git checkout -b articles
```

This command creates a new branch named `articles` as a duplicate of the current branch—`master`—and then switches to the newly created branch. To see a list of the branches in your project, we can use the *git branch* command:

```
$ git branch
```

```
* articles
  master
```

The output indicates we have two branches—articles and master. The asterisk in front of *articles* indicates that it's the *current* branch you're working on. To switch branches, use the git checkout command followed by the name of the branch you want to switch to:

```
$ git checkout master
```

```
Switched to branch 'master'
```

```
$ git checkout articles
```

```
Switched to branch 'articles'
```

The articles branch is the current branch again. We can confirm this by listing the branches again:

```
$ git branch
```

```
* articles
  master
```

Now, let's implement a new feature—an articles scaffold:

```
$ rails generate scaffold Article title:string body:text
```

```
      invoke  active_record
      create    db/migrate/20200427012944_create_articles.rb
      create    app/models/article.rb
      invoke    test_unit
      create      test/models/article_test.rb
      create      test/fixtures/articles.yml
```

```
invoke   resource_route
 route     resources :articles
invoke   scaffold_controller
create     app/controllers/articles_controller.rb
invoke     erb
create       app/views/articles
create       app/views/articles/index.html.erb
create       app/views/articles/edit.html.erb
create       app/views/articles/show.html.erb
create       app/views/articles/new.html.erb
create       app/views/articles/_form.html.erb
invoke     test_unit
create       test/controllers/articles_controller_test.rb
create       test/system/articles_test.rb
invoke     helper
create       app/helpers/articles_helper.rb
invoke       test_unit
invoke     jbuilder
create       app/views/articles/index.json.jbuilder
create       app/views/articles/show.json.jbuilder
create       app/views/articles/_article.json.jbuilder
invoke   assets
invoke     scss
create       app/assets/stylesheets/articles.scss
invoke   scss
create     app/assets/stylesheets/scaffolds.scss
```

Let's say we're done with the new feature changes. It's time to add the changes and commit them to the articles branch:

```
$ git add .
$ git commit -m "Adding Article scaffold"
```

```
[articles cb4bed1] Adding Article scaffold
 19 files changed, 351 insertions(+)
 create mode 100644 app/assets/stylesheets/articles.scss
 create mode 100644 app/assets/stylesheets/scaffolds.scss
 create mode 100644 app/controllers/articles_controller.rb
 create mode 100644 app/helpers/articles_helper.rb
 create mode 100644 app/models/article.rb
 create mode 100644 app/views/articles/_article.json.jbuilder
 create mode 100644 app/views/articles/_form.html.erb
 create mode 100644 app/views/articles/edit.html.erb
 create mode 100644 app/views/articles/index.html.erb
 create mode 100644 app/views/articles/index.json.jbuilder
 create mode 100644 app/views/articles/new.html.erb
 create mode 100644 app/views/articles/show.html.erb
 create mode 100644 app/views/articles/show.json.jbuilder
 create mode 100644 db/migrate/20200427012944_create_articles.rb
 create mode 100644 test/controllers/articles_controller_test.rb
 create mode 100644 test/fixtures/articles.yml
 create mode 100644 test/models/article_test.rb
 create mode 100644 test/system/articles_test.rb
```

When you check the git status command now, you see that you have nothing to commit in the articles branch:

```
$ git status
```

```
On branch articles
nothing to commit, working tree clean
```

The articles branch now has an articles scaffold, and the master branch doesn't. If you switch back to the master branch, notice that none of the articles scaffold files exist there:

```
$ git checkout master
```

```
Switched to branch 'master'
```

For fun, you could switch back to the *articles* branch and watch your articles scaffold files magically reappear. Hopefully the magic is a little clearer now; your branches can have different files in them, and depending on which branch is currently checked out, your filesystem will reflect the committed changes for that branch.

We could go on modifying the code in the `master` branch completely in isolation from the `articles` branch. But at some point, the feature being developed in the articles branch will be ready to be added to the "main" code branch, master. In Git terminology, that's a *merge*. Let's *merge* the `articles` branch into the `master` branch. We'll do that using the *git merge* command followed by the branch name you want to merge into the current branch:

```
$ git checkout master
$ git merge articles
```

```
Updating 15c012e..cb4bed1
Fast-forward
 app/assets/stylesheets/articles.scss               |  3 +++
 app/assets/stylesheets/scaffolds.scss              | 65
++++++++++++++++++++++++++
 app/controllers/articles_controller.rb             | 74
++++++++++++++++++++++++++++
 app/helpers/articles_helper.rb                     |  2 ++
 app/models/article.rb                              |  2 ++
 app/views/articles/_article.json.jbuilder          |  2 ++
 app/views/articles/_form.html.erb                  | 27
++++++++++++++++++++++++
 app/views/articles/edit.html.erb                   |  6 ++++++
 app/views/articles/index.html.erb                  | 29
++++++++++++++++++++++++++++
 app/views/articles/index.json.jbuilder             |  1 +
 app/views/articles/new.html.erb                    |  5 +++++
 app/views/articles/show.html.erb                   | 14 ++++++++++++++
 app/views/articles/show.json.jbuilder              |  1 +
 config/routes.rb                                   |  1 +
 db/migrate/20200427012944_create_articles.rb       | 10 ++++++++++
```

```
test/controllers/articles_controller_test.rb | 48
++++++++++++++++++++++++++++++++
 test/fixtures/articles.yml                   |  9 ++++++++++
 test/models/article_test.rb                  |  7 +++++++
 test/system/articles_test.rb                 | 45
++++++++++++++++++++++++++++++++
 19 files changed, 351 insertions(+)
 create mode 100644 app/assets/stylesheets/articles.scss
 create mode 100644 app/assets/stylesheets/scaffolds.scss
 create mode 100644 app/controllers/articles_controller.rb
 create mode 100644 app/helpers/articles_helper.rb
 create mode 100644 app/models/article.rb
 create mode 100644 app/views/articles/_article.json.jbuilder
 create mode 100644 app/views/articles/_form.html.erb
 create mode 100644 app/views/articles/edit.html.erb
 create mode 100644 app/views/articles/index.html.erb
 create mode 100644 app/views/articles/index.json.jbuilder
 create mode 100644 app/views/articles/new.html.erb
 create mode 100644 app/views/articles/show.html.erb
 create mode 100644 app/views/articles/show.json.jbuilder
 create mode 100644 db/migrate/20200427012944_create_articles.rb
 create mode 100644 test/controllers/articles_controller_test.rb
 create mode 100644 test/fixtures/articles.yml
 create mode 100644 test/models/article_test.rb
 create mode 100644 test/system/articles_test.rb
```

The output shows the effects of our merge; it shows which files have been updated and how many lines in each file were added or removed. (In our case, they were all additions.)

The task is complete: we "developed" a new feature in a separate branch without affecting the master branch; and when we finished, we merged those changes back into master.

There's much more to learn about these *git* commands; this is merely a brief introduction.

Remote Repositories and Cloning

As stated previously, Git is a distributed SCM; therefore, your repository is hosted locally on your machine, hidden inside your working copy directory. No one else has access to it.

However, if you want to set up a repository that you and your team can work on, you may want to create a *remote* repository that all of you can access and clone from. Your remote repository can be hosted on any machine that is available to all developers who need access to the repository and have Git installed. It can be hosted on your local network, online, or with a third-party Git hosting provider like the famous GitHub (https://github.com), which hosts Rails, as well as many, many other projects.

We used Git for this book's blog application, and we hosted the repository on GitHub. It's publicly available for you to browse and use; simply point your browser at https://github.com/nicedawg/beginning-rails-6-blog. This means you can clone a copy of the blog repository to your machine and browse the code locally. To do that, you need the Public Clone URL, which you find from the "Clone or download" button on the GitHub page for the repo. Let's clone the blog application repository using the git clone command:

```
$ git clone git@github.com:nicedawg/beginning-rails-6-blog.git
```

```
Cloning into 'beginning-rails-6-blog'...
remote: Enumerating objects: 499, done.
remote: Counting objects: 100% (499/499), done.
remote: Compressing objects: 100% (243/243), done.
remote: Total 1023 (delta 300), reused 424 (delta 253), pack-reused 524
Receiving objects: 100% (1023/1023), 265.83 KiB | 1.53 MiB/s, done.
Resolving deltas: 100% (537/537), done.
```

Now you have a local copy of the blog application repository cloned to your machine. You can change files and even commit them to your own local repository, but what you *cannot* do is share those commits with others. In order to *push* your changes, you need write access to the remote repository, which you don't have.

If you want to try that, sign up for a free account on GitHub and create a repository of your own there. You then have two URLs: a *public* URL that everyone can see and your *clone* URL, which gives you full access to this remote repository.

The concept is simple: after you clone your own repository using your own URL, you can work normally in your working copy, commit changes, and add and remove files. Whenever you want to share those commits with the rest of the world, you push them to the remote repository on GitHub using the `git push` command. If you have teammates pushing changes to the same repository, you can retrieve those changes by using the `git pull` command.

To sum up, you create a remote repository to allow more than one developer to work on the same repository. Although all developers on the team have their own copies, they still need to push their copies to the remote repository to allow the rest to pull from it and stay in sync.

When you sign up for a free account on GitHub, the repositories you create can be made publicly available for everyone to clone from. Or, if you want your repositories to be private, so only you and your teammates can access them, you can choose to make them private on GitHub, or you could host them on your own server with your own setup.

Learning More

Git is a great tool and has a lot of commands; however, this appendix has covered only the basic features and commands. We highly encourage you to read more. You can see a list of the most used Git commands using the `git help` command:

```
$ git help
```

```
usage: git [--version] [--help] [-C <path>] [-c <name>=<value>]
           [--exec-path[=<path>]] [--html-path] [--man-path] [--info-path]
           [-p | --paginate | -P | --no-pager] [--no-replace-objects] [--bare]
           [--git-dir=<path>] [--work-tree=<path>] [--namespace=<name>]
           <command> [<args>]

These are common Git commands used in various situations:

start a working area (see also: git help tutorial)
   clone          Clone a repository into a new directory
   init           Create an empty Git repository or reinitialize an
                  existing one
```

work on the current change (see also: git help everyday)
    add   Add file contents to the index
    mv   Move or rename a file, a directory, or a symlink
    restore   Restore working tree files
    rm   Remove files from the working tree and from the index
    sparse-checkout Initialize and modify the sparse-checkout

examine the history and state (see also: git help revisions)
    bisect   Use binary search to find the commit that introduced a
                     bug
    diff   Show changes between commits, commit and working tree,
                     etc
    grep   Print lines matching a pattern
    log   Show commit logs
    show   Show various types of objects
    status   Show the working tree status

grow, mark and tweak your common history
    branch   List, create, or delete branches
    commit   Record changes to the repository
    merge   Join two or more development histories together
    rebase   Reapply commits on top of another base tip
    reset   Reset current HEAD to the specified state
    switch   Switch branches
    tag   Create, list, delete or verify a tag object signed
                     with GPG

collaborate (see also: git help workflows)
    fetch   Download objects and refs from another repository
    pull   Fetch from and integrate with another repository or a
                     local branch
    push   Update remote refs along with associated objects

'git help -a' and 'git help -g' list available subcommands and some
concept guides. See 'git help <command>' or 'git help <concept>'
to read about a specific subcommand or concept.
See 'git help git' for an overview of the system.

To learn more about a specific command, you can use `git help COMMAND`, which shows that command's documentation and how to use the command.

Other SCM Systems

Although Git is the most talked-about SCM nowadays, you may either be required to use a different SCM or may want to investigate the alternatives. Here's a list of other SCMs you could choose:

- *Mercurial:* Just like Git, Mercurial is a distributed SCM. Mercurial is often compared with Git because of their similarities; feel free to try it if you want to explore another option. You can find out more about Mercurial from its official website: `www.mercurial-scm.org/`.

- *SVN (Subversion):* This was the most prominent SCM for a while, but it has since been overtaken by Git. You can find out more about Subversion from its official website: `https://subversion.apache.org/`.

- *CVS (Concurrent Versions System):* This was one of the earliest SCM systems (initial release in 1990). It's still popular, although because of some limitations, such as sparse Unicode support and expensive branching operations, developers have begun moving toward other version control systems like Subversion and Git. You can find out more about CVS from its official website: `www.nongnu.org/cvs/`.

Online Resources

After the beta launch of GitHub, Git received huge interest from developers, including the Rails core team; they decided to switch from Subversion to Git and host the official Rails repository on GitHub. This attention to Git encouraged more developers to try it, and a number of tutorials and blog posts began to appear in the community.

The following are some resources you can visit to dig deeper and learn more about Git:

- *http://gitimmersion.com*: A clean, organized step-by-step tutorial that shows how to use many of Git's commands

- *https://learngitbranching.js.org*: An interesting browser-based environment that helps you visualize what's happening with Git branches while you execute commands on them.

- *https://git-scm.com/doc*: An official list of resources, including a link to the excellent 2014 Apress book, *Pro Git*, by Scott Chacon and Ben Straub

Git is an amazing tool. It's tempting to primarily focus on developing mastery of your preferred programming language or framework, but don't neglect sharpening your Git skills; time you invest in learning Git will pay dividends through improving your efficiency and making your commits clearer and more understandable.

Index

A

Account model, 160

Action Cable
  broadcasting, 419
  channel, 418
  client side changes, 427, 428
  configuration, 420, 421
  connection, 418
  New article notification, 429
  Rails, 418, 419
  server side changes
    ApplicationCable, 422, 423
    ArticlesChannel, 423–426
  streams, 419
  subscriptions, 419
  web development, 417
  WebSockets, 417

ActionCable::Channel, 418

ActionCable::Connection, 418

Action Mailer
  components, 336
  configuration, 336
  configuring application
    settings, 342
  email (*see* Receiving emails)
  ISP, 336
  rails app, 335
  server connection strings, 337
  storing sensitive settings, 337–341
  web-based email application, 336

ActionMailer::MessageDelivery, 352

Action Pack
  action view helpers, 258, 260
  adding edit controls, 262–264
  articles have owners, 265–267
  controllers/templates, improving
    applying filters, 254,
      255, 257, 258
    article form, 248, 250, 252
    article index page, 247, 248
    authentication, filters, 253
    collection_check_boxes, 250
    filters, 252, 253
  custom helpers, 267–270
  formatting body field, 262
  generating controller (*see* Controller
    generator)
  HTML templates, 260
  layout, 271, 272, 279
  logging in user, 243–245
  logging out user, 245, 246
  nested resources (*see* Nested
    resources)
  session resources
    adding session, 241, 243
    path, 242
    sessions controller, 241
    named routes, 241, 242
  state, 240
  style sheet, 272, 274–278

© Brady Somerville, Adam Gamble, Cloves Carneiro Jr and Rida Al Barazi 2020
B. Somerville et al., *Beginning Rails 6*, https://doi.org/10.1007/978-1-4842-5716-6

P, Q

R

Printed in the United States
By Bookmasters